THE LAW OF POLITICAL ECONOMY

This book develops the law of political economy as a new field of scholarly enquiry. Bringing together an exceptional group of scholars, it provides a novel conceptual framework for studying the role of law and legal instruments in political economy contexts, with a focus on historical transformations and central challenges in both European and global contexts. Its chapters reconstruct how the law of political economy plays out in diverse but central fields, ranging from competition and consumer protection law to labour and environmental law, giving a comprehensive overview of the central challenges of the law of political economy. It also provides a sophisticated and multifaceted framework for further enquires while outlining the contours of new law of political economy.

Poul F. Kjaer is Professor of Governance and Sociology of Law, Department of Management, Politics and Philosophy, Copenhagen Business School, Denmark. His previous books include *Between Governing and Governance: On the Emergence, Function and Form of Europe's Post-National Constellation* (2010) and *Constitutionalism in the Global Realm: A Sociological Approach (2016).*

THE LAW OF POLITICAL ECONOMY

Transformation in the Function of Law

Edited by

POUL F. KJAER

Copenhagen Business School

CAMBRIDGE
UNIVERSITY PRESS

CAMBRIDGE
UNIVERSITY PRESS

University Printing House, Cambridge CB2 8BS, United Kingdom

One Liberty Plaza, 20th Floor, New York, NY 10006, USA

477 Williamstown Road, Port Melbourne, VIC 3207, Australia

314–321, 3rd Floor, Plot 3, Splendor Forum, Jasola District Centre, New Delhi – 110025, India

79 Anson Road, #06–04/06, Singapore 079906

Cambridge University Press is part of the University of Cambridge.

It furthers the University's mission by disseminating knowledge in the pursuit of education, learning, and research at the highest international levels of excellence.

www.cambridge.org
Information on this title: www.cambridge.org/9781108493116
DOI: 10.1017/9781108675635

First published 2020

Printed in the United Kingdom by TJ International Ltd, Padstow Cornwall

A catalogue record for this publication is available from the British Library.

Library of Congress Cataloging-in-Publication Data
Names: Law of Political Economy: Transformations in the Function of Law (Conference) (2017 : Handelshøjskolen i København) | Kjaer, Poul F., editor
Title: The law of political economy : transformations in the function of law / edited by Poul F. Kjær, University of Copenhagen
Description: Cambridge, United Kingdom ; New York, NY, USA : Cambridge University Press, 2020. | Includes papers "presented at the conference "The Law of Political Economy – Transformations in the Function of Law" which took place at the Department of Management, Politics and Philosophy, at the Copenhagen Business School on 15–16 June 2017" – ECIP Acknowledgement.
Identifiers: LCCN 2019056654 (print) | LCCN 2019056655 (ebook) | ISBN 9781108493116 (hardback) | ISBN 9781108675635 (ebook)
Subjects: LCSH: Law – Congresses. | Law and economics – Congresses. | Law – Political aspects – Congresses.
Classification: LCC K555 .L394 2020 (print) | LCC K555 (ebook) | DDC 343.07–dc23
LC record available at https://lccn.loc.gov/2019056654
LC ebook record available at https://lccn.loc.gov/2019056655

ISBN 978-1-108-49311-6 Hardback

This volume is dedicated to my supervisors,
Gorm Harste, Christian Joerges and Gunther Teubner.

CONTENTS

CONTRIBUTORS

MARIJA BARTL is Associate Professor at the Faculty of Law, University of Amsterdam.

EMILIOS CHRISTODOULIDIS holds the Chair of Jurisprudence at the School of Law of the University of Glasgow.

JAYE ELLIS is Associate Professor at the Faculty of Law, McGill University, Montréal.

MICHELLE EVERSON is Professor of Law at Birkbeck College, University of London.

ISABEL FEICHTNER is Professor of Law at the Faculty of Würzburg University.

STEFANO GIUBBONI is Professor of Labour Law at the University of Perugia, Department of Political Sciences.

CHRISTIAN JOERGES is Co-Director, Centre of Law and Politics, University of Bremen. Professor Emeritus for Law and Society, Hertie School of Governance, Berlin.

DAVID KENNEDY is Manley O. Hudson Professor of Law and Director, Institute for Global Law and Policy, Harvard Law School.

DUNCAN KENNEDY is Carter Professor of General Jurisprudence, Harvard Law School.

POUL F. KJAER is Professor at the Department of Management, Politics and Philosophy, Copenhagen Business School.

KARL-HEINZ LADEUR is Professor Emeritus at the Law Faculty, University of Hamburg.

HANS-W. MICKLITZ is Professor of Economic Law at the European University Institute, Florence.

JOTTE MULDER is Assistant Professor at the Utrecht School of Law.

GUNTHER TEUBNER is Professor Emeritus at the Law Department, Goethe-Universität Frankfurt.

RODRIGO VALLEJO is a Ph.D. researcher at the Department of Law, European University Institute, Florence.

LARS VIELLECHNER is Associate Professor of Constitutional Law, Constitutional Theory, Legal Philosophy, and Transnational Law, University of Bremen, Germany.

ACKNOWLEDGEMENTS

This book builds on insights first presented at the conference *The Law of Political Economy – Transformations in the Function of Law* which took place at the Department of Management, Politics and Philosophy, at the Copenhagen Business School on 15–16 June 2017. The insights were subsequently further developed and refined in several consecutive steps. A considerable part of the editorial work was carried out during a research fellowship at the Paris Institute for Advanced Study in Spring 2018.

The conference and the subsequent book project were generously funded by the European Research Council, within the framework of the research project 'Institutional Transformation in European Political Economy – A Socio-legal Approach' (ITEPE-312331). It also benefited from a Semper Ardens Grant from the Carlsberg Foundation.

Invaluable support was provided by Chris Engert, who carried out the linguistic editing of the manuscript. Finally, I would like to thank Finola O'Sullivan, Marianne Nield and the rest of the team at Cambridge University Press for their invaluable support throughout the publication process.

Poul F. Kjaer

ABBREVIATIONS

ACLU	American Civil Liberties Union
ACM	Authority for Consumers & Markets [Dutch Competition Authority]
Brexit	The Exit of the United Kingdom from the European Union
CJEU	Court of Justice of the European Union
CLS	Critical Legal Studies
CLT	Classical Legal Thought
DENIC	Deutsches Network Information Center eG
DG	Directorate-General
EC	European Communities
ECJ	European Court of Justice
ECOSOC	United Nations Economic and Social Council
EEC	European Economic Community
EN	*Energie Nederland*
EPL	European Private Law
ERC	European Research Council
ETUC	European Trade Union Confederation
EU	European Union
FCC	Federal Communications Commission (US)
FSC	Forest Stewardship Council
FTA	Free Trade Agreement
GAL	Global Administrative Law
GATT	General Agreement on Tariffs and Trade
GDP	Gross Domestic Product
GDPR	General Data Protection Regulation
ICANN	Internet Corporation for Assigned Names and Numbers
ICSID	International Centre for Settlement of Investment Disputes
ILO	International Labour Organization
IMF	International Monetary Fund
IP	Internet Protocol
IPCC	Intergovernmental Panel on Climate Change
IT	Information Technology
LGBTQT	Lesbian Gay Bisexual Transgender Queer Transsexual

LIBOR	London Interbank Offered Rate
M5S	Five Star Movement (*Movimento 5 Stelle*)
MIGA	Multilateral Investment Guarantee Agency
MS	Member States
NAACP	National Association for the Advancement of Colored People
NAFTA	North American Free Trade Association
NARAL	National Association for the Repeal of Abortion Laws
NGO	Non-Governmental Organisation
NIEO	New International Economic Order
OECD	Organisation for Economic Co-operation and Development
OMC	Open Method of Co-ordination
OPEC	Organization of the Petroleum Exporting Countries
PCIJ	Permanent Court of International Justice
PSNR	Permanent Sovereignty over Natural Resources
REACH	Registration, Evaluation, Authorisation and Restriction of Chemicals
SIN	Substitute It Now
SLT	Social Legal Thought
SVHC	Substances of Very High Concern
TEU	Treaty of European Union
TFEU	Treaty on the Functioning of the EU
TTIP	Transatlantic Trade Investment Partnership
TWAIL	Third World Approaches to International Law
UDRP	Uniform Domain Name Dispute Resolution Policy
UK	United Kingdom
UNGA	United Nations General Assembly
USA/US	United States of America
USD	United States Dollars
WTO	World Trade Organization
WWI	World War I
WWII/WW2	World War II

1

The Law of Political Economy

An Introduction

POUL F. KJAER

Introduction

The law of political economy is a contentious ideological field characterised by antagonistic relations between scholarly positions which tend to be either affirmative or critical of capitalist modes of economic reproduction. Going beyond this schism, two particular features appear as central to the law of political economy: the first one is the way in which it epistemologically seeks to handle the distinction between holism and differentiation (i.e. the extent to which it sees society as a singular whole which is larger than its parts, or, rather, as a mere collection of parts). Different types of legal and political economy scholarship have given different types of answers to this question. A third way has, moreover, emerged through an understanding of the law of political economy as being aimed at simultaneously separating and reconnecting political and economic processes in a manner which goes beyond the holism versus differentiation schism. The second feature of the law of political economy is the way in which it conceives of the relation between hierarchical and spontaneous dimensions of society, (i.e. between firms and the market, or between public institutions and public opinion). Also in this regard, competing approaches exist, just as the relation has been handled in radically differently ways within corporatist, neo-corporatist and governance-based institutional set-ups of political economy.[1]

[1] This double function is also at the heart of the following contribution to this volume by Christian Joerges and Michelle Everson.

I The Multiple Discourses on Law and Political Economy

Political economy themes have – directly and indirectly – been a central concern of law and legal scholarship ever since political economy emerged as a concept in the early seventeenth century,[2] a development which was reinforced by the emergence of political economy as an independent area of scholarly enquiry in the eighteenth century, as developed by the French physiocrats. This is not surprising in so far as the core institutions of the economy and economic exchanges, such as property and contract, are legal institutions.[3] In spite of this intrinsic link, political economy discourses and legal discourses dealing with political economy themes unfold in a largely separate manner. Indeed, this book is also a reflection of this, in so far as its core concern is how the law and legal scholarship conceive of and approach political economy issues. The focus is, in other words, on how law and legal scholarship internally reconstruct issues of political economy, and not on the political economy as such.

One reason for the relative estrangement between law and political economy might be found in the basic assumptions and focus of the dominant schools of political economy. As an ideologically contentious scholarly field, political economy tends, as mentioned, to be divided into approaches which are either affirmative or critical of capitalist modes of economic reproduction.

On the affirmative side, public and social choice stand out as umbrella terms for approaches which seek to transpose economic tools and perspectives, such as those derived from utility maximisation and game theory, into issue areas that are traditionally dealt with by public law and political science, that is, how individual decisions aggregate into collective decisions, and issues of individual, as well as social, optimisation of welfare.[4] New Public Management might be seen here as a related

[2] Antoine de Montchrestien, *Traicté de l'oeconomie politique*, edited by François Billacois (Geneva: Librairie Droz [1615] 1999).

[3] For illustrations of this, see, for example, Simon Deakin, David Gindis, Geoffrey M. Hodgson, Kainan Huang and Katharina Pistor, 'Legal Institutionalism: Capitalism and the Constitutive Role of Law' (2017) 45 *Journal of Comparative Economics*, 188–200; David Kennedy, *A World of Struggle. How Power, Law and Expertise Shape Global Political Economy* (Princeton NJ: Princeton University Press, 2016).

[4] See, for example, James M. Buchanan and Gordon Tullock, *The Calculus of Consent: Logical Foundations of Constitutional Democracy* (Ann Arbor MI: University of Michigan Press, 1962); James D. Gwartney and Richard E. Wagner (eds.), *Public Choice and Constitutional Economics* (Greenwich: JAI Press, 1988).

approach which seeks to develop 'business-like' forms of organisation and management in the public sector, for example, through the introduction of *quasi* markets.[5] These approaches tend – implicitly or explicitly – to be combined with normative undertakings aimed at expanding an economistic way of observing and evaluating social phenomena in areas of society not previously dominated by economic logics, thereby producing performative effects.

Critical political economy and associated left-Hegelian and Marxist-inspired approaches, on the other hand, have served as alternative ways of observing economic processes, essentially advocating the task of critical political economy as exposing the perceived inadequacies and simplifications of the basic concepts of mainstream economics, and engaging in the development of a conceptual framework capable of taking better account of the wider societal effects of economic reproduction.[6]

This divide between affirmative and critical approaches is furthermore based upon different methodological points of departure. Public and social choice and positive political economy in general depart from a methodological individualist perspective, maintaining individuals as their focal point. Critical political economy and Marxist-inspired approaches, on the other hand, tend to emphasise methodological collectivism, focusing on groups and structures, rather than on individual preferences. In this divide, rational institutionalism and Varieties of Capitalism might be seen as seeking to bridge the gap between left and right, departing from a 'centre-left position' while the section of positive economics which acknowledges the self-interest of the state and other collective formations, might be seen as engaged in the same exercise departing from a 'centre-right position.'[7]

In spite of the different points of departure, the various positions tend implicitly to share a number of assumptions. First, the primacy of the economy in so far as both the affirmative and critical approaches tend to see the economy as the central driver of societal evolution, with the in-built logics of profit generation, welfare maximisation, and creative destruction embedded in economic processes as the fuel. This is also

[5] Gernod Gruening, 'Origin and Theoretical Basis of New Public Management' (2001) 4 *International Public Management Journal*, 1–25.

[6] For an overview, see Gary Browning and Andrew Kilmister, *Critical and Post-Critical Political Economy* (Basingstoke: Palgrave, 2006).

[7] For positive economics, see Steven G. Medema, *The Hesitant Hand: Taming Self-interest in the History of Economic Ideas* (Princeton NJ: Princeton University Press, 2009), p. 197 et seq.

the case for those which explicitly seek to highlight the role of the state or the structural demand for a societal embeddedness of economic production processes, in so far as they tend to invoke the notion of capitalism, understood as an overarching process which integrates economic and political logics, thereby making it difficult to separate the political and economic dimensions of capitalist reproduction.[8]

Within legal discourse, a similar divide can be observed between the largely German ordoliberal school and the largely American law and economics approach. Both of them are primarily legal approaches, while being intrinsically linked to political economy and economics. At the same time, they reproduce the divide found within political economy, as the former provide a macro-approach, and the latter a micro-approach, derived respectively from methodological collectivism and methodological individualism. The two approaches therefore deal with different problem constellations. Ordoliberalism is a legal theory of societal ordering, which departs from an understanding of the economy and politics as different systemic processes in need of mutual stabilisation through law.[9] Law and economics, on the other hand, remain a toolbox for concrete problem-solving within market-based economic processes which does not derive an explicit macro perspective on society from it micro insights. The objectives guiding the two approaches therefore remain fundamentally different, as the latter, in essence, are concerned with questions of allocative efficiency, and the former with issues of power and stability in society. Thus, the two approaches do not serve as functional equivalents. This is also apparent in the area where the two have intersected the most, namely, in EU competition law and policy. The switch from a predominantly ordoliberal and legal approach to an economic approach, encapsulated as law and economics within the legal dimension of EU competition law and policy, have considerably altered the objectives and effects

[8] See, for example, Wolfgang Streeck, 'How to Study Contemporary Capitalism?' (2012) 53 *European Journal of Sociology*, 1–28.

[9] Franz Böhm, '*Privatrechtsgesellschaft und Marktwirtschaft*' (1966) 17 *ORDO: Jahrbuch für die Ordnung von Wirtschaft und Gesellschaft* (hereinafter *ORDO*), 75–151; Walter Eucken, 'Die Wettbewerbsordnung und ihre Verwirklichung' (1949) 2 *ORDO*, 1–99; Walter Eucken, 'Technik, Konzentration und Ordnung der Wirtschaft' (1950) 3 *ORDO*, 3–17. For a historical and conceptual reconstruction of ordoliberalism within the broader framework of neo-liberalism see; Thomas Biebricher, *The Political Theory of Neoliberalism* (Stanford CA: Stanford University Press, 2019). For the further development of ordoliberalism by Ernst-Joachim Mestmäcker and the long-term implications for Europe, see also the contribution of Christian Joerges and Michelle Everson to this volume.

produced by this policy regime.[10] In a simplified form, one might therefore argue that the ordoliberals are interested in the connection between political economy and law, while law and economics is interested in the connection between economics and law.

II The Law of Political Economy – A Sub-Case of a Grand Debate

The highly divergent assumptions and objectives guiding the various schools of political economy and of legal approaches to political economy means that exercises aimed at 'overcoming the differences' or developing a 'unified approach' within the scheme of a singular grand theory are likely to be futile. One might, however, fruitfully contextualise the existing approaches to law and political economy within the broader social scientific and epistemological realm, and position them according to a number of core dimensions.

II.1 Holism versus Differentiation

The grand theories of modern society from Hobbes and Hegel to Leibnitz and Luhmann all circulate around a trade-off between holism and differentiation. The diagnosis of society provided by such theories is, to a high extent, determined by the theoretical architecture put forward, and this architecture is pre-structured by the initial choice made between a holistic- or a differentiation-based world view, that is, between an understanding of society as a whole, which is larger than the sum of its parts, or an understanding of society as a mere collection of differentiated parts.

As also observable in the self-descriptions of society, the progressive advancement of modernity can be understood as a gradual move away from a holistic notion of society, and towards an increased reliance on a differentiation-based notion of society.[11] Hobbes' theory of the Commonwealth is, at least in the Anglo-American world, often considered the first theory of society based upon modern premises. But,

[10] For more on this, see Dzmitry Bartalevich, 'Do Economic Theories Inform Policy? Analysis of the Influence of the Chicago School on European Union Competition Policy', Ph.D. Dissertation, Copenhagen Business School, 2017. See also the contribution of Jotte Mulder to this volume.

[11] Reinhart Koselleck, *Begriffsgeschichten* (Frankfurt aM: Suhrkamp Verlag, 2006); Niklas Luhmann, 'Gesellchaftliche Struktur und semantische Tradition', in: Luhmann, *Gesellschaftsstruktur und Semantik, Band 1* (Frankfurt aM: Suhrkamp Verlag, 1980), pp. 9–71.

although a differentiation between state and society is implicit to the theory, its starting point is, as also illustrated by the famous frontispiece of Leviathan, a holistic (i.e. organic), notion of body politics.[12] In the Hobbesian world, there are many bodies in society, but they are all encompassed by the 'meta-body' of the state in the monarchical form. As such, Hobbes' theory introduces a modern element but never really escape the pre-modern understanding of society as a holistic whole. In a 'two steps ahead' and 'one step back' manner, the history of modern western thought from Locke and Montesquieu to Rousseau, Kant and Hegel are the history of the gradual shift – sometimes bemoaned and sometimes celebrated – from holism to differentiation. A movement which culminated in the theory of classical modernity, defined as the *époque* between 1789 and 1989, *par excellence*, in Hegel's *Philosophy of Rights*.[13]

A substantial degree of uncomfortableness with the modern condition can be detected in Rousseau's communitarian praise of the simple life prior to Hegel. A similar scepticism can be found in Kierkegaard's and Marx's subsequent critiques of Hegel through their explorations of the dark side of modernity by respectively looking at the individualised human condition and the implications of economic reproduction. Nonetheless, Hegel's theory was the first which made the structural conditions of modernity, a differentiated and temporalised society based upon a linear conception of time, rather than a holistic and static society reproduced through a circular notion of time, the explicit foundations for his theory, while, at the same time, systematically seeking to address the dark side of modern society by introducing a systematic notion of critique.[14]

The classical modernist narrative, as embodied in the advancements of the Atlantic Revolutionary movements, in Europe, North and South America, from the 1770s to the 1820s,[15] implied a focus on progress,

[12] Thomas Hobbes, *Leviathan: Or The Matter, Forme, & Power of a Common-Wealth Ecclesiasticall and Civil.*, edited by Ian Shapiro (New Haven CT: Yale University Press, 2010).

[13] Georg W.F. Hegel, *Grundlinien der Philosophie des Rechts oder Naturrecht und Staatswissenschaft im Grundrisse, Werke Band 7* (Frankfurt aM: Suhrkamp Verlag, [1821] 1970).

[14] Jürgen Habermas, 'Hegels Begriff der Moderne', in: Habermas, *Der philosophische Diskurs der Moderne* (Frankfurt aM: Suhrkamp Verlag, 1985), pp. 34–58.

[15] Hauke Brunkhorst, *Critical Theory of Legal Revolutions: Evolutionary Perspectives* (London: Bloomsbury Academic, 2014); Susan Buck-Morss, *Hegel, Haiti and Universal History* (Pittsburgh PA: University of Pittsburgh Press, 2009).

emancipation and freedom, while the 'dark side', from Hegel onwards, has been consistently problematised through terms such as *alienation* (Marx), *anomie* (Durkheim), *colonialisation* (Habermas), *de-differentiation* (Luhmann), *disciplination* (Elias and Foucault), *existential fear* (Kierkegaard), *rationalisation* (Weber), *reification* (Adorno and Horkheimer), and *technification* (Heidegger), upon the basis of what ultimately points in the direction of either a longing for, or at least serving as reflections on, the consequences of a lost world understood and observed in holistic terms.[16]

II.2 Holism and Differentiation in Economics and Political Economy

Within economics and political economy, a sub-variant of this debate has unfolded. With initial skirmishes unfolding from Smith and Ricardo to Hegel and Marx, the defining battle emerged with the constitution of economics as a largely self-contained academic discipline in the switch from the dominance of the German historical school, associated in various ways with von Schmoller, Weber, Schumpeter and others, to the analytical, model based, largely US-based economic discipline of today. The switch from the 'real world' (i.e. history), to analytical models is normally considered a switch from holism to differentiation because the German historical school ultimately subscribed to a particular holistic inspired philosophy of history.[17] This view, however, is highly questionable. Rather than representing an advancement of modernity, analytical economics remain stuck in the past, in so far as the axis around which modern economic theories circulates is a notion of 'equilibrium' and the idea that markets tend towards it. Any notion of equilibrium, or balance, however, presupposes a whole which can be 'in balance'. Contemporary economics is yin and yang science, where the whole (i.e. 'the market'), is a body which is greater than its parts (i.e. supply and demand). This is also expressed by the everyday stylisation of the market as a *persona* with autonomous

[16] Poul F. Kjaer, 'The Structural Transformation of Embeddedness', in: Josef Falke and Christian Joerges (eds.), *Karl Polanyi, Globalisation and the Potential of Law in Transnational Markets* (Oxford: Hart Publishing, 2011), pp. 85–104, at 89 et seq. See, also, Niklas Luhmann, *Paradigm Lost: Über die ethische Reflexion der Moral* (Frankfurt aM: Suhrkamp Verlag, 1990).

[17] Yuichi Shionoya, *The Soul of the German Historical School: Methodological Essays on Schmoller, Weber and Schumpeter* (New York: Springer Verlag, 2005).

agency, as expressed in statements such as 'the market expands', 'the market rebounds' or 'the market expects'.[18]

Whereas advanced social theories have shed any notion of equilibrium or balance a long time ago, and substituted them with notions of process and evolution, mainstream economics remains entrenched in holistic thinking of a seventeenth-century origin. This is also apparent from its built-in bias, which tends to see 'society', rather than the state or any other repository of public power, as the central driving force of social development, while, at the same time, 'society' is factually equalled to the market. Hence, 'private' is preferred to 'public', and public intervention is only deemed desirable in the unfortunate case of 'market imperfections'.

The above, somewhat crude, characterisation of the dominant traits of contemporary economics has, of course, been heavily criticised by the political economy discipline, which went its own way in the wake of the differentiation of economics from its neighbouring disciplines. But, even in contemporary political economy, the critique of 'market fundamentalism' and the crude world view concerning the nature of economic relations which dominates the economic discipline has, however, not implied an abandoning of the holistic premise, but merely a substitution of market holism with cultural holism. *The Three Worlds of Welfare Capitalism* approach, associated with Gøsta Esping-Andersen, advances, as is also apparent from the title, an image of distinct universes of welfare capitalism.[19] In a similar manner, *The Varieties of Capitalism* literature tends simply to speak of 'France', 'Germany' or the 'United States', assuming that they are unified and singular entities. From this perspective, the state/society distinction does not exist or is at least disregarded in so far as the objects of study are ontological presupposed and assumed to be 'culturally given' holistic national units, made up of all social communications unfolding within their respective borders and seen as tending to move towards some sort of institutional equilibrium.[20] In the German context, Fritz Scharpf and Wolfgang Streeck have, moreover, advanced an implicit culturalistic version of political economy, in which, for

[18] For a deconstruction of the notion of the market, see Geoffrey M. Hodgson, 'How Mythical Markets Mislead Analysis: An Institutionalist Critique of Market Universalism', *Socio-Economic Review*, published ahead of print 9 January 2019, available at: https://doi.org/10.1093/ser/mwy049.

[19] Gøsta Esping-Andersen, *The Three Worlds of Welfare Capitalism* (Cambridge: Polity Press, 1990).

[20] Peter A. Hall and David Soskice (eds.), *Varieties of Capitalism: The Institutional Foundations of Comparative Advantage* (Oxford: Oxford University Press, 2001).

example, the German political economy (i.e. the German capitalist state), is seen as a unitary and holistic system which includes all activities unfolding within the borders of Germany,[21] or through an understanding of the Eurozone as characterised by not only unbridgeable cultural divides, but also by static cultures which are essentially resistant to change.[22]

Due to the deficient conceptual tool boxes at their disposition both market-based economics and culturalist political economy are – for theory-constructing reasons – forced ontologically to assume the prior existence of some sort of given holistic unity which tends towards equilibrium upon the basis of mysterious forces. The essential nature of their respective constructions, therefore, only differs to a limited extent, because both types of theories lack the conceptual framework which would enable them to go beyond a holistic world view. As such, both strands can be understood as based upon foundationalism of an essential metaphysical character. Or differently expressed: Mainstream economics and political economy share the trait that they have not yet moved into the post-metaphysical era.[23]

The divide between market holism and cultural holism was particularly highlighted in the stand-off between Friedrich August von Hayek and Karl Paul Polanyi (*Polányi Károly* in Hungarian) which, to a large extent, continues to dominate contemporary debates on political economy.[24] In 1944, Hayek and Polanyi published *The Road to Serfdom* and *The Great Transformation* respectively and, in doing so, asked the same question: Why had totalitarianism emerged and

[21] Wolfgang Streeck, *Re-Forming Capitalism: Institutional Change in the German Political Economy*, 2nd edition (Oxford: Oxford University Press, 2010).

[22] Fritz W. Scharpf, 'The Costs of Non-disintegration: The Case of the European Monetary Union', in: Damian Chalmers, Markus Jachtenfuchs and Christian Joerges (eds.), *The End of the Eurocrats' Dream: Adjusting to European Diversity* (Cambridge: Cambridge University Press, 2016), pp. 29–49.

[23] Jürgen Habermas, *Nachmetaphysisches Denken* (Frankfurt aM: Suhrkamp Verlag, 1988). An important exception can, however, be found by Ngai-Ling Sum and Bob Jessop. In their version of cultural political economy, analyses of sense- and meaning-making are linked to instituted economic and political relations, thereby combining semiotic and structural features without falling into the trap of foundationalism. See Ngai-Ling Sum and Bob Jessop, *Towards a Cultural Political Economy: Putting Culture in its Place in Political Economy* (Cheltenham: Edward Elgar Publishing, 2013).

[24] See, for example, the contributions in (2018) 15 *Globalizations*, issue 7, special edition, entitled 'Questioning the Utopian Springs of Market Economy', guest edited by Damien Cahill, Martijn Konings and Adam David Morton, 887–1057.

succeeded?[25] The answers they gave were, however, diametrically opposed to one another. Hayek's answer was that the economy had not been differentiated enough from the rest of society (i.e. that society had become characterised by de-differentiation and a capture of the economy by politics). For Polanyi, the main problem was, on the other hand, a society in which the economy had become 'too detached' and dis-embedded from the rest of society. In short, the answers that they gave were yet another variation of the holism versus differentiation debate.

But even though Hayek seemingly opted for differentiation, his theoretical construction remained bound up on the ontological idea of the market, simultaneously understood as the sum of individual preferences and as a holistic universe in its own right, making it into more than the sum of individual preferences. In addition, both of them end up with lopsided theoretical constructions characterised by incongruous methodologies aimed at comparing 'apples and pears'. This is the case because they base their respective conclusions upon selective comparisons between empirical realities and highly idealised fictions. By Hayek, this is expressed in the comparison that he makes between the spontaneous order of the market as a fictional ideal, and the empirical reality of politics as selectively embodied in Stalinism and National Socialism. By Polanyi, on the other hand, the focus is on the empirical reality of market society, which is conceived of as essentially brutal and which is contrasted with the fictional ideal of a holistic and communitarian pre-modern world characterised by integrated and harmonic social exchanges.[26]

Yet another variant of the holism versus differentiation tension can be observed in the gradual substitution of the 1970s variant of structural Marxism with structural Liberalism (i.e. neoliberalism), as the fashionable ideology of the day. In theoretical terms, this merely implied a switch from one side to the other of the same coin, in so far as both assumed that society could be understood as being predominantly structured by economic interests and motivations, and that 'society' could be equalled to

[25] Friedrich A. Hayek, *The Road to Serfdom* (Chicago IL: University of Chicago Press, [1944] 1994); Karl Polanyi, *The Great Transformation: The Political and Economic Origins of Our Time*, 2nd ed. (Boston MA: Beacon Press [1944] 2001).

[26] An equally skewed reactionary-communitarian version of the Polanyian approach can be found in Wolfgang Streeck in his comparison between the real existing capitalist market economy and an ideal vision of democracy which, for Streeck, is equal to nationally constituted and embedded left-wing social democracy. For this capitalism versus democracy dichotomy within a nationalist frame, see, for example, Wolfgang Streeck, 'How will Capitalism End?', *New Left Review*, 87, May/June 2014, 35–64.

the economy. Both ideologies saw and see the economy and private power, and not the state and public power, as the true driving force of societal evolution, and, for both, state action ultimately remains guided by economic interests, leaving little autonomy for public power and law. If one digs deep enough behind both world views, one will find a holistic notion of society which is seen as the central source of meaning and evolution.[27]

II.3 Beyond Holism and Differentiation through Law

Within law, the holism versus differentiation debate has crystallised in another sub-debate on democracy versus rights and republican versus liberal approaches, often historically described as a relentless hollowing out of republican values and the rise of rights-based liberalism,[28] and continued attempts to square the circle between the two approaches.[29] The move towards a hollowing out of republican values can be understood as reflecting a progressive 'self-emptying of power'[30] through a substitution of politics with law.[31] Within political philosophy, the liberals versus communitarians debate of the 1990s might, furthermore, be seen as an offspring of the holism versus differentiation perspective on the world.

But, more fundamentally, law can also be seen as the social formation which – at least potentially – overcomes the trade-off between holism and differentiation. A central contribution of law to the rest of society is form giving, in which a social exchange becomes an economic exchange when given legal form and status through instruments such as contracts and property rights, and a social exchange becomes a political act when

[27] Poul F. Kjaer, 'Context Construction through Competition: The Prerogative of Public Power, Intermediary Institutions and the Expansion of Statehood through Competition' (2015) 16 *Distinktion*, 146–66.

[28] For example, Martin Loughlin, *What Is Constitutionalisation?*, in: Petra Dobner and Martin Loughlin (eds.), *The Twilight of Constitutionalism?* (Oxford: Oxford University Press, 2010), pp. 47–69.

[29] Most notably pursued by Habermas. See Jürgen Habermas, *Faktizität und Geltung. Beiträge zur Diskurstheorie des Rechts und des demokratischen Rechtsstaats* (Frankfurt aM: Suhrkamp Verlag, 1992).

[30] Jean Clam, 'What Is Modern Power?', in: Michael King and Chris Thornhill (eds.), *Luhmann on Law and Politics* (Oxford, Hart Publishing, 2006), pp. 145–62.

[31] Franz L. Neumann, 'The Change in the Function of Law in Modern Society', in: William E. Scheuerman (ed.), *The Rule of Law Under Siege: Selected Essays of Franz L. Neumann and Otto Kirchheimer* (Berkeley CA: University of California Press, [1933] 1996), pp. 101–41.

unfolded as formal legally framed decision making or when relying on legally constructed citizen rights, such as the right to vote, and other constitutional principles. Bridges between different spheres of society, such as the economy and politics, are also built through law, as, for example, expressed through the legal structuring and constitutional linking of taxation and representation.

In sociological terms, this means that it is through law that the functional differentiation of society is given form, in so far as law *simultaneously* separates and reconnects the different functional spheres of society. Law, in other words, has the *potential* to ensure the integration of society in a manner which goes beyond the zero-sum holism versus differentiation perspective. It is through law that a self-reflexive loop is established between a functional sphere (Hegel/Durkheim), social system (Luhmann) or field (Bourdieu) and the rest of society. Or to express it differently, it is through the coupling with law that a social system becomes a social system. Methodologically, this has profound consequences, as the very object of study becomes law, or, more correctly, the legal form. Following Hans Kelsen's identity thesis, the study of the state, for example, becomes the study of law, in so far as the state is the law and vice versa.[32] *If* one functional system takes up an overarching position in society, in the sense that it has a strategic position which enables it to serve as the central framework for the integration of society, it is therefore the legal system, and *not* the political or the economic system, because the legal system is what gives form to modern society. Again using the example of statehood, a modern state distinguishes itself from other types of ordering through the particular way in which it establishes a coupling with autonomous law through constitutional self-binding. The essential point concerning the nature of the state and other institutional repositories of political power (or, in fact, any other institutionalised social phenomena), is that states do not and cannot exist outside the law, and it is the law which constitutes the state and not the other way around. This is the case because there can be 'no sovereignty beyond legality',[33] or to

[32] See Hans Kelsen, *Pure Theory of Law* (Berkeley CA: University of California Press, [1934] 1960), p. 279 et seq.

[33] Hauke Brunkhorst, *Critical Theory of Legal Revolutions: Evolutionary Perspectives* (London: Bloomsbury Academic, 2014), p. 127. For more on this, see also the review by Poul F. Kjaer, 'Hauke Brunkhorst: Critical Theory of Legal Revolutions: Evolutionary Perspectives' (2015) 42 *Journal of Law and Society*, 312–18.

paraphrase Hannah Arendt, outside the law, there is no power only violence.[34] As argued by Franz Neumann, political freedom, both positively and negatively conceived, is therefore constituted through law, as it is rights, political, economic and social, which provide such freedom with its form, hereby, once again, underlining the constitutive function of law.[35]

The Marxist critique of law as an inseparable and constitutive element of capitalism is therefore both right and wrong. There is, indeed, no economy without law, and law is, indeed, intrinsic to economic reproduction.[36] But law is also intrinsic to all other institutionalised social formations. Modern political power, for example, is, as already indicated, legally constituted power.[37] But even more important, the modern version of this form-giving function of law established through simultaneous separation and reconnection of the functional spheres of society did not emerge from the dialectical stand-off between the economy and political power, but instead from the tension between religion and political power. The modern world emerged as an outcome of the tenth and eleventh century Investiture Controversy between the Pope and the Holy Roman Emperor. Modernity started with the central outcome of this Controversy, namely, the *simultaneous* differentiation and coupling of religion and law, giving religion, within the framework of the Church, a specific legal form. In short, the basic legal infrastructure of modern society was developed in the stand-off between politics and religion, and not in the stand-off between politics and the economy.[38] Later differentiations and couplings, such as the also legally mediated distinction between the economy and politics, as expressed in the law of

[34] Hannah Arendt, *On Violence* (New York: Harvest Books, 1970).

[35] Franz L. Neumann, 'The Concept of Political Freedom', in: William E. Scheuerman (ed.), *The Rule of Law Under Siege: Selected Essays of Franz L. Neumann and Otto Kirchheimer* (Berkeley CA: University of California Press, [1933] 1996), pp. 195–223.

[36] See, for example, the work of Grietje Baars. Especially, Grietje Baars, *The Corporation, Law and Capitalism. A Radical Perspective on the Role of Law in the Global Political Economy* (Leiden: Brill, 2019).

[37] Franz L. Neumann, 'The Change in the Function of Law in Modern Society', in: William E. Scheuerman (ed.), *The Rule of Law Under Siege: Selected Essays of Franz L. Neumann and Otto Kirchheimer* (Berkeley CA: University of California Press, [1933] 1996), pp. 101–41.

[38] Brunkhorst, *Critical Theory of Legal Revolutions: Evolutionary Perspectives*, n. 33 above; Harold J. Berman, *Law and Revolution: The Formation of the Western Legal Tradition*, Vol. I (Cambridge MA: Harvard University Press, 1983); Harold J. Berman, *Law and Revolution*, Vol. II: *The Impact of the Protestant Reformation in the Western Legal Tradition* (Cambridge MA: Harvard University Press, 2006), new edition.

political economy, are just variations of this first modern distinction. In the same manner as the emerging sovereign state *à la* Bodin and Hobbes was an imitation of the Kingdom of God,[39] the law of political economy is based upon recycled material emerging from the law of religion.

The breakthrough of modernity, at the time of the Atlantic Revolutions, implied a gradual shift of focus from religion to the economy, a development which, however, advanced slower than is often assumed, with the real shift only taking place in the first half of the twentieth century, a shift which, especially in the European context, has so far played out in three different institutional formations: those associated with the 'turn to corporatism' in the interwar period, the 'turn to neo-corporatism' in the immediate post-WWII era, and the 'turn to governance' since the late 1970s. All these shifts implied a recalibration of the function and status of law in general, and the law of political economy in particular. These shifts, as will become apparent below, might also be seen as different ways of approaching the relation between hierarchy and spontaneity in society through law, thereby providing an historical-empirical counterpart to the conceptual-theoretical distinction between holism and differentiation.

III The 'Turn to Corporatism' and the Suspension of Law

Contrary to popular perception, the factual realisation of the idea of legally constituted modern public power resting on legally constituted public sovereignty, which was advanced in the context of the Atlantic Revolutions, was a rather protracted affair.[40] Conglomerate *quasi*-feudal empires with strong privatistic and multilevel features, rather than nation states, to which the characteristics of modern legally constituted public power were attached, remained the dominant form of statehood on the

[39] Ernst H. Kantorowicz, *The King's Two Bodies: A Study in Medieval Political Theology* (Princeton NJ: Princeton University Press, [1957] 1997).

[40] The following illustrative historical-empirical reconstruction is largely limited to European developments though the insights might, in adjusted form, also be relevant for non-European settings. The reconstruction is based upon and expands, Poul F. Kjaer, 'European Crises of Legally-Constituted Public Power: From the "Law of Corporatism" to the "Law of Governance"' (2017) 23 *European Law Journal*, 417–30; Poul F. Kjaer, 'From the Crisis of Corporatism to the Crisis of Governance', in: Poul F. Kjaer and Niklas Olsen (eds.), *Critical Theories of Crises in Europe: From Weimar to the Euro* (London: Rowman & Littlefield, 2016), pp. 125–39; and Poul F. Kjaer, 'Context Construction through Competition: The Prerogative of Public Power, Intermediary Institutions and the Expansion of Statehood through Competition' (2015) 16 *Distinktion*, 146–66.

European continent right up to the implosion of the multinational Austro-Hungarian, German, Ottoman and Russian empires in the wake of WWI.[41] It was not until this point in time that modern nation statehood became the paradigmatic form of legal organisation in (continental) Europe.[42] With Czechoslovakia an important exception, the Central and Eastern states succeeding the continental empires all succumbed to different degrees of authoritarianism within a decade of their formation,[43] just as the democratic state of law inherent to modern statehood eroded or came under severe pressure throughout the rest of Europe as well.[44] This breakdown of legally constituted public power was intrinsically linked to the 'turn to corporatism' which unfolded throughout interwar Europe and which became the manifestation of the law of political economy. Drawing on earlier institutional formations, mostly related to the guilds and corresponding ideological articulations,[45] a diverse and multifaceted string of corporatist institutional formations and corresponding ideological movements gained momentum in the years following WWI, manifesting themselves in reactionary, totalitarian and progressive formats. The term 'corporatism' became the word of the day, gaining a level of popularity comparable with the popularity of the term 'governance' today, while also maintaining a similar illusive and catch-all character.[46] Factually, corporatism gained different institutional

[41] For two distinct approaches to the delayed modernity thesis, see Arno J. Mayer, *The Persistence of the Old Regime: Europe to the Great War* (New York: Pantheon Books, 1981), and Eugen Weber, *Peasants into Frenchmen: The Modernization of Rural France, 1870–1914* (Stanford CA: Stanford University Press, 1976).

[42] For Germany, see, for example, Franz L. Neumann, 'The Decay of German Democracy', in: William E. Scheuerman (ed.), *The Rule of Law Under Siege: Selected Essays of Franz L. Neumann and Otto Kirchheimer* (Berkeley CA: University of California Press, [1933] 1996), pp. 29–43. A similar case can be made in relation to the United States. See, also, Hauke Brunkhorst, *Critical Theory of Legal Revolutions: Evolutionary Perspectives*, n. 33 above.

[43] Balázs Trencsényi, 'The Crisis of Modernity – Modernity as Crisis: Toward a Typology of Crisis Discourses in Interwar East and Central Europe and Beyond', in: Poul F. Kjaer and Niklas Olsen (eds.), *Critical Theories of Crises in Europe: From Weimar to the Euro* (London: Rowman & Littlefield, 2016), pp. 37–52.

[44] Chris Thornhill, *A Sociology of Constitutions: Constitutions and State Legitimacy in Historical-Sociological Perspective* (Cambridge: Cambridge University Press, 2011), p. 275 et seq.

[45] Émile Durkheim, *De la Division du Travail Social* (Paris: CreateSpace, [1893] 2015), p. 10 et seq; Heinz-Gerhard Haupt, *Das Ende der Zünfte. Ein europäischer Vergleich* (Göttingen: Vandenhoeck & Ruprecht, 2004).

[46] Bob Jessop, 'Corporatism and Beyond? On Governance and its Limits', in: Eva Hartmann and Poul F. Kjaer (eds.), *The Evolution of Intermediary Institutions in Europe: From Corporatism to Governance* (Basingstoke: Palgrave Macmillan, 2015), pp. 29–46.

expressions in different national settings, from Austria, Germany, Hungary, and Italy to Spain, which all subsequently turned to authoritarianism or totalitarianism, at the same time that corporatism also gained considerable influence in democratic settings from France to the Netherlands and from Scandinavia to the United Kingdom.[47]

In spite of its multifaceted character, a number of core and shared features of corporatism, which were shared across ideological and national boundaries, can be distilled:

1. A holistic focus on 'society' in its entirety derived from an understanding of society as an organic body, rather than a focus on the state or other institutional repositories of public power. Overcoming the distinction between the public and private dimensions of society was, therefore, at the forefront of corporatist development;
2. A sectorial outlook, in *praxis* representing an in-built contradiction to the holistic outlook, emphasising the organisation of society along functional lines upon the basis of interest representation;
3. A rejection of the rule of law and legal formalism, since law and legal instruments came to be seen as a hindrance to efficient and goal-orientated planning and political action.

In general theoretical terms, corporatism can also be understood as reflecting a rejection of the spontaneous dimension of social processes and their substitution with planned and organised processes. Most functionally differentiated areas of society are characterised by a duality between hierarchically organised and spontaneously coordinated areas, as, for example, expressed in the distinction between firms and the market, the political system and public opinion, and between institutionalised religious congregations and their believers.[48] It was precisely this duality which came under attack through the corporatist intention to substitute spontaneous processes, including, but not only, market-based processes, with hierarchical structures which relied on organisation and planning. Not surprisingly, price control, rather than free price formation and

[47] Poul F. Kjaer, 'From the Crisis of Corporatism to the Crisis of Governance', in: Poul F. Kjaer and Niklas Olsen (eds.), *Critical Theories of Crises in Europe: From Weimar to the Euro* (London: Rowman & Littlefield, 2016), pp. 125–39.

[48] Gunther Teubner, *Constitutional Fragments: Societal Constitutionalism and Globalization* (Oxford: Oxford University Press, 2012), p. 88 et seq.

competition on the market, thus became a key aspect of the economic dimension of corporatism.[49] In its economic dimension, cartelisation thus became, at both national and transnational level, the dominant concrete organisational and legal form of corporatism.[50] This move to cartelisation factually implied the emergence of hybrid structures which cut across the public/private divide, allowing both the intrusion of states into the economy and an inclusion of private actors into public policy. Corporatism thus reflected, as, for example, was apparent in Weimar Germany, both an opening of the private realm to a high level of arbitrary state intervention, as well as a factual (re-)privatisation of public power as informal networks, most notably from industry, which, de facto, became an institutional actor of the state.[51]

Moreover, this factual suspension of the public/private distinction was, as indicated, connected to a more fundamental rejection of the rule of law. This rejection of law, which was taken to an extreme in Fascist Italy and National Socialist Germany, implied a dismissal of the modern form of statehood and legally constituted public power. As argued by Neumann, focusing on developments in the German context, the consequence was not only a strongly cartelised economy and a more general eradication of the separation between the state and the rest of society, but also the disappearance of the state, and, with it, the realm of public power. A state is constituted through the legal distinction between the state and the rest of society, and the dissolution of the distinction therefore also implies the dissolution of the state. In the German case, this process had already begun during the WWI through the introduction of a corporatist *war economy*, and gradually became more entrenched during the Weimar years, reaching its climax during the National Socialist regime. Rather than a 'strong state', National Socialism became characterised by a particular form of 'totalitarian pluralism' in which the notion of statehood had lost its

49 Wolfram Kaiser and Johan Schot, *Writing the Rules for Europe: Experts, Cartels, International Organizations* (Basingstoke: Palgrave Macmillan, 2014), p. 107 et seq.

50 Andrea Colli, *Dynamics of International Business: Comparative Perspectives of Firms, Markets and Countries* (Abingdon: Routledge, 2016), p. 134 et seq.

51 Ruth Dukes, *The Labour Constitution: The Enduring Idea of Labour Law* (Oxford: Oxford University Press, 2014); Chris Thornhill, 'The Constitutionalisation of Labour Law and the Crisis of National Democracy', in: Poul F. Kjaer and Niklas Olsen (eds.), *Critical Theories of Crises in Europe: From Weimar to the Euro* (London: Rowman & Littlefield, 2016), pp. 89–106.

meaning, as both the formal and factual distinction between the state and the rest of society had disappeared altogether.[52] Alternatively, one can, as argued by Ernst Fraenkel, speak of a 'dual state', since the legal system, continued partly as a 'normative state' (*Normenstaat*) and partly as a 'prerogative state' (*Maßnahmenstaat*), with the latter allowing for a continuation of social exchanges within the economy and other segments of society, for example, through the enforcement of contracts, while the latter *instrumentalised the law,* deploying legal instruments as a tool both in and for the advancement of arbitrary political objectives and for the suppression of resistance to the regime.[53]

IV The 'Turn to Neo-Corporatism' – Separation and Reconnection through Law

Against the background of the interwar experience, de-cartelisation and a competition-based market economy gained a central strategic status in the post-war European order, becoming central pillars of a new paradigm of the law of political economy. As already mentioned, Hayek and Polanyi simultaneously developed theories concerned with why totalitarian regimes had emerged but arrived at diametrically opposed conclusions in so far as the former argued that the problem was 'too little', and the latter 'too much', market and competition. In sociological terms, their respective positions can also be seen as focused upon whether the existence or the absence of a functionally differentiated society was the underlying reason for the emergence of totalitarianism. For Neumann, competition furthermore emerged as one of the 'four Ds' which subsequently became the pillar of the US-American occupation strategy in Germany: de-nazification, democratisation, de-militarisation, and finally de-cartelisation.[54] While not sharing Hayek's general stance on society

[52] Jürgen Bast, *Totalitärer Pluralismus. Zu Franz L. Neumanns Analysen der politischen und rechtlichen Struktur der NS-Herrschaft* (Tübingen: Mohr Siebeck, 1999), p. 279 et seq; Franz L. Neumann, *Behemoth: The Structure and Practice of National Socialism, 1933–1944* (Chicago IL: Ivan R. Dee ([1944] 2011), p. 467 et seq. For a somewhat similar view, see, also, Michel Foucault, *La naissance de la biopolitique. Cours au collège de France 1978–1979* (Paris: Seuil, 2004), p. 105 et seq.

[53] Ernest Fraenkel, *The Dual State: A Contribution to the Theory of Dictatorship* (New York: Oxford University Press, 1941).

[54] Neumann, *Behemoth: The Structure and Practice of National Socialism, 1933–1944*, n. 52 above.

and its central driving forces, as well as avoiding market holism, Neumann decisively opted for a functional differentiation approach, in so far as his central point was that de-differentiation between economic and political processes due to a suspension of generalised formal law was a central reason for the breakdown of the Weimar Republic. As such, he admitted a central strategic role to law as the framework which is aimed at simultaneously separating and reconnecting economic and political processes. Inspired by US antitrust policy, he came to see competition law and policy as a central instrument not only aimed at framing economic processes, but also aimed at preventing concentrations of resources and private power to a degree which enabled economic actors to exercise influence over or to undermine the autonomy of the political system. Neumann, in other words, granted competition law constitutional status, seeing it as a core pillar of the constitutional order.

Neumann's stance was unfolded within a wider ideological debate on the compatibility between the rule of law and the emerging welfare state.[55] The evolutionary answer was a double movement oriented at establishing institutional structures which served the dual function of internally stabilising functional, de-limitated spheres such as the economy, health, education, science, and religion, and providing frameworks for the compatibility between these spheres. This cluster of arrangements has traditionally been denoted as 'neo-corporatist', although it has, in fact, essentially nothing in common with earlier forms of corporatism. Although considerable variation can be observed,[56] the welfare-state conglomerates which emerged in Western Europe in the post-war period shared the feature that they had formal organisation and formalised positivist law as their key organisational components, and, as such, they were directly opposed to the core organisational ideal which had driven interwar corporatism. Neo-corporatist structures are characterised by hierarchically organised 'peak-associations' serving as negotiation systems (*Verhandlungssysteme*)[57] which mediate between the different spheres of society, most notably, but not exclusively, between the economy and the political system in the state form, with the objective of establishing mutual stabilisation of exchanges between the spheres in

[55] Christian Joerges, '*Rechtsstaat* and Social Europe: How a Classical Tension Resurfaces in the European Integration Process' (2010) 9 *Comparative Sociology*, 65–85.

[56] Gøsta Esping-Andersen, *The Three Worlds of Welfare Capitalism* (Cambridge: Polity Press, 1990).

[57] Helmut Wilke: *Ironie des Staates: Grundlinien einer Staatstheorie polyzentrischer Gesellschaft* (Frankfurt aM: Suhrkamp Verlag, 1992).

question.[58] What we, in mainstream language, have come to understand as nation states, rather take the form of configurational webs, which are mainly established at the level of organisations and regimes, in so far as the 'higher order' of nation states emerged through a mutual stabilisation of expectations and exchanges between multiple social spheres. Formal organisation became the form through which internal order was established within functionally delineated areas, just as they came to serve as the 'contact points' for inter-systemic exchange between, for example, national organised science, education, religion, health, mass media, economy and politics. The consequence is that a particular form of second order politics emerged. The internal form of stabilisation within functional spheres became a question which was channelled into formalised, often profession-based, organisational arrangements, which produced collectively binding decisions or the functional equivalents to collective decisions within their respective functional areas. It follows that a successful national configuration neither operates upon the basis of a total subordination of society to the modern form of political power in the state form, nor in a form in which the political only resides in the state. Rather, a certain gradualisation of the political can be observed, in the sense that some linkages between the state-based form of the political- and non-state-based forms remained tighter than others, just as the internal degree of hierarchy within the non-state forms differed from societal area to societal area.[59]

In this context, competition, especially within its ordoliberal variant, gained a specific function as the internal form of ordering within the economy. As pointed out by Foucault, this, however, had little to do with laissez-faire liberalism, in so far as competition became institutionalised and formalised as an objective, and its realisation became the task of an 'active policy' and 'governmental art'.[60] Consequently, the market and the state are not just in need of separation, but also in need of reconnection, in so far as 'pure competition' can only be produced through 'governmentality'. Especially in the German context, the form of this

[58] David Sciulli, *Theory of Societal Constitutionalism: Foundations of a non-Marxist Critical Theory* (Cambridge: Cambridge University Press, 1992), p. 73 et seq.

[59] Poul F. Kjaer, 'Law and Order within and beyond National Configurations', in: Poul F. Kjaer, Gunther Teubner and Alberto Febbrajo (eds.), *The Financial Crisis in Constitutional Perspective: The Dark Side of Functional Differentiation* (Oxford: Hart Publishing, 2011), pp. 395–430.

[60] Foucault, *La naissance de la biopolitique. Cours au collège de France 1978–1979*, n. 52 above, p. 121 et seq.

relationship was, however, essentially a legal one. The intervention of the state in the structuring of economic exchanges was based upon ordoliberal ideas, at least ideally, and based upon a double movement aimed at *simultaneously* separating and reconnecting the economy and politics through law. Thus, the objective was to maintain functional differentiation while reintegrating the economy and politics within a specific form. This, much neglected by Foucault, gives law a strategic position as the form through which expectations are stabilised, and exchanges and transfers take place between the economy and the political system in the state form. Foucault furthermore indicates that the structuring of the market becomes the overriding purpose of the state. While structuring the market indeed is a central function of the political system in the state form, this view probably underestimates the orientation of the state towards its own reproduction and the expansion of state power as well as the general function reproduced by states vis-à-vis society in its entirety.[61]

The constitutional coupling of law and politics is aimed at establishing the general convergence of the time structures of society and this is the central integrative contribution of states to society.[62] The convergence between the market and rest of society is just one dimension of this as the 'state-complex' of law and politics constitutes a common context through the structuring of relations and the convergence of time between a whole string of social spheres and regimes. This is also reflected in the societal reality of most post-war European settings, in so far as areas such as science, health, and education remained largely excluded from the market and were, instead, structured upon the basis of an ideal of professional autonomy. Like the market, this sort of autonomy was characterised by a dual set-up, simultaneously emphasising their self-regulatory nature and their reliance on an external legal basis provided by the state. Thus, in North Western Europe, the post-war period was marked by a massive strengthening of competition as an institutionalised form in relation to economic production processes and a simultaneous, legally structured, limitation of competition to the economic sphere, which enabled the political system in the state form to stabilise itself as the 'first among equals' within the larger conglomerate of the laterally related institutional

[61] Poul F. Kjaer, 'Context Construction through Competition: The Prerogative of Public Power, Intermediary Institutions and the Expansion of Statehood through Competition' (2015) 16 *Distinktion*, 146–66.

[62] Niklas Luhmann, *Recht der Gesellschaft* (Frankfurt aM: Suhrkamp Verlag, 1993), p. 427 et seq.

regimes which make up the nation state. Thus, also the so-called golden-age nation-state was not reflecting an outright state-centred society. What, in layman's language, is understood as the nation state should therefore rather be understood as considerably more complex configuration, in which the horizontal nature of relations between the state and other spheres of society remained a central feature, at the same time as the political-legal complex took up a strategically central position, enabling it to engage with other societal dimensions in an asymmetric manner.[63]

V The 'Turn to Governance' – Beyond the Form of Law

As a response to the 'turn to corporatism' and totalitarianism, Western Europe underwent a profound dual (trans-)national reconstitution process in the immediate post-WWII period, which implied a reinvigoration of public power within a neo-corporatist framework.[64] Together with *Les Trente Glorieuses* and the *Wirtschaftswunder*, this development provided for the expectation that Western Europe had finally arrived in modernity. However, since the 1970s, this has gradually changed due to a 'return of crisis',[65] as embodied in the stagnation crisis of the 1970s and the possibly interconnected financial crisis which became visible in 2007.[66]

It was in the context of this prolonged crisis trajectory that the 'turn to governance' gradually unfolded from the 1970s onwards. As was the case with the 'turn to corporatism', the emergence of

[63] Poul F. Kjaer, 'From Corporatism to Governance: Dimensions of a Theory of Intermediary Institutions', in: Eva Hartmann and Poul F. Kjaer (eds.), *The Evolution of Intermediary Institutions in Europe: From Corporatism to Governance* (Basingstoke: Palgrave Macmillan, 2015), pp. 11–28.

[64] Kjaer, 'From the Crisis of Corporatism to the Crisis of Governance', n. 40 above; Poul F. Kjaer, 'Towards a Sociology of Intermediary Institutions: The Role of Law in Corporatism, Neo-Corporatism and Governance', in: Mikael Rask Madsen and Chris Thornhill (eds.), *Law and the Formation of Modern Europe: Perspectives from the Historical Sociology of Law* (Cambridge: Cambridge University Press, 2014), pp. 117–41. More generally on the post-WWII reconstitution process, see Hauke Brunkhorst, *Critical Theory of Legal Revolutions: Evolutionary Perspectives*, n. 33 above, p. 436 et seq., and John Erik Fossum and Agustín José Menéndez, *The Constitution's Gift: A Constitutional Theory for a Democratic European Union* (Lanham MD: Rowman & Littlefield, 2011), p. 78 et seq.

[65] Hauke Brunkhorst, 'The Return of Crisis', in: Poul F. Kjaer, Gunther Teubner and Alberto Febbrajo (eds.), *The Financial Crisis in Constitutional Perspective: The Dark Side of Functional Differentiation* (Oxford: Hart Publishing, 2011), pp. 133–71.

[66] Wolfgang Streeck, *Gekaufte Zeit: Die vertagte Krise des demokratischen Kapitalismus* (Berlin: Suhrkamp Verlag, 2013).

the governance phenomenon has a dual character which is reflected in concrete institutional transformations, as well as in discursive articulations of particular intentions. The concept furthermore remains as multifaceted and elusive as the concept of corporatism, thereby depriving it of the status of a legal concept in the strict sense.[67] In terms of origin, two different strands can be detected. One mainly has nation-state origins and was closely associated with the introduction of New Public Management and concordant policies associated with the decentralisation, privatisation and deregulatory and re-regulatory reform programmes which took shape from the 1970s onwards. In terms of scholarly origin, this strand can furthermore be considered a further development of the theories of steering developed in the 1970s.[68] Another strand refers to transnational regimes centred on public international organisations such as the World Bank, the original creator of the concept, and public international organisations, such as the IMF and the OECD, and, of course, the EU.[69]

A common core of the various strands, however, shows certain affinities with the characteristics previously highlighted in relation to the 'turn to corporatism':

1. A holistic focus on 'society', rather than the state or other institutional repositories of public power. This implies an explicit intention to cut across the public/private divide, thereby undermining the distinction between state and society or equivalent distinctions between institutional repositories of public power and the rest of society. 'Society as such', rather than institutional realms of public power, thereby gains the front seat, being seen as both the object and the subject of policy making, while, at the same time, 'society' *de facto* is equalled to the 'economy';

67 Christoph Möllers, 'European Governance: Meaning and Value of a Concept' (2006) 43 *Common Market Law Review*, pp. 313–36. For an extensive analysis in the EU context, see Poul F. Kjaer, *Between Governing and Governance: On the Emergence, Function and Form of Europe's Post-national Constellation* (Oxford: Hart Publishing, 2010).

68 Renate Mayntz, 'Governance Theory als fortentwickelte Steuerungstheorie?', in: Gunnar Folke Schuppert (ed.), *Governance-Forschung. Vergewisserung über Stand und Entwickungslinien* (Baden-Baden: Nomos Verlag, 2006), pp. 11–20.

69 As expressed in the famous White Paper, *European Governance: A White Paper* (COM (2001) 428 final), 25 July 2001.

2. A sectorial outlook at policy making and legal regimes along functional lines, thereby making it closely aligned with the tendency towards the increased fragmentation of legal ordering. As such, the governance phenomenon is also characterised by a fundamental in-built contradiction as it simultaneously refers to society in its entirety and furthers the fragmentation of that society.
3. Instead of a focus on the decision-making processes themselves, the focus is externalised through an emphasis on output and efficiency, giving it a strong economistic touch.[70] The consequence is a pragmatic emphasis on decision making and the impact of decision making, paying less attention to the formal legal structuring of decision making and associated issues of accountability. Governance, therefore, implies a turn to informality which goes against the ethos of legal formalism.[71]

The fundamental difference between interwar corporatism and contemporary governance, therefore, seems to be the difference in normative intention, as corporatism, in essence, was about the constitution of a society-based political community unrestrained by formality and law, while governance is about the amelioration of economic efficiency through a loosening of the perceived grip of law and the 'red tape' of government regulation on the market or on market-mimicking social processes. Or, to put it in more abstract terms, whereas corporatism implied a dismissal of the spontaneous dimension of social processes and a re-enforcement of the hierarchical dimension, governance is aimed at ameliorating the spontaneous dimension and a downgrading of the hierarchical dimension. Governance, in other words, turns the intentions of corporatism upside down. But, at the same time, the two discourses share the focus on 'society', rather than the realm of public

[70] Christoph Möllers, 'European Governance: Meaning and Value of a Concept' (2006) 43 *Common Market Law Review*, pp. 313–36, at 314 et seq. For the switch from normativity to efficiency as the guiding thrust of 'governance law', see Sabine Frerichs, 'Taking Governance to Court: Politics, Economics and a New Legal Realism', in: Eva Hartmann and Poul F. Kjaer (eds.), *The Evolution of Intermediary Institutions in Europe: From Corporatism to Governance* (Basingstoke: Palgrave Macmillan, 2015), pp. 157–73.

[71] For an instructive overview of the implications and use of the term 'legal formalism', see Duncan Kennedy, 'Legal Formalism', in: Neil J. Smelser and Paul B. Baltes (eds.), *Encyclopedia of the Social & Behavioral Sciences*, Vol. 13 (Amsterdam: Elsevier, 2011), pp. 8634–38.

power, as their core object, just as they share the turn to informality and the downgrading of law, essentially dismissing the view that law provides the core infrastructure for the structuration of social exchanges and the integration of society. Or expressed differently: governance is corporatism turned upside down.

VI The Structure of the Volume

The holism versus differentiation and hierarchy versus spontaneity dimensions of the law of political economy highlighted above in relation to various historical phases do not and are not intended to provide a complete picture which gives justice to the many facets of law's dealings with political economy. It does, however, set some overall parameters which the other contributions to this volume relate to in various ways. The book is divided into four sections with the first one, in combination with this introductory chapter, setting the scene in a theoretical and conceptual sense. This is followed by a global outlook and then a zooming in on European developments before, in the final section, the dimensions of a new law of political economy are outlined.

The three contributions in the first section challenge the concept of governance and the concept of constitutionalisation, two of the most central prominent concepts of the last decades, arguing that both are 'totalising' concepts which do not recognise the existence of an outside world.

In the first section, Christian Joerges and Michelle Everson reconstruct the largely Germany-centred debate on economic constitutionalism. This is done through a contrasting of the ordoliberal vision of Ernst-Joachim Mestmäcker, which greatly influenced the early decades of the European integration process, with the 'alternative economic law' (*Alternatives Wirtschaftsrecht*) of Rudolf Wiethölter which was explicitly developed as a critique of ordoliberalism upon the basis of the idea an international *ordre public*. Joerges and Everson link up with this vision and engage in the development of a revised conflict-law perspective in the current European constellation, seeing it as a possible route out of the crisis of the last decade through an attempt to safeguard the proprium of law within that constellation.

In the following chapter, Emilios Christodoulidis exposes what he calls the myth of democratic governance, the idea that the move to flexible, decentralised, informal soft law modes of coordination provides an alternative to classical representative democracy. Rather, the turn to governance has facilitated a cutting adrift of the economy from political processes and the installation of the market principle as the central guarantor of both public interests and individual freedom, and has done so in a way which factually underlined the public/private divide and the concurrent distinction between public and private law. As such, the turn to governance implies the installation of the hegemony of market thinking which has no outside and thereby extends to all aspects of society.

Duncan Kennedy follows suit by arguing that law has become instrumentalised, used as a weapon aimed at striking down ideological adversaries. The progressive moves towards juridification, judicialisation and constitutionalisation of the contemporary legal order are seen in this light, as they reflect attempts to install a singular perspective as the higher and hegemonic order. The political economy of law is thus reflected in the continued attempts of collectivities that share material and ideological interests to constitutionalise their particular version of the common good. According to Kennedy, drawing mainly on US-American developments, the consequence of this development is a politicisation of the judiciary, a hollowing out of its claim to impartiality and the destruction of the faith in the methodology of law.

After the sobering contributions of the first section, the attention in the next section is turned to developments in the global political economy and the role of law in this context.

David Kennedy takes issue with the hereto-dominant perspectives on law and global political economy which have seen law as an ordering device aimed at introducing stability into the global political and economic systems while promoting peace, justice and prosperity. Instead, he suggests turning the focus to the law's constitutive role in the continued reproduction of injustice and inequality. Much like Duncan Kennedy, in the domestic US American setting, David Kennedy foregrounds the role of law in political and economic struggles in the global setting, recognising law as an instrument and weapon deployed in distributive struggles.

A clear example of this role of law is revealed in the following chapter in which Isabel Feichtner explores the law's role in the distribution and exploitation of natural resources, and the link between natural resource extraction and the financialisation of the global economy. She explores which bodies of norms shape the political economy of resource extraction, including norms of jurisdiction, ownership and use rights, and the justifications that accompany these norms of allocation, arguing that law has an in-built exploitation bias with respect to natural resource extraction, and that this bias has profound distributive effects. Through a historical reconstruction, she furthermore shows how this bias and related booms and busts in natural resource extraction are intrinsically linked to expansions in the financialisation of the economy.

Jaye Ellis adds another dimension by reminding us that a global perspective on the law of political economy necessitates an explicit anthropocenic view which takes the ecological impact of the law of political economy into account. Observing the current state of global law, she argues that political economy in the anthropocene remains dominated by cognitive instruments and practices, such as standards and indicators which are conditioned on scientific input and mainly operate though managerial governance, rather than law. However, she argues that legal norms have the potential to play a central role in the translation and condensation of scientific insights into components which are actionable in the political economy, thereby highlighting the form-giving function of law.

As becomes apparent in the following section, the global context of law and political economy provides a frame for observing European developments as well. Due to the particular intensity of transnational legal developments in the European context and the long standing European attempts to theorise the different aspects of the relationship between law and political economy, Europe might be seen as a particularly well-suited location for observing both factual as well as scholarly developments pertaining to the law of political economy.

Hans Micklitz sets the scene by establishing a link between the present 'Copenhagen book' and the 1989 'Bremen book' entitled *Critical Legal Thought: An American-German Debate.*[72] A substantial, though far from total, overlap exists among the contributors to the two volumes, allowing for a highlighting of the continuities and discontinuities of the past thirty years. Departing from a critical legal studies (CLS) perspective on the transformation of private law in the European context, he highlights how CLS scholars themselves became central actors in the attempt to construct a European internal market with a social face. This endeavour has, however, been challenged through the consecutive changes in the

[72] Christian Joerges and David M. Trubek (eds.), *Critical Legal Thought: An American-German Debate* (Baden-Baden: Nomos Verlagsgesellschaft, 1989), and Christian Joerges, David M. Trubek and Peer Zumbansen, 'Critical Legal Thought: An American-German Debate-Republication [with a New Introduction] Twenty-Five Years Later' (2011) 12 *German Law Journal*, 1–595, available at: www.germanlawjournal.com/volume-12-no–01.

function and status of law within the European integration process, as it has metamorphosed from 'integration through law' to 'integration through governance' and to 'integration beyond law'.

Marija Bartl follows suit with a reconstruction of the ideational imaginaries about economy and market which unfolds within European private law. By zooming in on European consumer law in particular, she reconstructs how different concepts and imaginaries of market and economy have shaped the integration project over the last thirty years. The transformation observed is essentially one which goes from the attempt to balance market- and non-market-based social formations to an attempt to optimise markets though deepened competition and marketisation. A transformation which is based upon a re-naturalisation of the idea of the market and the idea of the market as the preferred and most efficient form of resource allocation.

Within EU competition law, Jotte Mulder detects a similar transformation as the one observed by Bartl in consumer law. The cartel prohibition, in particular, has undergone a transformation which implies a structural shift which increasingly favours the demand side (consumers) over the supply side (producers). This development has been greatly accelerated since the modernisation and economisation of competition law at the turn of the millennium, which has curtailed the ability of Member States to take non-economic concerns into account. Mulder illustrates this in relation to the Commission's approach to liberal professions and provides two cases on ecological and environmental sustainability in the Netherlands.

Stefano Giubboni shifts the focus to labour law, highlighting the deeply ambivalent relation between labour law and capitalism, a relationship partly characterised by antagonism and partly by labour laws central role in enabling capitalist reproduction. This ambivalence, he argues, has been reinforced in the European context over the past three decades due to a fundamental transformation in the way in which European integration impacts upon national labour law systems. Through the 'internal market'-linked turn to governance, and subsequently through the economic and financial governance regime of the euro, the EU have moved away from safeguarding national autonomy in relation to labour law, thereby factually undermining such autonomy. This is particularly the case after the outbreak and expansion of the European debt crisis from 2009 onwards. The result has been the surge of 'populist' and 'sovereignist' countermovements throughout Europe.

The current state of both the global and the European political economy is marred by uncertainty and an erosion, possibly even an outright breakdown, of the institutional set-up put in place to stabilise economic and political exchanges. The massive transformations that have unfolded over the last four decades – as outlined in the previous chapters – seem to have led to a dead-end or cul-de-sac in the form of an ideational and institutional exhaustion. Against this background, the final section takes up the creative task of reflecting on the possibility of a new law of political economy, its substantial features, its purpose and its form.

Karl-Heinz Ladeur starts out with a radical proposal to go beyond hierarchical 'top-down law' based upon a doctrine of delegation and replacing it with 'serial law', which consists of temporalised experimental search processes characterised by *ex post*, rather than *ex ante*, control, a type of law-making which, he argues, can furthermore emerge from private and hybrid public/private sources, and rely on complex constellations of networked contracts, rather than pure public sources. Such a law, he argues, will correspond far more to the reality in which we now live, that is, a networked and fluid society characterised by data flows, social media, and rapid expansions in advanced technology.

Rodrigo Vallejo follows suit by unfolding a proposal for an understanding of current developments in relation to private regulation as amounting to the emergence of a private administrative law. Contrasting American and European approaches to private regulation, he argues that European rules of recognition concerning private regulation amount to a doctrinal construction containing institutional, formal and substantial dimensions. Thus, a new model of the law of political economy aimed a containing political economy struggles within the structural reality in which they unfold is emerging.

Lars Viellechner goes a step further by exploring the metamorphosis of constitutionalism, and in particular, the emergence of institutions of fundamental rights both within the transnational sphere and within 'private law'-based formations. Viellechner observes a double transformation of law: first an expansion of traditional international law into areas which traditionally have not or have only very slightly been touched upon by international law, such as environmental law, and certain aspects of criminal law and human rights law. Second, the emergence of contract-based transnational governance arrangements, such as the one guiding the Internet Corporation for Assigned Names and Numbers (ICANN), arrangements which, he argues, are based upon a new approach to the horizontal effect of constitutional rights which is capable of addressing the legitimacy demands of such transnational private arrangements.

Gunther Teubner generalises the above reflections by advancing a vision of rights as not only individual rights but also as trans-subjective rights of communicative, collective, and institutional formations in both the public and the private sphere. As such, Teubner argues for a radical expansion of law, allowing it to capture societal processes which are currently beyond its reach. In addition, the focus of rights needs to be expanded not only to focus on protection from the logics of politics in the form of state activity, but also from the logics of the economy and other societal dynamics. The expansion and transformation of the forms of economic reproduction as well as the intensification of other societal processes needs, in other words, to be addressed through a corresponding expansion and transformation of law.

In sum, the volume can be seen as providing a conceptual framework for the study of the law of political economy, a diagnosis of the current state of affairs within world society and specifically in Europe as well as outlining a vision for new law capable of encapsulating the future.

PART I

Studying the Law of Political Economy

2

The Legal Proprium of the Economic Constitution

CHRISTIAN JOERGES AND MICHELLE EVERSON

Une Querelle Allemande?

Writing in early 2019, the rate of challenge to post-war liberal constitutional settlement is breathtaking. Within the nation state, as within the EU, all the complacency that the 2008 financial crisis has been overcome has been blown away as constitutional-democratic processes totter and teeter, assailed by authoritarian leaders and so-called 'populist' movements. Is it at all possible to respond adequately to such fast-paced developments? Our chapter seems to avoid the effort altogether, dealing, instead, with two master thinkers of post-war German jurisprudence. It will, nevertheless, become readily apparent why each of these authors deserves this attention, and why they deserve it now. Our prime concern in our twofold homage reaches far beyond academic laudation, taking, instead, a systematic approach to their work with, we hope, contemporary relevance. We will present the work of our two protagonists, each a member of the same post-war generation, and thus each duty-bound to redefine the proprium of law. The projects developed by Ernst-Joachim Mestmäcker and Rudolf Wiethölter concern the 'ordering' of the economy, or its fruitful placement within the constitutional framework. These perspectives represent two distinct German *Sonderwege* of legal thought. We are also engaged in this contest and are clearly partisan in our conceptual allegiance. Nevertheless, we also pursue a far broader agenda of our own, seeking to deploy both projects, first to shed 'light' on Europe's crisis-ridden post-democratic constellation, and then to explore the potential for the preservation of the legal proprium within a political economy of profound transformation.

I The Economical and the Political

We take as our starting point the contributions made by Ernst-Joachim Mestmäcker and Rudolf Wiethölter to the *Festschrift*, '*Wirtschaftsordnung und Rechtsordnung*', which honoured Franz Böhm on his seventieth birthday in 1965.[1] Franz Böhm had been academic mentor to Mestmäcker for over a decade, and Mestmäcker was deeply indebted in his research to Böhm's seminal work on the 'economic constitution' (*Wirtschaftsverfassung*). Tellingly, in his contribution to the *Festschrift*,[2] he transferred the notion of the economic constitution to the European level, thereby elaborating on its latent supranational ambitions that reached far beyond individual EEC Member States. Wiethölter had received his first *Ruf* (professorial appointment) to Böhm's chair in Frankfurt. He submitted his 1964 inaugural lecture on the '*soziale Rechtsstaat*' (social [rule-of-law] state) to the Böhm *Festschrift*.[3] In his own working out of the social state concept, Wiethölter signalled his indebtedness to the legacy of Herman Heller and his commitment to the defence of the primacy of democratic legitimacy within economy and society. The divergence between these two *Sonderwege* seems so very obvious, yet is also far more complex. We will seek to decipher them by exploring, first, their methodological, and thereafter, their substantive, dimensions.

I.1 The Methodological Dimension

I.1.1 The Exercise of Freedom under General Rules

In a seminal 1972 lecture,[4] Mestmäcker elaborated on the methodological consequences of the constitutional premises that he had laid down in

[1] The idea of a theoretical comparison occurred to us in debate around a review by Christian Joerges of the most recent writings of Ernst-Joachim Mestmäcker (*Europäische Prüfsteine der Herrschaft und des Rechts. Beiträge zu Recht, Wirtschaft und Gesellschaft in der EU* (Baden-Baden: Nomos, 2018), and Christian Joerges, Review Essay, 'The Jurist as True Teacher of Law' (2019) 56 *Common Market Law Review*, 843–64).

[2] 'Offene Märkte im System unverfälschten Wettbewerbs in der EWG', in Helmut Coing, Heinrich Kronstein and Ernst-Joachim Mestmäcker (eds.), *Wirtschaftsordnung und Rechtsordnung. Festschrift zum 70. Geburtstag von Franz Böhm* (Karlsruhe: C.F. Müller, 1965), pp. 345–91.

[3] 'Die Position des Wirtschaftsrechts im sozialen Rechtsstaat', in: *Wirtschaftsordnung und Rechtsordnung*, n. 2 above, pp. 41–62.

[4] 'Macht, Recht, Wirtschaftsverfassung' (1973) 137 *Zeitschrift für das gesamte Handels- und Wirtschaftsrecht*, 97–111; English translation: Mestmäcker, 'Power, Law and Economic Constitution' (1973) 11 *The German Economic Review*, 177–92.

his contribution to the Böhm *Festschrift*, submitting that 'the issue is not merely to recognise the common problems of definition of jurisprudence and economics. It is just as important to develop economic policy solutions susceptible of being bound by legal and constitutional rules.'[5] Wiethölter observed a brief two years thereafter: 'there is little or no room left available for systematic legal logic (doctrine) when synchronisation between the operational techniques of lawyers and the creation of social theory that adequately reflects contemporary society is disturbed or destroyed'.[6]

Faux amis or ideational affinities? Both thinkers were clearly concerned that the law might have 'run out': Was there now a misfit between the logic of economics and the ability of law to order the economic within society? Their concerns were the same, their responses less so. For ordoliberal tradition, an inherent affinity between the legal and the economic had once been a core constitutive premise. In the words of a non-partisan observer, 'The juridical gives form to the economic, and the economic would not be what it is without the juridical.'[7] For Walter Eucken and Franz Böhm, the – somehow – prestabilised harmony between the legal and the economic could never be understood as an unconditional given, but instead required legal-constitutional underpinning for the simple reason that both the practice and the theory of law are moving targets. The conference that hosted Mestmäcker's cited lecture[8] questioned the legacy of Eugen von Böhm-Bawerk, a foundational figure within the Austrian School of Economics, who had argued that the logic of the economy would always – sooner or later – trump non-compliant political aspirations.[9]

5 Mestmäcker, n. 4 above, p. 183. The German original is clearer: 'Die Wirtschaftspolitik müsse sich "verfassungsrechtlich binden" lassen und "nach justiziablen Kriterien richten", Macht-Recht-Wirtschaftsverfassung', *Schriften des Vereins für Socialpolitik*, NF Bd. 47/I, S. 183 [=(1973) 137 *Zeitschrift für das gesamte Handelsrecht und Wirtschaftsrecht*, 97–111].

6 'Privatrecht als Gesellschaftstheorie? Bemerkungen zur Logik der ordnungspolitischen Rechtslehre', in: Fritz Baur, Josef Esser, Friedrich Kübler and Ernst Steindorff (eds.), *Funktionswandel der Privatrechtsinstitutionen. Festschrift für Ludwig Raiser zum 70. Geburtstag* (Tübingen: Mohr/Siebeck, 1974), pp. 645–95.

7 Michel Foucault, *The Birth of Biopolitcs. Lectures at the Collège de France 1978–79* (New York: Palgrave, 2014), p. 163.

8 German Association of Economists (*Verein für Socialpolitik*), Annual Meeting 1972 in Bonn on 'Macht und ökonomisches Gesetz'.

9 Eugen von Böhm-Bawerk, 'Control or Economic Law' (Macht oder ökonomisches Gesetz, 1914), Ludwig von Mises Institute: Auburn, Alabama, 2010. *Recht und ökonomisches Gesetz*, the title of an earlier collection of Mestmäcker's essays (Baden-Baden: Nomos, 1978), is his programmatic answer to Böhm-Bawerk.

Mestmäcker embraced this message that the 'rules' of the economy could not simply be assumed to achieve their own equilibrium. He did not, however, explicitly assign to the law any form of 'supportive' supremacy over the economic. On the contrary, his observations appear to us to be quite ambivalent within the established ordoliberal tradition. Although not explicitly disavowing the concretisation of economic policy within legal-constitutional prescription, Mestmäcker diverged to a degree from the views of the two founding ordoliberal fathers, Eucken and Böhm, observing that economic ordering cannot be directed to a given objective, for example, and vitally so, the idea of perfectly competitive markets.

Two reasons explain such caution. One was Mestmäcker's 'Hayekian turn'. Hayek's reconceptualisation of competition as a 'discovery procedure' was to reorient the ordoliberal school.[10] This was a reorientation of paradigmatic dimensions.[11] Competitive processes should only be guided, or limited, by 'abstract legal rules'; any substantive prescription was from now on to be perceived to be an 'anti-competitive' intervention within free market ordering. A further challenge was posed to inherited ordoliberal orthodoxy by the German turn to Keynesianism in the 1960s under the so-called 'super-minister', Karl Schiller. Under the '*Stabilitätsgesetz*' and the '*Konzertierte Aktion*' programmes, introduced in 1967, the political system was now expected to govern within a 'magic triangle' of (competing) goals of price stability, maintenance of the balance of payments, and economic growth. Mestmäcker's closest theoretical ally was among the strongest critics of this turn to economic managerialism.[12] Mestmäcker himself, however, was far more circumspect. His support for the practice of ruling by rules appeared defensive:

[10] Hayek's essay was published in English only in 2002 ((2002) 5 *The Quarterly Journal of Austrian Economics*, 9–23). The German original: '*Wettbewerb als Entdeckungsverfahren*' (Kiel: Institut für Weltwirtschaft, 1968); reprinted in Hayek, *Freiburger Studien* (Tübingen: Mohr Siebeck, 1969), pp. 249–65.

[11] Pierre Dardot und Christian Laval call this turnaround 'neo-ordoliberalism'; see their *The New Way of the World: On Neoliberal Society* (London: Verso Books, 2013), p. 194 et seq., 205 et seq. Dedicated defenders of the ordoliberal tradition tend to downplay the difference; see, recently, Peter Behrens, 'Laudatio', in: Reinhard Ellger and Heike Schweitzer (eds.), *Die Verfassung der europäischen Wirtschaft. Symposium zu Ehren von Ernst-Joachim Mestmäcker aus Anlass seines 90. Geburtstages* (Baden-Baden: Nomos, 2018), pp. 11–22.

[12] Erich Hoppmann (ed.), *Konzertierte Aktion. Kritische Beiträge zu einem Experiment* (Frankfurt aM: Athenäum, 1971); see, for a critical comment, Christian Joerges, 'Vorüberlegungen zu einer Theorie des Internationalen Wirtschaftsrechts' (1979) 43 *Rabels Zeitschrift für ausländisches und internationales Privatrecht*, 6–79, at 44 et seq.

'Up to the present, it has proved possible to administer general clauses by way of court rulings only where the structural similarity between private law and market economic process remains strong.'[13] What, however, of the situation where this structural similarity is distorted? Then, 'the judicial system cannot be wiser than contemporary economics in judging macroeconomic relationships'.[14] Is this merely a pragmatic concession to political power with a collateral impact upon the theoretical coherence of Mestmäcker's position? Or, does it represent something more? This query was never answered, losing its cogency in step with the rise of monetarism and neo-neoliberalism.[15] We will nevertheless necessarily return to this question in the course of our discussion of the present crisis (Part III).

I.1.2 Political Administration

Responding in his turn to this juridification wave, Wiethölter coined his own notion of 'political administration', a term which seeks to capture the specific characteristics of the *soziale Rechtsstaat* as home to:

> a form of law (once incorrectly called regulatory (*Maßnahmegesetze*)), which is distinguished from the classical rule of (substance) law that was derived from transcendental sources, by virtue of its planned and instrumental, or political purpose (goal) orientation. Such laws are neither frameworks, nor boundaries, nor moulds within which all manner of individual acts of legal disposition might be made; rather, they execute – directly or indirectly – a specific content-filled programme.

For Wiethölter, the foundational law of the ordoliberal economic constitution, namely, Ludwig Erhard's 1957 *Kartellgesetz*, as amended by the 1968 Act against Restraints of Competition, suggested itself as the exemplary case. This characterisation most surely has acted as a provocation to his ordoliberal colleagues, but was nevertheless wholly justified. The famed Antitrust Statute was indeed motivated by political objectives, debated in their time with great intensity in the quest for a new *leitmotif* for competition policy. An independent agency (the *Bundeskartellamt* in Berlin), staffed with an eye to necessary interdisciplinarity, with economists and lawyers, was charged with its implementation. The notion of 'political administration' captured these

[13] Mestmäcker (n. 4), 187.

[14] Ibid.; see, also, p. 190 et seq.

[15] See Peter A. Hall, 'Commentary. Brother, Can you Paradigm?' (2013) 26 *Governance: An International Journal of Policy, Administration and Institutions*, 189–92.

innovations well. For his part, rather than elaborate the technical, legal and interdisciplinary niceties, Wiethölter repeatedly refined his vision in thoughtful, brilliant, but also enormously complex, sketches,[16] which Jürgen Habermas has gently mocked: 'Thoughts are gathered meaningfully together like a maxim, only then in the next moment to mix explosively, detonating as ironic fireworks that project allegorical figures into the night sky, which are still in need of deciphering.'[17] But why was Wiethölter so idiosyncratically impatient? Why did he not engage, for example, with the debate on US experiences of the regulatory turn within the New Deal, on Ernst Forsthoff's post-democratic *Industriestaat*,[18] or on Hans Peter Ipsen's conceptualisation of the European Communities as '*Zweckverbände funktioneller Integration*' (special purpose association of functional integration).[19] Would that have made sense? In all of his pleadings for radical democratic innovation, Wiethölter always simultaneously identified the arguments that undermined his visions. The most telling example is a leading competition law case handed down in 1970 by the German Federal Court (*Bundesgerichtshof*).[20] Everything that Wiethölter had complained about in his critique of the premises and practices of German legal science (*Rechtswissenschaft*) became visible within the legalisation of the concerted oligopolistic behaviour of oligopolists: according to the Court, no anticompetitive '*Kartellvertrag*' had come into being (§1 GWB) since, as was the case under the Civil Code, contracts required offer and acceptance – our oligopolists, however, had not been so foolish as to coordinate their behaviour by means of formal contractual conclusion.

At this stage, we can sketch out a first summary: Mestmäcker sought to identify the conceptual conditions under which the market economy could be governed by law – but was forced to realise that these conditions had become fragile. Wiethölter identified the need for a paradigm shift in the coordination of politics and law – but realised that the law, as practised within the mainstream, operated as an insuperable barrier to innovative change. This methodological discrepancy is not easily

[16] See Rudolf Wiethölter, 'Privatrecht als Gesellschaftstheorie? Bemerkungen zur Logik der ordnungspolitischen Rechtslehre', in: Fritz Baur, Josef Esser, Friedrich Kübler and Ernst Steindorff (eds.), *Funktionswandel der Privatrechtsinstitutionen. Festschrift für Ludwig Raiser zum 70. Geburtstag* (Tübingen: Mohr/Siebeck, 1974), pp. 645–95.

[17] Jürgen Habermas, 'Der Philosoph als wahrer Rechtslehrer: Rudolf Wiethölter' (1989) 22 *Kritische Justiz*, 138–46.

[18] *Der Staat der Industriegesellschaft*, 2nd ed. (Munich: C.H. Beck, 1971).

[19] *Europäisches Gemeinschaftsrecht* (Tübingen: Mohr Siebeck, 1972), p. 176 et seq.

[20] BGHZ 53, 104 (=BGHSt 24,54) – '*Teerfarben*'.

categorised as being of a 'conservative' versus a 'progressive' disposition. It is, instead, rooted within more substantive concerns, leading us now to consider the material notion of *Wirtschaftsverfassung*.

I.2 Governance through Competitive Markets or Political Ordering of the Economy

Three years prior to the Böhm *Festschrift*, to which both Mestmäcker and Wiethölter contributed, Jürgen Habermas published his legendary *Strukturwandel der Öffentlichkeit*.[21] In chapter 16 of this work, Habermas addressed the restructuring of the relationship between society and the state, famously arguing that the once so firmly established separation between the two spheres had succumbed, leaving both realms interwoven with one another. It is precisely this blurring of a traditional rule of law conception that proved so troublesome within the search of each of our protagonists for the contemporary proprium of law.[22]

I.2.1 Mestmäcker's *Wirtschaftsverfassung*: The Precondition and Guardian of a Free Society

'*Wirtschaftsordnung und Rechtsordnung*' – a more paradigmatic ordoliberal maxim is scarcely imaginable, and the aptness of this appellation is only confirmed by the difficulty which we face in identifying an adequate translation: 'the order of the economy and the order of the legal' is enigmatic to the point of incomprehensibility. Yet the maxim is more easily deciphered with the help of three core ordoliberal messages:

1. 'The legal' and 'the economic' represent interdependent (mutually dependent) orders.[23]
2. A lack of respect for this interdependence on the part of supporters of the *laissez-faire* tradition impacted negatively on the coherence of law and society, in particular because it favoured the rise of an

[21] Subtitled: *Untersuchungen zu einer Kategorie der bürgerlichen Gesellschaft* (Neuwied-Berlin: Luchterhand, 1962) (*The Structural Transformation of the Public Sphere*) (Cambridge MA: The MIT Press, 1989).

[22] Close affinities with Duncan Kennedy's reconstructions are obvious; suffice it here to mention, 'The Stages of the Decline of the Public/Private Distinction' (1982) 130 *University of Pennsylvania Law Review*, 1349–57.

[23] Walter Eucken, *Grundsätze der Wirtschaftspolitik*, 1st ed., 1952, 7th ed., particularly pp. 332–7. The original text is even older: *Die Grundlagen der Nationalökonomie* (Jena: Fischer, 1940), 2nd ed., 1942); English translation by T.W. Hutchison, *The Foundations of Economics: History and Theory in the Analysis of Economic Reality* (London: William Hodge, 1950), reprint Berlin: Springer, 1992.

unaccountable economic power.[24] This was the reason why the invisible hand of the market had to be replaced by the visible hand of a legal system, which was perforce dedicated to protection of free competitive processes (i.e. the price mechanism) against its distortion by economic power.

3. It follows from the objectives of this type of law, that it must be administered by non-majoritarian institutions (courts and independent agencies); and it is inherent in this vocation that the establishment of this form of law is of constitutional importance.

This is a conceptual edifice of impressive coherence. One query, however, seems pressing: Where do politics come in? This is the query upon which Wiethölter insists in his essay, and which Mestmäcker discusses at greater length a decade later in a follow-up to the *Festschrift* for Böhm, this time entitled '*Wirtschaftsordnung und Staatsverfassung*'. Sharing its title with that of the volume, Mestmäcker's contribution[25] concludes after thirty-six pages:

> The academic school of thought which promotes the *Wirtschaftsverfassung* . . . is not committed to the elaboration of the political potency of the economic, in order to fall into the arms of the democratic regime, but rather seeks to place that regime in a position whereby it can independently and adequately perform its mandated rule of law and welfare tasks.

This is nevertheless a position which places Mestmäcker at odds with prevailing democratic practice, or the socialising aspirations of contemporary democratic societies. At the same time, it demonstrates blatant disregard for the social embeddedness of markets and the cultural dimensions of the economy.[26] In the first Böhm *Festschrift*,

[24] A tendency, which was lucidly diagnosed and criticised by the legal founding father of ordoliberalism, Franz Böhm in his seminal 'Das Reichsgericht und die Kartelle: eine wirtschaftsverfassungsrechtliche Kritik an dem Urteil des RG. vom 4. Febr. 1897, RGZ.38/155' (1948) 1 *ORDO: Jahrbuch für die Ordnung von Wirtschaft und Gesellschaft* (hereinafter *ORDO*), 197–213.

[25] 'Wirtschaftsordnung und Staatsverfassung' in Ernst-Joachim Mestmäcker and Heinz Sauermann (eds.), *Wirtschaftsordnung und Staatsverfassung. Festschrift für Franz Böhm zum 80. Geburtstag* (Tübingen: Mohr Siebeck, 1975), pp. 383–419; reprinted in: Mestmäcker and Sauermann, *Recht und ökonomisches Gesetz* (Baden-Baden: Nomos, 1978), pp. 29–64.

[26] The only discussion of the ordoliberal tradition in Polanyian perspective that we are aware of is David M. Woodruff, 'Ordoliberalism, Polanyi, and the Theodicy of Markets', in: Josef Hien and Christian Joerges (eds.), *Ordoliberalism, Law and the Rule of Economics* (Oxford: Hart Publishing, 2017), pp. 215–28.

Mestmäcker had defined the basis of his theory with greater clarity and less enigmatic mention of the political, under the title '*Offene Märkte im System unverfälschten Wettbewerbs in der EWG*',[27] whereby the institutional structures of the EEC were argued to operate as the visible hand for competitive ordering within the European system.[28] Transference of the *Wirtschaftverfassung* to European level had a strategic advantage, securing the (pre-political) theoretical core of the economic constitutionalist project. Mestmäcker continues to defend the doctrinal character of the integration project, which gains its normative potency from Kantian legal philosophy:[29] 'The fundamental, enforceable rights to freedom and the system of undistorted competition' are the constitution of the European community of law. This community derives its legitimacy, not from the 'continuing legitimation of member state legislatures ... but rather ... systematically ... in the mode of a rule of law ... by means of the justiciability of the freedoms guaranteed by the Treaty'.[30]

I.2.2 Wiethölter's Critique: *Wirtschaftsverfassung* as Stark Utopia and Democratic Failure

Wiethölter's inaugural address provides us with a comprehensive and concise account of the state of Germany's *Wirtschaftsrecht* debate.[31] His own position can be captured in two statements:[32]

[27] 'Offene Märkte im System unverfälschten Wettbewerbs in der EWG', n. 2 above.

[28] Friedrich von Hayek considered European federalisation as early as 1939(!). He assumed political differences between members would preclude the establishment of a European welfare state: 'The Economic Conditions of Interstate Federalism', in: Friedrich A. Hayek, *Individualism and Economic Order* (Chicago IL: University of Chicago Press, 1949), pp. 255–72 (reprinted from the *New Commonwealth Quarterly* V. 2, September 1939, 131–49).

[29] 'Kants Rechtsprinzip als Grundlage der europäischen Einigung', in: Götz Landwehr (ed.), *Freiheit, Gleichheit, Selbständigkeit. Zur Aktualität der Rechtsphilosophie Kants für die Gerechtigkeit in der modernen Gesellschaft* (Göttingen: Vandenhoeck & Ruprecht, 1999), pp. 61–72, cited from the reprint in Ernst-Joachim Mestmäcker, Wirtschaft und Verfassung in der Europäischen Union (Baden-Baden: Nomos, 2003), pp. 78–91.

[30] Ibid., p. 78 et seq.

[31] An important precursor was Horst Ehmke's, *Wirtschaft und Verfassung. Die Verfassungsrechtsprechung des Supreme Court zur Wirtschaftsregulkierung* (Karlsruhe: C.F. Müller, 1961), with a critical, often polemical, introductory chapter on the German debate (pp. 7–88).

[32] Repeated and elaborated two years later in his contribution on 'Recht', in: Gerd Kadelbach (ed.), *Wissenschaft und Gesellschaft* (Frankfurt aM: S. Fischer, 1977), pp. 213–75.

1. 'The overwhelming importance of the economy to the maintenance of political community, not only demands correspondingly-comprehensive legal intervention into spheres impacted by it, but also establishment of an economic law to act as the unifying parenthesis of the economic state.'[33]

Understood as a stark departure from the tradition of Germany's '*Bürgerliches Recht*',[34] Wiethölter's position was bound to encounter opposition both among mainstream academics and in the legal profession. Wiethölter had no illusions in this respect, but built confidently upon the transformative potential of Germany's post-war democracy. In the 1960s, democracy had indeed become a 'normative fact', a compound of sociological conditions, political life and reformist ideas, which motivated his second observation:

2. 'The modern democratic state is home to a broad and powerful demand for comprehensive social self-constitution ... this social state [is not afraid] to solve *the* economic law problem of the 20th century, or to determine the relationship to be maintained between political and economic power.'[35]

The addressee of this message is the ordoliberal school, in all of its allegiance to the vocation and potential of *law* to tame economic power by means an economically informed '*Staatsverfassung*', which is restrictive in its reach and objectives, but nevertheless strong in its commitment to the preservation of competitive ordering by independent agencies and courts acting beyond the political system. The critique returns as a *leitmotif* throughout the entire lecture: the notion that law could, and should, implement a self-sustaining, pre-political order is an ideological denial of the legitimacy of democratic, political will-formation and direction. At its core, the very idea of *Wirtschaftsverfassung*, recognised, both then and now,[36] as being Franz Böhm's greatest accomplishment, is no

[33] 'Die Position des Wirtschaftsrechts', n. 3 above, p. 44.

[34] This argument inspired the volume entitled, *Wirtschaftsrecht als Kritik des Privatrechts. Beiträge zur Privat- und Wirtschaftsrechtstheorie*, a collection of essays by Heinz-Diether Assmann, Gert Brüggemeier, Dieter Hart and Christian Joerges (Königstein: Athenäum, 1980).

[35] 'Die Position des Wirtschaftsrechts', n. 3 above, p. 46.

[36] See, for example, Mathias Siems and Gerhard Schnyder, 'Ordoliberal Lessons for Economic Stability: Different Kinds of Regulation, Not More Regulation' (2014) 27 *Governance: An International Journal of Policy, Administration, and Institutions*, 377–96.

more than a functionalist instrumentalisation of individual economic freedoms in the service of a competitive structuring of economy and society. Wiethölter's progressive break with tradition, however, impacted not simply upon ordoliberalism, but rather upon German tradition in its entirety. Legitimating his approach with reference to his distillation of the primacy of the political out of the constitutional theory of Hermann Heller and his followers within the Federal Republic,[37] Wiethölter concretised his critique around the very notion of the *Wirtschaftsverfassung* as such, or around the very idea of a pre-political economic constitution. The logical implication of democratic legitimacy for the *soziale Rechtsstaat* is clearly that the ordoliberal construction of economic ordering can no longer be invoked as a prohibitive barrier to the reach and the design of democratic governance. Wiethölter's critique nevertheless reaches deeper into the structures of ordoliberal theorising. The idea that law could, and should, implement a self-sustaining pre-political order, he argues, is not only incompatible with the legitimacy of democratic, political will-formation, it also rests upon unwarranted assumptions about the logic of the economic. As noted, the *Wirtschaftsverfassung* is built upon the functionalist instrumentalisation of economic freedoms in the service of the competitive structuring of economy and society. This gives rise to a questionable coupling, or a core weakness of ordoliberal economic theorising, to wit, its dependence upon anti-democratic assumptions. Inherent in this critique is a defence of the autonomy of labour law with regard to the subjection of industrial relations to competitive demands,[38] a particular *bête noir* within the process of European integration, and, latterly, within Europe's crisis politics (Part III).

[37] Heller was the most important opponent of Carl Schmitt in the Weimar Republic and is remembered as a constitutional theorist (see Agustín José Menéndez, 'Hermann Heller NOW' (2015) 21 *European Law Journal*, 285–94). His importance for economic law was first underlined in the legendary *Habilitationsschrift* of Horst Ehmke, *Wirtschaft und Verfassung: Die Verfassungsrechtsprechung des Supreme Court zur Wirtschaftsregulierung* (Karlsruhe: C.F. Müller, 1961). Both Wiethölter ('Die Position des Wirtschaftsrechts', n. 3 above) and Mestmäcker were aware of Ehmke's path-breaking study (see Mestmäcker's book review in: *Die öffentliche Verwaltung*, 1964, p. 606 et seq. (reprinted in Mestmäcker, *Recht und ökonomisches Gesetz* (Baden-Baden: Nomos (1978)), pp. 65–81)).

[38] See the remarks in Rudolf Wiethölter, *Rechtswissenschaft* (Frankfurt aM: Fischer, 1968), p. 249, and 'Recht', in: Gerd Kadelbach (ed.), *Wissenschaft und Gesellschaft* (Frankfurt aM: Fischer, 1977), pp. 213–75 (Section III).

II Wirtschaftsverfassung versus Sozialer Rechtsstaat

> This case is decided upon an economic theory which a large part of the country does not entertain. If it were a question whether I agreed with that theory, I should desire to study it further and long before making up my mind. But I do not conceive that to be my duty, because I strongly believe that my agreement or disagreement has nothing to do with the right of a majority to embody their opinions in law ... [A] constitution is not intended to embody a particular economic theory, whether of paternalism and the organic relation of the citizen to the State or of *laissez faire*. It is made for people of fundamentally differing views, and the accident of our finding certain opinions natural and familiar or novel and even shocking ought not to conclude our judgment upon the question whether statutes embodying them conflict with the Constitution of the United States.[39]

In his famous dissenting opinion, placing clear distance between himself and the economic constitutionalism of his colleagues, Justice Holmes revealed the core methodological problem within *Wirtschaftsrecht*: where law meets 'the economic', it must either reflect, respect or transform its make-up. But how is the law, or its judges, to assess and manage conflict about the correct nature of the economy, or the constitutive form of the economic? Our two contributions to the Böhm *Festschrift* approach this problem in two very different ways – and variation has only increased over time. Mestmäcker took an encyclopaedic approach, nevertheless never allowing his elaboration of the *Wirtschaftsverfassung*[40] to fall victim to the legal trivialities so often inherent in pernickety legal specialisation. Without once deviating from his own theoretical model,[41] he proved himself to be a true teacher of the law. Wiethölter, by methodological contrast, preferred – on his own admission – to play offside,[42] elaborating his economic law theory following the

[39] Justice Oliver W. Holmes dissenting in *Lochner* v. *People of State of New York*, 198 U.S. 45 (1905).

[40] See www.mpipriv.de/files/pdf5/SV_Mestmaecker.pdf.

[41] Recently, in particular: 'Gesellschaft und Recht bei David Hume und Friedrich A. von Hayek' (2009) 60 *ORDO*, 87–100; see, also, Ernst-Joachim Mestmäcker, *A Legal Theory Without Law – Posner v. Hayek on Economic Analysis of Law*, Tübingen: Mohr/Siebeck, 2007, available at: https://ssrn.com/abstract=1168422.

[42] *Utinam* (n. 3 above), 641; see, also, Rudolf Wiethölter, 'L'essentiel est invisible pour les yeux', in: Christian Joerges and Peer Zumbansen (eds.), 'Politische Rechtstheorie Revisited: Rudolf Wiethölter zum 100. Semester', ZERP Diskussionspapier 1/2013, Bremen 2013, 183–94.

end of the reformist politics in 1974 in a series of methodological sketches,[43] theoretical analyses,[44] and exemplary studies.[45]

We can neither do justice here to the full breadth of Mestmäcker's work, nor follow Wiethölter through the highways and byways of his ever-more sophisticated theoretical reasoning. We will instead restrict our comparative analysis to the debate on *Mitbestimmung* (co-determination), once again, a typically Germanic example, albeit one that allows us further to elucidate our two German *Sonderwege*. *Mitbestimmung* entails the institutionalisation of worker representation within the supervisory boards of private corporations, and, as such, is a challenge both to liberal market economies in general, and to the ordoliberal *Wirtschaftsverfassung* in particular. The same holds true for the effort to conceptualise and to defend the institutional potential of *Mitbestimmung* within the democratic constitutional framework. The essay by Mestmäcker which forms the basis for our discussion here,[46] was published a few years prior to the Federal Constitutional Court's seminal *Mitbestimmung* Judgment (1979),[47] Wiethölter's analysis three years thereafter.[48] Mestmäcker was thus not concerned with the judgment *per se*, but nevertheless dealt with comparable material, considering the issue of co-determination and its fraught relationship with his *Wirtschaftsverfassung*. Wiethölter focused squarely upon the Court's reasoning, describing how it resonated within his own understanding of the legitimation of the process of (extra-legislative) law production by means of the proceduralisation of the category of law. The discrepancy between the two approaches is, we will submit, of fundamental

[43] For example, 'Thesen zum Wirtschaftsverfassungsrecht', in: Peter Römer (ed.), *Der Kampf um das Grundgesetz. Über die politische Bedeutung der Verfassungsinterpretation* (Frankfurt aM: Syndikat, 1977), pp. 158–69.

[44] 'Social Science Models in Economic Law', in: Terence Daintith and Gunther Teubner (eds.), *Contract and Organisation. Legal Analysis in the Light of Economic and Social Theory* (Berlin-New York: Walter de Gruyter, 1986), pp. 52–67. [German original: 'Sozialwissenschaftliche Modelle im Wirtschaftsrecht' (1985) 18 *Kritische Justiz*, 126–39, reprinted Gert Brüggemeier and Christian Joerges (eds.), 'Workshop zu Konzepten des postinterventionistischen Rechts'. Materialien des Zentrums für Europäische Rechtspolitik (ZERP) 4/1984, 2–24.]

[45] 'Entwicklung des Rechtsbegriffs (am Beispiel des BVG-Urteils zum Mitbestimmungsgesetz und – allgemeiner – an Beispielen des sog. Sonderprivatrechts)' (1982) 8 *Jahrbuch für Rechtssoziologie und Rechtstheorie*, 38–59.

[46] 'Durch Mitbestimmung zum neuen Laissez-faire' (1974/1976) cited from the reprint in Ernst-Joachim Mestmäcker, *Recht und ökonomisches Gesetz* (Baden-Baden, Nomos, 1978), pp. 155–64.

[47] BVerfG 50, 290.

[48] 'Entwicklung des Rechtsbegriffs', n. 45 above.

importance in elucidating the primary schism in post-war scholarship on the place of the economic within society.

II.1 Mestmäcker: Supremacy of the Wirtschaftsverfassung

II.1.1 Co-Determination as an Exemplary Case

The constitutive roles played by *Mitbestimmung* and the social market economy (*soziale Marktwirtschaft*) within the societally integrative 'German Social Model' are well known, and, even outside Germany, are often closely associated with the ordoliberal legacy. This association is perhaps understandable in terms of daily political battle and the strategic play for votes. Nevertheless, the notion of *Mitbestimmung* has no conceptual place whatsoever within the ordoliberal *Wirtschaftsverfassung*. No less a figure than Franz Böhm was particularly clear on this point. Böhm's famous *Privatrechtsgesellschaft* (private law society) is composed of actors who coordinate themselves by means of the '*plebiscite de tous les jours*' in the exercise of their freedom of choice.[49] Mestmäcker has endorsed this concept on many occasions,[50] drawing crystal clear consequences from this premise: 'Co-determination within the corporation encroaches . . . upon the freedom of the firm to plan in accordance with its commercial freedom and entrepreneurial assumption of risk. It is therefore incompatible with the fundamental conceptions of the market order.'[51]

This assertion strikes us as doctrinaire in its rigidity. The long history of co-determination, the experience that has been built up around it, its sociopolitical legitimacy, the economic costs and advantages associated with it – all count for nothing, are '*en quelque façon nul*'. For Böhm, the only relevant measure is that of preservation of the constitutively functional preconditions for private law society. One might expect a more subtle and elegant approach from Mestmäcker, and indeed, his brief essay, '*Durch Mitbestimmung zum neuen Laissez-faire*'[52] meets such expectations to a large degree. Here, we find a history within which co-

[49] Franz Böhm, 'Privatrechtsgesellschaft und Marktwirtschaft' (1966) 17 *ORDO*, 75–151, at 138.

[50] For example, 'Die Wiederkehr der bürgerlichen Gesellschaft und ihres Rechts' (1991) 10 *Rechtshistorisches Journal*, 177–92.

[51] 'Franz Böhm und die Lehre von der Privatrechtsgesellschaft', in: Karl Riesenhuber (ed.), *Privatrechtsgesellschaft* (Tübingen: Mohr Siebeck, 2008), 35–50, cited from the reprint in Mestmäcker, *Prüfsteine*, n. 1 above, pp. 149–69, at 152.

[52] Note 45 above.

determination is given its place as a condition for, or challenge of, democratisation. Here, we also find reference to master and servant, tensions between capital and labour, as well as distributional conflicts. However, simultaneously, we find a framework which is *anything but* amenable to sociopolitical demands for change. The limits are set by the economic constitution itself, that is, by the economic and social preconditions for political freedoms, or for 'the functionality' of a decentrally steered and legally ordered market economy.[53] The approach once again owes itself wholly to Böhm. In the same volume, and alongside his essay on co-determination, Mestmäcker had, after all, penned his notable rebuttal of the critique that the economic constitution pre-empted constitutive democratic politics:

> The academic school of thought which promotes the *Wirtschaftsverfassung*... is not committed to the elaboration of the political potency of the economic, in order to fall into the arms of the democratic regime, but rather seeks to place that regime in a position whereby it can independently and adequately perform its mandated rule of law and welfare tasks.[54]

In short, a welfarist quality is imputed to the economic constitution that has, however, yet to be proven, and which remains the object of conflict.

II.1.2 Social Market Economy

To reiterate, the German social market economy is widely applauded as a significant achievement. Politics often cites its existence as proof of ordoliberal tolerance for welfarism. This assumption is nevertheless built on sand: even Alfred Müller-Armack, whose credentials as a 'true' ordoliberal are often doubted, in view of his expansive concepts of economic and social policy, never once sought to undermine the primacy of the economic. Social, labour and economic regulation should not be allowed to distort the working of the price mechanism.[55] Mestmäcker's position is better understood when we recall his Hayekian moment. Hayek made no secret of his disdain for

53 Ibid., p. 158 et seq.

54 'Wirtschaftsordnung und Staasverfassung', n. 25 above.

55 See, for example, Alfred Müller-Armack, 'Thesen zur Konjunkturpolitik' (1975) 24 *Wirtschaftspolitische Chronik*, 7–16; Müller-Armack, 'Die fünf großen Themen der künftigen Wirtschaftspolitik' (1978) 27 *Wirtschaftspolitische Chronik*, 9–34. In greater detail, Christian Joerges and Florian Rödl, '"Social Market Economy" as Europe's Social Model?', in: Lars Magnusson and Bo Stråth (eds.), *A European Social Citizenship? Preconditions for Future Policies in Historical Light. Preconditions for Future Policies from a Historical Perspective* (Brussels: Peter Lang, 2004), pp. 125–58.

'the social', a notion which he argued was no more than a 'weasel word', an exercise in 'the art of saying what you don't mean'.[56] It lacks any substantive content and is simply incompatible with liberal thinking.[57] This is not merely an observation on the use of the concept in different contexts, but rather a principled objection about the compatibility of social-policy ambitions with the rules that should govern political contestation in free societies. We return to this objection in the following section, contrasting Mestmäcker's reliance on the Hayekian discovery procedure with Wiethölter's law of collisions.

II.2 Wiethölter Reconstruction of the Mitbestimmungs-Urteil *and His Turn to Proceduralisation*

Beginning at the crux of the matter, Wiethölter tackles the same sociopolitical conflicts that he dealt with in his inaugural address, but sharpens the analysis to a point at which all paths out of the conundrum appear blocked. Where once the division made between labour and economic law seemed mundane, it now marked the explosive border between two incompatible sociopolitical aspirations: on the one hand, the demand for the application of an economic legal doctrine, according to which society should align itself to the functional preconditions of the economy; on the other, a democratising movement aiming at realisation of the self-determination demands of majoritarian social processes. Formal legal paradigms were the expression of one side, the concept of substantive justice the champion for the other. The conflict is immutable and cannot conceivably be overcome by means of compromise between formal and material notions of law: 'The fundamental transformation from legal guarantees [secured within formal law] to political guarantees for social positions [satisfying the demands of material justice] impacts upon the category of law at its very core.'[58]

From now on, each position would be called upon to place its faith within a process of 'proceduralisation', within which law would play its vital role, yet, for its part, would itself be driven by society-wide

[56] Friedrich A. von Hayek, *The Fatal Conceit: The Errors of Socialism*. The Collected Works of F.A. Hayek, edited by W.W. Bartley III (Chicago IL: University of Chicago Press, 1991), p. 114 et seq.

[57] F.A. von Hayek, 'The Political Order of a Free People', in: von Hayek, *Law, Legislation and Liberty*, Vol. 3 (London: Routledge, 1979; reprint, London: Routledge, 1982), pp. 40–50.

[58] Ibid., p. 42.

transformation processes.[59] Systematically detailing the proceduralisation paradigm on many occasions,[60] Wiethölter chose the Co-determination Judgment as the hook upon which he could hang his theoretical conceptions in order to test their operationalisability in a concrete juridical world.

In his essay on the development of the category of law ('*Entwicklung des Rechtsbegriffs*'), this effort ranges over a whole two and a half pages.[61] The Federal Constitutional Court had confronted a series of intractable issues with great bravura. Tricky issues, such as the appropriate approach to take towards legal conflict matter, the availability of prerogatives to deal with uncertainty, the existence of common law (experientially based) duties, and the suitable treatment of planning errors (political mistake), were all confronted explicitly; and, more laudably, were mastered without benefit of recourse to the more usual grandfathering (pre-emptive) rights secured within 'formal-liberal law', or to arbitrary application of the unlimited claims of material justice or 'substantive social law'. So, the Court decided, the democratically legitimated law-giver (legislature) could rightfully lay claim to a prognostic (planning) prerogative which might also be exercised lawfully 'in error'. By the same token, however, the legislature is then also subject to a duty to learn. The position of the private parties to the conflict was also clarified: a duty is laid upon them – 'loyally and fairly' – to tailor their forms of behaviour to the expectations found within legislative programmes. For Wiethölter, this subtle, careful, and procedural mode of dealing with the 'politics of law' creates the space for the development of a form of economic constitutionalism which can embrace and adjust both economic and labour law.

A further eighteen pages are dedicated, in characteristic argumentative density. to social-historical, legal-theoretical and socio-political developments and positions. Unlike Justice Holmes in our famous introductory citation, Wiethölter does not shy away from

59 Ibid., p. 42 et seq.

60 'Materialisierungen und Prozeduralisierungen von Recht', in: Gert Brüggemeier and Christian Joerges (eds.), *Workshop zu Konzepten des postinterventionistischen Rechts*, Materialien des Zentrums für Europäische Rechtspolitik (ZERP) 4, Bremen 1984, 25–64 (= 'Materialization and Proceduralization in Modern Law', in: Gunther Teubner (ed.), *Dilemmas of Law in the Welfare State* (Berlin-New York: Walter de Gruyter, 1986), pp. 221–49; Rudolf Wiethölter, 'Proceduralization of the Category of Law', in: Christian Joerges and David M. Trubek (eds.), *Critical Legal Thought: An American-German Debate* (Baden-Baden: Nomos, 1989), pp. 501–10.

61 Ibid., pp. 46–48.

the challenge of examining the potential of law. Quite on the contrary, the proceduralisation of the legal category is not in any manner commensurate with partisan adherence to the 'correct' social theory, but rather reflects the current 'state of legal and social science debate (touching less upon normative positions, and more upon procedural-functionalist processes of elimination within structured systems), or conceptual evolutions (in systematic scientific theories, steering and competition theories, decisional and game theory, evolutionary theories), which all have, as their theme, a connection between (each consequently delineated) investment opportunity and operational freedom (type: mutations–variations–selections)'.[62]

This may all appear to be too challenging. The difference in approach that each of our protagonists takes to the constitution of the economic is, however, clear enough. Just as Mestmäcker rejects all critique of his theoretical framework, and attempts, instead, to demonstrate the legal implications of his premises, he is subsequently and inevitably undone by insurmountable contradictions within the real world. Wiethölter, by contrast, ventures the *Wirtschaftsverfassung* as an incomplete task for the rule of law, the functional preconditions for which can be identified, but whose operationalisation cannot be programmatically predetermined. We conclude our comparative discussion of this contrast between pre-emptive theory and a competing faith in the powers of social development, moving on, instead, to interrogate the methodological conceptions adopted by our protagonists more closely.

III Competition as a Discovery Procedure versus a Law of Collisions as Constitutional Form

First a question: Does this section compare apples with pears? The answer depends on your particular perspective. We shall explore the commonalities between the two projects and the diversity of their ambitions. What the 'discovery procedure'[63] theorem and the notion of 'collisions as constitutional form'[64] share, however, is the conceptualisation of decision making as a creative activity. A categorical

[62] Ibid., at 55.

[63] Friedrich von Hayek, 'Competition as Discovery Procedure', n. 10 above.

[64] Rudolf Wiethölter, 'Begriffs- oder Interessenjurisprudenz:– falsche Fronten im IPR und Wirtschaftsverfassungsrecht. Bemerkungen zur selbstgerechten Kollisionsnorm', in: Alexander Lüderitz and Jochen Schröder (eds.), *Internationales Privatrecht und*

difference nevertheless arises, as each set of decision-making processes requires its own form of legitimation.

III.1 The Cognitive Demarcations of Hayek's Competitive Discovery Procedure

It would be reductionist to equate Mestmäcker's constitutionalism with that of Hayek's. It is nevertheless true that Mestmäcker's most important contribution to the ordoliberal tradition was his creative renewal of its methodological premises. This renewal impacted most evidently upon competition law and policy, but also reached out into the entire body of economic law and its constitutional design. This renewal was most closely informed by Hayek's notion of 'competition as a discovery procedure'; meanwhile, Mestmäcker's 'Hayekian turn' similarly reshaped the whole of his vision of economic constitutionalism and his work on economic law, both at national, and at European, level.

The promise that Hayekian thought holds out for Mestmäcker's economic constitutionalism is threefold in interdependent nature. First, comes his theory of the generation and use of knowledge, and of the functions of the rule of law. Since knowledge is dispersed throughout society in a form of such complexity and magnitude that it can never be properly accumulated and deployed by one mind, individuals instead use knowledge, complementing it and adjusting it by virtue of what they experience and learn. Following from this, the normativity at the core of Hayek's emphasis on the particular quality of these exchange and learning processes forms the basis of Mestmäcker's critique of Richard Posner's economic analysis of law: the Hayek-Mestmäcker discovery process can never be conceptualised as a rational act (logic of choice), or as an efficiency-driven activity; rather, market exchanges are cooperative activities with a productive potential, which creates a 'catallaxy', or spontaneous economy, to the degree that these operations respect the 'rule of law'. Last, but certainly not least, the catallaxy founded in unknown and unknowable exchange and learning processes stands as a bulwark, not simply to abuse of individual market power (in the manner of Böhm's price mechanism), but rather also to a more systemic 'scientism', or 'pretence of knowledge' which Hayek so convincingly critiqued in his 1974 Nobel lecture.

Rechtsvergleichung im Ausgang des 20. Jahrhunderts. Bewahrung oder Wende? Festschrift für Gerhard Kegel (Frankfurt aM: Metzner, 1977), pp. 213–63, at 226.

The catallaxy as a focus for creative cooperation, as a defensive bastion against all aggressive certainties, including those of arrogantly modelled economic theories, remains a conceptual achievement of no little import. Nevertheless, are its expectations ever actually met within a real world? The closer inspection of Mestmäcker's putative European Economic Constitution reveals expectations are rarely, if ever, met. It suffices here to mention only three concrete problems:

1. At both state and European level, the 'discovery procedure' is out of step with the multifaceted moralisation and politicisation of markets, which so often depends upon the integration of what might be argued to be an 'accepted certainty' of scientific expertise into their regulation.
2. EU legislative processes are, without doubt, imperfect. Yet, the suggestion that Europe should trust, instead, in 'regulatory competition', or 'methodological nationalism',[65] to discover the 'best' regulatory strategies leads only to a 'bad utopia', as notions of regulatory competition between states neglect processes of societal denationalisation that are particularly powerful within the EU.
3. A third objection is of particular relevance with regard to the, as yet unresolved, financial and sovereign debt crisis. The infamous no-bailout clause of Article 125 TFEU was bolstered by an underlying expectation that financial markets would discipline the financial policies of the Member States 'whose currency is the Euro'. Nevertheless, as convincingly argued by Lisa Herzog,[66] the knowledge communicated by markets is not available in the form that public authorities require in order to assess the performance of their economies.

III.2 Justifications of a Law of Society (Recht-Fertigungen eines Gesellschaften-Rechts)

'Be bold in Private International Law, give free rein to interpretation' – a play on Goethe's words[67] – this message was developed by Wiethölter

[65] See Michel Zürn, 'Globalization and Global Governance', in: Walter Carlnaes, Thomas Risse and Beth A; Simmons (eds.), *Handbook of International Relations* (Thousand Oaks CA-London: SAGE Publications, 2013), pp. 401–25, available at: www.wzb.eu/system/files/docs/ipl/gg/globalization_and_global_governance.pdf.

[66] 'Markt oder Profession? Die Politik zweier Wissenslogiken', Lecture at the Institute of Advanced Study Berlin of 18 January 2018 (on file with authors).

[67] 'Im Auslegen seid frisch und munter! Legt ihr's nicht aus, so legt was unter', Johann Wolfgang von Goethe, 'Zahme Xenien', in: Goethe, *Berliner Ausgabe. Poetische Werke*, Band 1, Berlin 1960 ff, pp. 671–87.

in his early writings and Frankfurt seminars on the *ordre public*. The thought is a direct forerunner of, but distanced by some time and by no little conceptual difficulty from his notion of law-(justification)-making processes within societal law and from his concept of law-(constituting)-law (*Rechtsverfassungsrecht*). We will eschew the task of academic reconstruction, however, and instead make use of the irritating suggestions made by Christian Joerges (as author and co-author) that a variety of legal principles and materials might usefully be re-construed as legal conflicts norms: to wit, the constitutional law of the combined European Treaties, the EU-internal conflict about nuclear energy, as well as WTO law. Can all of this legal material really be designated, even downgraded to the status of conflicts law, and what does this have to do with Rudolf Wiethölter anyway?

The assertion that Wiethölter inspired this approach is more than camouflage. Rather, the mouldering relic bequeathed to us by Private International Law is a one-sidedness, or blindness to the postnational, '*Kein Staat macht sich zum Büttel eines anderen Staates*' (No state will allow itself to become the overseer of another), or so intoned the leading German textbook as late as the year 2000.[68]

Thanks to Friedrich von Savigny, however, private law has always seen the world through very different lenses. The seeming symmetry deceives:

> The transactional conditions for all IPL provisions – conditions that guarantee the qualitative parity of legal orders and form the will for international co-operation between peoples – are the fruit of a pure private legal model that views private law as a pre-political product of *bourgeois* European society and therefore builds upon legal theories and social models rooted in a clear distinction between state and society; a distinction which is now obsolete.

Wiethölter had already riffed doctrinally and conceptually upon this argument in a report on the 'international *ordre public*': the entire realm of private and economic law was now reliant upon the creation of conflict norms whose operability was, above all, dependent upon similar endeavours in the internal world of states, wherein the conflict to be mediated was one formal law and material justice. The most forceful developmental reiteration was made in 1977 (*Festschrift für Kegel*, Wiethölter's academic mentor): 'Economic constitutional law', Wiethölter asserts from the outset, 'owes its character as a still surviving

[68] Gerhard Kegel and Klaus Schurig, *Internationales Privatrecht*, 8. Aufl. (Munich: C.H. Beck, 2000), p. 1094.

corpus of law . . . to the legal principles and substantive institutions of conflicts law (of national and international character)'. Twenty-five pages later, Wiethölter similarly reaches the conclusion that the '*Wirtschaftsverfassungsrecht* of the 1970s (WVR II) has left that of the 1950s and 1960s far behind'. Now, economic constitutionalism was concerned far more with 'the fundamental re-constitutive conflicts of material constitutional theory as social theory, whereby legal reconstruction interlinks with processes of social development'. Clearly, it would be foolish to attempt to trace the contours of contemporary political-economic conflict constellations back to the early years of the Federal Republic, and even less so to the current struggles between monetarists and 'fiscalists' (Keynesians). Nevertheless, a relationship can be identified between these contemporary conflicts and a longer-standing battle around the social (material) nature of a modern rule of law. Moreover, Wiethölter similarly gives us further orientation, as his work also gradually clarified the sociological dependency of law-(justification)-making processes, or their exposure to socially impactful conflicts between competing theoretical orientations and practical-political ambitions, as well as the collision norms that are developed as a consequence.

'*Exempla trahunt*', affords us renewed comfort: the debate on co-determination furnishes us with the exemplary canvas upon which we can first sketch out our comparison between our protagonists and then paint our explanation of conflicts-law-economic-constitutionalism. Mestmäcker's approach to the *Mitbestimmung* problem reveals that, for him, the concept of the discovery process serves as due protection for his theory of economic constitutionalism against the applicability of all other competing theories. For Wiethölter, by contrast, the proceduralisation of the legal category urges that reform projects should be allowed, albeit with the retention of exit and revision options.

And what of the suggested affinity between economic constitutionalism and 'conflicts law constitutionalism'? A close relationship can be identified with Karl Polanyi's economic sociology, which presages various aspects of conflicts-law constitutionalism:

1. Just as Wiethölter identified the complicity of law within social relationships, we can 'read' his work as the successor to Karl Polanyi's thesis of the 'always socially-embedded economy', in particular, when these theorems are interpreted as a 'cultural political economy'.

2. The rivalries between social theories and policies found within Wiethölter's writings might be favourably compared with Polanyi's observations on movements und counter-movements.
3. Last, but not least, Polanyi's insights into the Varieties of Capitalism within the final chapter of the *Great Transformation* have much within them with which the conflicts approach can work:

> ... with the disappearance of the automatic mechanism of the gold standard, governments will find it possible to ... tolerate willingly that other nations shape their domestic institutions according to their inclinations, thus transcending the pernicious nineteenth century dogma of the necessary uniformity of domestic regimes within the orbit of world economy. Out of the ruins of the Old World, cornerstones of the New can be seen to emerge: economic collaboration of governments and the liberty to organize national life at will.[69]

If we take the political autonomy of democratic societies seriously, we are called upon to respect their integral economic and sociopolitical character. Similarly, knowledge of the cultural dimensions of the economic equates with an awareness of just how resistant economies are to efforts to enforce their harmonisation. The guiding theorems of conflicts-law constitutionalism build upon these insights, just as the theory reaches for postnational and post-particularist formulations: 'Integration' within conflicts-law-constitutionalism is driven not by distinctions between legal orders, but by the inter-dependencies between societies, and does not force harmonisation, but rather seeks cooperative problem solving. The conflicts-law approach plumps for 'horizontal' constitutionalism, which derives its legitimacy from the quality of cooperative relationships.

IV European Crisis: Is the Law Running Out?

Back to the beginning, or to the commitment of our protagonists to the proprium of 'law'. We have emphasised the centrality of Mestmäcker's seminal 1972 lecture, in which he insisted upon the primacy of the legal over the economic: 'It is important to develop economic policy solutions susceptible of being bound by legal and constitutional rules.'

Mestmäcker is clearly concerned here with the defence of the economic constitution 'through law'. By contrast, and from the very outset, Wiethölter doubted the theoretical and practical feasibility of such

[69] Karl Polanyi, *The Great Transformation: The Political and Economic Origins of Our Time* (Boston MA: Beacon Press, 2001), pp. 253–54.

a defence in the face of the mass of legal provisions generated within the *soziale Rechtsstaat*. In making this comparison, we are undoubtedly partisan, but do also concede the inherent tensions and difficulties within Wiethölter's *Rechtsverfassungsrecht*, and, above all, recognise the irritating disjunction between his critique of the anti-democratic tradition of German *bourgeois* law (*Bürgerliches Recht*) and a continuing acknowledgement of the pragmatic virtues of doctrine within his theorems.[70] After all, what else guides the judges in their procedural sifting of the conflicts and policies of social evolution? Yet, moving on – in mid-2019 – to discuss one of Europe's many emergencies, the financial and sovereign debt crisis, we find that the challenges faced by both projects have only increased exponentially. The concept of 'law' is now itself strained to breaking point.

The misery extends far and wide, but can be summarised briefly: the Economic and Monetary Union, as it was established by the Maastricht Treaty of 1992, was a *lex imperfecta* in both the formal sense and in its conceptual design. The so-called 'stability community' existed only on paper; it lacked any meaningful sanctions. This formal imperfection was not accidental. It was the price that had to be paid for substantive political-historical deficits. Conceptually speaking, EMU was a hybrid of German ordoliberalism and French '*planification*', with Germany prescribing substantive (non-majoritarian) commitments, and France determining the procedural (politicised) framing. The functioning of the new regime was dependent on good economic luck and constant political processes of muddling through. No single, identifiable authority was entrusted with the necessary powers to ensure that the policies pursued both at European and at national levels of governance would be effectively coordinated in compliance with the legal criteria laid down in the Treaty. To reiterate: deficiencies within the framework were neither wilful nor accidental. Instead, the economic and fiscal policies of the Member States are embedded within their own particular economic and social conditions. This multifaceted and multicausal heterogeneity could not simply be dissolved by a common currency. As a consequence, the application of a uniform European monetary policy only became evermore dysfunctional. Meanwhile, it is less than surprising that

[70] See, for example, 'Privatrecht als Gesellschaftstheorie? Bemerkungen zur Logik der ordnungspolitischen Rechtslehre', n. 6 above.

corrective recourse has been made to intergovernmental bargaining, soft supervision and tentative coordination.

Nevertheless, legally under-determined processes have likewise generated a very rigid mode of 'new economic governance'. Considered and explained in exhaustive detail by academia,[71] we restrict ourselves here to highlighting three aspects of this transformation, which recall the leading *leitmotifs* of our arguments.

1. The first concerns the contest between the market domain and the countervailing powers of labour law and social policy. In this respect, the outcome of the crisis-driven transformation is uncontested: the priority of the new regime is the strengthening of the competitiveness of national economies through so-called structural reforms, *i.e.*, the dismantling of labour law and social entitlements.[72]
2. The conclusion that an ordoliberal version of economic constitutionalism is now in place would nevertheless be erroneous. New economic governance is, instead, incompatible with all varieties of economic liberalism. It is an *illiberal* regime, governed at best in its commitment to 'competitiveness' by utilitarian economic commitments to welfare maximisation ('scientism'),[73] is established outside the rule of law, and is governed, upon a day-to-day basis, within authoritarian management structures.[74]
3. Finally, however, we also draw on the work of Fritz W. Scharpf with regard to the excessive imbalance procedure as adopted in the Six-pack and the Two-pack regulations,[75] to underline the methodological peculiarities of the crisis regime: it is within the very logic of these instruments that 'dictates that it [the system of economic governance]

[71] See, for example, Michelle Everson and Christian Joerges, 'Between Constitutional Command and Technocratic Rule: Post Crisis Governance and the Treaty on Stability, Coordination and Governance ("The Fiscal Compact")', in: Carol Harlow, Päivi leino and Giacinto della Cananea (eds.), *Research Handbook on EU Administrative Law* (Cheltenham: Edward Elgar Publishing, 2017), pp. 161–87, with many references.

[72] See Roland Erne, 'How to Analyse a Supranational Regime that Nationalises Social Conflict? The European Crisis, Labour Politics and Methodological Nationalism', in: Eva Nanopoulos and Fotis Vergis (eds.), *The Crisis behind the Euro-Crisis: The Euro-Crisis as Systemic Multi-Dimensional Crisis of the EU* (Cambridge: Cambridge University Press, 2019), 2019.

[73] See here the echoes of Mestmäcker's critique of the Law & Economics movement (see n. 41 above).

[74] Everson and Joerges, n. 71 above.

[75] For a summary of the pertinent documents by the Commission, see: http://ec.europa.eu/economy_finance/economic_governance/sgp/index_en.htm.

> must operate without any pre-defined rule and that the Commission's *ad hoc* decisions must apply to individual Member States in unique circumstances rather than to EMU states in general. Regardless of the comparative quality of its economic expertise, the Commission lacks legitimate authority to impose highly intrusive policy choices on Member States.'[76]

Or, as Polanyi has observed, 'Laissez-faire was planned, planning was not'. Nobody planned the financial crisis of 2008 or the sovereign debt crisis that followed. Equally, although each and every phase of crisis was meticulously discussed and documented within European bureaucracy, national governments and expert circles,[77] neither the participants within these processes, not the general public at large believe that we are on our way to a 'final settlement'. Instead, be it in an optimistic Europeanist view,[78] or within a far more critical appraisal,[79] the talk is of an ongoing process of 'normalisation'.

But what of this normalisation? The architecture of 'new economic governance' is indeed impressive in its size and powerful in its impact. Nevertheless, this impact is so asymmetric in its effect that even the defenders of output legitimacy have difficulty subscribing to it. Granted, strong support for the normalisation thesis is to be found in the two landmark CJEU judgments on the crisis, yet at what price for the quality of law? In *Pringle*, for example, the CJEU held that the financial stability of the Eurozone (EU) as a whole, is the law's 'highest priority'. Similarly, in *Gauweiler*,[80] the Court added that the assessment of rescue measures undertaken by the ECB under its OMT programme is a matter for 'technical expertise', which, according to the TFEU is vested within the ECB.[81] The Court has likewise subjected

[76] Fritz W. Scharpf, 'Monetary Union, Fiscal Crisis and the Disabling of Democratic Accountability', in: Wolfgang Streeck and Armin Schäfer (eds.), *Politics in the Age of Austerity* (Cambridge: Polity Press, 2013), pp. 108–42, at 139.

[77] The most detailed reconstruction we are aware of is that of the historian Adam Tooze, *Crashed: How a Decade of Financial Crises Changed the World* (New York: Viking, 2018).

[78] See, for example, Thomas Beukers, Bruno de Witte and Claire Kilpatrick (eds.), *Constitutional Change through Euro-Crisis Law* (Cambridge: Cambridge University Press, 2017).

[79] Such as Christian Kreuder-Sonnen, *Emergency Powers of International Organization. Between Normalization and Containment* (Oxford: Oxford University Press, 2019), chapter 5.

[80] Case 370/12, *Pringle* v. *Ireland*, Judgment (Grand Chamber) of 27 November 2012, EU: C:2012:756. Pringle, para. 70.

[81] Case C-62/14 Peter Gauweiler EU:C:2015:400.Gauweiler, paras. 70 et seq.

the exercise of these powers to a proportionality test.[82] Nevertheless, this is but a very thin veneer of legal control without any corresponding legal bite.

This potential crisis within the rule of law also has an institutional dimension. The most important actor within the whole edifice of new economic governance is an actor with unprecedented autonomy, namely, the ECB, characterised memorably by Paul Tucker as an 'overmighty citizen',[83] and interrogated thoughtfully by the Princeton economist Ashoka Mody:[84]

> The legal and economic question of interest is whether the OMT tried to bypass the intent of the Treaty by creating a *de facto* fiscal union (a liability or transfer union in *Bundesbank* terminology). If so, without their explicit authorisation, countries had become fiscally responsible for the mistakes of other member countries.

To which he adds more pertinently, 'Can such a fiscal union be implicitly located in the ECB without the political willingness to transparently achieve that elusive goal?' The economist as true teacher of law?[85]

We do not and cannot know how stable this normalisation will be. We are not prepared to call it legitimate, let alone, democratic. We now wonder whether the new regime qualifies as 'law' at all. To the surprise of many, Mestmäcker was to observe, as late as in 2015, that 'law has proven to be the foundation for European integration in a manner that could not have been envisaged in 1962'.[86] In view of the new character of the new crisis regime and its 'macroeconomic relationships', this appellation is now particularly difficult to reconcile with Mestmäcker's quest 'to develop economic policy solutions susceptible of being bound

[82] Paras. 66 et seq.

[83] *Unelected Power: The Quest for Legitimacy in Central Banking and the Regulatory State* (Princeton NJ-Oxford: Princeton University Press, 2018).

[84] 'Did the German court do Europe a favor?', Bruegel Working Paper 2014/09, available at: http://aei.pitt.edu/52709/1/Did_the_German_court_do_Europe_a_favour%2D_(English). pdf.

[85] Ibid., at 6, 4.

[86] 'In a manner not predictable back in 1962, the law proved to remain the foundation of European integration.' Ernst-Joachim Mestmäcker, 'Die EU als Rechtsgemeinschaft', in: Peter Behrens, Markus Kotzur and Konrad Lammers (eds.), *Sechs Dekaden europäischer Integration – Eine Standortbestimmung, Symposium anlässlich des 60-jährigen Bestehens der Stiftung Europa-Kolleg Hamburg* (Baden-Baden: Nomos, 2015), pp. 31–55, at 31.

by legal and constitutional rules'.[87] Indeed, somewhat paradoxically, the practices that we have sketched out in all their troublesome quality are not so categorically different from what Wiethölter has characterised as the rise of 'political administration' in the *Sozialstaat*. He might, if called upon, even be prepared to value the involvement of so many actors within policy making, as well as the degree of contestation between them. Yet, it seems to us to be impossible to give this form of crisis governance, or its practices and regime, any form of legitimacy as *Rechtsverfassungsrecht*.

The problem is perhaps twofold. First, like Wiethölter, we find ourselves embarrassed by our own residual demand for doctrine within our rule of law. Legality does matter. Liberal impulses retain their status as bulwark against the undue exercise of power, or, in the Hayekian twist, gain potency in repelling the more systemic imposition of scientism, and the empty utilitarian promises of certainty. The conclusion is difficult, placing terrible duties upon a law and its judges, which and who, in our examples, have largely – with some fine exceptions[88] – failed in their mission to secure the legal proprium. But secondly, in contrast to the coldness of all 'regimes', we are also forcefully reminded in the crisis of the core transformative potential of social politics which is so central to Wiethölter's vision: on 23 March 2019, some two million citizens from all over the UK and the rest of Europe participated in the 'Put it to the People' march from London's Hyde Park Corner to Westminster. They represented, as *The Guardian* put it the next day, 'a formidable sea of humanity and powerful strength of feeling'. This genuine desire for a social, pluralist, free European society, was accompanied by strong arguments against the Brexiters in the UK government, society and media. Such aspirations reach far beyond Mestmäcker's sober vision of a European private law society and seem instead to encapsulate Wiethölter's more inspirational visions – and, in truth, the future of Europe lies very much in the hands of a transformative social politics, which must now assert itself both against the moribund discourse of traditional politics and against the more dangerous political forces seeking to take advantage of this *malaise*. But how can law react within such deep crises while it awaits the pleasure of sociopolitical transformation? The question is far from

[87] Mestmäcker, n. 44 above, p. 183.

[88] Above all, Justice Lübbe-Wolf of the German Constitutional Court; see, Michelle Everson, 'An Exercise in Legal Honesty: Rewriting the Court of Justice and the *Bundesverfassungsgericht*' (2015) 21 *European Law Journal*, 474–99.

new, forming the basis both of the works of Eucken and Böhm, and of those of Heller. Each of our protagonists' work was born out crisis, and, imperfect as each might be, it is surely the job of legal theorising to raise awareness within the law of the need for constant and vigorous self-reflection.

3

The Myth of Democratic Governance

EMILIOS CHRISTODOULIDIS

I 'Governance' and the Politics of Signifiers

'*Democracy is stirring*', begins Charles Sabel's 'Quiet Revolution of Democratic Governance',[1] with some aplomb. He is far from alone in celebrating the democratic energies of the 'new governance'. Janet Halley joins the chorus of approval on behalf of the 'governance feminists': 'I like the word "governance" because it suggests multiplicity, mobility, fragmentation, . . . as well as ready facility with non-state and para-state institutional forms. I use it to dodge the assumption that all legal power inheres in the state and comes down from a pinnacle of legitimate coercive power.'[2] The democratic project discovers 'the novelty and civil-society open-texturedness of "the new governance" and "global governance" to be quite hospitable', offering 'mobility' and institutional flexibility beyond anything that the rigidities of the state and government might have afforded. When it comes to law, new governance carries 'an

1 'Democracy is stirring. The economic turmoil and political revolts of the 70s and 80s, together with the globalisation of world markets that continues today, have brought renewal as well as disruption.' Charles F. Sabel, 'A Quiet Revolution of Democratic Governance: Towards Democratic Experimentalism', in: *Governance in the 21st Century* (Paris: OECD Publishing, 2001), pp. 121–48, at 121.

2 Janet Halley in 'From the International to the Local in Feminist Legal Responses to Rape, Prostitution/Sex Work, and Sex Trafficking: Four Studies in Contemporary Governance Feminism', Janet Halley, Prahba Kotiswaran, Hila Shamir and Chantal Thomas (2006) 29 *Harvard Journal of Law & Gender*, 335–425, at 341. Indicatively, also, is Chantal Thomas: 'Any account of Governance Feminism ("GF") first and foremost requires, to my mind, celebration of a social movement. Against very steep odds of governmental indifference and patriarchal hostility, feminism is succeeding in achieving recognition of and response to social justice claims on behalf of women everywhere. The feminist movement has proven truly international, and as such stands as an exemplar of the potential for "global governance".' Also in 'Four Studies in Contemporary Governance Feminism', *Harvard Journal of Law & Gender*, cited above in this note.

understanding of legal power as highly fragmented and dispersed'; it 'deemphasize[s] the politics/law distinction in order to work not only in the spectacularly legal domains of litigation, legislation, and policymaking, but also in personal pressure campaigns, consciousness raising, [etc]'; 'it seeks not a monopoly of these forms but rather a plentiful presence within them'.[3]

Let us approach the 'plentiful presence' of law in the structures of new governance from a different, more cautious, perspective and with a particular concern about how the *economic* system has cut itself adrift from *legal* regulation and, in the process, reconfigured its relationship to the law under the sign of 'governance'. The runaway economic system now presents a near-impossible challenge to the 'reflexivity' of law, inviting the latter to a renegotiation of function and foundation. Where, in the past, the distinction between public law and private law demarcated the spheres of the public interest and of individual freedom respectively, today we confront the pervasive move of market thinking that no longer pits them against each other but underwrites them both. This is what I will argue, and that, therefore, under the sign of *governance*, a substitution takes place: the market principle that was understood as the principle subtending the transactional nature of private law as distinct from public law, gradually becomes the arbiter of the separation itself and guarantor of the circulation ('balancing' in the preferred idiom) of public goods. And governance comes to lend a vocabulary to these foundational, tectonic, shifts, as signifier for plasticity, experimentalism and 'plentiful presence'.

The question of whether 'governance' might, as a result, be thought of as an '*empty signifier*' frames Claus Offe's 'sceptical reflections' on the concept and on its 'potential for political science'.[4] What unsettles Offe about the term 'governance' is, he says, its *polysemy*. As a question of syntactic structure, the concept oscillates between the transitive ('to govern') and the reflexive ('to govern oneself'); as a question of semantics it oscillates between the 'poles of structure and process',[5] and, as a result, the important distinction between subject and object is lost in 'curiously subject-less processes' that allow neither for 'imputability of actions' nor, for that matter, for any logic of attribution. But if much appears *floating* in Offe's account, there is curiously little that is *empty* about the

3 Halley, n. 2 above, at 341.

4 Claus Offe, 'Governance: An "empty signifier"?' (2009) 16 *Constellations*, 550–62.

5 Ibid., at 550.

signification in the circuits in which it is floated and in which it produces real effects to the addressees of governance practices, effects that are replete with content.[6] We will return to the distinction between an 'empty' and a 'floating' signifier in what follows, and we will look at the work that each of them performs. For now, we will stay with Offe's quandary.

What Offe queries more insistently about the empty signifier 'governance' is that it has no opposite, no 'mirror' or counter-concept that might pin down its semantic content. To take 'government' as its *aliud*, or 'other', is to miss the insight that the relationship between the two terms is the *stake* of the question of the definitional quest, rather than its departure.[7] What Offe finds unsettling about the absence of 'counter-concept' is the suspicion that 'governance' intimates a 'pure and innocent *power to*, while power of actors *over* is strongly de-emphasised', and that this smooth passage, he suggests insightfully, 'may suggest that ideological, premature and undifferentiated harmonization is one function of the concept and its discursive use'.[8]

The unresolved polysemy of governance, Offe will resolve with a topology of sorts. His 'plea' is

> to sharpen the concept of *governance* by introducing conceptual boundaries around it. On the one hand, a boundary must be set around the private and civil society sphere, where 'spontaneous' coordination of action, which has nothing to do with governance, occurs through associative as well as market transactions within a framework of social and legal norms. And, on the other hand, a boundary must be set around the core sphere of state institutions, for which one should retain the concept of *government*. For what point would there be in understanding statehood as a 'subset of governance,' . . . and thus drown the specific profile of

[6] For a similar argument, but with reference to the public/private distinction in law, see Veitch: 'The distinction [public/private] may be descriptively untenable . . . but it does conceptual work and has real effects'; Scott Veitch, 'Public/Private', in: Emilios Christodoulidis, Ruth Dukes and Marco Goldoni (eds.), *Research Handbook in Critical Legal Theory* (Cheltenham: Edward Elgar Publishing, 2019).

[7] The distinction between governing and governance is key to the analysis that Poul Kjaer offers of the processes of integration and constitutionalisation in Europe (in: Poul F. Kjaer, *Between Governing and Governance: On the Emergence, Function and Form of Europe's Post-National Constellation* (Oxford: Hart Publishing, 2010). As he puts it, the distinction between governing and governance allows for an understanding of the EU as a hybrid, consisting of a governing dimension, characterised by legal and organisational hierarchy, and a governance dimension which operates within a network form characterised by legal and organisational heterarchy.

[8] Offe, n. 4 above, at 551.

> distinctively authoritative state structures and processes ... in the gray area of an irredeemably overstretched concept?[9]

Offe proposes a delimitation of the concept of governance in order 'to capture the range of phenomena that extends *between* the poles of competitive markets and hierarchical expressions of state authority'.[10] Now this *in between* is a problematic location, and Offe's suggested topography largely elides the problem. Given how much hinges on delimiting the interstice on which to install 'governance', its subsequent definition by Offe as 'a concept employed to *bridge* and *blur* the differences that conventionally structure thought'[11] is singularly unhelpful. Not just because, obviously, 'bridging' and 'blurring' are mutually undercutting performances, but also because to bridge requires a certain solidity of the terrain, and the shifting *topoi* of market and state afford little such solidity. Moreover, Offe's topology, with the spatial delimitations that it suggests, stumbles on the limit of the metaphor that is 'public space'. And if one might switch for a moment from the spatial to the *temporal*, one might appreciate how the extraction of value associated with governance practices involves crossing and re-crossing those spatial boundaries as an *ongoing* process of 'bridging and blurring', of exploitation (of the market/state boundary) and flight (from processes of assumption and attribution of obligation).

So we must ask Offe who exactly is calling for the *resolution* of the polysemy of the 'irredeemably overstretched concept'? *For whom* is it overstretched, and what might its redemption look like? These questions go to the heart of theory construction and its stakes. Semantic correction – or the reining in of the 'overstretched' concept – addresses the dynamics of symbolic politics. Who gains from the overstretch, who from the floating signification? We will explore below how it is the very polysemy of governance that ensures, for its proponents, nothing short of a *democratic* redemption, couched in a language of democratic experimentalism. And the last thing that these 'experimentalists' would expect or demand is semantic discipline. A latent politics is played out on this terrain, on the one side, by those (still) defending a language of governing, institution and publicness, and, on the other, by those advocating the release of such 'rigidity' into polysemy, where the signifier 'governance' will attach to shifting correlations of collectivity and configurations of

9 Ibid., 552.
10 Ibid., 553, emphasis in the original.
11 Ibid., emphasis added.

publicness in a way that involves a renegotiation of political capacity, rationality and history. This is a renegotiation undertaken in the guise of expanding democracy. Processes of value extraction here are tightly knit to processes of the disarticulation and reconfiguration of conceptual schemes. And as far as the champions of governance are concerned, there is nothing at all that is 'irredeemable' about this 'overstretching'; the 'overstretching' is, instead, coincident with the expansion of democratic *reflexivity*.

The structure of the chapter is as follows. The next part (II) offers a brief genealogy of governance, in the sense of an excavation of what set it on its path and sent it along given trajectories, with an emphasis on the junctures where path dependencies were secured. On the one hand, the release of governance from the 'shackles' of (government) *planning* was secured by the successful attack of the (Hayekian) Right on 'overbearing' regulation and the necessarily inadequate knowledge on which it drew under conditions of increased complexity. This came coupled with the emancipatory idiom of the expansion, deepening, even 'radicalisation' of democracy. Part III will return to explore this 'myth' of *democratic* governance, with specific reference to the economy. It is a myth because the predication 'democratic', neither qualifying nor anchoring, becomes, instead, a sign of a self-referential operation that has internalised all its criteria in order that governance be able to define for itself what is democratic about it.

It is in anticipation of this move (of recursion and self-definition) that first we return to Offe, in the remaining part of this section, to pick up the concept of the '*empty signifier*', but this time resist his topography, with all its self-undermining and self-cancelling 'bridges' and 'blurrings', and focus instead on the emptiness, or void, of signification with the help of Ernesto Laclau's important theorisation of *empty signifiers*.[12] I have no idea whether Offe borrowed the notion from him, and Laclau does not appear in Offe's references. If we follow Laclau's theorisation of the empty signifier rather than Offe's, it is because the latter's is imprecise; Offe uses the term to denote indeterminacy of meaning ('polysemy'), and, in doing this, conflates 'empty' with 'floating' signifiers. We will stay, instead, with Laclau's insight about how the emptiness of signifiers informs a *hegemonic* gesture whereby a sign installs itself as a context

[12] Ernesto Laclau, 'Why do Empty Signifiers Matter to Politics?', in: Laclau, *Emancipation(s)* (London: Verso, 1996). See, also, Laclau, *On Populist Reason* (London: Verso, 2005); and Laclau, 'Populism: What's in a Name?', in: Francisco Panizza (ed.), *Populism and the Mirror of Democracy* (London: Verso, 2005).

and as a reference for a field, a totalising gesture that elevates the empty signifier – 'governance' in our case – to the position of signifier for a whole 'chain of equivalences'. We will take this gradually, and the first step is to address the distinction between floating and empty signifiers.

A *floating signifier* is one that does not attach unambiguously to a *signified*, but where, instead, 'either an over-determination or an under-determination of signifieds prevents it from being fully fixed'.[13] The important point to note is that the asymmetry that 'floats' the signifier, either as excess ('over-') or deficiency ('under-'), does not yet 'empty' it. In fact, Laclau tries to capture something very different, and significantly more complex, with the empty signifier. An empty signifier is, strictly speaking, a signifier *without* a signified, not, as in 'floating', in excess of one. 'But how would it be possible', he asks, 'that a signifier is not attached to any signified and remains, nevertheless, an integral part of a system of signification?' We are dealing, he answers his own quandary, 'with the precise theoretical possibility of something which points, from within the process of signification, to the discursive process of its own limits'.[14] The empty signifier, in other words, 'concerns the possibility of signifying the limits of signification as such'.[15] To understand this point, we will need to pick up the thread a few steps back.

Signification is differential inscription. From Ferdinand de Saussure, we know that every system of signification (of which language is a principal instance) is a system of differences. To name an identity is to draw out its difference within the system where every linguistic identity will be purely *relational vis-à-vis* all the others. The *contrasts between signs is* how signs derive their meaning.[16] And because identity is constituted as difference within the relational field, it enters into relations of equivalence with all

[13] Laclau, *Emancipation(s)*, n. 12 above, at 36.

[14] Ibid., at 36.

[15] 'If what we are talking about are the limits of a *signifying system*, it is clear that those limits cannot be themselves signified, but have to *show* themselves as the *interruption* or *breakdown* of the process of signification' (Laclau, ibid.).

[16] Signifiers attach to specific signifieds and the sign takes form as the associative link between the signifier and signified. A sign's 'meaning depends on its relation to other words within the system'. As the translator of Saussure's *Course in General Linguistics*, puts it in the introduction, '[t]he essential feature of Saussure's linguistic sign is that, being intrinsically arbitrary, it can be identified only by contrast with coexisting signs of the same nature, which together constitute a structured system' (Roy Harris, 'Introduction', to: Ferdinand de Saussure, *Course in General Linguistics*, edited and annotated by Roy Harris (La Salle IL: Open Court, 1983), p. x).

the other differences of the system, as differences become reconfigured and renegotiated in the emerging 'semiological chains' (Roland Barthes) and changing semiotic network of their linkage. Naming something as 'x' – deploying signs in linguistic usage – mobilises at once both a logic of difference and a logic of equivalence. The context of language, the *articulation* of difference and equivalence, is mobilised in every operation in which linguistic signs yield meaning.

It is against the background of this articulation of difference and equivalence that Laclau invites us to think about the function of *empty* signifiers. We talk of articulation because, linguistically, we can have neither pure difference nor pure equivalence; it is articulation that holds the two logics together and in tension. When signifiers lose their attachment to particular signifieds, to particular contents, when they become disconnected from the specificity of difference, then they can be floated across greater stretches of equivalence. They ride on ambiguity and extend their semantic reach across a broader field. We might say that their *extension* grows at the expense of their *intension*.[17] Where a purely differential content would attach a signifier to a single signified, an equivalential move loses that correspondence in a certain slippage on the symbolic plane, one that opens the signifier to a variety of rearticulations.[18] A particular signifier comes thereby to represent an 'equivalential chain', and the more it gains on the plane of equivalence, the more it loses its specificity on the plane of difference. There occurs a 'displacement', as Laclau puts it, 'from contents to form'.[19] And it is in the context of this displacement that we will locate the *empty* signifier. Signification is 'emptied' at the *threshold* where the equivalential *prevails over* the differential moment. 'Emptying' names a *performative* move. The 'empty signifier' performs what Laclau, following Antonio Gramsci here, describes as a *hegemonic* move.

Hegemony, it will be recalled with reference to Gramsci (and expressing a key focus of Laclau's most famous book),[20] expresses a substitution – of particularity for universality, class interest for general

[17] Laclau, 'Populism: What's in a Name?', n. 12 above, at 40.

[18] We know from Jacques Derrida that with the renegotiation of such specificity (between speaker, listener and observer) the possibilities of interpretation and reinterpretation become radicalised. For Mikhail Bakhtin, too, 'the interpretation of symbolic structures is forced into an infinity of symbolic contextual meanings'.

[19] Laclau, 'Populism: What's in a Name?', n. 12 above, at 44.

[20] Ernest Laclau and Chantal Mouffe, *Hegemony and Socialist Strategy: Towards a Radical Democratic Politics* (London: Verso, 1985).

interest – that becomes unchallengeable within a specific historical conjuncture by becoming coterminous with the conceptual possibilities of a system. In the terms that we have been using, it marks the point where the 'equivalential chain' that the signifier mobilises stretches across the entire field. It comes to delimit the very *describability* of alternatives. The signifier comes to name each and every rearticulation and provide for each and every re-description. The emptying of the signifier, its generalisation across the field of equivalence, is a totalising move that, at the point at which differential signification yields to equivalence, installs the 'empty signifier' as signifier of every instantiation and every dislocation, paradoxically 'empty' but not meaningless. 'Governance', the empty signifier that concerns us here, becomes the term generalised across a field of equivalence that displaces politics. Politics is displaced because politics *must* mobilise difference and distinction – public/private, collective/individual, class, gender, etc., – if only to provide for its conceptual possibility that things *could be otherwise*. Instead, at the point where the empty signifier takes hold, politics finds the field of differential inscription upon which it depends collapsed into the equivalence that governance names. Democratic politics, in other words, finds itself collapsed in the comprehensive inclusiveness of 'governance'. The hegemonic move is complete at the point at which a partial system of signifiers installs itself, through 'equivalence', as horizon and context of every possible description.

We now turn to the genealogy of the rise of governance in order to trace the history of its *hegemonic* ascendance and success in installing itself as context and register of 'democratic' thinking.

II The New Worlds of Governance

Governance does not properly make its appearance until the late 1970s. The oil crisis of 1973 had resulted in the loss of state revenues, and the fiscal crisis that followed made the commitment to welfare a much larger part of the national GDP of the developed world, and a prime target for the 'free market' ideology that was storming the political imaginary. Propelled by the new ideology, and against the loudly proclaimed 'failure' of Keynesian macro-economic planning, the new priorities for the state were pared back to, first, the control of monetary policy, with a view to securing a stable macroeconomic environment that would harbour and promote private sector activity and innovation and release the entrepreneurial energies of the nation, and, second, to the policing of the political and social unrest that would follow the clamping down on trade unionism and social rights. The champions of the New Right in the United States and the United Kingdom persuaded their political audiences that the market would fill the space vacated by the exhaustion of the energies of the post-War settlement. As with any paradigm shift, explanatory frameworks rose to organise the evidence around a new configuration of *explanans* and *explanandum*. The achievements of industrial democracy and of economic solidarity were abandoned as if, in a profound sense, they were *anachronistic*.

This is the context in which the paradigmatic *shift from government to governance* takes place, the latter associated, in the first wave of reform, with the attack on the regulatory state. Focused on micro-processes and interactions, and furnished with the philosophy of rational choice and decision theory, new governance was seen as a solution to the complexity and overload-induced inertia of the bureaucratic regulatory state, promising a more efficient, responsive, heterarchical, pluralistic pattern of rule.

The shift from government to governance is effected in, roughly speaking, two waves that follow distinct logics. The emergence of new governance as a *solution* depends on a narrative that understood 'regulatory fracture' as an inevitable pathology and expression of changing state functions. There were two prongs in the attack on the state. First, the post-war regulatory state was corporatist in organising state action and formulating public policy by reaching out to societal associations of organised interests and collective identifications, with a view to settling disputes, typically wage agreements in collective bargaining processes. What was *denounced* by the proponents of governance was the privileged inclusion and entrenchment of the political capacity of particular representatives of economic and professional interests. Secondly, the idea that the regulatory state could monitor and combine with the work of policy makers, social-welfare reformers, came under increased attack as embodying the discredited aspiration of command economies, as did the notion that it could tame the collective irrationalities of organised interests in the democratic process. The New Right attacked social welfare reform and associational democracy as philosophically naïve and politically dangerous. It is wrong however, as is sometimes argued, that this was an attack on the full range of the functions of the state, or that it led to its demise. Through monetary policy, the state would remain a necessary facilitator and guarantor of a stable macroeconomic environment, and, in moral terms, the lynchpin of national-communitarian 'belonging'.[21] If there is a turn away from the state because of globalisation, it involves neither a zero-sum shift to the transnational, nor a diminution of the significance of the state as a moral force behind identity-formation and community.

This first wave of the emergence and consolidation of governance, spearheaded in Britain, is coincident with the radicalisation of the agenda of the New Right in the 1970s and 1980s, on the axes of marketisation,[22] rational choice and utility maximisation. The state came under sustained attack as the site of overreach, inefficiency, cronyism and bureaucratic goal-displacement. A broad range of measures was developed and deployed in this first wave of governance reform: the removal of state functions from the economy; the opening up to competition to the detriment of any other basis of association; and, in certain European States in particular, the introduction of market thinking to public management, in what became the 'new public management' philosophies of organisation, which involved the reform of public sector management in accord with private sector techniques and the adoption of managerial and budgetary practices from private sector organisations.[23] 'Freedom to manage' would now be claimed *against* bureaucratic regulation and in the direction *of market discipline*, with the hallmark introduction of incentives and competitive pressures.[24]

[21] For this argument, see Maurice Glasman, *Unnecessary Suffering: Managing Market Utopia* (London: Verso, 1996), especially, p. xiv.

[22] 'The dominance of governance theory that places the market at the centre of its regulatory design has been relatively unabashed over the decades since the 1980s, and even the current financial and economic crisis does not yet seem to have induced its demise. At the same time we see that the engagements with "market" as governance category are untiring.' Peer Zumbansen, 'Knowledge in Development, Law and Regulation, or How are we to Distinguish between the Economic and the Non-Economic?', in: Gráinne de Búrca, Claire Kilpatrick and Joanne Scott (eds.), *Critical Legal Perspectives on Global Governance: Liber Amicorum David M. Trubek* (Oxford: Hart Publishing, 2015), pp. 103–25, at 119.

[23] See Mark Bevir, *Democratic Governance*, Princeton NJ: Princeton University Press, 2010), p. 71. See, also Ewan Ferlie, Lynn Ashburner, Louise Fitzgerald and Andrew Pettigrew, *The New Public Management in Action* (Oxford: Oxford University Press, 1996); and David Osborne and Ted Gaebler, *Reinventing Government: How the Entrepreneurial Spirit is Transforming the Public Sector* (New York: Plume-Penguin Books, 1992).

[24] A similar agenda of instilling market discipline was to be mobilised a decade later with particular brutality in the introduction of market discipline to the states of the former Warsaw Pact, in a reform strategy 'the likes of which no modern western nation had ever considered imposing on itself for fear of the effects it would have on people's lives and livelihoods'. For this argument, see Glasman, n. 21 above, at xiv.

The second wave of governance, which took hold in the 1990s, involved a partial retreat from the individualistic creed and the privatisation agenda, and its relaunch in terms of *joined-up governance*. Governance now shifts policy making towards *networks*. The discovery of networks as a new organising basis for society, as new points of entry of new actors in policy processes, and as organising structures to coordinate activities and allocate resources comes with an emancipatory idiom that changes the political imaginary. New spaces of participation, new understandings of 'stakeholding' (more on this below), the mobilisation of fragmented, cross-cutting, plural, mutually re-enforcing and cross-fertilising identities, the whole set of 'multi-perspectival' politics is hailed in to inform the processes of joined-up governance. They come with a new emphasis on the appropriateness of solutions to the complexity of the receiving field,[25] an emphasis on flexibility and responsiveness;[26] the acknowledgement that problems can be 'wicked';[27] the moulding of partnership structures to confront them, and the celebration of 'democratic experimentalism' as a source of innovation.

The successive waves of governance involve significant shifts in the *forms of analysis and explanation*, where formal modes of analysis come to pervade. Governance is constitutively coupled with forms of knowledge-production that, by centring the focus on outcomes and effects, seek solutions in terms of synchronic models of *functional* analysis, while bracketing historical-*causal* forms of explanation. The turn to functional analysis is accompanied by changes in the logic and form of legitimation. With the clear *impasses* into which the macro-supervisory role of the state had entered, and with public officials no longer seen as capable of guaranteeing procedures or supervising expertise in any realistic sense, political accountability had to be re-thought. It was re-thought in terms of a shift *from input to output legitimacy*, from overseeing procedure to auditing performance. The 'audit explosion' introduces indicator-based policy-production and implementation, the use of *performance measures* – the whole array of targets, standards and benchmarks – to audit outputs and relate them to budgets. The idiom of 'good governance' spreads across an increasing range of theory and to new levels of

[25] Gunther Teubner, 'Substantive and Reflexive Elements in Modern Law' (1983) 17 *Law & Society Review*, 239–86.

[26] Philippe Nonet and Philip Selznick, *Law and Society in Transition: Toward Responsive Law* (London-New York: Routledge, 1978).

[27] For a definition, see Bevir, n. 23 above, p. 77.

implementation, as it is adopted by both regional *blocs* (e.g., the European Union) and international bodies (e.g., the World Bank).

Now, if the first wave of reform gained its leverage from the critique of the bureaucratic state, with the second wave and the shift of focus to the *global* organisation of production, the structures of governance also migrated to the supranational level. What marked the first wave was the fragmentation of the state political system's 'publics', the proliferation of constituencies of stakeholders (more on stakeholding below), as internal to the nation state and as contained largely at that level. But with the generalisation of economic activity across national borders, the proliferation of networks now connects directly upward to the rise of regional blocks (second level)[28] and global governance (third level).[29] Clearly, there are differences and shifts of emphasis at each level, but the contribution of the new logic of governance is understood as largely being uniform at all levels, geared to the facilitation of the inclusion of new social actors, the emergence of new forms of expertise and processes of knowledge-production, and the rise of new forms of policy. Their implementation will undoubtedly engage the state, but in a new role that no longer involves it as embodiment, overseer or arbitrator of the common good, or shackled to the 'outdated' public/private distinction. Let us look at how a certain distinctive shift in the function of the state, consequently informs the logic of governance at regional and global levels.

Governance is 'multilevel' because with 'regulatory fracture' at the level of the state, the exercise of public policy migrates to supra- and sub-state levels. Supposedly, with this comes a 'new freedom': the breakdown of the hierarchy of rule allows a new 'heterarchy', and, with it, a new structure of regulatory competition,[30] a new freedom of jurisdictional allocation, and new opportunities of forum shopping and 'forum shifting'.[31] In European developments, it is becoming blatantly clear that, for any discussion to have any traction, it must be couched in the language of governance under the auspices of which labour protection,

[28] Indicatively, Charles F. Sabel and Jonathan Zeitlin, 'Experimentalism in the EU: Common Ground and Persistent Differences' (2012) 6 *Regulation and Governance*, 410–26.

[29] Indicatively, Gráinne de Búrca, Robert O. Keohane and Charles F. Sabel, 'Global Experimentalist Governance' (2014) 44 *British Journal of Political Science*, 477–86.

[30] Sol Picciotto, *Regulating Global Corporate Capitalism* (Cambridge: Cambridge University Press, 2011).

[31] John Braithwaite and Peter Drahos, *Global Business Regulation* (Cambridge: Cambridge University Press, 2000).

too, is thematised.[32] In contrast to the 'classic community method',[33] new governance in Europe has been ushered in to allow legislative processes to produce soft law and substantial flexibility. This flexibility buttressed by the key principles of subsidiarity and proportionality in EU law has been used to navigate policy towards harmonisation in areas of fiscal and social policy where the EU had limited powers. In this intermediate area where there was reluctance to cede competence to the EU, but where coordination was called for, the flexibility afforded by new governance was widely celebrated as securing the 'best of both worlds'.[34]

It is uniquely revealing that this 'achievement' is celebrated first and foremost on a *democratic* register. The normative dimension of the flexibilisation and spread of new governance comes widely to be expressed in the literature as a call for a re-thinking of democracy. One would have thought that the disaggregations, fractures and weakening of political representation would have been conceded as a weakening of democracy, the withdrawal of the capacity from the 'people' to form a will and transfer that will to the state for implementation. Not at all. Instead, the literature on new governance is resplendent with references to empowerment, 'bottom-up' deliberation, experimentalism, all clearly distinct from the stale and inward-looking *cul-de-sacs* of national democratic regimes and of states that have become poor aggregators of their citizens' interests. State regulatory functions, most notably in relation to the economy, are now exploded from within and harnessed to transnational frameworks where the national does not impede, and where, supposedly, nothing is taken for granted. It is thus that the significant *compensatory* gesture for the loss of the political in constitutionalism paradoxically involves the rediscovery of democracy in the varieties of the experimentalism of the new practices of 'democratic governance'. Here, networks and self-interested corporate actors emerge below, above and around the state institutional formations, so that the political is called to be re-thought in terms of this proliferation of subject positions that cut

32 Take the example of the *European Employment Strategy*, which is the first and most developed form of the *Open Method of Co-ordination*.

33 Joanne Scott and David M. Trubek, 'Mind the Gap: Law and New Approaches to Governance in the European Union' (2002) 8 *European Law Journal*, 1–18.

34 Jonathan Zeitlin, 'Social Europe and Experimentalist Governance: Towards a New Constitutional Compromise?', in: Gráinne de Búrca (ed.), *EU Law and the Welfare State: In Search of Solidarity* (Oxford: Oxford University Press, 2005), pp. 213–42. See, also, Charles F. Sabel and Jonathan Zeitlin, 'Learning from Difference: The New Architecture of Experimentalist Governance in the EU' (2008) 14 *European Law Journal*, 271–327.

across the traditional forms of representation. The relaunching of the function of governance runs alongside democracy as shorn of its national impediments, no longer beholden to the 'imperfect aggregations' of planning or the 'coercive transfers' of national welfare systems, pluralised as '*demoi*-cracies'[35] or other such absurd neologisms, and increasingly circuited to market dynamics at the transnational level.

It is in these terms that what is supposedly win-win about governance inscribes itself predominantly on a democratic register. New governance marks an 'expansion in the scope and intensity of civil society's role in decision-making processes' and with this mobilisation of civil society-wide resources, 'social dialogue' comes to install itself as a pervasive and enduring feature of EU governance;[36] examples include the creation of consultative *fora* on sustainable development in environmental issues, the use of voluntary agreements, widely hailed as exemplary[37] and of course 'social dialogue' (where it became nearly impossible to heed the reservations expressed by the ETUC for the ululations of its champions amongst EU policy makers, lawyers and discourse theorists). Suspended above these instantiations in every case, 'new governance' celebrates the advantages of participation and power sharing, with policy making 'a process of mutual problem-solving among stakeholders from government and the private sector',[38] the coordination at many levels of government achieving multilevel integration at the levels of locality, region, nation and supranational (European); the cultivation of diversity and the respect for subsidiarity against the uniformity of solutions imposed across the Union; the gains in flexibility offered by open-ended standards, flexible and revisable guidelines; the commitment to decentralised experimentation as generative of 'new knowledge: exchanging results, relating experience, benchmarking performance and sharing

35 Initially, Kalypso Nicolaïdis, 'Our European *Demoi*-cracy: Is this Constitution a Third Way for Europe?', in: Kalypso Nicolaïdis and Stephen Weatherill, *Whose Europe? National Models and the Constitution of the European Union* (Oxford: Oxford University Press, 2003). But now see, also, Jan-Werner Müller, 'The Promise of 'Demoi-cracy': Democracy, Diversity, and Domination in the European Public Order', in: Jürgen Neyer and Antje Wiener (eds.), *The Political Theory of the European Union* (Oxford: Oxford University Press, 2010), pp. 187–204.

36 For an acclamatory account, see Scott and Trubek, n. 33 above, p. 3. For a critical view, see Katherine Stone, 'Globalisation and the Middle Class', in: Gráinne de Búrca, Claire Kilpatrick and Joanne Scott (eds.), *Critical Legal Perspectives on Global Governance: Liber Amicorum David M. Trubek* (Oxford: Hart Publishing, 2015), pp. 163–84, especially at 173.

37 Scott and Trubek, n. 33 above, p. 3.

38 Ibid., p. 5.

best practices'. All of this, in turn, marks a significant increase in *responsiveness* – a term that preconceives the 'democratic' in reactive mode to the new exigencies: to increasing complexity and uncertainty; to irreducible diversity ('the systems of industrial relations and social protection vary tremendously'); to new developments in public administration and law.[39]

Let us stay with our fundamental query about what is *democratic* about democratic governance, taking as pivot, this time, the notion of the *common good.* Processes and interactions through which the exercise of public power now materialises in society reconfigure the meaning of public power, and its orientation to the common good, or 'public interest', in the process. Key to the paradigm shift from government to governance is the largely successful attack on the notion of the *common or public good* as tied to the state, the latter understood as the institutional form of the organisation of the national community. It was part of the post-war settlement that the social-democratic political consensus was expressed and enforced by the state that secured the implementation of the popular will as expressed through national legislation. With the acceleration of the global organisation of the economy, and the shift to supranational levels, the guiding democratic idea of the public good not only migrates away from the state, understood as the embodiment of the political community, as we saw, but also disconnects from the logic of *representation.* Institutions, as Alasdair MacIntyre powerfully argued,[40] embody a moral philosophy and a distinctive rationality, and their collapse comes at a cost. The cost is that with the migration to supranational settings what is 'common' about the 'good' loses its bearings. More precisely, the disarticulation of the 'good' from the 'common' collapses the meaning of what the two terms hold together, and the 'good', now adrift, comes to attach itself to a shifting pattern of commonality and constituency. The problem with the new 'pluralisms' in whose context the 'good' is now floated, is this: pluralising simultaneously both what is 'common' and what is 'good' of the guiding distinction of public policy, leaves the terms distinguished from each other and singularly underdetermined in themselves. What was irreducible (because 'common') about the 'public interest' was disaggregated in the first wave of

[39] All this replete with 'power sharing', 'participation', 'management by objectives', and a reminder that 'sometimes new governance' is the only way in which the EU can play a role in a particular domain. See, also, Burkard Eberlein and Dieter Kerwer, 'New Governance in the EU' (2004) 42 *Journal of Common Market Studies*, 121–42.

[40] Alasdair MacIntyre, *After Virtue* (London-New York: Bloomsbury Academic, 1981).

governance through rational choice assumptions and the generalisation of micro-level analyses, and then, in the second wave, harnessed to shifting patterns of stakeholder constituencies. With the 'good' losing its immanent connection and embeddedness in what was common, the 'common', now a sign for *any* discernible commonality of interest, can do little gathering work of its own, as it is loosely coupled to processes of dislocation and realignment on a global scale, too readily co-optable, too easily outwitted.

The grand project of de-structuring the common that is undertaken as new governance, gains its leverage and justification from the fact that it is effected on fluid terrain, on which governance professes to optimise the flow of streams, to counter bureaucratic inertia, to fragment rigid structures of decision making and realign processes to more flexible models of horizontal relationships and/within networks. Networks typically involve negotiated forms of coordination in 'horizontal', rather than hierarchical, patterns (of subsumption to state authority). Given that the turn to networks was largely a (second-wave) attempt to rethink social interaction beyond the theoretically rushed rational-action templates, for which any form of *bounded* rationality was already a pathological expression, one must see, as the foundational motivation of the theorising of networks, a concern to account for the mechanisms that secure the *second-order stabilisation of social formation*, whether these be thought in terms of the containment of contingency, or the countering of uncertainty.

How this systematic pluralising-cum-undercutting of political capacity is ideologically buttressed is revealing. An emancipatory idiom mediates the rise and rise of governance, so that compiling its lexicon involves the wholesale raiding of the inventory of democratic and critical thought. New governance, alternately though often also cumulatively, is celebrated as *participative, collaborative, deliberative, responsive, experimentalist, recursive, reflexive, revisable, multilevel, etc.* Take the terms in turn: *multilevel* secures that the new paradigm can claim purchase at all levels and, significantly, mediate hierarchisations and delimitations between them. Labile forms come to replace rigid demarcations of what should properly be decided at what level, and with this move not only are 'constitutionalisms from below' welcomed, but also constitutionalisation is surrendered to more flexible figurations. Subsidiarity, that cornerstone of European-level constitutionalism, which ensures responsiveness to, and self-determination at, more localised levels, can be both deployed *and* reflected on in the process. The reference to reflexivity, in this sense, undergirds and accompanies every one of the deployments.

Furthermore, new governance is *participative* because it is no longer a top-down affair. As coupled with constitutionalism from below, this *soft* form of law-making pivots on participation, rather than membership. Key connections are invoked to fill in the gaps, and, as these are drawn principally from the field of discourse-analysis, carry with them their own legitimatory and redemptive features. The participative element through the *deliberative* becomes both *responsive* (to the other) and *reflexive* at both level and meta-level. The reflexive dimension of dialogue and innovation carries across the spectrum. As deliberative, the participative turns *collaborative*; because the deliberative paradigm ensures that participation will only ever be collaboration and that any conflict that might have informed people's entry into the public sphere is *always-already* 'communal',[41] never antagonistic. Conflict positions are thus only ever entertained provisionally within the framing conditions of the projection of eventual consensus. Furthermore, the 'recursive' gives the 'collaborative' duration, while the 'responsive' secures adaptability to changing conditions. Further values build on this: 'learning oriented', rather than competitive or strategic, orientation furnishes the speaking positions, malleability maps on to contingency, and 'flexible' and 'revisable' become terms for listening to the other, responsively, open to learning, and dynamic. Crucially in all this, learning is supposedly released from path-dependency – or at least the single-track path dependency – of overbearing structure and overbearing theory. And if the objection is ever raised that this relaunching of governance elides a theory of justice to which it might be held, it is suggested that the undertaking itself, gaining leverage from, but no longer captive to, its presuppositions might fashion its own theory of justice, again, reflexively.[42] With this forever renewed gesture of inclusion, the 'empty signifier' of governance becomes the sign of the field of equivalence, installing itself as the horizon of every possible instantiation of

[41] For the notion of communal conflict, see Georg Simmel, *Conflict*, trans. K. Wolff (New York: The Free Press, 1955), and Lewis Coser, *The Functions of Social Conflict* (New York: The Free Press, 1956). For the *ideological* function of the distinction communal/non-communal conflict, see Emilios Christodoulidis, *Law and Reflexive Politics* (Dordrecht: Kluwer Academic Publishers, 1996).

[42] For this suggestion, see Gráinne de Búrca: 'Another possible answer is that the philosophy of experimentalism – which is premised on the recursive, deliberative, and inclusive working out of shared solutions to common problems – should over time produce its own theory of justice, since our theories of justice derive ultimately from the exercise of public reason.' In: Gráinne de Búrca, 'New Governance and Experimentalism: An Introduction' (2010) *Wisconsin Law Review*, 227–38, at 238.

democracy and justice. It is this usurpation of language, the collapse of critique into affirmation in the modalities of the forever renewed, meaning-depriving inclusion, which come to sustain and buttress the myth that is democratic governance.

III 'Stakeholding'

Remember Offe's topography: governance should properly be relocated to the middle ground between, on the one hand, government, which refers to the 'shrinking realm of manifest state power', and, on the other, the 'private and civil society sphere' where '"spontaneous" coordination of action . . . occurs through associative as well as market transactions'.

> If one accepts these two delimitations, there still remains a large set of phenomena that a concept of governance, thus defined, would capture. This includes, on the one hand, the regulation of *publicly relevant issues by non-state strategic actors* – e.g. large corporations, employer associations, unions, churches, chambers of commerce, the mass media, etc. And on the other hand, this would include actors, on whose cooperation state policy depends without being able to mandate and sanction such cooperation. These phenomena encompass activities which can be subject to very different normative evaluations. The shaping of publicly relevant affairs through private actors can be seen as the exercise of foresighted *responsibility* and an obligation oriented toward the *common good*.[43]

Hence,

> . . . the proposed delimitation of the concept of governance aims to capture the *range of phenomena* that extends between the poles of competitive markets and the hierarchical expressions of state authority.[44]

There is much to note here. First, let us note the smooth passage between the 'associative' and the 'market transactions' as both relegated to the civil society sphere, a sphere from which governance is, properly understood, to be distinguished. Second, let us note the reference to the 'regulation of publicly relevant issues' by non-state actors, what the list includes, and the emphasis on the concepts of 'responsibility' and the 'common good'. Finally, it should be noted that the proposed delimitation captures a range of phenomena as now locatable at the interstice between the two poles.

We might begin from the latter point. The notion that governance applies to phenomena that fall between state and market perspectives

[43] Offe, n. 4 above, at 552–3, my emphasis.
[44] Ibid., at 552–3.

involves a *curious ontology*, given that the range will be thematised in mutually exclusive ways by both the market and the state. Their 'phenomenality' – to introduce a basic notion from the phenomenological tradition – does not pre-exist their emergence – that is, their individuation *as* phenomena – on the competing templates. How something emerges as a problem, what conditions its emergence as a theme, and what path-dependency grants it meaning, are tied to the mutually exclusive frameworks (of market and state), and their own understanding of what falls within and outside. This is a boundary that can only be observed from the inside; in the case of the market, it distinguishes between what can be priced and what constitutes an externality, and, in the case of state policy-making, what falls within and outside the regulation of the common good. Nothing mediates or 'inter-dicts' (we might say with Alain Supiot) 'total market thinking'[45] and state planning in order to set up the 'range of phenomena' on a commonly de-limited plane and as relevant to the logic of the third – governance. Instead, the latter must 'bridge and blur' to fashion a space for itself, and the equivocations here between associative and market are indicative of a functional turn, away from 'deficient state capacities' and towards 'its [governance] greater problem-solving capacity'.[46]

Offe's reference, as we saw, was to the 'regulation of publicly relevant issues' by non-state actors, with an emphasis on the concepts of 'responsibility' and the 'common good'. But, first, the reach of governance has to be settled because it must navigate and synthesise (Offe borrows from Bob Jessop here) 'several simplistic dichotomies that inform the social sciences',[47] including the likes of state/society, political/economic action, structure/process, domestic/foreign, subject/object, etc. Their synthesis and (circum-)navigation involves a sobering fastening onto problem-solving, that avoids the tendency to 'over-aggregate' phenomena, but instead to deal with them *as they appear*.

> One may fall back on governance as a comparatively 'soft' mode of substituting for state and government while avoiding the political costs of conflict, so goes the attractive promise, everywhere where state capacity is deficient, on the one hand, and pure market coordination has little

[45] Alain Supiot, *Governance by Numbers: The Making of a Legal Model of Allegiance* (Oxford: Hart Publishing, 2017).

[46] Offe, n. 4 above, at 554, quoting Julia von Blumenthal, 'Governance – eine kritische Zwischenbilanz' (2005) 15 *Zeitschrift für Politikwissenschaft*, 1149–80, at 1157.

[47] Ibid., at 553, quoting Bob Jessop, 'The Rise of Governance and the Risk of Failure: The Case of Economic Development' (1998) 155 *International Social Science Journal*, 29–45.

> prospects of success, on the other. Jessop interprets this recourse to 'governance' as a pattern of mutually beneficial exchange: ... the state gives up part of its capacity for top-down authoritative decision making in exchange for influence over economic agents and more effective overall economic performance.[48]

There are clearly problems with this new emphasis on problem solving, with which Offe is also somewhat ill at ease. His own paper finishes with a warning about 'blindspots' and persisting questions, and he is clearly not comfortable with the way that governance has enabled 'third way' politics in the United Kingdom and elsewhere to travel the trajectory of the 'state-organised unburdening of the state'[49] or informed theories of 'autonomous societal self-organisation' (presumably of the 'societal constitutionalism' variety). I leave a question mark over all this, not just because Offe leaves us with ambivalence, but more because it does not matter that he does. What he *has* given us is a topography that is evocatively, and instructively, problematical, with its constitutive orientation to functionality (problem solving) and its suggested (and here clearly endorsed) dis-articulation of the common good from the state, and subject positions from citizen and corporatist figurations. His invitation is to adopt the identification of the 'collective action problem' from the governance scholarship: the 'horizontal problem', as it is customarily put, of the 'production of collective goods'.[50] His invitation is to address the problem of collective action by releasing it from redundant patterns and attaching it, instead, to fluid conceptions of stakeholding.

Stakeholding, a concept that we have already repeatedly encountered, is an organising category in new governance thinking. For Gráinne de Búrca:

> the two most crucial features of an experimentalist-governance system, and those without which the system will fail in addressing the problem, are (1) the broadest possible degree of stakeholder participation compatible with effective decision-making, and (2) effective and informed monitoring.[51]

[48] Ibid., at 554, quoting Jessop, at 36.
[49] Ibid., at 555.
[50] Offe, n. 4 above, at 556.
[51] In de Búrca, 'New Governance and Experimentalism: An Introduction', n. 42 above, at 227.

If stakeholding gives us the answer to the 'collective action problem', it is because it successfully breaks with the concept of 'representation' and the traditional structures that tied it to the institutions of government. As an organising concept in the new dispensation ('stakeholder society'), the concept of 'stakeholding' promises reflexivity in two directions: regarding the determination of the problem (*stake*holding), and regarding the determination of the subject position (stake*holding*). It is indeed reflexivity that holds the clue here for how governance is expressed (and redeemed) as a democratic achievement. It is in the name of the democratic questioning of stakeholding that reflexivity is invited, regarding both *how* to understand the problem and *who* has a stake in its solution. The notion of 'representation' is thereby *destabilised* in the direction, supposedly, of more democracy. Stakeholding as an organising category of new governance allows an insight into how new governance effects a reconfiguration of democratic politics along temporal, material and social dimensions. Let us look at this more closely.

As a question of the new temporality, first, the *time* of governance with its staggered, incremental, step-by-step approach, both recursive and revisable, locates itself in the modality of the present/future and avails itself of 'learning': and learning, of course, involves a surrender of normativity, to the extent that disappointed expectations – over what is at stake – are not held onto, but are discredited in the face of better knowledge.[52] An older democratic politics, one insistent on the mandates that a people had entrusted to its representatives in government, involved no such surrender: a normative commitment was, after all, something onto which one intended to hold. Implementing the mandated word was the test of the truth of representation. But governance, as Alain Supiot writes, 'implemented as programmes of self-adjustment to received signals in real time, is incompatible with keeping one's word'.[53] Governance shifts the temporal modality to become, instead, a question of 'the capacity of human beings to adapt their behaviour to changes in the environment in order to survive'.[54]

[52] On the difference between normative and cognitive expectations around the question of 'learning', see Niklas Luhmann. Briefly, a cognitive expectation 'learns' from disappointment, because it is thereby discredited, whereas a normative expectation is maintained in the face of disappointment.

[53] Supiot, n. 45 above, pp. 26 and 28. 'The replacement of government by governance is an expression of a new cybernetic imaginary' (ibid., p. 30).

[54] Ibid., p. 30.

But stakeholding allows a reconfiguring also of material and social givens. Along the material axis, the stake is re-thematised, and the 'interests' that constellate around it are not pre-given, but are discursively formed. In the self-proclaimed, heavily pragmatic, social theory that new governance locates itself, institutional *fora* enable practices of negotiation and settlement (in participatory councils, in processes of 'social dialogue', etc.) where, to use the words of one of its champions, 'interests values and [the] institutions [themselves] can always become the starting point of their redefinition'.[55] Reflexive stakeholding of this kind, reflexive here over the definition of the 'stake', will additionally draw from local contexts as apposite to the truly participative thrust of new governance: its key is the horizontal articulation of particular interests and knowledge as opposed to any top-down imposition; 'heterarchy' rather than hierarchy. If, in the temporal dimension, stakeholding re-directs democracy to learning, and, in the material dimension, explodes fixed interests (or corporate bodies and state citizenries amongst others) in the direction of democratic renegotiation, it is in the social dimension that it secures its democratic pedigree *par excellence*: structures of representation are no longer the starting point or vehicle of representation, but stakeholders emerge reflexively in renegotiations of fixed subject positions (say, of corporate, class or national identities). The reflexivity of stakeholding becomes the democratic corrective to representation, and to the 'collective action' problem (as above), in the direction of better knowledge.

As experimentalism writ large, 'new governance' ticks all the boxes. The problem that it now faces is how to reconcile the promises harboured at the level of theory-construction with the reality of a field of application replete with power asymmetries. It cannot, of course, afford to treat asymmetries of power as definitive of, or structural to, the receiving field, or in any way as being compromising or debilitating of reflexivity. It is here that the recourse to discourse theory is invoked to provide the necessary leverage. Why is the recourse, and the leverage, 'necessary'? Because it does not take great sociological insight to discern that those with specific and targeted aims, those with clearly staked-out interests and the leverage to press them will do better in the competition over the definition of the stakes and of holding them. And that, even if new governance keeps alive a certain level of recognition of stakeholding,

[55] Charles F. Sabel, 'Learning by Monitoring: The Institutions of Economic Development', in: Neil J. Smelser and Richard Swedberg (eds.), *The Handbook of Economic Sociology* (Princeton NJ: Princeton University Press, 1994), pp. 137–65, at 158.

the reality of participation in institutional procedures is erratic, incremental, only selectively inclusive. And that, in temporal terms, full inclusion (however understood) and unlimited opportunity of participation (however envisaged) would make procedures too cumbersome to yield any results, so that, in practice, they *have to* be curtailed, shrunk in temporal terms and appended to substitute operations (e.g., 'social dialogue' in European industrial relations). To counter this *impasse*, 'new governance' will typically draw on the resources of discourse theory.

And at this juncture, like all theories that draw on the paradigm of discourse for their justification, the typical gesture of the proponents of new governance will involve importing a projected intersubjectivity of stakeholding operating under ideal conditions, *counterfactually* back to real conditions. This *importation-back* from ideal to real onto the terrain of political debate, the contributions to which will, as a matter of fact, be asymmetrical, performs the following significant ideological function. The ideal situation holds the promise that, should the real conditions be improved in the direction of the ideal situation, and should certain thresholds – although these are typically only reflexively stipulated – be met, whatever consensus is formed will receive full justification. The series of slippages involved should be noted: it is the actual conditions of engagement that stand in the way of the aspired-to intersubjectivity, consensus and truth; these can be procedurally propped up or improved in the direction of the ideal speech situation, but ideal consensus is – by definition – aspirational and therefore unattainable, and thus must give way to the more modest ambition of a 'well-grounded' consensus;[56] conditions for what counts as 'well grounded' cannot and should not be imposed *a priori*, and therefore must emerge dialogically, reflexively, from actual practice. Participants in actual practice will redefine what is at stake, in whatever direction, although, of course, only ever provisionally. And the substitution of real for ideal continues at each step of the

[56] Habermas replaces the criterion of actual consensus with that of 'well-grounded' consensus as criterion of truth: 'The meaning of truth lies not in the circumstance that some consensus is actually achieved, but rather in this: that at any time and in any place if we but enter into discourse, a consensus can be achieved under certain conditions which prove this to be a well grounded consensus' Jürgen Habermas, 'Wahrheitstheorien', in: Helmut Fahrenbach (ed.), *Wirklichkeit und Reflexion: Festschrift für Walter Schultz* (Pfullingen: Neske Stuttgart, 1973), pp. 211–65, at 239, quoted in Robert Alexy, *A Theory of Legal Argumentation: The Theory of Rational Discourse as Theory of Legal Justification* (Oxford: Oxford University Press, 1989), at 111.

way. What is distinctive throughout this process of substitution is that the 'ideal' conditions are doing the redemptive work, while the real conditions are producing the results. It is on the back of this series of slippages that an approximation is effected between the counterfactual and the real conditions of engagement. Such is the power of this approximation that gradually the fact of *there being a dialogue at all* secures, on this model, the guarantee that there will be openness, the filtering out of prejudice, learning, consensus and truth. The gap between the ideal and the real is there to be closed, an assumption carried in nothing less than the conditions of linguistic usage and the openness of communicative exchange. Louis Althusser famously saw the function of *bourgeois* ideology as consisting in securing that the appearance of emancipation that it promises is not undercut by the truth of the domination that it organises.[57] Such organisation is precisely what is being secured in this succession of slippages. And if, in effect, the ideal intersubjective conditions that would *redeem* current practices find *no purchase in* those practices, then the promise that a genuine project of self-determination will democratically be hoisted out of them is a lie. That is the lie of new governance.

And in this it inflicts what Jean-François Lyotard calls a *wrong*, an unrecoverable damage: through the gesture that is typical of ideology, redress, cannot find a point of inscription at all on the democratic register. Because what is remarkable about new governance, '*democratic*' governance, is that it forces a reorientation of 'democratic' thinking to accommodate itself around the new functionality that, as we saw, comes to coincide with the 'common' or 'public good'. We can trace the same line of argument now in terms of stakeholding, and the paradox that needs to be suppressed in its regard. The paradox lies in the fact that, if the question is over *what is at stake*, the assumption of the speaking position of stakeholder unravels; clearly, I cannot assert the position of stakeholder if the very stake that furnishes my speaking position is at stake, so to speak. In other words, if the object of holding becomes questionable, so is my subject-position as holder. The spectre of exclusion at this point spreads at least as quickly as the promise of inclusion. It will take the form: '*I do not recognise your stake in*

[57] Louis Althusser, *Sur la reproduction* (Paris: Presses Universitaires de France, 1995), at 269.

this.' How this resonates with the spectre of exclusion of those unable to negotiate the 'entry point' into stakeholding, the systematically excluded, the world's redundant populations that lack (Hannah Arendt's) 'world-making capacity', and who bring nothing to appearance except their needs. In all this, what is left is the collapse of the speaking position of those whose relationship to stakeholding becomes untenable: typically, those deprived of the opportunities to make any difference to the discussion, and whose participation had previously been claimed on grounds of belonging, actually or potentially, to the material reproduction of society, and on grounds of equal membership in the body politic through structures of political representation.

IV Conclusion

In this chapter, we have traced how Offe's allegedly 'unresolved polysemy' of 'governance' has been emphatically resolved by governance scholars in two directions, semantic and functional. First, on the *semantic* level, we looked at how the floating signification ('polysemy') of the concept crossed the threshold of indeterminacy to become 'empty' at the point at which the field of difference collapsed into the field of equivalence. The floating, and then the emptying, of the sign 'governance' marks the loss of the ability of a political society to hold on to specific differences, and therefore specific determinations of the meaning of the *common good*. With governance introduced to carry the organising concept of politics into the new, post-state, dispensation, the term was divested of its *differentia specifica*, floated across the boundaries of public/private, citizenship/market, and lost to the field of equivalence where it names both everything and nothing in particular. This loss of terms, I argued, is, nevertheless, productive to the consolidation of *hegemony*, understood as a totalising inclusion in which particular designations (of what was common, good, associative *because* irreducible to the logic of price) are universalised. The terms are lost at the point at which they can no longer sustain themselves as signifiers of particular signifieds, defined through mutual differentiation. We saw how hegemony constituted the political field in the sense of delimiting (and policing) what counts as rational within it. It involved pitting the practicable against the utopian, the rational against the insane, the attainable against the impossible; with this gesture of delimitation it also established the meaning of renegotiation, redefinition, intelligibility, describability and thus what, within its ambit, was possible as rational consensus,[58] already inclusive, as we said, of every political instantiation and every 'rational' contestation.

What, at the semantic level, collapses the meaning of political terms, at a second, *functional*, level, mobilises them as functional equivalents within governance's problem-solving vernacular. Different aggregations and optimisations arise here to harness governance to problem solving as pragmatic, sobering, objective, and crucially free of the collective irrationalities and biases that riddled the 'collective action problem' when it used to be cast in corporatist or class terms. The 'collective action problem', the democratic question *par excellence*, is recast in the modalities of stakeholding. With collectivity and the common adapted to more flexible figurations, the scope of governance now expands, and with it the operation of functional equivalence between problem-solving mechanisms with little more than optimisation and efficiency left as criteria for its success.

Because governance releases 'collective action' from fixed constituencies and channels of representation, governance comes to identify with democratic experimentalism, involving the explosion of given subject positions, both individual and collective: a reflexivity is supposedly imported at the very level at which these subject-positions used to be taken for granted, taken, in other words, as the *entry points to* the democratic game, rather than as the *results of* it. New governance invites new pluralities and reconfigures the plane of societal association. Except that these are also now pluralities without history. Divested of such encumbrances, stakeholding can only but mutate into an economic category. The radicalisation of the point of entry into stakeholding is at the same time a dramatic reduction of political capacity: the stakeholder is invoked and called forth in the only way possible in the wake of the collapse of collective categories and corporate identities, as *utility-maximiser*, as self-interested rational chooser, whose affiliation to the stakes of social and political action can only be external. With stakeholding

[58] Compare Glasman: 'Politics, especially during periods of transformation, is a struggle over the terms of definition of that world, an argument over what is and what is not unalterable in it. . . . . The social scientific fallacy is that agents act within a fixed rationality that is not itself the site of a struggle over re-definition' (ibid., n. 21 above, at 106).

replacing self-determination, the 'self' having been cut free from the register in which macro-identities and stakes were mutually constituted, the loss of collective categories and corporate identities is a loss with many facets, involving (i) the loss of the value of *participation as such* in collective practices; (ii) the loss of the social meaning of democratic participation at the level of the *constitution of collective identities*; and (iii) with the decoupling of the stake from antagonistic positions, the language of antagonism gives way to the language of competition, sometimes dignified as agonism. In the substitutions effected, the *eclipsing* of democratic thinking is tied to its alleged 'experimentalist' *affirmation* as governance.

4

A Political Economy of Contemporary Legality

DUNCAN KENNEDY

Introduction

This chapter starts with an observation: contemporary élite jurists pursue, *vis-à-vis* one another, a 'hermeneutic of suspicion', meaning that they work to uncover hidden ideological motives behind the 'wrong' legal arguments of their opponents, while affirming their own right answers allegedly innocent of ideology.[1] The rise of the hermeneutic of suspicion is a striking manifestation of the contemporary transformation of the relationship between legal élites and political/economic élites. This transformation accompanies and corresponds to the progressive juridification, judicialisation and finally constitionalisation of the contemporary social order.

The 'political economy' that my title proclaims as method for understanding all of this means incorporating at least the following elements of the social whole. There are groups, understood not just as collections of individuals but as collectives (usually, but not always, loose) with goals and strategies that are based on shared material and ideological, or 'ideal' interests. They cooperate in all the aspects of social production and reproduction and are, at the same time, in conflict with each other over

[1] This chapter is a thoroughly revised version of Part II of Duncan Kennedy, 'The Hermeneutic of Suspicion in Contemporary American Legal Thought' (2014) 25 *Law & Critique*, 91–139. Earlier formulations of the hermeneutic of suspicion idea: Duncan Kennedy, *A Critique of Adjudication: (fin de siècle)* (Cambridge MA: Harvard University Press, 1997), chapter 8, p. 180; Kennedy, 'Political Ideology and Comparative Law', in: Mauro Bussani and Ugo Mattei (eds.), *The Cambridge Companion to Comparative Law* (Cambridge: Cambridge University Press, 2012), pp. 35–56. I revised the version in the *Law & Critique* piece and published it as Duncan Kennedy, 'A Social Psychological Interpretation of the Hermeneutic of Suspicion in Contemporary American Legal Thought', in: Justin Desautels-Stein and Christopher Tomlins (eds.), *Searching for Contemporary Legal Thought* (Cambridge: Cambridge University Press, 2017), pp. 365–85.

the distribution of stakes that are both material and 'ideal', and include the resources necessary for success in the next iteration of the process. The conflict is situated within institutionally established rules of the game. These are given at any particular moment, but are also in constant modification since the rules of the game are among the objects of the game. Relations of domination and subordination are pervasive. Marx's *The Eighteenth Brumaire of Louis Bonaparte* is, for me, a canonical example, but the *schema* is very general, across the many forms of social division and antagonism.[2]

With the exception of a cursory, but instructive, reference to German constitutionalism, this is an essay on contemporary American legal thought and legal institutions. My interpretation of these American developments is heavily influenced by my prior work, trying to develop an account of transnational legal consciousness evolving through three stages: Classical Legal Thought (1850–1930), Social Legal Thought (1890–1968), and what was, when I developed the theory, Contemporary Legal Thought (1945–2000).[3] Up to World War II (WWII), in this account, the United States was a massive importer of European legal thought, and an innovator, but with negligible impact elsewhere, except for Latin America. After WWII, the United States stopped importing or even relating to legal developments abroad, except to try to influence them in our various imperial ventures.

At the same time, the rest of the world fell under various kinds and degrees of American legal hegemony.[4] For this reason, my account of contemporary American legal thought has only minimal reference to

[2] Two other examples among many that I find inspiring are W.E.B. Du Bois, *Black Reconstruction* (New York: The Free Press, [1935] 1998), and Yves Dezalay and Bryant Garth, *The Internationalization of Palace Wars: Lawyers Economists and the Contest to Transform Latin American States* (Chicago IL: University of Chicago Press, 2002). Antonio Gramsci, *Selections from the Prison Notebooks*, edited by Quentin Hoare and Geoffrey N. Smith (New York: International Publishers, 1971), is another inspiration. I attempted political economy inspired analyses in Duncan Kennedy, 'Legal Economics of U.S. Low Income Housing Markets in Light of "Informality" Analysis' (2002) 4 *Journal of Law in Society*, 71–98; Kennedy, 'African Poverty' (2012) 87 *Washington Law Review*, 205–35; and Kennedy, 'Commentary on Anti-Eviction and Development in the Global South', in: Lucie E. White and Jeremy Perelman (eds.), *Stones of Hope: How African Activists Reclaim Human Rights to Challenge Global Poverty* (Stanford CA: Stanford University Press, 2010), pp. 41–50.

[3] Duncan Kennedy, 'Three Globalizations of Law and Legal Thought: 1850–2000', in: David. M. Trubek and Alvaro Santos (eds.), *The New Law and Economic Development: A Critical Appraisal* (Cambridge: Cambridge University Press, 2006), pp. 19–73.

[4] An important work on this process, including its 'two-way' character, is Diego Lopez Medina, *Teoría Impura del Derecho. La transformación de la cultural juridical latinoamericana* (Bogotá: Legis, 2008).

foreign developments, although German and French legal thinkers have strongly influenced my analysis. It might nonetheless be interesting in legal contexts where importation from the United States is a welcome or unwelcome reality. I am afraid that what I write here will be much less intelligible and so less interesting to readers who have not read at least a little of this earlier work, but I will try, as I go along, to give as much quick background as possible.

I The Hermeneutic of Suspicion

The charge of abuse of legal method with ideological intent (conscious or unconscious) is so common in contemporary legal culture that it seems fair to say that it is haunted by a 'hermeneutic of suspicion' towards claims of legal necessity.[5] The most familiar form of the accusation is the claim that there was a right answer, but the jurist, who might be a judge, an advocate or a professor, disregarded it in order to produce a wrong answer that fit his or her ideological predispositions. The motivated reasoning error can be a wrong use of any of the extant types of legal reasoning (precedent, deduction, teleology, etc.) or more commonly a wrong use of many at the same time.

The defining aspect of this form is that the jurist claims not just that his opponent chose the wrong answer for the bad reason of covert ideological preference, but that there *was* a right answer, which countered the preference, and which the opponent was bound by fidelity to law to adopt. This fits the sense shared between popular observers of the system and élites with strong ideological commitments that 'the law' (defined by the constitution, justice, human rights, freedom, the nation) is intrinsically on their side, so that when the jurist defines the law against them there is something more than just error, something more like cheating or betrayal going on. There is no admission that their answer will be subject to an exactly analogous suspicion-hermeneutic as the one just critiqued. But every sophisticated jurist is acutely aware of this possibility, and of the impossibility of knowing for sure when suspicion will conquer certainty.

In developing the notion of a hermeneutic of suspicion as something common to Freud, Nietzsche and Marx, Paul Ricoeur insisted that it is part of a matched pair, or has a twin, called 'hermeneutics as the restoration of meaning': 'The contrary of suspicion, I will say bluntly, is

[5] See n. 1 above.

faith. What faith? No longer, to be sure, the first faith of the simple soul, but rather the second faith of one who has engaged in hermeneutics, faith that has undergone criticism, post-critical faith.'[6]

Ricoeur uses interpretation in contemporary studies of religious consciousness as exemplary of the two hermeneutics, and treats the second mode as 'post-critical' because it does not simply affirm the truth of the sacred that lies behind and animates the texts in question, but acknowledges that they are contested. For American jurists, the hermeneutic of restoration that is the twin of suspicion as I will be developing it here, is also post-critical, chastened by the vicissitudes of faith, from the reactionary 'horrors' of *Lochner* v. *New York*[7] to the liberal activist 'overreaching' of the Warren Court.[8]

The hermeneutic of the restoration of legal meaning animates the method of construction in induction/deduction, or the positing of overarching purposes of the legal order in teleological reasoning. It is a disposition, like the disposition of its twin to doubt and unmask, a tendency, in this case, to search for and find values immanent in the body of legal materials, to believe in those values, and to deploy the techniques of legal argument to develop and apply them to shape the legal order through time. I sympathise with the suspicion-hermeneutic and not with the restoration-hermeneutic, but reject its insistence on legal wrong answers as the *locus* of legal sin. To my mind, ideology is mainly present not via betrayal but through professionally legitimate legal work on the legal materials that exploits or generates or eliminates open texture.[9]

Suspicion is a psychological propensity or tendency or disposition. The hermeneutic is a contemporary phenomenon. Although it has its origin in the critique of Lochnerism, in that phase it was a critique of

6 Paul Ricoeur, *Freud and Philosophy: An Essay on Interpretation*, Denis Haven (trans.) (New Haven CT: Yale University Press, [1965] 1970), p. 28.

7 In this case, the United States Supreme Court invalidated as unconstitutional a state law establishing minimum work hours for bakers, creating a precedent subsequently developed to invalidate a large part of the progressive agenda for reform of labour/capital legal relations. *Lochner* v. *New York*, 198 U.S. 45 (1905).

8 See Learned Hand, *The Bill of Rights* (Cambridge MA: Harvard University Press, 1958); Alexander M. Bickel, *The Supreme Court and the Idea of Progress* (New Haven CT: Yale University Press, 1978); John H. Ely, 'The Wages of Crying Wolf: A Comment on Roe v. Wade' (1973) 82 *Yale Law Journal*, 920–49.

9 See Kennedy, *A Critique of Adjudication*, n. 1 above, chapter 7, 'Ideologically Oriented Legal Work', pp. 157–79, and chapter 8, 'Strategizing Strategic Behavior in Interpretation', pp. 180–214.

a serious deviation from good practice, rather than an expectation about everyday practice across the whole domain of law. At a very abstract level, its contemporary rise makes sense to me because I see it as an important aspect of a Weberian 'disenchantment narrative' that begins with religion, moves on to natural rights and eventually reaches law, the last bastion.[10] But world historical narratives are not self-realising. Has something changed in contemporary law, either in the way it is practised or in our awareness or understanding of it, that would help explain this disenchantment, not another, now rather than at some other time?

The long-term development of what might be called extreme sceptical legal theory, both academic and as part of the legal consciousness of the bar, is certainly part of the story. An extreme sceptical view had already emerged at the end of the nineteenth century as part of the attack on Lochnerism (although something like it had long been a part of populist lay legal consciousness). It was one tendency (but by no means the only one, or even the dominant one) within the German Free Law School of the first decade of the twentieth century,[11] among the American legal realists[12] in the 1930s, and among the 'crits' in their 1980s heyday.[13] In this view literalism, induction/deduction and single purpose teleology are always abusive, and proportionality tests are 'inherently' political. They mean that, no matter what the configuration of the legal materials, there is '*never* a single right answer', although they are not clear as to how that absolutist claim could be supported.[14]

The typical practitioner of the hermeneutic in its common contemporary form deploys the critical techniques developed by sceptical legal

[10] Duncan Kennedy, 'The Disenchantment of Logically Formal Legal Rationality, or Max Weber's Sociology in the Genealogy of the Contemporary Mode of Western Legal Thought' (2004) 55 *Hastings Law Journal*, 1031–76.

[11] Gnavius Flavius, 'The Battle for Legal Science', Cory Merril (trans.) (2011) 12 *German Law Journal*, 2005–30.

[12] Felix Cohen, 'Transcendental Nonsense and the Functional Approach' (1935) 35 *Columbia Law Review*, 809–49. Jerome Frank, *Law and the Modern Mind* (New York: Routledge [1970] 2017).

[13] For example, Gary Peller, 'The Metaphysics of American Law' (1985) 73 *California Law Review*, 1151–1290.

[14] For my view that legal analysis can and often does have the 'effect of necessity' on a relevant legal audience so that the answer is right in the sense of not presently opposable, see Duncan Kennedy, 'A Left Phenomenological Alternative to the Hart/Kelsen Theory of Legal Interpretation', in: Kennedy, *Legal Reasoning: Collected Essays* (Aurora CO: The Davies Book Publishers, 2008), pp. 153–74, available at: http://duncankennedy.net/documents/Photo%20articles/A%20Left%20Phenomenological%20Alternative%20to%20the%20HartKelsen%20Theory%20of%20Legal%20Interpretation.pdf, last accessed 25 January 2019.

theory, but strongly rejects the extreme sceptical conclusion. This is implicit in the affirmation that there is a correct legal answer that we should adopt in this particular case (the answer may be 'deference'[15]), once we understand the ideologically motivated legal error of the other side. In other words, this particular form of contemporary legal consciousness deploys the suspicion-hermeneutic and the hermeneutic of the restoration of meaning, one after the other, in tandem. There is nothing necessary about the connection since each can be – and often is – practised without the other.

I suggest in this chapter that the intensity of the hermeneutic is intelligible as a response to the changing relations between, on the one hand, ideological intelligentsias working for and against contemporary transformations of economic and social life,[16] and, on the other, the corps of jurists. This interaction has produced three striking developments that provide the context for the hermeneutic.

First, the juridification of social life through the rise, over the first half of the twentieth century, of the regulatory/administrative state, theorised and implemented by jurists who had developed social legal thought[17] as a critique of the theory and practice of Classical Legal Thought.[18] Second, the judicialisation of that juridified regime, as part of the reaction against the social after WWII. Third, its constitutionalisation, beginning in the

[15] See Duncan Kennedy, 'Proportionality and "Deference" in Contemporary Constitutional Thought', in: Tamara Perišin and Siniša Rodin (eds.), *The Transformation of Reconstitution of Europe: The Critical Legal Perspective on the Role of Courts in the European Union* (Oxford-Portland OR: Hart Publishing, 2018), pp. 29–58.

[16] For definitions of ideology and ideological intelligentsia, as I am using them here, see Kennedy 'Political Ideology and Comparative Law', n. 1 above; Kennedy. *A Critique of Adjudication*, n. 1 above, chapter 3, 'Ideological Conflict over the Definition of Legal Rules', pp. 39–72, and chapter 11, 'Adjudication in Social Theory', pp. 264–98. An ideology in this chapter is a set of positions that are 'universalising', rather than avowedly 'partisan', and claim to represent Weberian 'ideal interests', as opposed to particular material interests. On intelligentsias, see Gramsci, *Selections from the Prison Notebooks*, n. 2 above, pp. 5–23. On universalising political discourse, see Jürgen Habermas, *The Theory of Communicative Action. Vol. 1: Reason and the Rationalization of Society*, Thomas McCarthy (trans.) (Boston MA: Beacon Press, [1981] 1984), pp. 16–19.

[17] On social legal thought, see Duncan Kennedy, 'From the Will Theory to the Principle of Private Autonomy: Lon Fuller's Consideration and Form' (2000) 100 *Columbia Law Review*, 94–175, and Kennedy, 'Three Globalizations of Law and Legal Thought: 1850–2000', n. 3 above.

[18] On classical legal thought, see Duncan Kennedy, *The Rise and Fall of Classical Legal Thought – With a New Preface by the Author '30 Years Later'* (Washington DC: Beard Books, [1975] 2006), and Kennedy, 'Three Globalizations of Law and Legal Thought', n. 3 above, p. 25.

1960s, as an aspect of a shift of power not just to the judiciary, but also within it and within the professional corps of jurists.[19] An important subplot is the emergence of 'ambitious believers' pursuing sometimes frankly ideological, although strictly internal, professional projects, aimed, in Ricoeur's vocabulary, at the restoration of meaning to law as a whole through abstractions like efficiency or human rights, rather than at the local level.

The three developments combine (paradoxically? predictably?) with the gradual loss of faith in the determinate character of the techniques of legal reasoning that the judges are supposed to apply to their vastly expanded task of legal regulation. These techniques are roughly literalism, precedent, induction/deduction, teleology (also known as 'policy') and proportionality (also known as 'balancing'). The societal demand that they be applied in a strictly 'neutral', 'objective' and 'apolitical' manner has become ever more insistent, as the judges have become more powerful, just as competing critiques have undermined confidence in their capacity to play the role assigned to them. As I have argued at length elsewhere, the hermeneutic of suspicion is intelligible as a response to this situation by 'projection', here of the actor's sense of the inevitability, but also unacceptability of ideology in legal judgment, onto the opposing party.[20] The rest of this chapter explores the political economic preconditions for this response, keeping it in tense relationship with its twin hermeneutic aimed at the restoration of meaning.

II The Juridified Universe

II.1 Horizontal Spread of Administration

The oft-remarked 'juridification of social life' is obviously complex to say the least.[21] I hope that, for our purposes, a very reductive summary will be enough, a summary that emphasises the place of the process of

19 For these developments as important aspects of contemporary legal thought, see Kennedy, 'Three Globalizations of Law and Legal Thought', n. 3 above.

20 Kennedy, 'A Social Psychological Interpretation of the Hermeneutic of Suspicion in Contemporary Legal Thought', n. 1 above; Kennedy, *A Critique of Adjudication*, chapter 8, 'Strategizing Strategic Behavior in Interpretation', n. 9 above, at 180.

21 Lauren B. Edelman and Marc Galanter, 'Law: Overview', in: Neil J. Smelser and Paul B. Baltes (eds.), *International Encyclopedia of the Social & Behavioral Sciences*, first edition (Oxford: Elsevier, 2001), pp. 8538–44; Gunther Teubner (ed.), *Juridification of Social Spheres: A Comparative Analysis in the Areas of Labor, Corporate, Antitrust and Social Welfare Law* (Berlin-New York: Walter de Gruyter, 1987).

juridification in the progression from Classical Legal Thought (CLT) to the Social to contemporary legal thought.

When people talk about juridification, the previous regime with which they are contrasting the current situation is CLT, modified by the social. The CLT regime was characterised by the existence of large pockets, or areas, in which private parties, administrators, legislators and national governments had discretion to set rules and make determinations. Discretion meant that there was no institutional actor charged with applying constraining criteria of legal validity to their decisions. This was strikingly the case for the exercise of patriarchal power in the family, the control of persons in state custody, and international relations.

Outside the pockets, economic life had been commodified (land, labour and capital).[22] The ensuing market economy was fully juridified in the sense that it was governed by a judicially enforced regime of private law based upon autonomy of the will. But there was little judicial, legislative or administrative regulation or oversight of the terms of the contracts that were the legal form of virtually all market relationships.[23]

The social regime had, as its principal objective, to fill in the empty spaces and regulate the contracts.[24] The vehicles were legislation and administration. The key to understanding the social regime is that the typical techniques were (i) the 'separation out of social law'[25] by the creation of regulatory regimes, typically with inspectorates, through techniques like licensing, enforced by low-level criminal or civil penalties without private rights of action; (ii) the creation of bureaucracies to administer the regimes of social insurance (accidents, unemployment, health care) and welfare; and (iii) the 'move to institutions', meaning the development of new organisational forms.[26] This third technique is the least familiar: in the market, it included labour unions, professional associations with regulatory powers, large public and semi-public

[22] See Karl Polanyi, *The Great Transformation: The Political and Economic Origins of Our Time* (New York: Farrar & Rinehart, 1944).

[23] See Franz L. Neumann, 'The primary function of the state is to create a legal order which will secure the fulfilment of contracts'. Franz L. Neumann, 'The Change in the Function of Law in Modern Society', in: William E. Scheuerman (ed.), *The Rule of Law Under Siege: Selected Essays of Franz L. Neumann and Otto Kirchheimer* (Berkeley CA: University of California Press, [1933] 1996), pp. 101–41, at 116.

[24] Jacques Donzelot, *L'invention du social: essai sur le déclin des passions politiques* (Paris: Fayard, 1984); Kennedy, 'Three Globalizations of Law and Legal Thought', n. 3 above.

[25] Franz Wieacker, *A History of Private Law in Europe with Particular Reference to Germany*, John Weir (trans.) (Oxford: Clarendon, 1995).

[26] David Kennedy, 'The Move to Institutions' (1987) 8 *Cardozo Law Review*, 841–985.

housing projects, public service corporations running utilities; in the law of custody, juvenile facilities, orphanages, vast prison expansion, mental hospitals, both voluntary and involuntary, run by psychiatrists; in international law, beginning with the League of Nations, the proliferation of organisations from the ILO to the refugee regime.

All these developments involved new 'staff', expanded police forces, social work, lawyer economists in securities regulation agencies, and hosts of inspectors of everything from food and water to atomic energy. The ethos was professional and technical, with the schemes to be devised and also administered by experts, working in the 'public interest' upon the basis of the natural and social sciences.

The new institutions, the regulatory agencies and the welfare state bureaucracies operated according to a model in which the inmates or residents or beneficiaries of the various social institutions were understood as objects of administration. Theirs were 'privileges rather than rights', and the 'Social' or 'public' interest rather than the individual interest was both the justification of the existence of the programmes and the guide to how they should be structured and operated on the ground.[27] The emerging international regime was based on treaties obliging states to one another with no rights at all for persons (as, for example, the minority protection regime).

What is important here is that, although law, in the form of statutes and regulations and treaties, is pervasive, indeed, all-pervasive, judges definitely are not: juridification without judges. (The exception being the turn-of-the-century progressive romance with new courts for social problems.[28]) It is true that, in all the relevant countries, administration was formally subject to the jurisdiction of courts, specialised or not, so the new regimes were formally within the conventional notion of the rule of law. But it was a rule of law that deliberately granted maximum discretion to the administrators. If courts wanted to do more than very passively and distantly oversee, they had to do battle with the ethos of the time, which regarded them as the historic enemies of the social project, and their power as a threat to its successful execution.

And, like judges, rights, and particularly individual rights, were not only not central to the legal theorisation of the social, they were positively anathema. It was all about social needs, social purposes, groups, classes,

[27] See Karl E. Klare, 'Judicial Deradicalization of the Wagner Act and the Origins of Modern Legal Consciousness, 1937–1941' (1978) 62 *Minnesota Law Review*, 265–339.

[28] For example, Michael Willrich, *City of Courts: Socializing Justice in Progressive Era Chicago* (Cambridge: Cambridge University Press, 2003).

functions, and against the 'individualism' of CLT. If there must be rights, they were social rights (e.g. the social Catholic 'right to family life') understood as guides to legislation.

II.2 Politics in the Juridified Universe

The juridification of much of social life, in the sense of its subjection to legislation and administration in the name of the public interest, meant that it was politicised in a new way. The issue was no longer the abstract one of whether to 'intervene in' or 'reform' the more or less *laissez-faire* late-nineteenth century regime. Nor was it the more concrete one of whether to favour a particular new regime of, say, labour law. The social regime once in place, the issue was how it would evolve in practice, how major or minor changes in it would unfold, against the background of the major ideological confrontations that had brought it into existence.

The old ideological formations, say, free market conservatism or progressivism, or consumerism or unionism or social Catholicism or civil libertarianism, or, in Western Europe, socialism and communism and fascism, constantly found that new battles, within the regime, rather than over its existence, required them to take positions on small issues and to develop strategies for the long term on large issues. The outcomes of micro and macro questions of adaptation to change would determine whether a given regime would develop or atrophy or unwind, whether liberal innovations would serve conservative ends and vice versa, and so forth.

After World War II, new ideological formations came onto the scene, with strong agendas for the reform or repeal or radicalisation of the social regimes established over the previous decades. These included neoliberalism on the right,[29] favouring massive deregulation of the economy. Neoliberals allied with social conservatives whose primary concern was the erosion of 'traditional' values (and social hierarchies) supposedly dominant in a fantasised national past.

The liberals on the left initially favoured an ambitious programme to transform ineffectual social regulatory regimes for the market, the family, and the state, thereby completing the redistributive programme of the New Deal. As time passed, influence shifted in the direction of advocates

[29] Three canonical right-wing critiques of the social: Friedrich A. von Hayek, *The Road to Serfdom* (Chicago IL: University of Chicago Press, 1944); Ronald H. Coase, 'The Problem of Social Cost' (1960) 3 *Journal of Law and Economics*, 1–44; and Christopher Lasch, *Haven in a Heartless World* (New York: Basic Books, 1977).

for individual rights (civil, constitutional, universal, social and economic, or human) as the basis for fighting against discrimination (*de jure* or *de facto*) upon the basis of identity.

Both right and left were somewhat fragile coalitions not corresponding to (in the US) Democrat/Republican party lines. The identity-rights-oriented liberals shared with the neoliberals (but not with the social conservatives or the distributively oriented New Dealers) a civil libertarian critique of the forms of power that had emerged in the new public and private organisations and regulatory and welfare bureaucracies.

III 'Judicialisation' of the Juridified Universe

After World War II, the socially oriented legislators and administrators, with their jurist allies, continued to build their juridified universe into the 1960s (up to the famous fiscal crisis of the (welfare) state).[30] But during the post-war phase of the social, accelerating through the 1970s and after, judges began to play a more and more important role in the definition of the rules and practices of social law broadly conceived.[31] As contemporary legal thought began to differentiate more and more from social legal thought, it was characterised by an across-the-board increase in the modalities of judicial intervention in the various juridified domains.[32] This phenomenon seems to have developed first, and to have gone furthest, in the United States, but it has long since become characteristic, to one degree or another, of contemporary law worldwide.[33]

Like many others in the history of the transformations of legal consciousness, this development is difficult to explain in any straightforward causal way. It is certainly useful to advert to Ugo Mattei's striking and original theory of American 'exaggeration' of British strong judging and at the same time of German devotion to legal science based in legal education.[34] According to him, these traits combine with post-realist technical mastery, and the sophistication forced by a multi-jurisdictional but also hierarchised federal system, to produce a judiciary (particularly,

30 James O'Connor, *The Fiscal Crisis of the State* (New York: St. Martin's, 1973).

31 Martin Shapiro and Alec Stone Sweet, *On Law, Politics and Judicialization* (Oxford: Oxford University Press, 2002).

32 Abram Chayes, 'The Role of the Judge in Public Law Litigation' (1976) 89 *Harvard Law Review*, 1281–1316.

33 Ibid.

34 Ugo Mattei, 'A Theory of Imperial Law: A Study on US Hegemony and the Latin Resistance' (2002) 10 *Indiana Journal of Global Legal Studies*, 383–448.

the federal judiciary) that is capable, albeit in a 'reactive' way, of exercising major power at the expense of a relatively 'weak state' (by European standards). This theory helps to explain how judicialisation could happen, but leaves the question of why 'all of a sudden' after WWII.

Another way to understand it, I am going to argue, is as the emergence of a new form of interaction between the élites that dominate economic, social and political life, and the 'legal subsystem', as Gunther Teubner might have it,[35] operated by the professionally specialised 'corps' of the jurists socialised to understand their role as very different from that of the ideological intelligentsias[36] of the larger society.

Accurately assessing and explaining the very uneven diffusion of judicialisation across the globe is obviously difficult, and I will not attempt it here, other than to mention, in a conclusory way, the three schemas of imposition by force, bargaining (as in IFI 'rule of law' conditionalities), and prestige.[37]

III.1 'Outside' Ideological Intelligentsias Motivate the Process of Judicialisation by Their Allied 'Inside' Legal Intelligentsias as Part of the Critique of Social Law

Judicialisation, in this account, is both the product of and the cause of the development of a small but, I would argue, disproportionately important subset of activist jurists (lawyers, professors and judges). As ideological intelligentsias realised that judicial power was crucial to the success or failure, not to speak of the day-to-day guidance of their projects, they developed their own legal specialists. In the beginning, they were liberals, sometimes the defenders of the social project and sometimes rights-oriented critics of it.

When they go to work for a union side law firm doing strategic litigation or for the ACLU or the NAACP Legal Defense Fund, NARAL-Pro-Choice America, the Environmental Defense Fund, the Legal Services Corporation, Human Rights Watch, an LGBTQT or an indigenous peoples' public interest law firm, they understand themselves and are understood by 'others in the know' to be situated exactly at the intersection of 'outside' ideological projects and the 'inside' requirements of legal

35 Gunther Teubner, *Autopoietic Law: A New Approach to Law and Society* (Berlin-New York: Walter de Gruyter, 1988).

36 For a definition and sources for the idea of an ideological intelligentsia, see n. 15 above.

37 Kennedy, 'Three Globalizations of Law and Legal Thought', n. 3 above.

form. The same is true for firms specialising in employment discrimination cases and a significant part of the plaintiff side products liability bar. Sometimes, they have ideologically defined organised interests as their 'clients', but sometimes they 'represent' diffuse interests that they amalgamate themselves for their own purposes, for example, through consumer class actions. It was a striking development of the 1980s that a more or less mirror image 'conservative legal movement'[38] reproduced this structure at the other end of the political spectrum, joining the already thoroughly established 'defence bar' that represented corporate institutions against the day-to-day lawsuits made possible by the juridified social regime.

Depending on which party is in power, this is the pool from which chief executives draw appointees for law-related government jobs at all levels of the federal system and law schools recruit teachers of the more ideologically charged topics in the curriculum. Although they are a small minority of judges and government lawyers, a larger minority of law professors and a tiny minority of the bar, they are relatively visible members of the (American) political élite, as drivers of legal change, rightward as much as leftward.

As already mentioned, the many activist groups pursuing politically progressive reform agendas shared with the neoliberals a civil libertarian, proceduralist critique of the juridified social regime, the regime created and controlled by legislators and administrators. The 'objects of administration' were allowed few, if any, challenges to any aspect of official behaviour within the myriad social institutional settings. The left activist jurists (including judges and professors) developed a multi-front attack on the statutory frameworks, the mass of administrative regulations, and the day-to-day administrative practices that constituted the social regime.

They were able to recruit crucial proto-neoliberal allies ('Liberal Republicans') as long as the claim was for procedural justice rather than for redistribution. Their challenge was nonetheless to the ethos of the whole, as well as to the rule structure, to the arbitrariness of the experts, whose claims to professional knowledge had come to seem suspect rather than sacrosanct (medical malpractice is paradigmatic for this) and whose appeal to the public interest over the interests of individuals came to seem hollow or even hypocritical.

[38] Steven M. Teles, *The Rise of the Conservative Legal Movement: The Battle for Control of the Law* (Princeton NJ: Princeton University Press, 2007).

In the prevailing post-war context of legislative stalemate and administrative agency capture, the judiciary (systematically excluded in the development of social legal thought) was the only group of sovereign power holders likely to harbour potential allies in the programme of reform. Not surprisingly, the reformers tried to mobilise them, chiefly by public and then judicial exposure of scandalous administrative abuses, the very techniques that the muckraking social reformers had used against the regime of CLT. Together, they developed varied legal strategies based on litigation, sometimes as a supplement to strategies of legislative or regulatory change, but sometimes exclusively judicial, and so independent of the political fluctuations of legislative and executive power. If there was one thing they had in common across a very wide sweep of proposals it was the transformation of social protections into individual entitlements.[39]

One move was to demand micro-level judicial supervision of what had once been practically unreviewable, for example, by the mass appeal of routine administrative orders terminating welfare payments.[40] Another was class action litigation designed to get judges to more or less take over dysfunctional institutions, from prisons to mental hospitals to public housing projects to labour unions to failing public/state schools.[41] Yet a third was to press for substantive judicial review of statutes, regulations and informal administrative practices (say, of police interrogation or hospital disclaimers of liability).[42]

A fourth, and, in some ways, the most dramatic, was the 'socialisation' of private law,[43] meaning adding judicially enforceable contract, tort and property rights to the social regime of administrative regulations, inspectorates, low-level criminal penalties, and minimal or non-existent rights to appeal. Activists gave up on housing code enforcement through city administrators and litigated for judicial creation and the enforcement of the individual tenant's 'warranty of habitability'. The tools of judicialisation thus included constitutional law but also the non-constitutional

[39] Charles A. Reich, 'The New Property' (1964) 73 *Yale Law Journal*, 733–87.

[40] Frances Fox Piven and Richard Cloward, *Poor People's Movements: Why they Succeed, How they Fail* (New York: Vintage, 1978).

[41] Chayes, n. 32 above.

[42] *Miranda* v. *Arizona*, 384 U.S. 436 (1966); *Tunkl* v. *Board of Regents*, 60 Cal.2d 92 (1963).

[43] Jay Feinman, 'Un-Making Law: The Classical Revival in the Common Law' (2004) 28 *Seattle University L.aw Review*, 1–59; Martijn Hesselink, *CFR and Social Justice: A Short Study for the European Parliament on the Values Underlying the Draft Common Frame of References for European Private Law: What Roles for Fairness and Social Justice?* (Amsterdam: Sellier Europa Law Publishing, 2008).

norms of administrative law, micro- or macro-level statutory interpretation and common law precedent.

Up until 1970 and the demise of the Warren Court, the central preoccupation of activist jurists in the US was 'American apartheid', a complex race regime that like its namesake, was – and is – pervasively a legal one.[44] In the beginning, the neoliberals allied with social conservatives and their allies in the agencies under attack against all attempts to expand New Deal redistributive programmes and against the ambitious liberal programme of rights for black people. But, as the liberals were discouraged or defeated on the fronts of race and redistribution,[45] a new configuration emerged. Once black demands for radical change in the race regime had been suppressed, the neoliberals joined the left challenge to the social regime in the name of groups (e.g., women, mental patients) and practices (e.g., non-straight sex, unconventional speech) that the social regime had quite self-consciously left out.

The liberals pushed both new interventions and deregulation at the same time in the domain of sexual practices and indeed cultural control in general. This is captured by the simultaneous demand for a radical expansion of protection against domestic violence and discrimination on the basis of gender, with decriminalisation of contraception, abortion, adultery, fornication, homosexual sodomy and pornography. The neoliberals, heirs of the libertarianism that had always been a minority tendency within the Republican Party, joined this liberal project when the doctrine of colour-blindness allowed them to give it an anti-black spin. They split from their right-wing social conservative allies, who found themselves suddenly allied with the radical and cultural feminist backlash against the liberalised gender regime. On the left, the redistributivist camp, allied with the white working class, was ambivalent about many aspects of identity politics. The result was a modernist/traditionalist opposition that cross-cut the left/right divide.

44 Daniel Fusfeld and Timothy Bates, *The Political Economy of the Urban Ghetto* (Carbondale IL: Southern Illinois University Press, 1984); Douglas S. Massey and Nancy A. Denton, *American Apartheid: Segregation and the Making of the Underclass* (Cambridge MA: Harvard University Press, 1998).

45 Kimberle Crenshaw, 'Race Reform and Retrenchment: Transformation and Legitimation in Antidiscrimination Law' (1988) 101 *Harvard Law Review*, 1331–87.

III.2 *The Politics of Legal Discourse in a Judicialised Universe*

In order for there to be a dramatic increase in the role of judges in the juridified social universe, it was not necessary that all the activist initiatives, or even very many of them, should succeed. As long as some succeeded, and as long as it was easy to see that there were an indefinite number of others that might plausibly succeed, then the dispersed defenders of existing institutions, governmental and corporate, and of the ethos of the order as a whole, had to be prepared to defend themselves. They developed a pervasive practice of pre-empting attack by modifying the various regimes to make them less vulnerable to the reformers' demands. The result was a kind of managerial juridification, as large organisations of all kinds formalised the internal procedures governing both their treatment of their employees and clients, and horizontal workplace relations, for example, in the domains of discrimination and sexual harassment, that might generate liability for the institution.[46]

While it was, above all, the progressive, individual-rights-oriented groups that began the process, judicialisation is now a simple fact of life for all tendencies. For contemporary legal consciousness, it is the normal situation for the endless questions of adapting, evolving, reforming, expanding, and contracting all the different regimes and sub-regimes of the juridified social universe to be referred to the expanded corps of lawyers and to end up regularly as legal questions settled in litigation.[47]

Empowering judges as decision makers, at the expense of administrators or legislators, brought with it new court-centred procedural rules and also rigid discursive requirements. Ideologically motivated actors who used to spend their time with legislators and administrators now have to spend it trying to persuade judges. They have to develop legal arguments, rather than the familiar overtly political arguments for legislators, or policy arguments for rule-making administrators.

The binding conventions of legal discourse require them to adopt a bizarre fiction. It is that the answer to any big or little question of legal evolution, no matter how clearly it is significant mainly or exclusively for its ideological content, is determined in advance by the 'sources': statutes, administrative regulations, judicial decisions, and

46 Richard Michael Fischl, 'Rethinking the Tripartite Division of American Work Law' (2007) 28 *Berkeley Journal of Employment and Labor Law*, 163–216.

47 Robert Kagan, *Adversarial Legalism: The American Way of Law* (Cambridge MA: Harvard University Press, 2001).

constitutional provisions, with a flavouring of law review commentary. No matter how implausible, they have to do it all with literalism, precedential reasoning, induction/deduction, teleology and balancing, all the while proclaiming that there is no choice but only legal necessity.

The activist jurists worked with the resources available in the legal materials, and the conflicting overarching orienting conceptions of Classical and Social Legal Thought. These had once been highly flexible 'modes', available as a language for the justification of an indefinitely large number of specific innovations in the interests of the full range of ideological tendencies. The modes permitted, but also channelled, legal argument that was overtly technical, and not political or ideological, on whatever the judges had to decide.

In the United States today, legal argument disposes major and minor ideological stakes through highly patterned arguments, along with equally standardised counter-arguments, that are templates for parry and thrust that will be contextualised to fit large numbers of problems of judicial interpretation.[48] There are many examples, but the most familiar may be the standardised argumentative repertoire for debating whether to expand or contract freedom of contract,[49] in myriad settings from consumer protection to labour law to family law to corporate law to international investment law to treaty law, and recently to Obamacare.

It is striking that the legacies of CLT and the Social are both omnipresent and transformed.[50] The characteristic CLT mode of argument was based on the will theory, a sharp public/private distinction and the idea that the holders of rights and powers should be 'absolute within their spheres' as defined, if possible, by inductive/deductive method. These arguments are with us today, but oddly politicised: neoliberal lawyers and informed laymen deploy the CLT arguments in the economic sphere to support the claims of economic power holders against weak parties in all domains. The cluster of arguments supporting freedom of contract and against regulation in the economy, like the argument for absolute property rights, is available as a template to be deployed against every new left initiative.

But, in the domain of civil society, family, religion, health, education, culture, the same CLT arguments are left-identitarian: for absolute

48 Duncan Kennedy, 'A Semiotics of Legal Argument', in: Kennedy, *Legal Reasoning: Collected Essays*, n. 14 above.

49 Ibid.

50 Kennedy, 'Three Globalizations of Law and Legal Thought', n. 3 above, last section on 'Contemporary Legal Thought', p. 63.

individual rights, both against other individuals and against the state, rights to abortion, marriage equality, anti-discrimination, affirmative action, etc., in the same mode of induction and deduction that characterised the neoliberal economic arguments.

The social has undergone a similar politicisation combined with internal polarisation, in the reverse sense. In the economy, the arguments of the social for interdependence, solidarity, planning, regulation and institutional innovation beyond the public/private dichotomy, all to deal with omnipresent inequality of bargaining power, are left redistributive arguments. They underpin critiques of freedom of contract, and are very much on the defensive. In the civil society domains, on the other hand, the social arguments are social conservative, for protecting the fetus, organic family relationships, the native-born against immigrants, and, in general, the collective investments and accomplishments that depend on cultural or religious homogeneity and hierarchy.

The standard modes of legal argument of the two historical periods were once non-ideological in the sense that there was a right, a centre and a left CLT, and a left, a centre and a right Social. These two argumentative modes displaced, more or less, their predecessors' reliance on directly moral, religious or instrumental argument. When they politicised in this odd polarised way, so that each is left in one domain and right in the other, they produced a situation in which the surface of supposedly non-ideological argument suggests the very thing that it firmly denies. The jurist's ideological preference can be predicted in advance from his doctrinal vocabulary, even before we know his substantive positions.

A not surprising consequence was the slow but steady and ultimately pervasive politicisation of the selection of judges. Judges were vetted by reference to their relationships to the 'internal' legal-ideological intelligentsias, displacing the regime in which notables of the bar had substantial influence exercised in the name of supposedly non-political professional ethics and competence.[51]

III.3 The Politics of the Separation of Powers

Left and right intelligentsias are not mere passive recipients of the political logic of judicialisation. As repeat players in the game of

[51] Anthony T. Kronman, *The Lost Lawyer: Failing Ideals of the Legal Profession* (Cambridge MA: Harvard University Press, 1995).

litigation,[52] they assess it from the point of view of how its expansion or contraction will affect their interests. When considering different dynamics, they will have a general estimate of the relative sympathy for their projects of the different separated powers, legislative, executive, and judiciary.

If, on balance and over a fairly long run, the judiciary is likely to be more sympathetic to a given ideological project than the executive or the legislature, it may make sense to try to persuade their judicial allies to increase their intervention in the domain in question. A lot depends on whether they think that the legal materials that govern the domain are sufficiently open textured so that there will be many occasions for ideologically oriented interpretation that will dispose significant stakes, and on the course of judicial selection over time.

Of course, the opposite conclusion about the judges will lead to a strategy of trying to keep them out, reinforcing the autonomy of the administrators and corporate managers who run the institutional complexes of the social, and preserving the balance of power among private actors. For actors (inside as well as outside the judiciary) who are trying to instrumentalise or neutralise the judges as power holders, judicialisation and anti-judicialisation have become possible strategic 'moves'. There will now be a 'politics of the separation of powers', just as there is a politics to all the substantive regimes that the judges monitor or control outright.

Judicialisation was, and is, the product of hundreds of discrete initiatives by activist jurists (including judges and professors as well as lawyers) pursuing uncoordinated but closely analogous strategies across dozens of legal doctrinal domains. Each instance of judicialisation or de-judicialisation is at once a victory or defeat for the substantive positions of the litigants, and a change in the rules of the game of future conflict within that particular sphere. The players understand that the rules of the game are stakes of the game, and strategise upon that basis.

It is easy to see why the reformers of the social chose the judiciary (as already noted: legislative gridlock and agency capture), and that conservative activists had no choice but to create a countervailing 'conservative legal movement' in response. In

[52] Marc Galanter, 'Why the "Haves" Come out Ahead: Speculations on the Limits of Legal Change' (1974) 9 *Law & Society Review*, 95–160.

these cases, it is the agendas of the 'outside' or general political intelligentsias that push for or against judicialisation, whether left wing (redistributive/rights identitarian) or right wing (neoliberal/social conservative).

The left and right ideologies and their subdivisions are commonly understood to be responsive both to the material interests and to the principled aspirations of the groups that put them forward as grounds for political decision. A vulgar formulation might be that neoliberals represent capital, the redistribution-liberals represent the old and new working classes, the rights-identitarian liberals represent professional/educational capital, and the social conservatives represent traditional cultural capital.

A general transformation in the direction of judicialisation, along with the rise of litigation as the dominant mode of social policy making, was never an explicit demand or proposal of any of the above, be it left, right, modernity or tradition. It seems worth asking whether, apart from path dependence as given interests tried to take advantage of the peculiar institutional structure of the separation of powers, there were material or ideal interests driving the transformation towards judicialisation.

The legal activist élite (including principled anti-activists) is 'liminal' in the sense of being situated on the border between lay and legal domains, translating lay demands into the discourse required in order to influence the judges. It seems plausible that the activist lawyers are the group that had a material class interest (transcending the left/right modern/traditional divides) in judicialising the juridified social universe. Within each intelligentsia, it meant a dramatic shift in power and, perhaps even more strikingly, in raw numbers and financial resources, between the outside and the inside, the general political and the legal sectors of the élites.

It meant a dramatic increase in legal activist power *vis-à-vis* all other political actors because of their possession of a legal discourse that defines the politically permissible but is in a flexible technical form that is incomprehensible to and thus not critiquable by the lay public. It arguably meant a decrease in the relative power of groups outside the consensus of the liberal democratic centre left and centre right. Those outside groups are not generally represented in the élite bar and consequently lack access to the opaque legal discourse necessary to play the game of judicialised power.

III.4 *Ideal Interests of Legal Activists: Suspicious Believers and Realists*

Reducing the role of legal activist jurists in judicialisation to the promotion of their own material interest in jobs, budgets and clout would be 'reductionist'. In any case, calculating the impact of judicialisation on their class power (disregarding the left/right division) would be impossible. But, at a deeper level, judicialisation has not been clearly in the activist interest because the accompanying politicisation of legal discourse threatens the appearance of political neutrality that is one basis of their power (exercised through the judges). It gives rise, in short, to the hermeneutic of suspicion.

I defined the hermeneutic as a disposition to uncover hidden ideological motives behind the 'wrong' legal arguments of their opponents, while affirming their own right answers to be allegedly innocent of ideology. As the lists in the previous paragraphs illustrate, the judicialisation of the juridified social universe was also the judicialisation of most important and very many unimportant questions with all kinds of ideological stakes. First and foremost, the vast array of ideologically charged questions raised by the overlay of the domain of contested social law on the domain of contested classical law. The apparent political valence of the newly polarised CLT and Social Legal Thought (SLT) arguments in the economy and civil society beg for an attitude of suspicion, or even outright rejection of the claim to neutrality.

The situation might be less dire were it not for the progress, or devolution, of legal reasoning from induction/deduction to teleology to proportionality in the movement from CLT to the Social to contemporary legal thought. This development parallels the sequence of juridification and judicialisation (and ultimately constitutionalisation) that we have been tracing, along with the politicisation of the orienting discourses of CLT and SLT (as in the freedom of contract example). As large and small ideological stakes came more and more to be disposed by judges, the task of distinguishing legal reasoning from political or merely moral reasoning became both more important and more difficult. At the same time, the legal techniques available became more vulnerable to internal critique.

The rise of teleology in Germany, France and the United States after World War I was the alternative of SLT to the discredited Classical method of induction/deduction.[53] The rise of proportionality after

[53] Kennedy, 'From the Will Theory to the Principle of Private Autonomy', n. 17 above.

World War II was in part, a response to equally devastating critiques of teleology, most trenchant in the United States.[54] The internally critical destructive part of the hermeneutic of suspicion had undermined 'pre-critical' faith in legal reason to the point that a new 'last resort' seemed necessary. But balancing as a last resort is particularly vulnerable to the charge of easy manipulability for covert ideological purposes.[55]

One might have thought (some of us did think[56]) that the parallel developments at the institutional and technical argumentative levels would combine to produce a 'legitimation crisis'.[57] And I am indeed arguing that this double development explains (in large part) the intensification of the hermeneutic of suspicion, and is an important factor in the various 'populist' revolts against liberal-democratic judicial power that developed across the post-industrial West after the crisis of 2008. Yet paradoxically, albeit quite understandably, claims that baldly deny this sociologically 'obvious' fact seem as strong as ever, perhaps stronger.

The public response of ideological élites and their liminal legal representatives has been denial that contemporary legality has any problems at all of any kind, other than having to deal with 'authoritarians' who, overtly or covertly, reject the whole premise of the rule of law. But this is pretence for the lay public, treated by the mainstream of the profession as simplistic and good for consumption only by the unwashed. There are many versions of a more 'sophisticated' professional understanding.

Many legal activists might be described as 'realist cause lawyers'. In my experience of them, under the right circumstances, they confess that they just 'pretend' to believe that the sources plus legal reasoning determine right answers in a way that excludes ideology. They practise the hermeneutic of the restoration of meaning, doing the legal work of interpreting apparently conflicting or ambiguous materials as leading inevitably to a conclusion. But the conclusion is not 'up for grabs' as they do the work,

[54] Duncan Kennedy, 'A Transnational Genealogy of Proportionality in Private Law', in: Roger Brownsword, Hans-W. Micklitz, Leone Niglia and Stephen Weatherhill (eds.), *The Foundations of European Private Law* (Oxford-Portland OR: Hart Publishing, 2011), pp. 185–220.

[55] Kennedy, 'The Hermeneutic of Suspicion in Contemporary American Legal Thought', n. 1 above, Part I, p. 92.

[56] Duncan Kennedy, 'Comment on Rudolf Wiethölter's 'Materialization and Proceduralization in Modern Law' and 'Proceduralization of the Category of Law', in: Christian Joerges and David M. Trubek (eds.), *Critical Legal Thought: An American-German Debate* (Baden-Baden: Nomos, 1989), pp. 511–24.

[57] Jürgen Habermas, *Legitimation Crisis*, Thomas McCarthy (trans.) (Boston MA: Beacon Press, [1973] 1975).

but ideologically predetermined. They consciously manipulate legal discourse in the ideologically desired direction, but accept the duty to obey in good faith when there is no legally plausible route to the ideologically correct outcome, hoping that this will not happen in too many or too horrible cases.

They practise the critical branch of the hermeneutic of suspicion with cynical vigour, unmasking their opponents' legalisms as error in the service of bad politics, and apply it from time to time to their own side and to the judges they admire. They believe in their own legal correctness, but in a self-consciously, non-dogmatic way. They see the judges as legitimately powerful, but also meaningfully constrained, political actors, directly contrary to the simplistic version of the separation of powers with its distinction between 'making' and 'interpreting' law.

The 'suspicious believers' that I introduced in Part I above are also practitioners of the negative side of the hermeneutic of suspicion, but they deny that their practice of the hermeneutic of the restoration of meaning is manipulation for ideological purposes. They say they act and I think many of them *do* act on the presupposition that the law itself immanently commands its own transformation to correspond to their particular ideological projects. The universalising claims of the project are true (all ideologists believe this, by definition), and it so happens that law already contains that truth, at least so far as the work of interpretation is concerned.

This notion seems to me to be adopted not by all, but by significant numbers of jurists whose intellectual/political commitment is to law and economics, neoliberalism, religiously based social conservatism, civil liberties, feminism, identity-based anti-discrimination, or human rights. This attitude provides a clue to the currently unfolding constitutionalisation of the judicialised universe.

IV Constitutionalisation of the Judicialised Universe

Constitutionalisation, I will argue here, is a process of change in the contemporary (liberal democratic industrial/post-industrial welfare capitalist) mode of social ordering through law, occurring within the already juridified and judicialised universe. Within a particular domain, a constitutional court changes an earlier approach by henceforth reviewing a recurring ideologically sensitive practice by application of a test derived directly from the constitution. Constitutionalisation is interesting and important when it becomes cumulative, occurring in a patterned way across many areas, always in the same direction of greater supervision of public actors of all kinds (and some private ones as well) by the highest constitutional court in the system.

At some indefinite point, quantity becomes quality, and we can say that constitutional lawyers are operating a new paradigm, within a new political economy of the separation of powers. The various intelligentsias and those they represent will gain and lose according to their ability to operate the new system. Along with a shift of power upwards towards élite lawyers and élite courts and away from everyone else, the new paradigm represents the triumph of Ricoeur's hermeneutic of the restoration of meaning. It realises an ambitious internal legal project of believers to unify liberal democratic law, opposed by the camp of modest sceptics of the necessary powers of judicial reason. The development as a whole intensifies, perhaps to the point of crisis, the paradox of concentrating élite judicial power as judicial method slowly succumbs to the suspicion-hermeneutic.

IV.1 Constitutionalisation as Normative Change in a Direction

The following are US examples of constitutionalising normative change. The new heightened level of top court supervision can take the form of a rule or a standard:[58]

- In judicial review of any police interrogation the first question is whether the police violated the constitution by violating court-ordered rules (e.g., Miranda warning) explicitly designed to protect the suspect's right against forced self-incrimination.
- In the regulation of abortion, the court will ask whether any statute or administrative practice that has an effect on women seeking abortion wrongly balances the state's generic legitimate regulatory interest against the woman's generic right to privacy.
- The Court will test statutes criminalising obscenity for compatibility with the first amendment and then review the application of the statute under the same test.
- Whenever a regulation significantly changes the value of a property interest, the owner can challenge it under a constitutional test of 'regulatory taking' based upon multi-factor balancing case by case.

[58] Duncan Kennedy, 'Form and Substance in Private Law Adjudication' (1976) 89 *Harvard Law Review*, 1685–775.

- The practice of disciplining of prisoners in prisons is subject case by case, or under court-established rules, to a constitutional test of 'cruel and unusual punishment' or a 'dignity' based equivalent, and a procedural due process test, and the same is true for every imposition of the death penalty.
- Constitutional norms forbidding discrimination on identity grounds are applied directly to review statutes and regulations restricting sexual and cultural practices, as in rules about 'sodomy' and same-sex marriage.
- The private law rules of creditor conduct in debt collection by repossession must comply with the debtor's constitutional property, privacy and due process rights, to be determined case by case in balance with the constitutional protection of freedom of contract.
- Every application of the tort law of defamation must pass the test of compatibility with the first amendment rights of the defendant, and that includes deciding on constitutional grounds whether the plaintiff is a public figure and what level of care the defendant exercised.

For the United States, the number of such examples could be multiplied many times, and the process certainly appears to be cumulative. Competent activist lawyers have long since turned constitutionalisation into a technique for generating a constitutional issue and then constitutionally required remedies, for ideologically controversial practices of public or private actors. Their opponents have standard answers at the ready to be adapted to each new case. In a striking discussion of German law, called 'Who Is Afraid of the Total Constitution?', Mathias Kumm claims that:

> Under the guardianship of the Federal Constitutional Court the German Basic Law had, over the course of the second half of the 20th century, developed to become what Schmitt might well have referred to as a total constitution. If a total state is a state in which everything is up for grabs politically, a total constitution inverts the relationship between law and politics in important respects ... The constitution serves as a guide and imposes substantive constraints on the resolution of any and every political question. The validity of any and every political decision is subject to potential challenge before a constitutional court that, under the guise of adjudicating constitutional rights provisions, will decide whether such an act is supported by good reasons. The legislative parliamentary state is transformed into a constitutional juristocracy.[59]

[59] Mathias Kumm, 'Who Is Afraid of the Total Constitution? Constitutional Rights as Principles and the Constitutionalization of Private Law' (2006) 7 *German Law Journal*, 341–71, at 343.

Political decisions, in this analytic, can include the definition of the rules of private law. In other words, following Carl Schmitt, Kumm assumes that private law, once understood as the product of legal science working on universally shared ethical premises, is now no less political than private law.

> A key function of constitutional rights is to provide the basis for claims against public authorities to intervene on behalf of rights claimants in response to threats from third parties. These third parties can be terrorists threatening to kill a hostage, nuclear power plant operators imposing dangers on neighboring residents, creditor banks enforcing a contract against a debtor, employers firing an employee, or landlords threatening to evict a tenant. The public authorities to whom these claims are addressed can be the legislator . . . the executive . . . or the judiciary.[60]

For Kumm, constitutionalisation has a major positive side because it subjects politics to a (judicial) test of 'good reasons', by which I take him to mean a relaxed Dworkinian idea of principled decision that does not categorically exclude policy argument, and permits proportionality tests. A much darker view, in which the relations of force between law and politics are more balanced, with politics threatening to 'corrupt' law, or at least force it to 'adapt' to an alien rationality, is proposed by Gunther Teubner:

> In its relationship to politics, judicial constitutional review of legislation has presented the model that, so far, exists only rudimentarily in relation to other sub-systems. In what respect does the law have to adjust to the intrinsic rationality of the other sub-systems, and to what extent must influences that corrupt the law be warded off? The constitutional review of political legislation has developed extensive review techniques that neutralize party-political decisions, translate result-oriented 'policies' into universal legal principles, fit political decisions into legal doctrine in accordance with legal criteria of consistency, and, in the worst case, pronounce legislative acts to be unconstitutional. On the other hand, constitutional law has liberated the intrinsic logic of politics by 'politicising' the law itself: teleological interpretation, policy orientation, balancing of interests, impact assessment and result-orientation are indicators for an adaptation of law to the rationality of politics.[61]

[60] Ibid., p. 344.

[61] Gunther Teubner, 'Societal Constitutionalism: Alternatives to State-Centred Constitutional Theory?', in: Christian Joerges, Inger-Johanne Sand and Gunther Teubner (eds.), *Transnational Governance and Constitutionalism* (Oxford-Portland OR: Hart Publishing, 2004), pp. 3–28, at 25.

Without the obscurantist language of 'rationalities', Teubner is describing the disintegration of the law/politics boundary in adjudication, and identifying it with the rise of teleology, policy analysis and proportionality that followed the discrediting of literalism, precedent and induction/deduction. I agree with this view rather than with Kumm as Polyanna, and I think it well describes the United States as well as Germany. But, to be convincing, we need an account of the relationship between constitutionalisation and politicisation.

IV.2 Constitutionalisation as a Development beyond Judicialisation

What has been constitutionalising slowly within the movement of judicialisation is the law that the judges developed into the heterogeneous juridified regime that succeeded CLT. As outlined in Part III.1 above, they took over oversight of the classical/social amalgam through a range of techniques, including statutory interpretation, rationality review of agency law making, insistence on strict compliance with procedural or evidentiary requirements, and common law development of new private law rules. Constitutional law was, at first, one of this diverse set of tools, although in the United States it was a bigger part of the story than anywhere else. Jurists thought of it as a list of specific or general requirements (procedural due process, the prohibition of religious 'establishment', and so forth) that would serve to strike down a specific rule or an application of a rule of the classical or the social legal regime.

The early reformers and their judicial allies had no intention of developing, through reformist case law, a new coherent theory of constitutional law under which, to use Kumm's description of contemporary German law, 'the constitution serves as a guide and imposes substantive constraints on the resolution of any and every political question'.[62] The self-conscious minimalism of their approach was part of the reaction against the 'pre-critical' believing, conservative activist courts of the high classical era. The conservative jurists, according to the reformers, interpreted the federal constitution as a coherent document whose logic was inconsistent with progressive reforms. This was the reformers' 'realist' methodological critique of Lochnerism as bad law driven by bad ideology. They believed that they had banished it from mainstream American legal thought.[63]

[62] Kumm, n. 59 above.

[63] See Alexander Bickel, *The Least Dangerous Branch: The Supreme Court at the Bar of Politics* (New Haven CT: Yale University Press, [1962] 1986).

Constitutionalisation is a paradigm shift, not a function of the number of provisions in the document, and it is no less likely in an old fragmentary constitution like the American than in the highly theorised modern ones. It is based on a re-conception of constitutional doctrine in which all legal actors in all their actions are exercising either rights or powers, all rights conflict with other rights, and with powers, and all powers conflict with other powers. Constitutional interpretation is the task of settling these conflicts as they arise, harmonising with other interpretations on the presupposition that the document is a coherent statement, but without the hope of eliminating them for the future.

The text has transformed, to use an old analogy, into something more like a Continental civil law code, interpreted as a coherent whole applicable to every case. It is no longer like a set of unrelated, contingently motivated, common law statutes, each one modifying an item of the judge-made common law, seen as the true domain of coherence.

Subsumption is based on the complex patterns of argument about key issues understood to arise in multiple diverse policy contexts that jurists worked out when they moved the social into the courts. Left, right, traditionalist and modernist jurists adapt their complex argument-sets to the indeterminate constitutional language (e.g., due process and equal protection), understood as creating and limiting rights and powers. This process was driven first by the Warren Court's massive development of constitutional protections for civil, social and some economic rights of minorities and weak parties. Left constitutionalisation provoked neoliberal and social conservative constitutional backlash.

Today, both the right and the left, traditionalists and modernists, deploy their versions of the Lochner apparatus of absolute individual rights, as though they had never been discredited, along with a brand new post-WWII discourse of positivised human rights (e.g., constitutional privacy).[64] In what seems like an ironic 'overcoming' of the opposition of Lochnerism and realism, modern constitutionalists argue, through rival contradictory coherentist theories providing 'under the guise of adjudicating constitutional rights provisions', plausible opposite legal answers

[64] See Samuel Moyn, *The Last Utopia: Human Rights in History* (Cambridge MA: Harvard University Press, 2010).

to questions of the 'validity of any and every political decision' by any and every actor wielding discretionary legal power.[65]

IV.3 The Politics of Constitutionalisation

Constitutionalisation, as I am developing it here, has a second aspect, along with the paradigm shift to the constitution as code. The shift is interesting because it has gone with a dramatic intensification of judicial supervision of the juridified universe. Rather than develop 'deference' as the key to operating the new paradigm,[66] constitutionalising courts exercise supervisory power to restrict the power or autonomy of a legal actor, often, but not necessarily, increasing the freedom of action of another actor. That is, they narrow the zones where decisions are granted strong presumptions of validity, or a wide 'margin of appreciation', or, conversely, tightly constrained by bright line rules and intrusive standards. Successful resistance to the process preserves whatever relations of power among legislative, administrative and private actors existed within the spheres of autonomy defined by the status quo.

An example: in the case of *Lindsey* v. *Normet* in 1972, the US Supreme Court decided that landlord/tenant law was normal economic regulatory law and therefore subject only to judicial constitutional review for minimum rationality, rather than to a more strict review based upon the notion that the interests of tenants were 'fundamental', like those, say, of racial minorities to equal treatment. Landlord/tenant rules had been and continued to be subject to minimum rationality review. But the decision was nonetheless a victory for the anti-constitutionalising forces, because stricter review would have meant more Supreme Court control of the then highly ideological issue of tenants' rights.

> Appellants argue, however, that a more stringent standard than mere rationality should be applied both to the challenged classification and its stated purpose. They contend that the 'need for decent shelter' and the 'right to retain peaceful possession of one's home' are fundamental interests which are particularly important to the poor and which may be trenched upon only after the State demonstrates some superior interest. They invoke those cases holding that certain classifications based on unalterable traits such as race and lineage are inherently suspect and must be justified by some 'overriding statutory purpose'. They also rely on cases where classifications burdening or infringing constitutionally

[65] See Kumm, n. 59 above.

[66] See Kennedy, 'Proportionality and "Deference"', n. 15 above.

> protected rights were required to be justified as 'necessary to promote a compelling governmental interest'.
>
> We do not denigrate the importance of decent, safe, and sanitary housing. But the Constitution does not provide judicial remedies for every social and economic ill. We are unable to perceive in that document any constitutional guarantee of access to dwellings of a particular quality, or any recognition of the right of a tenant to occupy the real property of his landlord beyond the term of his lease without the payment of rent or otherwise contrary to the terms of the relevant agreement. Absent constitutional mandate, the assurance of adequate housing and the definition of landlord-tenant relationships are legislative, not judicial, functions.[67]

For ideological intelligentsias, the only question posed by activist constitutionalism as a general trend or in a particular legal domain is whether or not it favours their ideologically defined group interest. The imposition of new constraints on the legislature, executive or private sector is important not for the jurists' reasons of legal theory, but because the domain that is being narrowed is the *locus* of some balance of power between competing ideological tendencies. When the sphere is narrowed, there will be a new balance of power, favourable or not to each particular ideological tendency. When the sphere is widened, a different new balance emerges, depending on which ideological actors can take advantage of the new possibilities.

For example, *Lindsey* v. *Normet* was a major defeat for tenants' rights lawyers, and activists on behalf of the poor in general, because it signalled that the Supreme Court was not going to intervene on their behalf in the way in which it had intervened (up to quite recently) on behalf of minorities. Everyone understood that a high standard of review would have meant that state law rules that favoured landlords would be under attack in a way not possible with a minimum rationality test. The mere decision to increase the rigour of the test would have meant that many of those rules would not survive the change (otherwise why do it?).

In this case, constitutionalisation was a strategy of the left liminal legal intelligentsia I described in the last section, and the case was a victory for the newly emerging but already better funded right-wing liminal legal intelligentsia. Suppose a constitutional court is controlled by judges whose ideological sentiments seem to the suspicious observer to be significantly to the right of those prevalent in the legislature and the executive. Whatever it may have argued in

[67] *Lindsey* v. *Normet*, 405 U.S. 54 (1972), 74.

Lindsey, the left legal intelligentsia will argue here against constitutionalising private law rules favouring property owners, and in defence of legislation changing those rules to grant public access to beaches.

IV.4 Constitutional Ambition versus *Modesty as 'Internal' Politics*

As was true with judicialisation, it is tempting to regard constitutionalisation as simply one of the instrumental strategies of activist lawyers as they pursue goals set in the general political policy universe outside the legal discursive sphere. We might add the interest of élite activist lawyers and their élite opponents, since they are the ones who are the masters of constitutional argument in the federal courts all the way to the US Supreme Court. Up until recently, constitutionalisation intensified the effect of judicialisation in empowering the ideological centre left and centre right, together, against the danger that the vagaries of the electoral process would produce radical left or radical right legislation upsetting to the *status quo* consensus of liberals and conservatives. The movement to tighter control by a smaller number of élite judges is part of a counter-majoritarian agenda rather than a supposed 'difficulty'.[68]

A difference between the two processes is that judicialisation was not the avowed programme of any of the interest groups in presence. The same is not true of the development we have just been tracing. On the contrary, in a case like *Lindsey*, the Court's refusal to intensify constitutional scrutiny of landlord/tenant law was a right-wing ideological move, *and also* an incident in a continuing dispute within legal theory, distinct from the ideological disputes of the larger society. In that debate, jurists favouring constitutionalisation as a general phenomenon, the 'Ambitious' as I will call them, square off against those opposing it, who I will call the 'Modest'.

The ambitious are typical proponents of suspicious belief, practising the hermeneutic of the restoration of meaning on a grand scale. When right-wingers re-constitutionalise neoliberal ideas and left-wingers work to make the Constitution seem like a derivation from the Universal Declaration of Human Rights, they are taking the restoration far beyond

[68] See Ran Hirschl, *Towards Juristocracy: The Origins and Consequences of the New Constitutionalism* (Cambridge MA: Harvard University Press, 2004), for an analogous line of argument about the globalisation of judicial review.

what is necessary to make a distinctly legal case for some particular outcome.

The idea is that internal and contextual analysis of the Constitution reveals, as its governing elements, the normative principles (human rights or efficiency, for example) that they themselves believe are valid. Construction can be by induction/deduction or through the location of governing teleological principles. Ambitious suspicious believers can be civil libertarians, identity-based anti-discrimination advocates, neoliberals, advocates of the efficiency norm in adjudication, religious social conservatives, and very strikingly human rights lawyers. What they share, if they are indeed suspicious believers and not just masquerading realist cause lawyers, is that the process of constitutionalisation is, for them, much more than a tactic, more even than a strategy. When they work to interpret the document in line with their ideological projects, they are not instrumentalising it, but rather 'working it pure' or realising it. They suspect the hesitancies of the 'modest' as covertly motivated by bad ideology (the enemy), or by a more or less craven principle-deficit (so-called friends).

The opponents of constitutionalisation have typically based their objection in part on a sceptical view of judicial reason. Since the project depends on a supreme court as the final arbiter, its claim to transcend politics fails if interpretive technique is open to ideological manipulation. This was a key part of the Southern argument against Marshall's federalism,[69] and then the sociological jurists' and realists' argument against Lochnerism.[70] It was reborn in the 1950s and 1960s in Felix Frankfurter's and Learned Hand's professedly regretful liberal arguments against Warren Court activism,[71] and has been revived in reaction to the judicial activism of the Reagan/G. Bush/G.W. Bush/Trump Courts.[72]

The ambitious programme for public international law was set out in an explicitly 'post-critical' way by Hans Kelsen in his Holmes Lectures

69 William Jr. Rawle, *A View of the Constitution of the United States of America* (Clark NJ: The Lawbook Exchange, [1829] 2014).

70 Felix Frankfurter in *Baker* v. *Carr* 369 U.S. 186 (1962), Dissenting Opinion, 369 U.S. 266.

71 Learned Hand, n. 8 above.

72 Mark Tushnet, *Taking the Constitution Away from the Courts* (Princeton NJ: Princeton University Press, 2000); Tushnet, *Weak Courts, Strong Rights. Judicial Review and Social Welfare in Comparative Constitutional Law* (Princeton NJ: Princeton University Press, 2009); Jeremy Waldron, 'The Core Case against Judicial Review' (2006) 115 *Yale Law Journal*, 1346–1406; Waldron, 'Judicial Review and Judicial Supremacy' (2014) New York University Public Law and Legal Theory Working Papers, 495.

at Harvard Law School in 1941.[73] The uncontroversial goal of world peace is best secured by the construction of a global legal order, based on a coherent, but as yet merely potential, scheme of democratically legitimated rights and powers overseen by a world court. A unitary order of principle has to be constructed by legal interpretation working within the existing order, which is fragmentary and gap-filled, and permits, both in theory and in practice, a vast amount of action that is inconsistent with minimum ideas about democracy and rights. In other words, the basic tool for the jurist with this approach is the method of construction, whether pursued inductively/deductively, teleologically or through balancing.

In the European context, Joseph Weiler's 'The Transformation of Europe'[74] is a classic study of constitutionalisation, nothing if not ambitious, and his 'Eurocracy and Distrust'[75] brings the 'counter majoritarian difficulty', renamed 'the democracy deficit' in close analogy to the US problematic. Christian Joerges' proposal that the harmonisation of European private law should be conceived as a conflict-of-laws problem is an example of sophisticated modest theorising, explicitly critical of the dangers of ambition.[76] The same structure of argument appears with respect to the international economic order (are the WTO rules 'constitutional'?) and, according to a very interesting article of Gunther Teubner already quoted,[77] the order of transnational non-state organisations of many different kinds.

The 'modest' have the view that, in many instances, a movement towards principled unity under judicial supervision would be a bad thing, because it necessarily suppresses differences that should be encouraged. It may be desirable, in a particular case, to reduce the level of internal coherence and unitary application of the existing order, rather than increase it, for example, by increasing the deference accorded to some

[73] Hans Kelsen, *Law and Peace in International Relations: The Oliver Wendell Holmes Lectures, 1940–1* (Cambridge MA: Harvard University Press, 1942); David Kennedy, 'The International Style in Postwar Law and Policy' (1994) 10 *Utah Law Review*, 7–104.

[74] Joseph H.H. Weiler, 'The Transformation of Europe' (1991) 100 *The Yale Law Journal*, 2403–83.

[75] Weiler, 'Eurocracy and Distrust: Some Questions Concerning the Role of the European Court of Justice in the Protection of Fundamental Human Rights within the Legal Order of the European Communities' (1986) 61 *Washington Law Review*, 1103–42.

[76] Christian Joerges, 'Conflicts-law Constitutionalism: Ambitions and Problems', *ZenTra Working Paper in Transnational Studies*, 10 (2012), available at: http://ssrn.com/abstract=2182092, last accessed 6 November 2018.

[77] Teubner, n. 61 above.

particular governmental actor, or reducing judicial supervision, say, of an area of contract law or of the law of marriage.

In this view, legitimate profound differences, and also conflicts of economic interests, should often be handled by bargaining leading to negotiated agreement or voting or exit, rather than settled by the rational application of principles whose legitimacy supposedly transcends that of the various actors in conflict. In this view, judges are not the right people to settle the deepest kinds of conflicts of interest or of principle (i.e. ideological conflicts).

The 'modest' charge the ambitious with 'neo-formalism'. The 'formalism' part is a systematic tendency to abuse induction/deduction to make preferences into legal necessity. It is 'neo' because it is a revival of the methods of late-nineteenth century legal thought, aiming at making the law coherent by bringing out an immanent rationality corresponding to a particular vision of society. Because it is 'post-critical', it is chastened: incremental, conscious of the dangers of backlash, wary of sounding Lochnerist.[78]

Neo-formalist projects that turn ideology into constitutional law, while at the same time turning the constitution into ideology, make the perfect object for the hermeneutic of suspicion. It is not only the more sceptical cause lawyers and self-avowed ideological neutrals who wield it against ambition. The constitutionalising projects totalise in contradictory ways, for example, neoliberalism against human rights, and ambitious suspicious believers deploy the hermeneutic against one another. They scavenge the critical resources left high on the beach with each flooding and ebbing of the critical tide, from sociological jurisprudence to legal realism to critical legal studies, for use in merciless attacks on their rivals.

I don't, myself, have a 'right answer' to the conflict between the 'modest' and the 'ambitious'. I see each as representing a value that has to be compromised with the other, and, unless the case for one or the other is very clear, I anticipate that I will subordinate the 'internal' debate to my own sense of what is politically fair and just (in other words, to my own ideological orientation).

Conclusion

I think it is commonsense among legal theorists today that law in liberal democratic post-industrial welfare capitalism is neither mere superstructure

[78] For the private law variant of this tendency, see John Goldberg, 'Introduction: Pragmatism and Private Law' (2012) 125 *Harvard Law Review*, 1640–63.

nor autonomous. When we think of, or refer to, contemporary capitalism in this mode, its juridification is a defining feature. It 'is what it is' because it is juridified. Judicialisation is more or less complete in the United States, Britain and its settler colonies, and the German sphere in Western Europe. Constitutionalisation, and resistance to it, have a much more limited scope, but include the United States and Germany and the range of powerful transnational institutional systems. These specific positive law doctrinal developments 'constitute' capitalism 'relatively autonomously', through the work of legal intelligentsias across political divides.

For contemporary capitalism, it is still a key legitimation claim that conflict occurs within a framework that is stable, neutral between persons, and democratically legitimate. These characteristics are direct consequences of the idea that the framework is legal, in accordance with a pre-critical idea of law that is still prevalent across the social space. Why is the hermeneutic of suspicion a predominant disposition of jurists in this moment? I think the answer for the United States is that the gradual but enormous increase in the power of judges to determine the winners of ideological conflicts, some significant, some small but still visible, has come along with the undermining of faith that they have a method that is immune to ideology. Absent a method, their power to decide ideological conflict for one side or the other is arguably democratically illegitimate (counter-majoritarian difficulty, democracy deficit). The hermeneutic responds to this danger to the legitimating myth by denouncing ideology in the other, while affirming the legal correctness of one's own answer, thereby reaffirming the rule of law.

A last paradox. The 'ambitious' suspicious believing programme is also a response to the potential (or actually unfolding as I write) legality-legitimation-crisis. Ambitious believers aim to rebuild liberal democratic legitimacy by constitutionalising one ideological project or another, neoliberal, social conservative, liberal-identitarian or redistributivist, under the supervision of a constitutional court. In another version, the believer aspires to constitutionalise several of the conflicting ideological projects that are represented diffusely throughout the constitutional materials by proportionality analysis.

This means concentrating more and more power in a single institution, the constitutional court, supported by a super-élite subset of an already unrepresentative lawyer class, ruling through a discourse inaccessible outside their circle, but easily recognisable to the whole public as supreme political power. Integrating the structure simultaneously makes it appear stronger and increases its vulnerability to unravelling. But the court's opaque discourse of power is experienced as legitimate by those subject to it only because of some mediation between the ruling legal élite and the public, carried out through the cultural and political intelligentsias of the society. As they polarise, and deal with their various populists, the destructive side of hermeneutic threatens to engulf the positive affirmation of legal correctness. It seems plausible, but by no means inevitable, that securing legitimacy through concentrating more and more power ('total' constitution) at a higher and higher level, will eventually reveal the temple as a house of cards, or a whole wardrobe of the emperor's new clothes. Always acknowledging the plausible counter-narratives of Chicken Little ('the sky is falling') and 'The Boy Who Cried Wolf'.[79]

[79] See Paul Veyne, *Did the Greeks Believe in Their Myths? An Essay on the Constitutive Imagination*, P. Wissing, trans. (Chicago IL: University of Chicago Press, 1988), pp. 27–39 (chapter 3: 'The Social Distribution of Knowledge and the Modalities of Belief'). Veyne's description of the ambivalent attitudes of the Greeks towards their myths seems to apply strikingly well, *mutatis mutandis*, to the attitudes of contemporary jurists towards the rule of law. Likewise his anti-necessitarian claim about the fate of their belief systems.

PART II

Transformations of the Law of the Globalising Economy

5

Law in Global Political Economy

Now You See It, Now You Don't

DAVID KENNEDY*

Introduction

International legal intellectuals today have a hard time grappling with law's constitutive role in the world's political economy or in the distributions of wealth and authority among individuals, groups, sectors or nations. This is strange because globally oriented legal élites on the shores of the North Atlantic have spent the last hundred and more years developing the philosophical, doctrinal and institutional tools that strategic actors use every day around the world to pursue their interests, defeat their rivals and consolidate their gains. They developed those tools precisely to render law useful and significant for political and economic actors. How can it be so difficult to see what they have wrought?

In this chapter, I review ideas about law in global affairs which have been broadly shared among North Atlantic legal professionals over the last century to figure out how we got here. These men – and they overwhelmingly *were* men – shared the foreign policy projects and perspectives of their time and place. Pursuing them seemed to require repeated innovation in their ideas about how law might be understood to function in global political and economic life. The result was a diversity of ideas about law and a dispersion of legal professional activity which they interpreted as the construction of a pragmatic global legal order oriented to peace, justice and prosperity. Although shaken by the events of the last decades, North Atlantic legal intellectuals have generally continued in this vein: the legalisation of everything adds up to a kind of ordered governance.

* Manley O. Hudson Professor of Law and Director, Institute for Global Law and Politics, Harvard Law School.

Unfortunately, thinking in this way makes it more difficult to see law's entanglement with injustice, inequality and conflict. Indeed, the specialised legal disciplines – international law, comparative law, international economic law, private international law – actually distort understanding, narrowing our sense for the law that is out there, overstating its coherence and obscuring its malevolence. They obscure its role in the reproduction of injustice and inequality, even as they enable it. I attribute this to the persistence of an image of law beyond the nation state as a weak ordering and regulatory system rather than a constitutive element in the ongoing tumble of transnational life.

As an antidote, I propose a different set of professional goggles which foreground law's role in political and economic struggles rather than its promise of order, its distributional impact rather than its peace building or humanitarian potential. I propose that we learn to see legal arrangements more as strategic actors already do – as tools of combat and records of gains and losses rather than as bricks in an evolving system. Seeing this way, I hope, will make it easier to identify and pursue alternatives to our current arrangements. After all, where the world's political, economic and social arrangements have been forged in legal terms through struggle, they could be remade the same way.

I Be Careful What You Wish For: A Century and a Half of International Legal Innovation

The professional projects that animated the effort to strengthen a legal fabric overlaid on diplomatic and commercial life changed over the last century with the turning of generations and major shifts in global political life. I focus on élite thinking about the limited thing called 'international law', although doing so leaves out much of what was significant in the legalisation of global life. Nevertheless, it is a place to begin. The story has a simple narrative arc. At the start of the last century, international law seemed cut off from global politics, if useful for commercial life; by mid-century, law seemed intertwined with both political and economic arrangements; in the years after the end of the Cold War, law seemed to have won out. The effort to nurture a global legal order 'at a distance' from political and economic activity had reached its apogee. The political and economic disruptions of the last twenty years raise the obvious question: If law triumphed, is it not also somehow implicated in things we deplore? In political incapacity, rising inequality, environmental catastrophe? If you are asking such a question, my aim is to explain how it might be answered – and why doing so has been so difficult.

In the late nineteenth century, the European legal élites who set the agenda for North Atlantic thinking pursued two projects in parallel: consolidating a cosmopolitan order among European 'civilised' states while cementing control of colonial possessions. In the United States, the preoccupations were commerce, the protection of American citizens (including missionaries) and investments abroad, and then our own colonial management in the Caribbean, Central America and across the Pacific.

After World War I, the dream of a cosmopolitan legal order among civilised European cultures had been smashed. The élite looked out on a world divided between a civilisation to rebuild and more primitive peoples to be brought progressively towards it. Dreams of legal order took a back seat to the urgent tasks of remaking the political geography of defeated and collapsing empires, stabilising the management of their colonies, containing the passions of nationalism.[1] Perhaps it made more sense to focus on rebuilding a global political system of collective security – the League of Nations – for which law would be – at best – an occasional tool.

For the international law establishment, international law and politics were distinct spheres. At best, lawyers could try to identify – perhaps codify – norms which had survived, or contribute to dispute resolution when sovereigns thought it useful, drawing on private and commercial law analogies. Meanwhile, commercial lawyers, judges and colonial officers were developing ever more flexible legal strategies to pursue their interests, harnessing pragmatic ideas about the social function of law.

In the years following World War II, North Atlantic legal and policy élites – now shifted more fully to our side of the Atlantic – focused on rebuilding a shared legal and institutional order as a bulwark in the Cold War and platform for economic reconstruction. Theirs was a world of sharp ideological, economic and military division between East and West, of proxy wars and nuclear terror – and of decolonisation and development in the South. Law and politics merged into a complex policy process to stabilise a politically divided world while revitalising transnational economic activity on our side of the Iron Curtain – including the

[1] See Nathaniel Berman, *Passion and Ambivalence: Colonialism, Nationalism, and International Law* (Leiden-Boston MA: Martinus Nijhoff, 2012).

newly discovered 'developing world'. Commercial and diplomatic legal professionals were playing with the same set of cards institutionally, intellectually, and doctrinally.

Skipping ahead to the heady years after 1989, law seemed to have gained the upper hand over politics, constraining even hegemons while serving as the vehicle for consolidating the 'liberal peace' among democratic states, the newly global liberal economy, and a newly universal commitment to human rights. The world remained divided, but softly – between democratic and non-democratic, developed and developing nations – all within a progressively advancing global civilisation, beyond which only outliers, failed states, criminal gangs and terrorists.

II Their Images of Law in Global Society

These successive professional projects and images of the world were accompanied by innovations in thinking about the nature of law itself. If a century ago cosmopolitan legal intellectuals worried whether law was even *possible* outside the nation state, today the world is awash in legal norms, institutions, professional practices and frames of reference. It took more than a hundred years of intellectual and practical work to make law so ubiquitous and the legality of transnational law so plausible. It is worth revisiting this history of innovation in order to understand how effectively élites reinvented law itself in pursuit of their political and economic agendas as world managers.

At the start of the last century, many international legal intellectuals doubled down on what they remembered from nineteenth century 'positivist' legal science, reviving John Austin's challenge: Could there be law 'properly so called' among such powerful political sovereigns?[2] A distinct normative legal field demanded a catalogue of valid rules agreed by sovereigns and interpreted by

[2] John Austin, *The Province of Jurisprudence Determined* (London: J. Murray, 1832), p. 208:

> 'And hence it inevitably follows, that the law obtaining between nations is not positive law: for every positive law is set by a given sovereign to a person or persons in a state of subjection to its author. As I have already intimated, the law obtaining between nations is law (improperly so called) set by general opinion. The duties which it imposes are enforced by moral sanctions: by fear on the part of nations, or by fear on the part of sovereigns, of provoking general hostility, and incurring its probable evils, in case they shall violate maxims received and respected.'

international jurists. In 1922, this idea gave us Article 38 of the Statute of the Permanent Court of International Justice.[3]

But Article 38 was a harsh taskmaster. Little of the diverse material available to legal professionals thinking about law in global affairs in the early nineteenth century – people like John Marshall, for example – could be pushed through its sieve. No seizing fishing smacks in time of war, but beyond that?[4]

As people – including the Permanent Court of International Justice (PCIJ) justices – tried to use law, they modified or augmented this remembered positivism with a series of new ideas. The movers here were less international legal theorists and judges than commercial men, diplomatic and colonial officers and national judges managing routine transboundary problems. Over the course of the century, international law 'properly so called', if I can put it that way, waxed and waned in relation to the many legal arrangements required for international trade, investment and finance, to foreign relations law and the changing military practices of leading states. As legal professionals acted across these all fields, innovations came quickly.

First, *a move to principles and purposes*: where codified rules could not be settled, jurists could find solutions elsewhere, in private law analogies, in social observations about the nature of international society, in deductions from the idea of sovereignty itself. The *S.S. Lotus* case was probably the most famous example.[5]

And then *a more sociological turn*: judges should be guided by facts and realities. Here is Judge Pound, in 1933, leaving the niceties

[3] Article 38 of the Statute of the Permanent Court of International Justice:

> The Court shall apply: 1. International conventions, whether general or particular, establishing rules expressly recognized by the contesting States; 2. International custom, as evidence of a general practice accepted as law; 3. The general principles of law recognized by civilized nations; 4. Subject to the provisions of Article 59, judicial decisions and the teachings of the most highly qualified publicists of the various nations, as subsidiary means for the determination of rules of law. This provision shall not prejudice the power of the Court to decide a case ex aequoet bono, if the parties agree thereto.

[4] The Paquete Habana (1900) 175 U.S. 677 (affirming a customary law norm prohibiting the seizing of fishing smacks during a lawful blockade in war after an exhaustive historical survey of precedent).

[5] *France* v. *Turkey* (S.S. Lotus Case) (1927) Permanent Court of International Justice, Ser. A, No. 10 (deducing a priority for territoriality over citizenship from the nature of sovereignty in permitting Turkey to exercise criminal jurisdiction over a French national for actions on the high seas).

of *de jure* recognition to the State Department: ' ... what is Soviet Russia? ... We all know it is a government ... If it is a government in *fact*, its decrees have [legal] force ... '[6]

By mid-century, norms could be found in social life – in what were *enforced* as norms, *interpreted* as norms, seemed *persuasive* as norms, in a rough and tumble policy process, underwritten by shared values. International rules, national laws and corporate norms, hard law and soft, policies and principles, formal rules and informal practices, even explicitly non-binding arrangements could have legal consequences.[7] It made more sense to focus on modes of interaction than norms, on processes and procedures for handling claims, defining actors and understanding the normative implications of horizontal sovereign-to-sovereign activity. Transnational law was all about overlapping powers, jurisdictions, dispute resolution machinery, wherever located.[8] States were rethought as the sum of jurisdictions effectively exercised – rather than as mystical entities which contemplated whether or not to exercise jurisdiction.[9]

With the sociological turn came a more *functional, problem solving* family of legal ideas. Law as what works, in a new focus on substantive results and pragmatic problem solving. Here is Judge Cardoso, in 1920, on the status of treaties:

> International law today does not preserve treaties or annul them, regardless of the effects produced. It deals with such problems pragmatically, preserving or annulling as the necessities of war exact. It establishes standards but does not fetter itself with rules. When it attempts to do more, it finds that there is neither unanimity of opinion nor uniformity of practice.[10]

Boundaries between legal fields were artificial, obstacles to pragmatic action. For that, one should cultivate situation specific work, harvesting

[6] *Salimoff & Co.* v. *Standard Oil*, New York Court of Appeals, 1933, 262 N.Y. 220 (at 226), 186 N.E. 679 (giving legal effect in the United States to a confiscation decree by the unrecognised Soviet government).

[7] See Oscar Schachter, 'The Twilight Existence of Nonbinding International Agreements' (1977) 71 *The American Journal of International Law*, 296–304.

[8] As exemplified in Henry Steiner and Detlev Vagts, *Transnational Legal Problems: Materials and Text* (Mineola NY: Foundation Press, 1968).

[9] Robert Malley, Jean Manas and Crystal Nix, 'Constructing the State Extraterritorially: Jurisdictional Discourse, the National Interest, and Transnational Norms' (1990) 103 *Harvard Law Review*, 1273–1305.

[10] *Techt* v. *Hughes*, New York Court of Appeals, 1920, 229 N.Y. 222 (at 241), 128 N.E. 185, cert. denied, 254 U.S. 643 (asserting the competence of the court to decide on the validity and enforcement of treaty provisions in times of war).

rules and principles and institutional authorities as they seemed useful.[11]

By late in the century, the regulatory, administrative and dispute settlement functions for global life had been redefined as activities which might be done anywhere. Cities do it, states do it, corporations do it, NGOs do it – even rock stars do it. Indeed, to solve global problems, one must become a norm entrepreneur, repurpose your institution as a site for 'governance', develop institutional techniques to encourage favourable normative development.[12] In exuberant moments, it could seem that, wherever two are gathered in its name, there is international law, there is community, there is consensus.

And maybe *law is more symbol than substance*, more thought than institution: a shared consciousness which could be shocked, a measuring rod for legitimacy, the expression of a universal civilisation.[13] It became possible to speak openly of international law as an *ideology*, parallel to the ordoliberal and neoliberal imaginaries which accompanied global economic policy. Here is Lori Damrosch introducing students to human rights: '... with the end of the Second World War, the idea of human rights became a universal political ideology and a central aspect of an ideology of constitutionalism'.[14]

All this intellectual and practical innovation came not as a resigned retreat from positivist rectitude, but as the result of people enthusiastically expanding law's role and potential in global economic and political life. And expand it they did. Each set of ideas suggested finding law in new places, using it in new ways, applying it to new domains. At the end of the century, international legal theory and practice seemed to reinforce one another: developing new

[11] Philip Jessup, 'Functional Approach as Applied to International Law', *Proceedings of the Third Conference of Teachers of International Law* (1928), pp. 134 et seq.

[12] The expression 'norm entrepreneur' was coined by Cass R. Sunstein, 'Social Norms and Social Roles' (1996) 96 *Columbia Law Review*, 903–68, at 909, 929, 947 and 968. See, also, Ian Johnstone, 'The Secretary-General as Norm Entrepreneur', in: Kofi Annan and Simon Chesterman (eds.), *Secretary or General? The UN Secretary-General in World Politics* (Cambridge: Cambridge University Press, 2007), pp. 123–38.

[13] Hilary Charlesworth and Christine Chinkin, 'The Gender of Jus Cogens' (1993) 15 *Human Rights Quarterly*, 63–76, at 66: 'Much of the importance of the *jus cogens* doctrine lies not in its practical application but in its symbolic significance in the international legal process.'

[14] Lori Damrosch and Sean Murphy, 'Foundations of Human Rights in Law', in: *International Law: Cases and Materials* (6th ed.), (St. Paul MN: West Academic, 2014), pp. 915–1006, at 915.

answers to the Austinian question – how can there be law among sovereigns? – offered new tools for practice. As a result, legal professionals had access to a grab bag of diverse ideas about what law is and how it functions, any of which could be drawn on strategically. People who used these tools to consolidate their own gains could imagine themselves to be striking a blow for law itself, for order, for the system.

The result was an enormous legal dispersion. The less decisive, determinative or univocal law seemed, the more prevalent it became. And the more useful to people with projects: including projects of dominance and submission, ownership and dispossession, projects to corner markets and garner gain, consolidate authority and reinforce dependency. Soon, people everywhere articulated and pursued their interests in legal terms, relying on legal arrangements to consolidate their gains, their identities, and their authority.

Twenty years ago, North Atlantic élites celebrated law's global ubiquity as a great achievement – the emergence of a global order, an international system, a network of networks, a normative transnational legal process, a regime of universal values which could bring economic prosperity and underwrite democratic justice for people everywhere.

My sense now is that the legal intelligentsia is more uneasy. The result was not a universal legal order of shared values. The world remains a terribly unjust place of intractable problems and political division. More than a century of creative efforts to place law at the centre of global life have led us to a world of technocratic élites and managerial rule. And it has given us a cultural and political backlash against expert governance which offers no alternative but itself and worries that things may fall apart. This may well be a classic case of 'be careful what you wish for'.

Along the way, people who use law routinely, exploiting its porosity and strategic usefulness, often developed a kind of *pragmatic disenchantment*: a disbelief in all the details which makes it easier to strategise, to speak truth to power in the morning and make a deal with them in the afternoon. For reasons that remain obscure, disenchanted professionals also seem to need to be anchored by faith in the vocabulary as a whole: its virtue, coherence or inevitability. There is an appetite for reassuring accounts of how all their disaggregated activity coheres. Even the International Law Commission felt the need to step in, reassuring us we had the professional techniques to manage so much dissonance and fragmentation.[15] They were not the only ones. The scholarly community generated innumerable pictures of the order law had – or might soon – conjure from a disparate world. A (professional) community with a - consciousness.[16] A transnational process.[17] A brocade of interlocking networks.[18] A constituted whole.[19] Regulatory capitalism.[20] A global administrative space.[21]

Looking back, I think people credited law with so many magical shape-shifting forms not only because it seemed useful, but because they felt they had to. It was Hans Kelsen who most eloquently asked us to recognise – to *choose* to recognise – that only the 'efficacy of the legal order' underwrote the legal order.[22] We should *choose*, as a matter of professional faith, to see all that disaggregated political and economic activity as *legal* – law abiding, law creating. We had had politics in the early twentieth century and we knew where that led – what was needed was law. To see it, to affirm it, was also to make it true.

This continues to function as an article of professional faith: for the world to continue the arc towards peace and justice – and prosperity –

15 Martti Koskenniemi, 'Report of the Study Group of the International Law Commission: Fragmentation of International Law: Difficulties Arising from The Diversification and Expansion of International Law', A/CN.4/L.682, 2006.

16 For example, Oscar Schachter, 'The Invisible College of International Lawyers' (1977) 72 *Northwestern University Law Review*, 217–26. See, also, Peter Sutch, 'Evil in Contemporary International Political Theory: Acts that Shock the Conscience of Mankind)', in: Bruce Haddock and Peri Roberts, *Evil in Contemporary Political Theory* (Edinburgh: Edinburgh University Press, 2011), pp. 101–23 (arguing for a conception of evil drawn not from first principles but from international law's expression of 'deep commitments' of the 'international community of states').

17 Harold Hongju Koh, 'Transnational Legal Process' (1996) 75 *Nebraska Law Review*, 181–207.

18 Anne-Marie Slaughter, 'Disaggregated Sovereignty: Towards the Public Accountability of Global Government Networks' (2004) 39 *Government and Opposition*, 159–90; Slaughter, *A New World Order* (Princeton NJ: Princeton University Press, 2009).

19 Jeffrey Dunoff and Joel Trachtman, *Ruling the World? Constitutionalism, International Law, and Global Governance* (Cambridge-New York: Cambridge University Press, 2009); John Jackson, *The World Trading System: Law and Policy of International Economic Relations*, 2nd ed. (Cambridge MA: The MIT Press, 1997), p. 299.

20 John Braithwaite, *Regulatory Capitalism: How it Works, Ideas for Making it Work Better* (Cheltenham-Northampton MA: Edward Elgar Publishing, 2008).

21 Benedict Kingsbury, Nico Krisch and Richard Stewart, 'The Emergence of Global Administrative Law' (2005) 68 *Law and Contemporary Problems*, 15–61.

22 Hans Kelsen, *Law and Peace in International Relations: The Oliver Wendell Holmes Lectures, 1940–41* (Cambridge MA: Harvard University Press, 1942), p. 81.

law must be consistently affirmed. To keep the faith, it is better to leave the tawdry details of struggle unseen: the coercion of losers, the embedded hierarchies and inequalities. Everything, in short, you would need to see to understand law's role in political economy, in the distribution of authority, resources and status. The result is a kind of unholy alliance: the dream of legal order and the facilitation of ceaseless distributive struggle.

III A Dream Too Good to Be True

It is important to recall how attractive – intoxicating – this combination can be. It is hard not to be nostalgic for the idea of a global order, centred in the North Atlantic, which could be effectively mobilised by bankers and generals, diplomats and businessmen, bureaucrats and citizen activists. Not *all* bankers or businessmen or diplomats or citizens, of course. In every interaction, the order was harnessed *by* someone *against* someone. But this was easy to overlook if you focused only on the general categories – citizens and governments, public and private, civilian and military. Wow, everyone can play!

To North Atlantic élites, the post-war order, like any order one gets used to, seemed both *natural* and *stable.* All those sovereigns exchanging courtesies in diplomatic routines and institutions, settled expectations about what leaders and media stars could say and do – while the global market moved resources to their most productive use as if by an invisible hand. It felt *hard won* – the global market rescued from national protectionism, a legal order wrung from inter-sovereign competition. For political stability to replace war and great power conflict, particularly in Europe, required enormous commitment and effort. After all this effort, there seemed *no going back.* Going back could only mean returning to an unattractive state of nature: to WWII, to the economic catastrophes of the Great Depression, to colonialism or a world of religious wars.

And the order seemed remarkably *resilient* – it had survived the Soviet era, absorbed decolonisation, the 1960s, the oil shock. It had underwritten and survived repeated global economic crises and wars all around the periphery, as well as dramatic changes in technology, communication, the structure of manufacturing and finance. Why wouldn't it also survive today's challenges? After all, everyone was joining the institutions that we'd created – first, the GATT, then the WTO. They were signing trade agreements, honouring investment obligations, even responding to the naming and shaming of human-rights advocacy. Not just because it was the only game in town. It also promised stability – even *stability in the interest of all.* And if American or Western hegemony underwrote the whole thing, this was less a worry than a relief. At least somebody was paying attention to what all require: a benign hegemony for which one should be grateful, given the historical alternatives.

Taken together, a comforting dream. But dreaming the world also had its dark sides. We know, for example, that in dreams, things can magically turn out all right. The post-war order was a dream like that. Law was a kind of *ersatz* global sovereign or reassuring father, at once problem solver and ethical lodestar. A good thing, on the right side of things, solving problems, affirming values. Law protects the environment, resolves disputes, affirms human dignity, reduces the violence of war. Even if, in every concrete situation, law may have been harnessed for just the opposite result. People who *want* things to be unequal have long since located the levers to garner and protect their gains, hired lawyers to find them, use them, hide behind them. A 'law become many things' will be used in many ways: will also comfort the environmental despoiler, protect private right from public power, and heighten the intensity of disputes when all sides come to believe their cause is just. And in a world in which it is no one's job to attend to world public interest, there's no reason to expect law *in general* or *on average* or *over time* to be benevolent.

In dreams, moreover, intractable differences can disappear or fade from view. Dreaming about a global legal order, élites can imagine that social conflicts and contradictions have been domesticated, turned into contending principles and interests to be balanced by inspired statesmen, or into 'disputes' which might be settled by the appropriate institutional machinery. In dreams, a law that contained all things could settle all things, expressing the commitments of an international community, beyond which there were only failed states and historical throwbacks. But dissonance didn't disappear. From the peripheries, whether that's Bangladesh or a forgotten region of England or Arkansas, the global game is much more difficult to play. The legal arrangements are not your ally, they are the tools of your disempowerment. The struggles continue, the winners win and the losers lose, while the dream which legitimated it fades from view.

And we now know how provincial – albeit globally influential – this series of preoccupations and projects has been. Recent historical work has recaptured the élite projects, ideas and professional practices in the peripheries of the North Atlantic as they came to terms with their own traditions, their situation(s), their national and collaborative projects for global society.[23] Their projects shifted things around, opened possibilities, provided vehicles for resistance as well as assimilation, even if they were not able to reverse the hierarchy of centres and peripheries. It turns out that you can consolidate your superiority over the colonial world in a wide range of legal vocabularies, from natural law to bilateral investment treaties.

I can't help wondering how the story of law in global society would look if you started in China, let us say, with the Unequal Treaties of the late nineteenth century and proceeded through all the twists, turns and ruptures in Chinese political and intellectual history over the hundred and fifty years that followed. What images of law in global affairs, what shared projects among the legal and professional élites? How to understand the genealogy of the contemporary Chinese professional conversations about such matters? How do they dream?

When you are dreaming, there are lots of things you don't see, perhaps prefer not to see, or see only dimly. Take the challenges of injustice. In international legal dreams, they somehow seemed balanced by the order's built-in progressivity – that arc of history bending towards liberal values, peace, prosperity. The way things were – at least in the North Atlantic, at least most of the time, or as élites imagined them – prefigured how they might one day be for the world. That's why people thought working *for the order* – and preserving what they had built for ourselves – was also to work towards a more just future for all mankind.

We knew there were stronger and weaker powers, developed and underdeveloped societies, leading and lagging sectors. But the post-war order was open-ended: anyone could join, participate, and then catch up. Development was available to any country with the right policy, just as

[23] See, for example, Bhupinder Chimni, *International Law and World Order: A Critique of Contemporary Approaches* (New Delhi: Sage Press, 1993); Balakrishnan Rajagopal, *International Law from Below: Development, Social Movements and Third World Resistance* (Cambridge: Cambridge University Press, 2003); Antony Anghie, Bhupinder Chimni, Karin Mickelson and Obiora Okafor (eds.), *The Third World and International Legal Order: Law, Politics and Globalisation* (Leiden: Kluwer Law International, 2003); Antony Anghie, *Imperialism, Sovereignty, and the Making of International Law* (Cambridge: Cambridge University Press, 2005); Anghie, 'TWAIL: Past and Future' (2008) 10 *International Community Law Review*, 479–81; Arnulf Becker Lorca, *Mestizo International Law: A Global Intellectual History, 1842–1933* (Cambridge: Cambridge University Press, 2014); Luis Eslava, *Local Space, Global Life: The Everyday Operations of International Law and Development* (Cambridge: Cambridge University Press, 2015); Liliana Obregón, 'Empire, Racial Capitalism and International Law: The Case of Manumitted Haiti and the Recognition Debt' (2018) 31 *Leiden Journal of International Law*, 597–615.

liberal democracy might come to any nation with the right constitution. The global consensus and the institutional arrangements that it underwrote were open to anyone with the right values. The trade regime as well, if you joined the WTO, made the necessary concessions. The global financial architecture also, if you managed your national accounts, protected investor rights, and joined the regime of bilateral investment treaties. The European Union and the euro have paths to membership. Even the Rule of Law could be injected by the development agencies of the Global North. If outsiders cannot be assimilated, it is only because they present existential threats.

When international legal professionals are dreaming, there is no 'other' – just a persistent feeling of insecurity, a vague awareness of the barbarians 'out there'.[24] Domination and unequal powers were somewhere at the margins, *outside* the order, before it, beneath it – conditions to which it responded. It was hard to see inequality as an active project, to imagine the established arrangements making things worse, winners feathering their own nests while making promises they could not keep. It was hard to see the 'structure' as a collection of levers winners use to defeat losers, consolidate and legitimise their gains.

And when you're dreaming, there really is no alternative. You have to keep dreaming. So it has been for the post-war legal order: it is all well and good to critique it, but what alternative is there? Although the post-war order had been many things in its short life – a regime of capital controls, then of free movement; of national economic development, then of open economies; of Cold War division, then of triumphant universalism – its very complexity and ubiquity precluded other arrangements. When the order is threatened – by backsliding, by outsiders – the solution is vigilance, security cooperation and the reinforcement of existing institutional arrangements. The only response to an unsatisfactory Europe is more Europe, an unsatisfactory NAFTA a new NAFTA. Beyond that, only the power of 'no': of religion in a secular world, of nationalism, tribalism and racism against a cosmopolitan order. You might try to go back, back to the sovereignty and local control and the politics that you remember – Brexit perhaps, or Make American Great Again. But there is no Brexit, no return to American pre-eminence. There is only an endless

[24] Anne Orford, *International Law and its Others* (Cambridge-New York: Cambridge University Press, 2006).

negotiation of a thousand technical questions. Like the 'Hotel California',[25] the order can always be reformed, but you can never leave.

IV Waking Up in the Twenty-First Century

So where are we now? In 2018, the US Council on Foreign Relations publication *Foreign Affairs* led off with a series of six short articles responding to the question: 'Which world are we living in?'[26] Is it a '*realist world*' of political struggle among great powers? A '*liberal world*' of universal institutional and legal commitments structuring commerce and providing guardrails for national political action? A '*tribal world*' of ethnic, religious, gender and national identities? A '*Marxist world*' of economic competition and struggle among industrial sectors, regions and classes? Is it a '*warming world*' whose twenty-first century history will be determined by now uncontrollable changes in global temperatures? Or is it a '*techno world*' of new technologies, modes of communication, artificial intelligence, blockchain – which will transform the nature of work and family and political and economic life beyond what can be imagined? Each essay had a point – but the most striking thing is simply this: the foreign policy élite does not know what world they are living in.

The last twenty years have been a series of wake-up calls for the intelligentsias of the North Atlantic. Ceaseless and unsatisfying post-9/11 wars. The great recession. Global warming. Global inequality. The rise of China; the decline of the West. And, of course, Trump and Brexit and populism. It is ever harder to imagine that the global system is up to it: the managerial class must be either part of the problem or asleep at the wheel. The sites where global problems might be addressed are manned by people with more parochial mandates, interests and projects. There simply is no global location or authority – not even a hegemon – credibly pretending to take responsibility for the global public interest. And it is hard to identify a place where politics remains possible, where decisions can be contested, where people can share responsibility and participate in the making of winners and losers. It is not surprising so many ask what

[25] Title track from the Eagles' album of the same name, released in 1977: 'You can check out any time you like / But you can never leave.'

[26] Gideon Rose, 'Which World are we Living in?' (2018) 97 *Foreign Affairs*, at 9.

happened to sovereignty – to decentralisation, to local control, to the ownership of the decisions which matter.

But waking up from a powerful dream is hard – it can leave you lying there, in a bit of a stupor. Even a dozen years ago, my students all seemed to have projects – a global problem that they were going to solve, often single-handedly on summer break. If they needed an institution, they'd set one up. Those days are gone – students come now with a deeper sense that everything needs to be rethought down to the foundation, but without a sense that it can be done. Or done in time. They are open to rethinking – but it often seems they harbour a secret plan to find a career and a gated community on high ground. And can we blame them? After endless education and cutthroat competition, their opportunities to do otherwise are few in a world whose gatekeepers keep doubling down on the very arrangements that got us into this mess.

It is difficult for a student of international law to understand global political economy as something that law had a hand in making and could do something about. A gap has opened between the way in which legal professionals think about law in global affairs when asked to describe it, teach it or write about it, and when they engage in it. As if the intellectual project took the high road, articulating an order, a direction, a project for global society which would have to be abandoned – and might be undermined – were we to dip down to the road where people use law to garner and secure gains, exclude others and ensure the stability of unequal powers.

It was not always like this: for most of the last century, efforts to extend law in practice seemed to confirm the emergence of the legal order being imagined by theory. People struggling for gain expanded the plausibility of the dream by pushing the boundaries of what law can be in global affairs while the intellectual peregrinations necessary to keep the dream alive forged the tools – and legitimated the outcomes – of all that struggle. At the same time, the notion that distributional struggles all add up to – or take place in – an order oriented to peace, prosperity and shared notions of justice helped to keep the struggle ruthless.

But something has shifted. It is becoming difficult to overlook law's persistent role in economic inequality, political dysfunction, and conflict. The growing salience of law in political and economic struggles *both* reinforced *and* undermined confidence in the idea of a cosmopolitan legal order above, outside, or innocent of political economic injustice and conflict. As a result, managing the paradox of seeing and not seeing law's distributive significance is part of being a legal professional in global affairs. It requires effort and shapes professional activity – encouraging people to insist, for example, on the differences between theory and practice, or between the world in which we work and the one we are working towards, or between the good work of law and the sorry state of everything else. Or to borrow balance-of-power models from political science or market models from economics which posit lots of self-interested activity generating a stable and beneficial equilibrium. It is in professional anxiety management practices like these that the role of law in distributive conflict, injustice and structural inequality gets lost.

Over the last few decades, the most prominent scholars have offered ever more complex accounts of law's global possibility and promise, encouraging their readers to affirm law in the world as a fragile and imperfect substitute for – or a primitive version of – a responsive global government. If you have woken to twentieth-century worries about human survival, economic inequality and political instability, an imperfect and primitive governance potential will seem ... imperfect and primitive. And it will be difficult to look beyond this weakness to grapple directly with law's powerfully constitutive role in the problems which worry you.

Take the image of legal norms infiltrating decentralised national institutions in a transnational 'normative legal process' through which norms 'percolate up' through national courts and bureaucracies, ensnaring even the most recalcitrant state.[27] A kind of 'deep state' for the world at large. This certainly does happen. And attention to the role of national courts or bureaucracies would be crucial in mapping the role of routine legal work in global patterns of distribution. But the inquiry would need to shift from the old question of international law's normativity to the constitutive role of legal practices in the distribution of resources, status or authority. Fewer norms percolate up than effects percolate out.

Or take the idea that global life is animated by a shared consciousness or ideology of governance which can be promoted and intensified through the techniques of human rights or environmental activism.[28] It was a major advance to identify élite ideas about what

[27] Koh, n. 17 above. Koh has reiterated his view over time. See, also, Harold Hongju Koh, 'Why Transnational Law Matters' (2006) 24 *Penn State International Law Review*, 745–53. And, more recently, Koh, 'The Emerging Law of 21st Century War' (2017) 66 *Emory Law Journal*, 487–512.

[28] See, for example, Louis Henkin, *International Law: Politics and Values* (Dordrecht, Boston: M. Nijhoff, 1995); Philippe Sands, *Greening International Law* (New York: New Press, 1994).

is 'reasonable' or 'appropriate' as part of the legal fabric to be influenced by activism. Legal preconceptions about the global priority of property, freedom of commerce or investor rights and the national limits of sovereign 'public policy' authority, for example, are a central normative component of global political economy. Institutions like the GATT were designed to encourage a shared sense for the natural forms of national sovereign authority in a global economy.[29] Unfortunately, however, focusing on the promise of 'human rights' or 'corporate social responsibility' or the 'precautionary principle' as *limits* on political and economic activity encourages the notion that states and corporations are otherwise natural phenomena subject only to such weak limitations, rather than being legally constructed in ways which could be changed.

It is now common to describe global legal activity as the disaggregated performance of familiar governance functions. Beyond the plethora of dispute resolution procedures – conciliation, arbitration, national litigation, adjudication – we are encouraged to see a 'global administrative space', 'regulatory capitalism', or simply 'new governance'.[30] Again, it is useful to identify the dispersion of legal coercion we associate with 'administration' or the legislative authority we associate with 'regulation' across a range of public and private institutions with global impact. Among other things, doing so helps us identify the concentration of power: of regulatory authority in a few cities, of coercive power in leading 'private' firms.

The difficulty arises in imagining these functions as *governance* activities somehow parallel to what we know as legislation, administration or adjudication from civics class. This suggests, for example, that mechanisms of accountability familiar in domestic law could be grafted onto the 'global administrative space' despite the absence of a global political authority to whom all this coercive authority could be held accountable. It suggests that norm-making and application, dispersed worldwide, is somehow undertaken in the 'public interest' when that's nobody's job

[29] Wilhelm Röpke, 'Economic Order and International Law' (1954) 86 *Recueil des Cours*, 203–73.

[30] See Kingsbury, Krisch and Stewart, n. 21 above; Braithwaite, n. 20 above. See, also, Orly Lobel, 'New Governance as Regulatory Governance', in: David Levi-Faur (ed.), *The Oxford Handbook of Governance* (Oxford: Oxford University Press, 2012), pp. 65–82; Gráinne de Búrca, Robert O. Keohane and Charles F. Sabel, 'New Modes of Pluralist Global Governance' (2013) 45 *New York University Journal of International Law and Politics*, 723–86.

even though everyone is articulating their parochial objectives in these terms. When lead firms in global value chains or the world of finance use law to pursue and protect their interests, they do displace what we used to call 'sovereigns'.[31] Thinking of this as some kind of public governance function, however, obscures its motive and impact. It makes it all too convenient to focus on actions which correspond to what a benevolent public authority might have done – that's corporate social responsibility – rather than the broad range of coercive legal powers deployed for other purposes.

No one heading out for a day's work defending their property, their market share, their national political interests, thinks that what they are doing is 'governing'. They think they are working. And somewhere, they imagine, *other* people are governing, setting the terrain on which they work, addressing – or failing to address – the difficult problems we all face. This helps to explain why professional confidence in the ability to alter economic or political affairs to one's advantage – or that of one's client – rarely translates into the feeling that something could be done about – or anyone has responsibility for – injustice. We *intended* to move people from the country to the city, transform peasants into factory workers, remodel low-wage industries into innovation clusters, but no one intended inequality. People *intended* to liberate capital here, expand liquidity there, open these markets, restrict access to credit somewhere else, manage exchange-rate fluctuation, and expand opportunities for securitised investment, but no one intended fiscal 'imbalances'.

All these images of global legality and dispersed governance make this innocence plausible. It doesn't seem to matter whether people think of an international legal system, an infinite series of functionally specialised and differentiated regimes, each with its own logic, defending its authority and pressing for priority, or as something far more nebulous – a constellation of networks somehow sutured together by law. The idea that there is a WTO and a UN and an international legal order out there somewhere regulating trade, addressing global problems, governing relations among states – however imperfectly – like the strange fantasy that, in each 'nation', there is an entity aggregating interests and 'governing' – keeps the distributions which result from their daily activity from

[31] The IGLP Law and Global Production Working Group, 'The Role of Law in Global Value Chains: A Research Manifesto' (2016) 4 *London Review of International Law*, 57–79. For an analysis of power differentials in global value chains, see Gary Gereffi, John Humphrey and Timothy Sturgeon, 'The Governance of Global Value Chains' (2005) 12 *Review of International Political Economy*, 78–104.

appearing to be anyone's responsibility. They are doing their job – it is someone else's job to clean up the mess. What we can do is contribute to the further dispersion of legal arrangements and professional vocabularies.

It will be difficult for legal professionals to leave these tendencies behind. Lawyers come to global affairs with a picture of law at home as a 'system': the French legal system or the American system. It seems obvious that law in global affairs should be imagined analogously: as 'governance', both primitive, compared to national governments, and sophisticated in having dispensed with politics all together in order to focus on shared values and problem solving. It seems irresponsible not to imagine oneself acting *on behalf of* the system, reforming it, describing it, in order to perfect it. In this light, it hard not to overestimate the orderliness and the desirability of current arrangements, and to underestimate the opportunities – or stigmatise the motives – for disrupting them. If you are thinking about the world as a 'system', conflict is the exception. On the economic side, lawyers think of trade, like contract, as a 'bargained for exchange'. Yes, unequal bargaining power might skew the results, but the legal system is oriented to bargain. On the political side, sovereigns are equal – that's the whole point of being a nation, self-determination. Yes, politics and geography and history and economics can skew things, but legally, at least, the system is one of equal participation – all those flags lined up at the UN. It will be difficult to get from here to understanding how law is implicated in inequality and injustice, in the dynamics of hierarchy and the distribution of wealth and misery.

V From Governance System to Distributional Struggle

Focusing on law's role in *struggle* – rather than order or governance – would improve our grasp of law's role in global political and economic life. We might begin the way someone with a political or economic project might begin: with a 360 degrees audit of the status of forces, identifying the powers and vulnerabilities of those who might impede or assist in realising the project. It is helpful to think of people coming to struggle with little backpacks of legal entitlements, powers and vulnerabilities. These legal arrangements are a record of past victories and defeats, defining what it means to be a 'corporation' or 'state' or 'citizen', and authorising some actors to exclude others, change the rules affecting others, or expose them to risk.

Drawing on the resources in their backpack, people assert powers and rights, attribute identities and responsibilities, articulate reasons and necessities as they seek to capture and hold gains from economic or political interaction. When people articulate their interests in legal terms, they transpose parochial objectives into matters of ostensible agreement or fact: I am sovereign or this is my property. When these assertions are effective, people yield to one another's authority or exclusive access. The outcome is a distribution of economic and political authority.

Legal arrangements distribute when they affect the bargaining power of people or groups struggling with one another, or simply mark the line where coercion will enforce an allocation, excluding others from political authority or economic gain. Because struggle is an iterative affair, people fight for an improved starting position in the next round by locking in gains and defending their dominance. The fault lines between winners and losers mark the outcomes of past struggle and affect the alliances and trajectories for the next round. This will not be new to those for whom the world order was *always* more struggle than system, nor to strategic actors right at the centre of things. Multinationals eagerly lobby for rules which will consolidate their market power and close out their rivals. Teams of lawyers work to identify levers to place income here and losses there.

Over time, gains and losses compound as legal entitlements and authority, sparking dynamics of inequality between groups, sectors, regions and nations. From colonial governance to modern trade and investment, legal arrangements have consolidated the distribution of rents from global economic activity and the political authority of those committed to the stability of the outcome. A map of law's role in domination and distribution would illuminate the ways in which regimes which seem impartial, even benevolent, participate in making an unequal and unjust world. The legal institutions of the European Union and the financial hegemony of London and Frankfurt, for example, allow monetary union to become a recipe for debt bondage, just as the European Court of Justice interprets free movement for the periphery and social protection at the centre in ways which become an engine for relative wealth and stagnation.[32]

[32] See David Kennedy, 'Turning to Market Democracy – A Tale of Two Architectures' (1991) 32 *Harvard International Law Journal*, 373–96. On the centre–periphery dynamic

One effect of struggle by law is to reduce the experience of direct conflict or hierarchy. Articulating interests in legal terms reframes distributional outcomes as pre-existing facts or marginal adjustments required by technical considerations. Eventually, law infiltrates our commonsense about the distributions that are just, the interests which can be heard, the gains which are legitimate. The result can be world making, enabling patterns of inequality and entrenching hierarchies of authority. By managing the contested boundaries of social aggregates like 'the economy and politics' or 'the international and the national' or 'the public and the private' legal professionals make their current forms seem both adjustable and inevitable.

For example, as lawyers distinguish 'market supporting' from 'market distorting' regulations – or 'private rights' which travel from 'public policies' which typically do not – they solidify the conceptual and institutional arrangements which keep the global economy and national politics at a distance from one another.

As a result, legal arrangements offer a bright red thread to identify the effects of legal power in global political economy. You can begin to develop a map of law's impact most anywhere, by identifying a rule, a judicial opinion, a field of jurisprudence, a professional attitude, a practice, an institution, an argumentative habit – a legal something – which allocates a surplus among individuals or groups in political or economic competition with one another. And then you start working adjacently. What other legal arrangements support this effect? Made it possible? Make it reproducible? As you go along, it may appear that the allocation you have identified is a function of a social, political or economic 'fact' – or is simply a function of 'power'. Here, you go back to Step One, asking what legal arrangements, ideas, practices enabled the 'fact' of union density. And through what legal and institutional forms did this 'power' operate?

Thinking this way turns our attention to law's background role in the foundations of political and economic life: in the shape of credit, property, money, capital, labour, citizenship, sovereignty. Law's distributional significance is most pronounced here: not in the way it 'regulates' or 'administers', but in the way it puts the pieces together in the first place.

within the European Union, see Ermal Frasheri, 'Of Knights and Squires: European Union and the Modernization of Albania' (2016) 42 *North Carolina Journal of International Law*, 1–73; Damjan Kukovec, 'Hierarchies as Law' (2014) 21 *Columbia Journal of European Law*, 131–93.

In this light, many 'facts' might be rethought as legal arrangements. For example, people often attribute the distribution of 'gains from trade' to facts like 'bargaining power', the relative 'productivity' of factors or the 'competitiveness' of actors. 'Bargaining power' or 'competitiveness' depend on the legal and institutional arrangements that affect things such as costs of production and barriers to entry, the structure of traded industries, the relative power of labour and capital invested in them, the monopoly power of producers and so on. Economic words like 'competitiveness' and 'productivity' have their parallels in political terms like 'leverage' or 'persuasiveness'. Each apparent fact ('he had more leverage, she was more persuasive') rests on legal entitlements, institutional arrangements, and vernaculars of persuasion that could be organised in different ways and are themselves worth struggling over.

Many economists, for example, speak about the strategic imperative for companies – and countries – to enter and hold 'high-value' segments of the global production process. They imagine a ladder from natural resource exploitation through processing to assembly, manufacturing, design, branding, and invention. This ladder generates a rule of thumb: 'innovation' or 'knowledge-based' activities will pay higher wages and allow firms to capture a greater portion of the overall gain from economic activity, if only because there is more competition at lower rungs on the ladder. But the ladder is a function of legal arrangements which could be changed. A shift in intellectual property law and labour law, for example, might sharply diminish the exclusivity of innovation-based activities and reduce the privilege to access low-wage labour. At the margin, regulatory shifts in the many rules governing access to returns from different activities in global value chains could alter what is and is not a 'high-value' activity. It is no wonder, therefore, that we also see intense struggle over these rules, undertaken in an extremely unruly and disparate fashion, among producers, consumer groups, investors, firms, cities, and nations.

Without a map of the legal arrangements, it is tempting to explain inequalities and hierarchies as the effect of 'power'. We might say, for example, that the colonial centre has the 'power' to extract gains from their colonies. But how exactly? The power in a colonial relationship needs to be exercised through institutions, be they social, military, or legal. Did the imperial power take colonial products by force? Did they prevent trade with other countries? Did they compel purchase of their products in the colony at above market prices? Perhaps there was a complex tax system – or a set of currency controls and licences – that ensured the prices paid in the two countries distributed the gains to consumers – or the tax office – in the imperial centre. Or perhaps the institution doing the work is a social one: colonial élites so enamoured with products branded in the mother country that they were willing to pay more. And things could be arranged the other way around: perhaps consumers in the mother country were compelled to purchase colonial products at higher prices as part of the overall colonial arrangement. Each of these distributive mechanisms requires legal institutional form and practice.

VI Thinking this Way Perhaps We Can Change the World

A careful map of law's power in global political economy makes it easy to see trade more as hierarchy than bargain, world politics as domination rather than a system of sovereign equality, and global political life as conflict embedded in legal arrangements until it sinks from sight and can be reimagined as equilibrium, peace – or simply as fact.

More importantly, such a map identifies points of choice, openings to contest the political and economic hierarchies and unjust distribution, alternatives to our current institutional arrangements. For every legal arrangement allocating authority or gain, there was an alternative. And at stake in struggle is not only the distribution of gains, but the large-scale direction of society. Economies configured differently will operate differently, just as different allocations of legal capacities and authority will generate divergent polities. Tracing the impact of legal arrangements on economic and political actors, and the activities they constitute, one can identify choices among different political and economic trajectories. Knowing how things have been put together, people can struggle to identify and build alternative, even equally efficient or democratic, modes of economic and political life with diverging patterns of inequality, alternate distributions of political power and economic benefit, more or less space for experimentation or contestation.

It is true that the room for national initiative and experimentation has been eroded by small and large changes made in the name of 'globalisation'. Laws enabling free movement of goods and services have made territorial regulation more difficult. The erosion of the tax base has bound sovereigns in the service of global investors. But these things were not inevitable. They were made – victories over alternatives. Indeed, wherever there was struggle, there were alternatives. Where money, credit, labour and capital, political power and right have been legally constructed, there was a moment when they could have been put together differently. Had they been, the legal boundaries between economics and politics or between those private and public actors might be otherwise. And then *that* might seem normal, commonsensical – factual.

Today, the gulf between a global economy and a national politics seems an unbridgeable chasm: a difference in scale disempowering politics and leaving global economic affairs unmoored from prudential safeguards. It doesn't have to be that way – we *know* how to link economic life to territory and community – just as we know how to distribute opportunities for political choice across institutions beyond the national capital and the professionals we call 'politicians'. It has been done before. To get there, we would need to reorient expert work from managing the separation to arranging their connection.

It is not that we lack the ability to rearrange distribution when we want to. The machinery to link the dispossessed productively to companies and nations which benefit from global markets, mobilities and technologies is not mysterious. Those who have ensured their disconnection know how it could have been done. Just as we could disperse sites for political engagement and link economic actors to communities, we could reshuffle legal arrangements to mitigate dualist dynamics.

Think of local content, employment, technology transfer, or investment requirements that link firms benefiting from privileged market access or free trade zones to their periphery. Or corporate mandates that prioritise links with communities or unions alongside shareholders, lending requirements targeting credit to peripheral actors, zoning practices linking an office tower downtown with the establishment of a shipping facility in the ghetto and so on. Corporations could be discouraged from offloading workers on national states for tax and transfer welfare, and encouraged or required to find something these workers might productively do. Capital flight could be restrained, capital investment in developing regions required. Go-slow provisions could prevent the rapid inflows and outflows of speculative capital in thin peripheral markets. By tracing the impact of legal arrangements on political and economic trajectories, we might illuminate alternative directions for the routine work of managing the 'system', adjusting the entitlements and expectations that link people in relationships of relative privilege and vulnerability.

One of the tragedies of our contemporary situation is a collective amnesia about the very real alternatives lying all around us – an entire history of heterodox analyses, proposals and real-life experiences. Rearranging things will not be easy. We will need to be savvy and strategic. People will resist. But changing the world is not done by system or order. It requires struggle on the terrain where inequality is established and maintained. Many are already hard at it. I hope that people of good heart everywhere will learn to join in.

6

Law of Natural Resource Extraction and Money as Key to Understanding Global Political Economy and Potential for Its Transformation

ISABEL FEICHTNER

I A Global Economy of Extraction

The global political economy is characterised to a significant extent by value extraction[1] through the exploitation, *inter alia*, of natural resources. Despite calls for resource efficiency and for transition to a circular economy, natural resource extraction is continuously expanding – as illustrated by recent endeavours to establish legal frameworks for mineral mining in areas beyond national jurisdiction, in the deep seabed and in outer space.[2] In trying to understand (international) law's constitutive role in political economy and, in particular, its implication in the expansion of exploitation, as well as the resulting ecological destruction and social inequality, this chapter focuses on the law governing extractive resources (in particular minerals) and the law of money. I choose this focus not only because both – raw materials extraction as well as money – are at the centre of exploitative relations. Moreover, both money and raw materials can be situated at the intersection of political organisation and the economy. Money is not only the medium of the economic system,[3] it is also a creature of the state.[4] Nature and natural resources are, at the same time, habitat, they are considered the common heritage of political

[1] On value extraction (as distinct from value creation), see Mariana Mazzucato, *The Value of Everything. Making and Taking in the Global Economy* (London: Allen Lane, 2018).

[2] Isabel Feichtner, 'Mining for Humanity in the Deep Sea and Outer Space. The Role of Small States and International Law in the Extraterritorial Expansion of Extraction' (2019) 32 *Leiden Journal of International Law* 255–274.

[3] Niklas Luhmann, *Die Wirtschaft der Gesellschaft* (Frankfurt aM: Suhrkamp Verlag, 1988), p. 14 et seq.

[4] Georg Friedrich Knapp, *The State Theory of Money* (London: Macmillan, 1924).

communities, and they constitute factors of economic production. Finally, both evidence parallel developments, linkages and interdependencies, the examination of which may yield insights into the constitution and transformation potentials of political economy.[5]

My motivation in this examination of the law and institutions of natural resources and money is to obtain a better understanding of the drivers of exploitation. I also hope to prepare the ground for identifying ways in which the law may reconfigure and transform the current political economy. This line of research arises from a number of discontents with certain strands of research in political theory, global justice, law and governance. An increasing body of global justice and political theory literature focuses on extractive resources.[6] Yet, when asking, for example, whether the principle of permanent sovereignty over natural resources produces just distributive outcomes, such literature frequently ignores the fact that questions of extraction and resource trade are situated in a larger historical, political and economic context, and that much of what these theories take as given, are characteristics which are (co-)produced by law.[7] Thus, demand for access to specific natural resources and extraction is often treated as a fact, as is scarcity of exhaustible resources and a particular geographic distribution. Questions as to what drives demand for a particular resource, what turns a certain mineral into a resource (i.e. renders it economically valuable), why certain locations are particularly attractive for exploration and exploitation are being sidelined. I have similar discontents regarding the growing literature in international law that addresses the governance of natural resource extraction. Here, too, we can observe a neglect of the political and economic structures which underlie exploitation and the proposal of remedies for symptoms, not causes, such remedies including,

[5] To get a fuller picture of the constitutive role of law in political economy, one may (and should) add an analysis of labour law – human labour also being simultaneously inextricable from social and political life and subject to commodification. For a seminal analysis of political economy that focuses on land, money and labour, see Karl Polanyi, *The Great Transformation: The Political and Economic Origins of Our Time* (New York: Farrar & Rinehart, 1944).

[6] See, for example, Thomas Pogge, *World Poverty and Human Rights* (Cambridge: Polity Press, 2002); Mathias Risse, *On Global Justice* (Princeton NJ: Princeton University Press, 2012); Margaret Moore, *A Political Theory of Territory* (Oxford: Oxford University Press, 2015); Leif Wenar, *Blood Oil: Tyrants, Violence, and the Rules that Run the World* (New York: Oxford University Press, 2016); Chris Armstrong, *Justice and Natural Resources: An Egalitarian Theory* (Oxford: Oxford University Press, 2017).

[7] See, also, the contribution by David Kennedy in this volume (Chapter 5).

in particular, 'better' human rights protection, environmental regulation, and anti-corruption measures.[8] It is not seldom that these remedies are presented as win-win situations, as mutually beneficial solutions (for home states, host states, investors and local communities alike), while neglecting the persistence of distribution conflicts.[9]

In this chapter, I explore the distributive effects that law generates – by allocating jurisdiction, by allocating exploitation rights, by submitting distribution conflicts either to resolution through political procedures or through market mechanisms – as well as the dominant and stabilising rationalisations for such allocations, in particular, justifications in terms of the pursuit of public interests, and the desirability of leaving distribution either to politics or the market. I use the terms 'politicisation and politics' and 'marketisation and market' in order to refer to particular modes of decision making and distribution. Politics, in the sense in which I employ the term here, is based upon the premise that irreconcilable conflicts of interests exist between different groups and classes, such as resource-producing and resource-consuming states, that may be but temporarily appeased through political compromise and decision making. By contrast, marketisation – the transfer of the powers of allocation and decision making to 'the market' – is predominately being justified by pointing to 'the market's' ability to achieve optimal and efficient allocation, to attain equilibria. I want to stress that when I refer to 'the market', I do not endorse the view that there is such a thing as 'the market'; the whole point of this chapter being to contribute to our understanding of markets being co-produced by law (and politics), and thus taking different forms and shapes, and resulting in different distributions.

The chapter cannot outline an alternative political economy and ecology of natural resource extraction. Rather, it points to past junctures when institutional alternatives were proposed and debated, and certain

[8] See, for example, Elena Blanco and Jona Razzaque (eds.), *Globalization and Natural Resources Law. Challenges, Key Issues and Perspectives* (Cheltenham: Edward Elgar Publishing, 2011); Daniëlla Dam-de Jong, *International Law and Governance of Natural Resources in Conflict and Post-conflict Situations* (Cambridge: Cambridge University Press, 2015); Isabel Feichtner, Markus Krajewski and Ricarda Roesch (eds.), *Human Rights in the Extractive Industries: Transparency, Participation, Resistance* (Heidelberg: Springer, 2019).

[9] For calls to analyse international law's constitutive role in an exploitative political economy, see Susan Marks, 'Exploitation as an International Legal Concept', in: Marks (ed.), *International Law on the Left: Re-examining Marxist Legacies* (Cambridge: Cambridge University Press, 2008), and Marks, 'Human Rights and Root Causes' (2011) 74 *Modern Law Review*, 57–78.

paths were chosen over others, and indicates possibilities for destabilising prominent rationalisations of a law that sustains the current political economy of natural resource exploitation.

II Permanent Sovereignty Over Natural Resources and Monetary Sovereignty: Setting the Stage for Resource and Money Politics

I begin my sketch of the international law of natural resources and money with the post-WWII era of decolonisation – a juncture in time when the state, as a form of political organisation, became universal, when formerly colonised peoples were promised political sovereignty to be exercised both within and through the state.[10] This sovereignty came to be understood to encompass what international law denotes as 'permanent sovereignty over natural resources' (PSNR) (and 'monetary sovereignty'). Yet, at the time, such an understanding of sovereignty was not fixed, and alternative conceptions were also part of international discourse. In the following, I allude to such alternatives and conclude with the observation that the legal principles of PSNR and monetary sovereignty set the stage for an international politics concerning resource trade as well as exchange rates and balance of payments.

During the transition from the colonial to the postcolonial era, PSNR did not appear as the only form that jurisdiction over the natural resources located within a sovereign state's territory could take. At least two further options were envisaged, as concerns jurisdiction over, and administration of, natural resources. One option, favoured by Wilhelm Röpke, wanted to see international resource trade freed from political obstacles. Röpke – writing in 1944–45 – bemoaned the politicisation of international resource trade. He argued against political intervention and in defence of free international trade, which would ensure access to raw materials for all economies, including those lacking resource deposits.[11] The other option, proposed by the United States with respect to oil, was to establish international institutions for the administration of raw material deposits – even if they were located within national jurisdiction.

[10] See Sundhya Pahuja, *Decolonising International Law: Development, Economic Growth and the Politics of Universality* (Cambridge: Cambridge University Press, 2013).

[11] Wilhelm Röpke, *Internationale Ordnung* (Erlenbach-Zürich: Rentsch, 1945), p. 120 et seq. Today, the view that free markets form the precondition for a just distribution of raw materials is promoted by the European Union. In its raw materials diplomacy, it pursues, *inter alia*, international legal prohibitions of restrictions on raw material exports, such as export tariffs, see n. 93 below.

The United States aimed to establish an International Petroleum Council to prevent oil-producing countries from claiming control over oil production. The justification put forward for establishing such an institution also was that it would secure an equitable international distribution of oil.[12]

That neither of these alternatives to PSNR prevailed is not surprising given the newly independent states' desire to realise international law's promise of political sovereignty. In the context of decolonisation, the principle of PSNR – asserted in a number of United Nations General Assembly resolutions,[13] as well as in both international human rights covenants[14] – is initially to be read as being primarily an assertion of external sovereignty.[15] The principle clarifies that the territorial sovereignty of states encompasses jurisdiction over natural resources and shields states against claims of foreign actors – be they states or private investors – to their resource wealth. This clarification must be understood not only as a response to past imperial exploitation – enabled and legitimised by international law – but also as a response to the above-mentioned political initiatives that sought to place certain strategically important natural resources under international administration. In this external dimension, PSNR becomes the international legal basis for nationalisations and other state-imposed restrictions on foreign investment in extraction projects, as well as on exports of natural resources, and thus for the politicisation of the international resource economy that liberals such as Röpke criticised.

[12] Timothy Mitchell, *Carbon Democracy: Political Power in the Age of Oil* (London: Verso Books, 2011), pp. 113 and 114; see, also, Nico Schrijver, *Sovereignty over Natural Resources* (Cambridge: Cambridge University Press, 1997), pp. 37 and 38 (referring to a similar proposal submitted in 1947 by the International Co-operative Alliance to ECOSOC).

[13] UNGA Res. 523 (VI) (1952); UNGA Res. 626 (VII) (1952); UNGA Res. 1803 (XVII) (1962).

[14] Article 1:2 of the International Covenant on Civil and Political Rights and the International Covenant on Economic, Social and Cultural Rights.

[15] It does, however, also entail an internal dimension which is increasingly mobilised to support demands for a democratisation of resource extraction, as well as to support the rights of indigenous communities to self-determination with respect to natural wealth; see Lillian Aponte Miranda, 'The Role of International Law in Intrastate Natural Resource Allocation. Sovereignty, Human Rights, and Peoples Based Development' (2012) 45 *Vanderbilt Journal of Transnational Law*, 785–840. Ricardo Pereira and Orla Gough, 'Permanent Sovereignty over Natural Resources in the 21st Century: Natural Resource Governance and the Right to Self-Determination of Indigenous Peoples under International Law' (2013) 14 *Melbourne Journal of International Law*, 1–45.

As explained in more detail below, monetary sovereignty as the right of a state to issue and administer its own currency, similar to PSNR, set the stage for an international monetary politics. It was the International Monetary Fund (IMF) that state representatives, negotiating the post-war international economic order at Bretton Woods, designated as the public institution responsible for monetary politics. Its politics-enabling function was to be twofold: first, the Bretton Woods system was to ensure the autonomy of states to pursue domestic policy aims, for example full employment, without having to subordinate them to maintaining an external balance of payments and thus freeing domestic politics from the constraints that had existed under the gold standards;[16] second, the IMF was to become the forum for international monetary politics concerning balance of payments and exchange rates.[17]

III From International Resource Law to Transnational Economic Law and the Proliferation of Markets

Sovereignty over natural resources and the assertion of political control over domestic resource economies was the basis upon which states, and in particular the newly independent states, then attempted to employ international law in order to reconfigure the global political economy and mitigate global inequality. This international law as part of the New International Economic Order (NIEO), *inter alia*, was to enable an international resource politics. Yet, in a parallel development – and in part as a reaction to the NIEO – there emerged a transnational economic law that came to severely restrict the space for resource politics. It was not only transnational economic law, however, that promoted a depoliticisation of the natural resource economy. Rather, the very act of asserting governmental control over natural resources contributed to an expansion and proliferation of resource markets.

[16] The reconciliation of international liberalism with domestic policy autonomy that the Bretton Woods system was to achieve has come to be known as embedded liberalism, after John G. Ruggie, 'International Regimes, Transactions, and Change: Embedded Liberalism in the Postwar Economic Order' (1982) 36 *International Organization*, 379–415.

[17] Barry Eichengreen, *Globalizing Capital: A History of the International Monetary System*, 2nd ed. (Princeton NJ: Princeton University Press, 2008), p. 91 et seq.

III.1 Attempts to Establish an International Resource Politics and Administration

Collective Action to Promote Distributive Justice

One objective of the international resource law as envisaged by newly independent states was to enable the producers of primary commodities to reap a greater share of profits in transnational production chains and to reduce dependency on the production of primary commodities through the establishment of a manufacturing industry.[18] The core demands of the newly independent states' agenda for the establishment of a New International Economic Order (NIEO) included technology transfers, unconditional financial assistance, and the conclusion of international commodity agreements.[19] The latter were to establish international organisations in which both resource-producing and resource-consuming states were to be represented and that would – upon the basis of an international resource politics – intervene in international commodity trade through quotas, buffer stocks and price indexing. The main aim of such market intervention was to stabilise prices and enhance the export earnings of the resource-producing and resource-exporting states.[20]

Such reorganisation of the international economy was justified in terms of public interests, or – in the terminology of many international lawyers at the time – the common interests of international society. In the view of a number of third world, but also western, international lawyers, the common interests of the international society of states had significantly changed with the accession of the newly independent states, and, in order to remain viable, international law had to adapt to the new situation.[21] Some lawyers, including Bernard Röling and Wilfred Jenks, analogised international law to the law of the welfare state, and argued that international law had to take account also of the needs of the poorer

[18] Raúl Prebisch, *Towards a Dynamic Development Policy for Latin America* (New York: United Nations, 1963).

[19] Declaration on the Establishment of the New International Economic Order, UNGA Res. 3201 (S-VI)(1974); Programme of Action on the Establishment of a New International Economic Order, UNGA Res. 3202 (S-VI) (1974); Charter of Economic Rights and Duties of States, UNGA Res. 3281(XXIX)(1974).

[20] On the history and law of international commodity agreements, see Bhupinder Chimni, *International Commodity Agreements. A Legal Study* (London: Croom Helm, 1987).

[21] On the reform of international law after colonialism in order to protect and promote common interests, see, for example, R.P. Anand, *New States and International Law* (Delhi: Vikas Publishing, 1972); Georges Abi-Saab, 'The Newly Independent States and the Rules of International Law. An Outline' (1962) 8 *Howard Law Journal*, 95–121.

and disadvantaged members of international society.[22] Ultimately, however, the appeal to a common interest in greater global economic equality did not yield the institutional reforms desired by the newly independent states.[23] While the next section offers a brief explanation for the lack of success of the NIEO, it should be noted that its institutional proposals, in particular for international commodity agreements, have become part of what we may call the 'institutional toolbox' of international law. Thus, when commodity prices soared during the financial crisis of 2008, these proposals were being revisited.[24]

III.2 The Emergence of a Transnational Economic Law: Private Enterprise and Markets as Guarantors of Development and Fair Distribution

The establishment of international commodity organisations in which resource-producing and resource-consuming states were to be represented and to decide together on market interventions was meant to politicise natural resource extraction and trade. Yet, the attempt to bring into existence an international resource politics was met with a countermove towards depoliticisation, *inter alia*, through a transnational economic law.[25] The primary beneficiaries of this transnational economic law were transnational corporations, its most important institutions were arbitral tribunals, and it was justified with reference to the market as the optimal distribution mechanism, and to economic liberalisation as a win-win

[22] Bernard V.A. Röling, *International Law in an Expanded World* (Amsterdam: Djambatan, 1960), p. 83 et seq; Wilfred Jenks, *Social Justice in the Law of Nations* (Oxford: Oxford University Press, 1970), p. 1. A distinction should be drawn, however, between, on the one hand, the NIEO objective to change the structures of the global economy, and, on the other hand, the provision of welfare assistance – even if both sought to address global inequality in the name of common interests.

[23] Producer cartels were one option that resource exporting states could pursue without the cooperation of resource importing states. OPEC, founded in 1960, has been the most effective of these cartels. However, only few extractive industries exhibited the features conducive for the successful establishment of cartels.

[24] Brian Wright, 'International Grain Reserves and Other Instruments to Address Volatility in Grain Markets' (2009) *FAO Investment Centre Working Paper*, available at: www.fao.org/3/a-i3338e.pdf; Christopher Gilbert, 'International Agreements for Commodity Price Stabilisation: An Assessment' (2011) No. 53 *OECD Food, Agriculture and Fisheries Papers*, available at: http://dx.doi.org/10.1787/5kg0ps7ds0jl-en.

[25] For an elaboration on how the emergence of transnational economic law undermined attempts to establish an NIEO, see Antony Anghie, *Imperialism, Sovereignty and the Making of International Law* (Cambridge: Cambridge University Press, 2005), chapter 4.

situation that would be mutually beneficial to resource-producing as well as resource-consuming states.

Transnational economic law, together with international trade and investment law, incrementally established a legal framework which secured to the resource-importing states and their industries access to the resources of their former colonies and other capital-importing and resource-exporting states.[26] It can be read not only as the result of an effective strategy of highly industrialised states to meet their supply needs, but also as a successful redefinition of the international public interest.[27] This transnational economic law was only in part created by states (e.g. through bilateral investment treaties), but was also substantially developed by non-state actors, namely, arbitrators and experts in the secretariats of international institutions, in particular the World Bank and the IMF.

Its main elements are investment protection and policy prescriptions aimed at economic liberalisation and privatisation. The protection of foreign investment is effectuated through international investment arbitration – at first mainly based upon investor-state contracts and later increasingly on bilateral investment agreements embodying not only the legal basis for the jurisdiction of arbitral tribunals to adjudicate investor state disputes, but also substantive protection standards.[28] The reprivatisation of natural resource industries (that had been nationalised upon independence) has been promoted through the international financial institutions which advocated and assisted in the establishment of investor-friendly legislation and administration, and made financial assistance conditional upon the privatisation of mining enterprises.[29]

The emergence of a transnational economic law – which, it should be noted, was highly asymmetric in that, effectively, it mainly obliged states from the Global South and benefited corporate actors form the Global North – also entailed a redefinition of the international public interest and the means to achieve it. The overarching public interest invoked to justify law and policy making by intergovernmental institutions as well as

[26] Stephen D. Krasner, *Defending the National Interest: Raw Materials Investments and US Foreign Policy* (Princeton NJ: Princeton University Press, 1978).

[27] I have expanded on this argument in Isabel Feichtner, 'International (Investment) Law and Distribution Conflicts over Natural Resources', in: Stephan W. Schill, Christian J. Tams and Rainer Hofmann (eds.), *International Investment Law and Development: Bridging the Gap* (Cheltenham: Edward Elgar Publishing, 2015), pp. 256–84.

[28] Charles Leben, *The Advancement of International Law* (Oxford: Hart Publishing, 2010).

[29] See Section IV.1 below.

investor-state dispute settlement became economic development, replacing the notion of distributive justice.[30] And economic development, according to the neoclassical economic doctrine which came to dominate policy prescriptions, in particular those of the international financial institutions, was to be achieved mainly through private economic activity and liberalised markets. Accordingly, transnational economic law as well as privatisation policies promoted by international institutions could be justified with reference to a coincidence of the public interest in economic development with the private interests of investors. Happily, these interests also coincided with the interests of the highly industrialised states dependent on access to natural resources abroad. According to this justification, which regards private enterprise and unencumbered markets as the drivers of economic development, political intervention into the global political resource economy became both unnecessary and undesirable. While it would have been the function of the law of international commodity organisations to enable an international resource politics,[31] the main function of transnational economic law became the protection of private entitlements and investments. Advocates of transnational economic law lauded this depoliticisation of international economic relations as one of its major achievements.[32]

III.3 (Unintended) Consequences of Asserting Political Control over Natural Resource Wealth: Expansion and Proliferation of Markets

The assertion of political control over natural resources by governments not only prompted the development of a transnational legal framework for the protection and promotion of privatised resource extraction, it also triggered the expansion and proliferation of commodity and derivatives markets.

[30] As Sundhya Pahuja convincingly argues, the employment of international law in pursuit of economic development has rendered international law's promise of political self-determination for the countries of the Third World increasingly elusive; see Pahuja, *Decolonising International Law*, n. 10 above; for a more far-reaching argument that the form of international law promotes economic exploitation, see China Mieville, *Between Equal Rights: A Marxist Theory of International Law* (Leiden: Brill, 2004).

[31] Trade in raw materials did not (or only to a very small extent) come to be regulated by international commodity agreements, but was covered instead by the rules of the GATT 1947 and later the WTO.

[32] See Ibrahim F.I. Shihata, 'Towards a Greater Depoliticization of Investment Disputes. The Roles of ICSID and MIGA' (1986) *ICSID Review – Foreign Investment Law Journal*, 1–25.

The nationalisation of extractive industries was a factor which contributed to a significant change in the structure of the trade in raw materials and energy resources in the 1970s and 1980s. Until the early 1970s, energy resources and metals had predominately been traded either within large vertically integrated firms or through long-term supply contracts.[33] The nationalisation of extractive industries in the course of decolonisation cut these links between enterprises engaging in extraction and enterprises engaging in production. Consequently, the high degree of vertical integration which had characterised extractive industries in the 1950s and 1960s could no longer be maintained.[34] As a further consequence, natural resources were increasingly traded on spot markets and via commodity exchanges.[35] Daniel Yergin gives the example of British Petroleum, which was once seen as 'a quasi governmental bureaucracy' but then chose a trading-oriented approach.[36] Nationalisation was not the only reason for the change in trading structure. In a situation of surplus production, trade via exchanges could appease the worries on the part of the producers about access to potential buyers.[37] Moreover, prices of natural resources that are traded through exchanges can be more responsive to changes in supply and demand than prices determined by long-term supply contracts, even though the latter frequently made use of price indexation.[38] For natural resources to be tradable on spot markets

[33] WTO, *World Trade Report 2010. Trade in Natural Resources* (Geneva: WTO, 2010), p. 61; Christian Kirchner, Erich Schanze, Fabian G. von Schlabrendorff, Albrecht Stockmayer, Thomas W. Wälde, Michael Fritzsche, Reinhard Patzina and Ralph W. Beha *Rohstofferschließungsvorhaben in Entwicklungsländern. Interessenrahmen, Verhandlungsprozeß, rechtliche Konzeptionen* (Frankfurt aM: Metzner, 1977), p. 195; Daniel Yergin, *The Prize: The Epic Quest for Oil, Money and Power* (New York: Free Press, [1993] 2009), p. 703 et seq. (for the petroleum industry).

[34] It was, however, not only nationalisations that were responsible for reverse integration. Resource-oriented corporations such as the German *Preussag*, which had operated their own mines, gave up the mining business due to falling prices (in the 1980s), the lack of profitability of mining operations, and the ability to satisfy their resource demands on the world market; see Stefan Beißwenger, 'Nationale Versorgungssicherheit, internationale Rohstoffpolitik und nachhaltige Entwicklungszusammenarbeit. Eine Gleichung ohne Lösung?' (September 2013) *BIGS Studie*, 11.

[35] By 1982, according to Daniel Yergin more than half of internationally traded crude oil was either traded through the spot market or its price was keyed to the spot market while until the end of the 1970s no more than 10 per cent of oil traded internationally was traded on spot markets, see Yergin, *The Prize*, n. 33 above, p. 704; WTO, *World Trade Report 2010. Trade in Natural Resources*, p. 61.

[36] Yergin, *The Prize*, n. 33 above, p. 704.

[37] Ibid., p. 703.

[38] WTO, *World Trade Report 2010. Trade in Natural Resources*, n. 33 above, p. 61.

and through exchanges, they needed to be turned into fungible commodities. As concerns oil, fungibility was achieved through the standardisation of different types of oil.[39]

A further effect of the shift in trading structure was that trading in raw materials itself provided increasing commercial opportunities due to the proliferation of derivative markets.[40] The proliferation of markets for commodity futures and options was a consequence of the emergence of spot market and exchange trading of primary commodities.[41] These commodity derivatives allow sellers and buyers of primary commodities to hedge against the risk of price volatility, which is generally high for primary commodities. At commodity exchanges, these derivatives are traded through standardised contracts with the exchange functioning as the contractual counter party. This makes the derivative contracts also fungible.[42] Clearing houses that are linked to commodity exchanges perform financial processing functions. They mark-to-market the derivative contracts, and the parties have to pay losses as they occur. Clearing houses thus reduce the danger that the parties to derivative contracts will renege on their obligations.[43] Today, the volume of trade in these derivatives far exceeds that of trade in the primary commodities themselves. A reason for the exponential increase in commodity derivatives trade was a loosening of regulatory strictures, for example, through the US Commodity Futures Modernization Act of 2000.[44] In the course of the financial crisis of 2008, a number of scholars and international institutions have argued that the financialisation of commodities is responsible for an increased volatility of natural resource and food prices; that price hikes are caused by speculation and do not merely reflect changes in trade fundamentals such as the supply of and the demand for the respective primary commodity.[45]

[39] Yergin, *The Prize*, n. 33 above, p. 703; Donald MacKenzie, *An Engine not a Camera: How Financial Instruments Shape Markets* (Cambridge MA: The MIT Press, 2006), p. 13 (for grain).

[40] Yergin, *The Prize*, n. 33 above, p. 705.

[41] A future being a promise to deliver a good at a fixed price, time and place in the future; an option being an opportunity to buy or sell products at a fixed price, time and place in the future, see James M. Falvey and Andrew N. Kleit, 'Commodity Exchanges and Antitrust' (2007) 4 *Berkeley Business Law Journal*, 123–76, at 126.

[42] Ibid., 'Commodity Exchanges and Antitrust', p. 126 et seq.

[43] Ibid.

[44] Lynn A. Stout, 'Derivatives and the Legal Origins of the 2008 Credit Crisis' (2011) 1 *Harvard Business Law Review*, 1–38.

[45] See, for example, UNCTAD, *Price Formation in Financialized Commodity Markets: The Role of Information* (New York-Geneva: United Nations, 2011).

IV The Law of Money and Finance in the Political Resource Economy

Beyond the financialisation of the extractive resource trade, natural resource extraction and institutions of money and finance are linked in myriad further ways. In this section, I roughly sketch, first, the role that transnational trade in natural resources played in transformations of the international monetary system – the breakdown of the Bretton Woods arrangement of fixed exchange rates, the liberalisation of capital markets, and the consolidation of the US dollar as the world's main trading currency. Second, I indicate the effects, which, in turn, the current law of money and public finance has on natural resource extraction. While the changes in the international monetary system further reduced the space, not only for international monetary politics and domestic welfare politics, but also for international and national resource politics, an examination of the law of money and public finance calls into question public interest justifications for extraction, in particular the notion of securing the public's fair share in the financial gains from extraction and the notion of market supply.

IV.1 The Breakdown of the International Monetary System of Bretton Woods, Capital Market Liberalisation, and the Consolidation of the US Dollar as the World's Main Trading and Reserve Currency

To clarify further the links between the assertion of political control over natural resources – in particular, by oil-exporting states through the nationalisation of the petroleum industry and the formation of OPEC as a cartel to administer oil prices – and the transformation of international monetary law and capital markets, I reconstruct two developments, taking particular account of the role played by resource trade. The first is the demise of the Bretton Woods system of pegged, but adjustable, exchange rates. The second is the active promotion of the liberalisation and the transnationalisation of financial markets by the United States in order to maintain and consolidate the US dollar's status as the main international trading currency.

At Bretton Woods in 1944, the negotiating states had agreed (based mainly upon plans by John Maynard Keynes and Harry Dexter White) on a system of pegged, but adjustable, exchange rates.[46] The Articles of

[46] On the negotiations and the Keynes and White plans, see Richard Gardner, *Sterling-Dollar Diplomacy* (New York: Oxford University Press, 1956), pp. 71–100; Benn Steil, *The*

Agreement of the International Monetary Fund, which entered into force 27 December 1945, obliged IMF members to declare par values of their currencies in terms of gold or a currency convertible into gold.[47] The US dollar was pegged to gold at 35 USD per ounce in this system, and, with the United States at that time being the world's strongest trading economy, the dollar became the international monetary system's leading reserve currency.[48] The United States' Treasury was committed to exchange US dollars submitted to it by official foreign holders into gold. Here, too, it should be noted that this version of an international monetary regime was chosen over institutional alternatives with potentially different trajectories. Two characteristics, in particular, distinguish the law of the IMF, as it was instituted in 1944, from the International Clearing Bank proposed by Keynes. First, under the law of the IMF, the dollar functioned (and still does so today) as the main international reserve currency, whereas Keynes' proposal had envisaged the creation of an international central bank money, the Bancor. Second, under the law of the IMF, the burden of adjustment for balance of payment disequilibria mainly falls on debtor countries, whereas Keynes' proposal had envisaged that creditor countries were also to take adjustment measures (or be sanctioned).[49]

Under the 'gold-exchange standard' system, as it was instituted with the IMF Articles of Agreement, not only were industrialised states able to exert political power by threatening the conversion of their foreign reserve holdings,[50] but resource-exporting poor states could also put pressure on the international monetary system by way of shifting their export earnings.[51] Thus President Kaunda of Zambia in 1966 threatened to sell off Zambia's sterling holdings (accumulated mainly through the

Battle of Bretton Woods. John Maynard Keynes, Harry Dexter White and the Making of a New World Order (Princeton NJ: Princeton University Press, 2013).

47 Article XX IMF Articles of Agreement; exchange rates could be adjusted, generally by up to 1 per cent and by up to 10 per cent in cases of fundamental disequilibrium; see Eichengreen, *Globalizing Capital*, n. 17 above, p. 95.

48 Another important reserve currency was the British pound sterling used as trading currency within the sterling bloc.

49 Gardner, *Sterling-Dollar Diplomacy*, n. 46 above, pp. 92–4.

50 On France's attempt to weaken US power by attacking its position in the international monetary system through rhetoric, conversion of dollar holdings into gold, and obstruction of international cooperation, see Jonathan Kirshner, *Currency and Coercion: The Political Economy of International Monetary Power*, 3rd ed. (Princeton NJ: Princeton University Press, 1997), pp. 192–203.

51 Ibid., p. 192 et seq. The shifting of export earnings remained a danger to financial stability even after the demise of the Bretton Woods system of pegged exchange rates; see C. Fred

sale of copper) in order to coerce Great Britain into intervening militarily in Rhodesia and overthrowing the white rebel regime under Ian Smith, who had proclaimed Rhodesian independence in 1965.[52] Even though Kaunda's threat to sterling did not achieve the aim of British military intervention in Rhodesia, Nathan Kirshner observes, that it sufficed to obtain increased aid payments from Great Britain.[53] Kirshner further comments that menaces of this kind could not only endanger the position of reserve currencies within the international monetary system, but also the stability of the international monetary system as a whole.[54]

The system came under increasing pressure when, due to the high growth rates in Western Europe and Japan, as well as the rising payments deficit of the United States, more and more US dollars and other US official liabilities were held abroad.[55] These foreign dollar holdings raised doubts as to whether the US would be able to maintain the dollar-gold exchange rate of 35 USD per ounce. For a while, a number of international cooperation initiatives sought to stabilise the system. With the creation of the Gold Pool, for example, industrialised states agreed not to present their dollar reserves to the US administration for conversion into gold.[56] The willingness to join in cooperative efforts to support continued dollar-gold convertibility faded, however, when the United States, instead of making efforts to reduce its payments deficit, under the presidency of Lyndon Johnson increased domestic spending as well as military expenditure related to the war in Vietnam. In 1971, the Nixon administration – faced with a choice of either addressing the deficit or defaulting on its obligation to convert foreign official dollar holdings into gold – decided no longer to convert US dollars into gold, and devalued the dollar.[57] Other states followed in devaluing their currencies, and, in 1976, the system of pegged, but adjustable, exchange rates was formally abandoned with the second amendment of the IMF's Articles of Agreement.[58]

Bergsten, 'The Threat from the Third World' (1973) *Foreign Policy*, No. 11, 102–24, at 109 et seq.

52 This announcement was combined with the further threat to change the currency for copper trading from sterling to the US dollar.

53 On this episode, see Kirshner, *Currency and Coercion*, n. 50 above, pp. 203–12.

54 Ibid.

55 Eichengreen, *Globalizing Capital*, n. 17 above, pp. 126 and 127.

56 Eichengreen, *Globalizing Capital*, n. 17 above, pp. 121, 122, 127 and 128.

57 Ibid., p. 131.

58 Today, the Articles of Agreement merely require orderly exchange arrangements, Article IV, Sec. 1.

It was not the export earnings of the resource-exporting countries by themselves which brought down the Bretton Woods monetary system, but rather a combination of factors, the most important of which was the growing payments deficit of the United States as issuer of the international de facto reserve currency.[59] Nonetheless, resource-exporting states contributed to its instability as the system of fixed exchange rates provided them with significant power to pursue political aims by threatening, what Kirshner calls, systemic disruption.[60]

After the demise of the Bretton Woods system of pegged, but adjustable, exchange rates, the United States actively sought to maintain the dollar's status as the international trading currency. This status allowed the United States to maintain what Giscard d'Estaing had called an 'exorbitant privilege'.[61] The term has come to denote the United States' privilege, due to the worldwide demand for US dollars, to sustain a persistent trade deficit and finance consumption-based growth with the savings of other countries which invest their export earnings in US sovereign bonds. To achieve the aim of consolidating the dollar as an international trading currency, it was crucial that the dollar continued to function as the predominant currency for trade in natural resources, especially petroleum.[62] Two (interlinked) elements are of particular significance in explaining how the United States' government attained its aim: first, US governmental support for the liberalisation of transnational financial transactions, and, second, the transnational 'recycling' of petrodollars through US financial institutions.

Transnational financial markets had not been on the agenda of the Bretton Woods negotiations for a post-war international economic order. While the Bretton Woods institutions pursued the promotion of international trade as their key objective,[63] they did not aim to liberalise

[59] A number of scholars have convincingly shown that, despite its monetary power, it was not OPEC, with its concerted action to raise oil prices, which was responsible for the demise of the Bretton Woods system; see Eichengreen, *Globalizing Capital*, n. 17 above.

[60] For a theoretical underpinning of systemic disruption, see Kirshner, *Currency and Coercion*, n. 50 above, p. 170 et seq. (making the argument that opportunities for systemic disruption are greater in systems of fixed exchange rates than in systems of floating exchange rates).

[61] William Tabb, *Economic Governance in the Age of Globalization* (New York: Columbia University Press, 2004), p. 120; Kirshner, *Currency and Coercion*, n. 50 above, pp. 192–203.

[62] Mitchell, *Carbon Democracy*, p. 111 (pointing to the 'neglect of oil in standard accounts of international finance').

[63] Article 1 of the World Bank's and the IMF's Articles of Agreement.

transnational capital movement. On the contrary, the Bretton Woods system of pegged exchange rates accorded a particular significance to capital controls. While the IMF Articles of Agreement included a general prohibition on payment restrictions as a barrier to international trade,[64] they permitted the adoption of capital controls.[65] Keynes, in particular, considered capital controls crucial for enabling states to pursue domestic objectives of economic expansion and full employment through monetary and economic policies without having to fear speculative attacks on their currencies.[66] The United States, even if not a strong supporter of capital controls, accepted their employment by other IMF member states, and, in 1965, the US government itself adopted a capital controls programme in an attempt to reduce its payments deficit and take pressure off the dollar.[67] Yet, the United States simultaneously supported the emergence of a transnational financial market, namely, the eurodollar market. The eurodollar market had been established in the late 1950s and was located in London. It allowed trade in foreign currencies, mainly US dollars, relatively free from regulation. Thus, when, in 1965, the US government itself opted for capital controls, it could appease New York banks and corporations, which were opposed to such controls, by encouraging them to move their business to London's eurodollar market.[68] The eurodollar market also provided an incentive to foreign investors to hold dollars or assets denominated in US dollars.[69]

After the United States had ceased converting foreign official dollar holdings into gold and devalued the dollar in 1971, Western European states, together with Japan, and within the framework of the IMF, aimed at reforms to save the system of pegged exchange rates. To make capital controls a more effective instrument, they proposed an amendment of the IMF's Articles of Agreement that would have given the IMF the competence to oblige its members to cooperate in imposing and enforcing capital controls.[70] Apart from providing for more effective capital

[64] The general prohibition is included in Art. VIII, Sec. 2(a) (providing for an exception if the IMF approves a restriction). Exceptions are found in Art. VII, Sec. 3(b) (scarce currency clause) and Art. XIV, Sec. 2 (for transitional arrangements).

[65] Capital controls are only prohibited if they restrict payments for current transactions (Art. VI, Sec. 3).

[66] Eichengreen, *Globalizing Capital*, n. 17 above, p. 94.

[67] Eric Helleiner, *States and the Reemergence of Global Finance: From Bretton Woods to the 1990s* (Ithaca NY: Cornell University Press, 1994), p. 84 et seq.

[68] Ibid.

[69] Ibid.

[70] Helleiner, *States and the Reemergence of Global Finance*, n. 67 above, p. 102 et seq.

controls, some IMF members further called for replacing the US dollar with an international, reserve currency to effectively reform and stabilise thy system of pegged exchange rates.[71] The French government, in particular, supported by its chief economists, had for a long time been a strong critic of the position of the US dollar as the system's key currency.[72] With the United States' unwillingness to address its balance of payments deficit and the unilateral decision to terminate its commitment to gold convertibility, the case for the creation of an international reserve currency became even stronger. Yet, the United States was not ready to lose its privilege, which was based upon the global demand for the US dollar as the preferred reserve currency. The United States therefore objected to such reform plans and prevented their adoption. Instead of joining in efforts to maintain a system of fixed exchange rates, the United States became a supporter of floating exchange rates[73] and of the liberalisation of financial markets in order to strengthen the position of the dollar.[74] Floating and the dismantling of capital controls eventually led to a significant expansion of transnational capital markets and trade in financial instruments not directly related to trade or direct investment.[75]

To keep global demand for the US currency high, it was furthermore important that natural resources, in particular petroleum, continued to be traded in dollars. Petrodollar recycling through US financial institutions became a way of binding oil-exporting states to the dollar. The extreme rises in oil prices in the 1970s – not only triggered by OPEC's exercise of its cartel power, but, in part, also caused by the high inflation rates in the United States[76] – meant that OPEC members held large amounts of dollars. These were not fully absorbed by investments in their domestic

[71] Eichengreen, *Globalizing Capital*, n. 17 above, p. 127.

[72] Kirshner, *Currency and Coercion*, n. 50 above, p. 192 et seq.

[73] The permission of floating exchange rates was codified in an amendment to the IMF's Articles of Agreement of 1978.

[74] Tabb, *Economic Governance in the Age of Globalization*, n. 61 above, p. 120. The US position was also supported by an increasing number of economists, among them von Hayek and Friedman, who supported floating as a market solution to the pricing of currencies.

[75] Ibid., p. 121.

[76] Legalisation of floating meant that governments were not prevented by international monetary law from engaging in monetary financing of their deficits leading to high inflation rates in many countries; see Eichengreen, *Globalizing Capital*, n. 17 above, p. 138.

economies.[77] The liberalisation of capital markets facilitated transnational investments of these 'petrodollars'. The United States government provided OPEC members, in particular Saudi Arabia, with a number of incentives to invest in US treasury bills, to deposit dollar reserves in US bank accounts, and not to diversify their portfolios through acquiring assets not denominated in US dollars.[78] Extensive investment in US securities by Saudi Arabia had the effect that the Saudi Arabian government did not support initiatives within OPEC to shift to a trading currency other than the US dollar.[79]

As a consequence of the petrodollar investments, US banks were holding significant amounts of petrodollars and had an interest in using them profitably. One such use was the extension of loans to developing countries, which was facilitated by the removal of restrictions on transnational capital transactions.[80] A justification for the extension of loans to developing countries was provided, *inter alia*, by the US government, which argued that unless the capital surplus of OPEC exporters was distributed to states that incurred payments deficits, it would pose an obstacle to global economic development.[81] A significant share of these loans was extended to developing countries which were themselves oil-exporting countries, such as Mexico, their oil deposits serving as a security.[82] The commercial banks making the loans to governments saw them as a safe alternative to foreign direct investment, given the inhospitable 'investment climate' in many developing countries due to their pursuit of import substitution industrialisation policies which involved nationalisation and other far-reaching

[77] Mahmoud El-Gamal and Amy Myers Jaffe, *Oil, Dollars, Debt and Crises: The Global Curse of Black Gold* (Cambridge: Cambridge University Press, 2010), p. 9.

[78] According to Tabb, Secretary of State Kissinger 'made clear that any effort to use dollars to buy control of American companies would not be tolerated', see Tabb, *Economic Governance in the Age of Globalization*, n. 61 above, p. 123; for implied threats by the US administration to influence OPEC investments, see, also, David Spiro, *The Hidden Hand of American Hegemony: Petrodollar Recycling and International Markets* (Ithaca NY: Cornell University Press, 1999), p. 31; El-Gamal and Myers Jaffe, *Oil, Dollars, Debt and Crises*, n. 77 above, p. 10.

[79] El-Gamal and Myers Jaffe, *Oil, Dollars, Debt and Crises*, n. 77 above, p. 174 (for a reaffirmation of this position in 2008).

[80] Money was also deployed for speculation in foreign exchange markets; see Tabb, *Economic Governance in the Age of Globalization*, n. 61 above, p. 123.

[81] Spiro, *The Hidden Hand of American Hegemony*, n. 78 above, p. 29.

[82] El-Gamal and Myers Jaffe, *Oil, Dollars, Debt and Crises*, n. 77 above, p. 84.

interventions by governments into the economy.[83] Developing country governments, on their part, welcomed these loans, as they were not tied to conditions as loans from official lenders such as the World Bank and the IMF were.[84] When the indebtedness of developing countries to US banks rose significantly, IMF managing director Johan Witteveen issued a warning in 1974 and recommended that lending should be channelled through official institutions such as the IMF in order to enable an equitable and prudent process. Yet, the US administration objected and banks downplayed the risks of lending and the resulting high levels of sovereign debt.[85]

It is well known how this story of 'petrodollar recycling' unfolded. Interest rates on the loans followed the London Interbank Offered Rate (LIBOR). And when, in 1979, the US Federal Reserve Board, under its newly appointed chairman Paul Volcker, raised interest rates to halt inflation in the United States, LIBOR surged and third-world indebtedness multiplied.[86] A further factor aggravating the debt crises in developing countries was the global recession and the fall in the prices of raw materials as well as the massive capital flight.[87] In a number of cases, starting during the 1982 debt crisis with Mexico, new loans were extended to the debtor states and the debt renegotiated. A crucial part of these rescue programmes was the conditionality of the aid, which required compliance with structural adjustment programmes prescribed by the IMF and the World Bank.[88] Frequently, not only were austerity measures part of conditionality, but also the reprivatisation of extractive industries, trade liberalisation and the promotion of foreign direct investment, *inter alia*, through the facilitation of administrative procedures.[89]

[83] Ibid., p. 110.

[84] Bergsten, 'The Threat from the Third World', n. 51 above, p. 103 et seq.

[85] Spiro, *The Hidden Hand of American Hegemony*, n. 78 above, p. 42 (noting that the US government actively discouraged international cooperation in petrodollar recycling).

[86] Vijay Prashad, *The Poorer Nations. A Possible History of the Global South* (London: Verso Books, 2012), p. 53 (noting that, when, in 1973, their external debt had amounted to 130 billion USD, in 1982 the debt level was 612 billion USD).

[87] El-Gamal and Myers Jaffe, *Oil, Dollars, Debt and Crises*, n. 77 above, p. 34; El-Gamal and Myers Jaffe make petrodollar recycling responsible not only for the debt crises in the 1970s but also subsequent ones (p. 19).

[88] Helleiner, *States and the Reemergence of Global Finance*, n. 67 above, p. 176 et seq.

[89] Zambia is a case in point, see John Craig, 'Putting Privatization into Practice: The Case of Zambia Consolidated Copper Mines Limited' (2001) 39 *Journal of Modern African Studies*, 389–410; Alastair Fraser and John Lungu, *For Whom the Windfalls? Winners & Losers in the Privatization of Zambia's Copper Mines* (CSTNZ/CCJDP, 2007).

Eric Helleiner points out that agreement to structural adjustment programmes on the part of Latin American states was not without alternative; that potential alternatives, such as obligatory capital repatriation and the implementation of strict capital controls, were not adopted because the élites in these countries themselves adhered to the neoliberal thought that informed structural adjustment.[90]

I wish to conclude this section with a number of observations: even though PSNR attributes jurisdiction over natural resources to peoples and governments as their representatives, the assertion of sovereignty and political control over extractive industries was accompanied by developments which have resulted in natural resource extraction today being largely market-led and transnationalised. The market has become the preferred allocation mechanism for exploitation and distribution.[91] Resource extraction in many countries has been reprivatised and become the subject of foreign direct investment protected by transnational economic law; primary commodities are predominately traded via exchanges and commodity derivatives provide a growing business for the financial industry. With the expansion and proliferation of commodity and capital markets, the scope for a natural resource politics – national as well as international – has diminished significantly. Resource-exporting countries experience difficulties when they wish to implement policies to reap a greater share of profits from extraction. High mobility of capital, for example, has made the taxation of corporate profits more difficult,[92] and an increasing number of trade agreements prohibit export tariffs which provide an alternative to taxation for governments to share in extraction profits.[93] The shift in trade from long-term supply contracts to spot-market trading provides an example of the limited opportunities for an international resource

[90] Helleiner, *States and the Reemergence of Global Finance*, n. 67 above, p. 181 et seq; on the weak collective bargaining power of debtor states due to the ad hoc nature of crisis lending, see Susan Strange, *States and Markets: An Introduction to International Political Economy* (London: Pinter Publishers, 1988), pp. 110 and 111.

[91] Olivier De Schutter and Katharina Pistor, *Governing Access to Essential Resources* (New York: Columbia University Press, 2015), p. 4.

[92] Reuven S. Avi-Yonah, 'Globalization, Tax Competition, and the Fiscal Crisis of the Welfare State' (2000) 113 *Harvard Law Review*, 1573–676.

[93] While the GATT itself does not prohibit export tariffs, a prohibition of export tariffs is included in a number of WTO accession protocols. The negotiation of export tariff prohibitions is moreover part of the EU's raw materials strategy, see Communication from the Commission to the European Parliament, the Council, the European Economic and Social Committee and the Committee of the Regions, 'Tackling the Challenges in Commodity Markets and on Raw Materials', COM (2011) 25 final.

politics. Trade through long-term contracts had allowed the parties to the contract not only to adjust and renegotiate the contractual terms in order to take account of changing interests and preferences, but also to strike deals which allowed them to exchange natural resources for other goods such as technology.[94] Such negotiated deals are not possible when primary commodities are traded via exchanges.

The turn from politics to markets has been accompanied by a shift in the function of law. On the one hand, the liberalisation and integration of financial markets has significantly curtailed the scope for politics and market intervention facilitated through law (e.g. market interventions negotiated within the framework of international commodity agreements or the adoption of capital controls) – this restriction being lauded by the proponents of neoliberalism as a 'disciplining' of governments. On the other hand, it has become a main function of law, international institutions and expert networks, such as the Bank for International Settlements, the Basle Committee on Banking Supervision (BCBS), and the International Organization of Securities Commissions, to protect financial stability in order to sustain these capital markets, given their proneness to recurring crises.[95]

IV.2 The Law of Money and Finance as Driver of Natural Resource Exploitation

The previous section focused on how developments in the political resource economy contributed to the dismantling of international monetary law (and politics) and the liberalisation of capital markets. In this section, now, I change perspective and take a closer look at how the political resource economy is being shaped by the law of money and public finance. I, first, turn to the law of public finance. I argue that a legal framework that strictly separates fiscal and monetary policy contributes to the dire state of public finances in many countries and thus incentivises resource extraction. Within a legal framework of austerity, resource extraction presents itself as an opportunity for both government and the public to reap a 'fair share' of the profits generated by transforming natural wealth into money. Second, I seek to deconstruct the notion of

[94] See Mahnoush Arsanjani, *International Regulation of Internal Resources: A Study of Law and Policy* (Charlottesville VA: University of Virginia Press, 1981), p. 187; China, in recent years, has concluded agreements with governments of African States to exchange development assistance for access to natural resources.

[95] See Helleiner, *States and the Reemergence of Global Finance*, n. 67 above, chapter 8.

'market supply' by outlining how private money creation stimulates extraction driven by a profit motive.

The conceptualisation by much of economic and legal scholarship of money as itself constituting a commodity – the main function of which is to serve as a medium of exchange – provides the justification for a strict separation between fiscal policy (as the responsibility of democratic government) and monetary policy (entrusted to independent central banks).[96] In the EU, this separation – and the concomitant isolation of monetary policy from democratic politics – is most pronounced. It finds expression, *inter alia*, in the 'prohibition of monetary financing' codified in Article 123 of the Treaty on the Functioning of the European Union. As a consequence of this prohibition, a state, in order to finance its budget, must either generate sufficient revenue through taxation, or borrow on capital markets. It cannot (and nor can the political organs of the EU) use sovereign monetary powers to generate public credit. The prohibition of the use of monetary powers to finance public expenditure, in combination with constitutionalised debt brakes and the mounting difficulty of governments to generate public revenue through taxation,[97] pave the way not only for austerity politics, but also for the sale of public – including natural – wealth.

When natural resources are not considered private property but the common heritage of a political collective (individual states or the international community), it is tempting for governments to consider them a potential source of public revenue.[98] Public

[96] I expand on the conceptual separation between monetary and fiscal policy in public law and scholarship, in Isabel Feichtner, 'Public Law's Rationalization of the Legal Architecture of Money: What might Legal Analysis of Money Become?' (2016) 17 *German Law Journal*, 875–905.

[97] Reasons are not only tax evasion and avoidance or tax competition but also lack of popular support for taxes if taxes do not translate into tangible benefits for taxpayers but rather serve to pay off sovereign debt and finance budget deficits, see Wolfgang Streeck and Daniel Mertens, 'Politik im Defizit: Austerität als fiskalpolitisches Regime' (2010) 3 *Der moderne Staat*, 7–29.

[98] On deep seabed mining as a potential source of revenue to finance economic development of poor states, see Richard N. Cooper, 'The Oceans as a Source of Revenue', in: Jagdish N. Bhagwati (ed.), *New International Economic Order, The North-South Debate* (Cambridge MA: The MIT Press, 1977), pp. 105–19. See also US President Donald Trump's Statement on the Paris Climate Accord of 1 June 2017: 'We have among the most abundant energy reserves on the planet, sufficient to lift millions of America's poorest workers out of poverty. Yet, under this agreement, we are effectively putting these reserves under lock and key, taking away the great wealth of our nation . . . '; available at: www.whitehouse.gov/briefings-statements/statement-president-trump-paris-climate-accord.

revenue can be derived from natural resource exploitation either if extraction is conducted by state enterprises whose profits flow directly into the public budget,[99] or if private miners pay royalties or taxes on their profits.[100] In the last decade, not only Latin American governments have turned to natural resource extraction as a strategy for economic development, prompting what a number of commentators criticise as neo-extractivism.[101] Small Pacific island states, too, seek to generate revenue from extraction. By becoming sponsors of deep-seabed mining enterprises they hope to share in the profits from mining deep seabed minerals that Article 136 of the United Nations Law of the Sea Convention designates as the common heritage of mankind.[102] And also in the highly indebted European states there has been renewed government interest in extraction. In 2012, at the height of the Eurocrisis, the Greek Prime Minister, Antonis Samaras, supported the Canadian mining company Eldorado's investments in large-scale gold-mining projects. As a consequence of intensified gold mining, Greece sought to become the largest exporter of gold in Europe.[103]

The growing interest in gold prompts the question of what makes gold attractive for investors – given that only a small fraction of the extracted

[99] A number of resource-rich states have established Sovereign Wealth Funds for the investment of resource revenues; see Macartan Humphreys, Martin E. Sandbu, 'Resource Funds', in: Macartan Humphreys, Jeffrey Sachs and Joseph Stiglitz (eds.), *Escaping the Resource Curse* (New York: Columbia University Press, 2007), pp. 194–234.

[100] Some economists argue that profits from natural resource extraction, as they are to be understood as economic rents should be taxed up to 100 per cent, see, for example, Paul Collier, *The Plundered Planet: Why we must – and How we can – Manage Nature for Global Prosperity* (Oxford: Oxford University Press, 2010), p. 88.

[101] Ulrich Brand, Kristina Dietz and Miriam Lang, 'Neo-Extractivism in Latin America. One Side of a New Phase of Global Capitalist Dynamics' (2016) 11 *Revista de Ciencia Política*, 125–59; Maristella Svampa, 'Resource Extractivism and Alternatives. Latin American Perspectives on Development', in: Miriam Lang and Dunia Mokrani (eds.), *Beyond Development: Alternative Visions from Latin America* (Transnational Institute/Rosa Luxembourg Foundation, 2013), pp. 117–43.

[102] I elaborate on the attempts by states to gain revenue from deep seabed mining in Isabel Feichtner, 'Sharing the Riches of the Sea. The Redistributive and Fiscal Dimension of Deep Seabed Exploitation' (2019) 30 *European Journal of International Law* 601–633.

[103] Deepa Babington and Lefteris Papadimas, 'Insight: Gold Mine Stirs Hope and Anger in Shattered Greece' (13 January 2014), *Reuters*, available at: www.reuters.com/article/us-greece-gold-insight/insight-gold-mine-stirs-hope-and-anger-in-shattered-greece-idUSBREA0C0DG20140113.

gold is used in (technology) production.[104] The reason may be found in an immediate money motive – not only of the governments licensing the mining operations (despite the devastating impact that gold-mining has on the environment and on the health of mine workers and local populations) – but also of private investors. Even though gold does not officially have the status of money, it does serve a monetary function. In times of political and economic instability, in particular, gold functions as a store of value, and demand for gold increases.[105] Thus, the interests of private investors and governments in extraction mutually reinforce each other: sovereign debt crises prompt investor demand for gold, and, in turn, this demand promises an opportunity for states to generate much needed revenue by licensing gold mining.

The justification of natural-resource extraction with the need to generate public revenue can be criticised by pointing to the flaws of treating money as a commodity and to the potential of monetary redesign to overcome a perpetual state of austerity.[106] A wealth of literature has sought to discredit the notion that money is a particular kind of exchange commodity, to reveal the credit function of money and its dependence on government power.[107] This line of scholarship can inform a redesign of monetary institutions that aims at making money and money's credit function serve the public, for example, in the form of a job guarantee.[108]

[104] See World Gold Council, Gold Demand Trends, available at: www.gold.org/goldhub/research/gold-demand-trends/gold-demand-trends-full-year-2018 (showing that the greatest share of demand relates to jewellery followed by bar and coin demand).

[105] Samuel K. Gayi and Janvier D. Nkurunziza, 'Trends in Minerals, Ores and Metals Prices', in: Paul A. Haslam and Pablo Heidrich (eds.), *The Political Economy of Natural Resources and Development: From Neoliberalism to Resource Nationalism* (London: Routledge, 2016), pp. 35–52, at 46; see, also, James Rickards, *The New Case for Gold* (New York: Penguin, 2016). It is not only gold, but also other natural resources, such as food, that have become a preferred object for financial investors in order to diversify and protect their portfolios from losses in times of economic recession.

[106] For John Maynard Keynes' critique of gold mining along these lines, see Maynard Keynes, *General Theory of Employment, Money and Interest* (Basingstoke: Palgrave Macmillan, 1936), chapter 10, section VI.

[107] See Knapp, *The State Theory of Money*, n. 4 above; Alfred Mitchell-Innes, 'What is Money?' (1913) *The Banking Law Journal*, 377–408; David Graeber, *Debt. The First 5,000 Years* (New York: Melville House, 2011); Christine Desan, *Making Money: Coins, Currency, and the Coming of Capitalism* (Oxford: Oxford University Press, 2014).

[108] For proposals to make monetary sovereignty serve public financing needs, see, for example, Abba P. Lerner, 'Functional Finance and the Federal Debt' (1943) 10 *Social Research*, 38–51, at 38 and writings of the so-called modern money theorists, for

I now turn to my second claim in this section, namely, that the current legal framework of money and finance calls into question justifications for extraction that rely on the notion of 'market supply'. Rather than the demand for minerals – for example, of societies that seek to implement substitution of fossil fuels with renewable energy – it may also be profit expectations that drive extraction. Above, I indicated how the conceptualisation of money as a commodity serves to restrict governments' monetary sovereignty, their power to spend money into existence, for example, by paying for public goods and services with government-issued money. Here I want to draw attention to the fact that most of today's money supply is not created by central banks, but by commercial banks. Profit expectation as the driving force for this private money-creation steers investment towards the extraction of natural resources as long as such extraction proves profitable, independent of any actual societal demand for the extracted minerals.

The rhetoric of resource policies, initiatives and strategies, be it on the part of the EU Commission, the German Federal Ministry of the Economy, or the Association of German Industry, regularly employs the notion of 'the market' as if the market was a natural occurrence. This market, thus the rhetoric goes, responds to the supply needs of the real economy; it should be kept free from distortions – this being a main claim of the EU resource initiative – so that it can ensure a fair distribution of natural resources.[109] Obviously, markets are highly contingent on the respective legal framework. Yet, while it is recognised that legislation shapes and transforms markets, be it through tax incentives or regulation, insufficient attention is paid to the market-shaping impact of private money creation. When German mining law, for example, is informed by the premise that mining licences are requested because the real economy demands extractive resources and that, consequently, mining enterprises fulfil a public-utility function by supplying industry with raw materials,[110] it ignores the fact that private money creation incentivises natural-resource extraction, and promotes natural-resource

example, William Mitchell, Randall Wray and Martin Watts, *Modern Monetary Theory and Practice: An Introductory Text* (North Charleston: CreateSpace, 2016).

109 See Communication from the Commission to the European Parliament, the Council, the European Economic and Social Committee and the Committee of the Regions, 'Tackling the Challenges in Commodity Markets and on Raw Materials', COM(2011) 25 final.

110 Federal Constitutional Court, *Garzweiler II*, judgment of 17 December 2013, 1 BvR 3139/08, 1 BvR 3386/08.

exploitation to an extent not necessarily related to the needs of the real economy.

As money theorists do not tire of stressing, it is a myth that banks are mere intermediaries between the depositors and the investors of money. Rather, private banks engage in money creation.[111] With each loan that they extend, they create a deposit, and thus so-called book money. Control by central banks of private money creation is limited. Commercial banks are required to hold a certain amount of reserves with the central bank, and this requirement is meant to restrict the amount of loans that they can extend. In practice, however, reserve requirements do not determine the volume of commercial loans. Instead, the reserve creation by central banks follows the decision of private banks to extend loans.[112] This private money creation is the motor for private economic enterprise. Banks extend credit to commercial enterprises that invest this money. In their investments, enterprises are driven by a profit motive, as they not only need to pay back their loans with interest, but also seek compensation for the entrepreneurial risk. Thus, the system of private money creation sets in motion a system based upon the pursuit of profit.[113] In this system, geared towards profit making and growth, the use of natural resources is particularly attractive. Contrary to workers, nature need not be compensated for her labour, and, as long as ongoing exploration and the spatial expansion of extraction prevents an actualisation of resource scarcity, the rents that the owners of natural resources (i.e. states or the international community) can demand are rather limited.[114] Moreover, and as I indicated above, financialisation and derivatives trade, to some degree, may have uncoupled investments in extractive resources from the needs of the real economy.[115]

111 See Michael McLeay, Amar Radia and Ryland Thomas, 'Money Creation in the Modern Economy' (2014) Q1 *Bank of England Quarterly Bulletin*, 14–27.

112 Thomas Mayer, *Die Neue Ordnung des Geldes. Warum wir eine Geldreform brauchen* (Munich: FBV, 2014), 36.

113 Hans Christoph Binswanger, *Die Wachstumsspirale. Geld, Energie und Imagination in der Dynamik des Marktprozesses*, 4th ed. (Marburg: Metropolis-Verlag, [2006] 2013); private money creation also promotes financial speculation which does not contribute to value creation in the real economy, but periodically leads to financial crises; see Hyman Minsky, *Stabilizing an Unstable Economy* (New Haven CT: Yale University Press, 1986).

114 Binswanger, *Die Wachstumsspirale*, n. 113 above, p. 192 et seq.

115 See n. 45 above.

Here, too, it should be noted that the extraction bias is an effect of the legal design of monetary and financial institutions. Institutional alternatives may prevent largely unrestricted private money creation or attenuate the linkage between credit and profit. In the course of the financial crisis, a number of institutional proposals for increased control of private money creation,[116] as well as for monetary (policy) design to steer money towards sustainable investments,[117] were presented and some have been taken up by politics, an example being the initiative by the government of Iceland to explore implementation of Josef Huber's plain money proposal.[118]

V Conclusion: Transformation of the Global Political Economy through Law?

Taking the international law principle of permanent sovereignty over natural resources as a starting point, this chapter has traced a number of transformations in political economy that have enhanced its exploitation bias, including through the transnationalisation of economic law, the demise of the Bretton Woods System of pegged exchange rates, as well as the liberalisation and proliferation of capital markets. By trying to understand law as a constitutive element in political economy, and not just as a potential remedy to exploitation, it sought to complicate global justice and governance accounts of, and their prescriptions for, resource extraction. The chapter may be read as a story of necessity explained by the

[116] See Gunther Teubner, 'A Constitutional Moment? The Logics of "Hitting the Bottom"', in: Poul F. Kjaer, Gunther Teubner and Alberto Febbrajo (eds.), *The Financial Crisis in Constitutional Perspective: The Dark Side of Functional Differentiation* (Oxford: Hart Publishing, 2011), pp. 3–42 (building on plain money proposals by economist Josef Huber and arguing that destructive tendencies of the economic system may only be contained by directly tackling and restricting the medium of the economic system, namely, money); others suggest to link money creation to resource use, see, for example, Richard Douthwaite and Bernard Lietaer, *The Ecology of Money* (Cambridge: Green Books, 1999).

[117] See, for example, Richard Murphy and Colin Hines, *Green Quantitative Easing. Paying for the Economy we Need* (Norfolk: Finance for the Future, 2010), available at: http://openaccess.city.ac.uk/16569.

[118] Frosti Sigurjonsson, 'Monetary Reform. A Better Monetary System for Iceland. A Report Commissioned by the Prime Minister of Iceland' (2015), building on Joseph Huber, *Monetäre Modernisierung. Zur Zukunft der Geldordnung: Vollgeld und Monetative*, 6th ed. (Marburg: Metropolis-Verlag, 2018).

industrialised economies' hunger for raw materials, structural state power, and the profit orientation of capital. Contingency enters the picture when I observe that, at various junctures in history, governments were confronted with choices and might have opted for alternative laws and institutions. Recognising structural causes for the expansion of extraction as well as exploring the institutional repertoire that may be derived from historical and comparative inquiry both are necessary prerequisites to engage in experimental institutional design with the aim of transforming political economy.[119] In this chapter, I merely indicate how a redesign of the legal institutions of money and finance might contain the expansion of extraction. Such redesign, for example, may enable political collectives to rely on other sources of credit and finance than capital markets and the exploitation of their natural wealth. As a consequence, permanent sovereignty over natural resources might indeed be operationalised so as to allow for democratic politics to determine how natural wealth should be treated, including the option not to extract.

[119] See Roberto Mangabeira Unger, *Democracy Realized: The Progressive Alternative* (London: Verso Books, 1998); Unger, *Free Trade Reimagined: The World Division of Labor and the Method of Economics* (Princeton NJ: Princeton University Press, 2007); Unger, *False Necessity: Anti-necessitarian Social Theory in the Service of Radical Democracy. From Politics, a Work in Constructive Social Theory* (London: Verso Books, 2004).

7

'Social Nature'

Political Economy, Science, and Law in the Anthropocene

JAYE ELLIS

Wotan: Geheimniss hehr hallt mir dein Wort:
weile, daß mehr ich wisse!
Erda: Ich warnte dich; du weißt genug:
sinn' in Sorg' und Furcht![1]
Richard Wagner, *Das Rheingold*

I Introduction

Will Steffen, a renowned climate scientist and scholar of the Anthropocene, wrote, in 2011, that '[h]umanity itself has become a global geophysical force, equal to some of the "great forces of Nature" in terms of Earth system functioning'.[2] But, as Dipesh Chakrabarty reminds us, there is a great distance between humanity as a global force and humans as agents.[3] Humanity has acquired awesome destructive capacities, but humans have little idea how to wield them.[4] This gap between knowledge and power – or, more

[1] *Wotan:* With mystic awe fills me thy word: go not till more thou tellest!
Erda: I warned thee; thou know'st enough; brood in care and fear!
Frederick Jamieson transl.

[2] Will Steffen, et al., 'The Anthropocene: From Global Change to Planetary Stewardship' (2011) 40 *AMBIO: Journal of the Human Environment*, 739–61, at 741.

[3] Dipesh Chakrabarty, 'Postcolonial Studies and the Challenge of Climate Change' (2012) 43 *New Literary History*, 1–18, at 14.

[4] This latter view is not universally shared: witness champions of the 'good Anthropocene', Ted Nordhaus and Michael Schellenberger, who made their name with their 'death of environmentalism' argument: Ted Nordhaus and Michael Schellenberger, *Break Through: From the Death of Environmentalism to the Politics of Possibility* (New York: Houghton Mifflin Harcourt, 2007); Ted Nordhaus, Michael Shellenberger and Jenna Mukuno, 'Ecomodernism and the Anthropocene' (2015) *Breakthrough Journal*, available at:

precisely, the means of deliberately channelling power to attain specific ends – remains stubbornly wide, despite the work of organisations such as the Intergovernmental Panel on Climate Change operating at the boundary between science and governance, and scientists such as Steffen, who have been working tirelessly to articulate and promote concepts such as the Anthropocene and its companion concept, the planetary boundaries, in the hope of providing political authorities with the context and frameworks which they need to articulate and pursue ecological objectives.

Scientists have become adept at communicating information about ecological risk, explaining the implications of their observations and conclusions in terms that resonate with the media, political authorities and civil society. Yet these notions of ecological risk are not readily translatable into political risk, such as the risk to a political party of losing office after having promoted, or failed to curtail, ecologically harmful activities. Political authorities do take legislative action against environmental risks, and these efforts have resulted in slowing of the rate of acceleration of environmental degradation in some regions, but the risk of ecological collapse continues to grow. One could also think in terms of ethical risk, but the complexity of causal chains, and the ethically neutral or positive nature of much behaviour harmful in its environmental consequences, muddy the translation from scientific knowledge to ethically informed behaviour, even if that knowledge may be the grounds for ethical conviction and political engagement.

One set of actors does seem attuned to scientific communications about ecological degradation: to wit, economic actors. Firms do seem capable of responding to communications about ecological risk under certain conditions, and other actors, including civil society organisations, have developed mechanisms for tapping into and amplifying the correlation made by economic actors between ecological and economic risk. One narrative about this correlation depends on the existence of a form of rationality operating at a societal level: the destruction of the ecological resources upon which humankind depends is irrational, and economic actors must

https://thebreakthrough.org/journal/issue-5/ecomodernism-and-the-anthropocene. For a critical response, see Clive Hamilton, *Earthmasters: The Dawn of the Age of Climate Engineering* (New Haven CT: Yale University Press, 2013).

be brought to understand that their own survival depends upon the exercise of restraint. But the nexus between ecological and economic risk is manifesting itself in a different, much less direct, way, one which operates through the individual rationalities of societal systems.[5] In broad outline, scientific communications are packaged for maximum ethical-political resonance, generating media attention, the development of ethical convictions, and the emergence of social movements. This process renders economic actors that profit from environmentally harmful behaviour potentially vulnerable, to the extent that channels and vehicles are created to translate ethical-political conviction into consumption and investment decisions. These channels and vehicles function by signalling to consumers and investors which firms are behaving in line with their convictions. As a result, the political economy becomes one of the most important *loci* for environmental regulation. These signals take the form of promises (consumption of this product is consonant with your ethical-political convictions) and threats (failure to abide by these standards will close off economic opportunities) that operate through, and alter, economic incentive structures.

At first glance, the heightened importance of translation processes among science, politics, and economics seems to leave law to one side. It is more accurate to say that a certain conception of law, whereby political consensus within a territorially bound population is expressed in a material law whose validity depends on the pursuit of political objectives, is of diminished relevance in global society. Indeed, leaving this concept of law to one side presents important advantages. A global law operating through the political economy crosses jurisdictional boundaries as freely as do money, products, and hazardous substances. Its norms do not depend on consensus-producing collective decision making, nor do they rely on cumbersome regulatory agencies or legal instruments whose substance is rapidly made obsolete. But, although one of the most important roles of global ecological law may be to structure the translation from scientific to economic logic, this does not mean that it will thereby lose all normative functionality. The normativity of global

[5] Niklas Luhmann, *Ökologische Kommunikation. Kann die moderne Gesellschaft sich auf ökologische Gefährden einstellen?*, 5th ed. (Wiesbaden: VS Verlag für Sozialwissenschaften, 2008), chapter.

ecological law arises, in particular, from its attunement to the normativity inherent in the production of scientific knowledge.[6]

Cognitive instruments, such as indicators, standards, benchmarks, and criteria for quantifying the performance of firms, constitute an important and growing part of global law, but require other types of legal norms in order to function as part of a system. These instruments, and the networks both through which they are transmitted and which give them their effectiveness, are constituted, put in motion, and irritated, by law. Scientific knowledge is built, after all, on processes of evaluation, weighing, and judging, as well as persuasion, all depending on norms that govern the scientific enterprise, stabilising expectations about what counts as good, rigorous, reliable science. By productively misunderstanding these norms as legal norms,[7] the processes through which these cognitive instruments are developed come to be governed by law. As Harm Schepel has put it, law comes to provide not 'regulation, but regulation of self-regulation'.[8]

In what follows, I will discuss two boundary objects that attempt to bridge the gap between scientific insights and responses on the part of political and legal authorities, the Anthropocene and planetary boundaries. Both concepts represent attempts by scientists to communicate to governance authorities the urgency of ecological crises and the need for a swift and decisive response. I then address two broad categories of responses to these concepts, based upon Bruno Latour's distinction between *jus naturalis* – assuming that the content of law must be dictated by the non human world – and *jus gentium*, through which the otherness of the non-human world is recognised although the means may nevertheless be available to engage with it. Taking my cue from the concept of *jus gentium*, I acknowledge that global ecological law will continue to be characterised by cognitive instruments and practices, such as standards and indicators whose content depends on scientific inputs and which operate mainly through the political economy. However, I argue that there remains scope for normativity, that is, legal norms that are resistant to learning in the face of disappointment, and which steer both the confection and the operation of these instruments.

[6] William Rehg, *Cogent Science in Context: The Science Wars, Argumentation Theory, and Habermas* (Cambridge MA: The MIT Press, 2009).

[7] Gunther Teubner, 'The Two Faces of Janus: Rethinking Legal Pluralism' (1991) 13 *Cardozo Law Review*, 1443–62.

[8] Harm Schepel, *The Constitution of Private Governance: Product Standards in the Regulation of Integrating Markets* (Oxford-Portland OR: Hart Publishing, 2005), p. 29.

II Science at the Boundary

A number of prominent earth systems scientists have – apparently – concluded that it is not enough to generate data and scientific communications about environmental degradation; they need to speak more directly to society and not just to a small group of interlocutors within governments. Two highly influential concepts generated for these purposes are the Anthropocene and planetary boundaries. The concept of the Anthropocene was introduced in a note written by two scientists, one a Nobel laureate,[9] who argue that the scale and scope of the human impact on the planet has led the Earth out of the relatively stable conditions characteristic of the Holocene into a new geological epoch. The concept has proven to be immensely influential, and has provoked much debate regarding the implications for the ethical obligations of humans towards the non-human world, and, building on such arguments, for politics. Less attention has been paid to the implications for law, though Bruno Latour, as mentioned above, has opened an interesting debate on two possible approaches, *jus naturalis* and *jus gentium.* Latour acknowledges the loss of (perceived) human control over the forces of nature, which come, once again, to be conceived of as savage and uncontrollable:[10]

> Since the scientific revolution, the objectivity of a world without humans had offered a solid ground for a sort of undisputed *jus naturalis* – if not for religion and morality, at least for science and law. At the time of the counter-Copernican revolution, when we turn toward the former solid ground of natural law, what do we find? The traces of our action are visible everywhere! And not in the older way that the Male Western Subject dominated the wild and savage world of nature through His courageous, violent, sometimes hubristic dream of control. No, this time we encounter, just as in the old prescientific and nonmodern myths, an agent which gains its name of 'subject' because he or she might be subjected to the vagaries, bad humor, emotions, reactions, and even revenge of another agent, who also gains its quality of 'subject' because it is also subjected to his or her action. It is in this radical sense that humans are no longer submitted to the diktats of objective nature, since what comes to them is also an intensively

[9] Paul J Crutzen and Eugene F. Stoermer, 'The "Anthropocene"' (2000) 41 *Global Change Newsletter*, 17–18. For a more fulsome and highly influential presentation and analysis of the concept, see Will Steffen, Paul J Crutzen and John R McNeill, 'The Anthropocene: Are Humans now Overwhelming the Great Forces of Nature?' (2007) 36 *AMBIO: Journal of the Human Environment*, 614–21. Steffen is a chemist and renowned climate change scientist.

[10] William Cronon, 'The Trouble with Wilderness, or Getting Back to the Wrong Nature', in: Cronon (ed.), *Uncommon Ground: Rethinking the Human Place in Nature* (New York: W.W. Norton, 1996), pp. 69–90.

> subjective form of action. To be a subject is not to act autonomously in front of an objective background, but to share agency with other subjects that have also lost their autonomy.[11]

In response, Latour argues that '[t]he best we can hope for is to stick to a new sort of *jus gentium* that would protect us against one another and against … "the revenge of Gaïa".'[12] In other words, it is not Gaïa who gives us law; rather, a law that forms the basis for negotiating and interacting with this foreign subject is crafted within society. Importantly, this *jus gentium* does not depend on complete and holistic knowledge of the subject which it purports to govern; quite the opposite: it is a law for strangers, based upon assumptions of structural uncertainty and unknowability.

We must now consider who the 'we' who are crafting this law might be, and how to conceive of the subject that 'we' ourselves face. As we have seen, one influential implication of the Anthropocene is humankind as a planetary force.[13] Many scholars have responded by concluding that the lesson of the Anthropocene is that there is no longer a meaningful distinction between inside (society) and outside (nature).[14] This (mis-)appropriation of the concept of social nature, or the construction of the concept of nature by humans,[15] may be due to confusion of the categories of humankind and the human agent. Humankind crosses one planetary boundary after another as an *inadvertent* result of human agency. As Chakrabarty puts it, 'human beings have tumbled into being a geological agent through our own decisions', but ecological modification on a planetary scale 'has been an unintended consequence of human choices'.[16] Humans as agents deploy this agency within increasingly narrow limits: as Clive Hamilton notes, unprecedented power is acquired

[11] Bruno Latour, 'Agency at the Time of the Anthropocene' (2014) 45 *New Literary History*, 1–18, at 5.

[12] Ibid., at 5. James Lovelock, *The Revenge of Gaia: Why the Earth is Fighting Back – and How we can Still Save Humanity* (London: Penguin Books, 2006). Gaïa is the term borrowed from Greek mythology by James Lovelock to represent the Earth as a living organism: James Lovelock, *Gaia: A New Look at Life on Earth* (Oxford: Oxford University Press, 2000).

[13] Dipesh Chakrabarty, 'The Climate of History: Four Theses' (2009) 35 *Critical Inquiry*, 197–222, at 206. Chakrabarty, n. 3 above, at 9.

[14] See, for example, Jedediah Purdy, *After Nature: A Politics for the Anthropocene* (Cambridge MA: Harvard University Press, 2015).

[15] Bruce Braun and Noel Castree (eds.), *Remaking Reality: Nature at the Millenium* (London: Routledge, 1998).

[16] Chakrabarty, n. 13 above, at 210. Chakrabarty notes that '[w]e have stumbled into it'. Ibid., at 217.

along with unprecedented vulnerability.[17] There can be no comprehensive political response to the Anthropocene because 'there is no "humanity" that can act as a self-aware agent . . . no corresponding "humanity" that in its oneness can act as a political agent'.[18] One can go further and argue that there is no society that can respond to ecological crisis, either. As Niklas Luhmann points out, we already know what needs to be done: reduce emissions, restrain or reverse population growth, curtail resource exploitation. But, in stating the problem (and its solution) in this manner, Luhmann argues that society is taken for an agent whose behaviour could be changed by way of information and exhortation.[19] Not only is society not an agent, but it has no summit or centre; none of its subsystems is capable of making and implementing decisions on behalf of society.[20]

The planetary boundaries concept is a declination of the Anthropocene, identifying a series of boundaries which, if respected, might permit the avoidance of catastrophic environmental change. The concept was proposed by a group of mainly natural scientists in a 2009 article entitled 'A Safe Operating Space for Humanity'.[21] The authors identify nine key Earth system processes[22] and seek to quantify the boundary beyond which degradation or perturbation of each process would result in unacceptable environmental change. The authors are at pains to point out that the boundaries and supporting data are no more than a 'proposed framework' subject to multiple sources of uncertainty.[23]

[17] Clive Hamilton, *Defiant Earth: The Fate of Humans in the Anthropocene* (Cambridge-Malden MA: Polity Press, 2017), chapter 4. Ibid., at chapter 2.

[18] Chakrabarty, n. 3 above, at 14.

[19] Luhmann, n. 5 above, at 164.

[20] Ibid., at 166.

[21] Johan Rockström, et al., 'A Safe Operating Space for Humanity' (2009) 461 *Nature*, 472–5. Johan Rockström, et al., 'Planetary Boundaries: Exploring the Safe Operating Space for Humanity' (2009) 14 *Ecology and Society*, 32.

[22] Highly provisional numeric boundaries were proposed for climate change, ocean acidification, stratospheric ozone, the biogeochemical nitrogen and phosphorous cycles, global freshwater use, land system change, and rate of loss of biodiversity. Two additional, non-specified, boundaries are chemical pollution and atmospheric aerosol loading: Rockström et al., 'Planetary Boundaries' n. 21 above.

[23] The authors state:

> Much of the uncertainty in quantifying planetary boundaries is due to our lack of scientific knowledge about the nature of the biophysical thresholds themselves, the intrinsic uncertainty of how complex systems behave, the ways in which other biophysical processes such as feedback mechanisms interact with the primary control variable, and uncertainty regarding the allowed time of overshoot of a critical control variable in the Earth System before a threshold is

Among the responses prompted by the paper have been those of political scientists, which are evocative of Latour's *jus naturalis*:[24] the laws of nature, as revealed by scientific research into Earth systems, are taken up as laws for society. These scholars have generally taken as read that the institutional response must be global – or, more specifically, international.[25]

This instrumental approach, in which governance is reduced to a planning exercise, fails to capture the potential of the planetary boundaries concept to mediate between science and other social systems, such as law, politics, and economics. The boundaries are, in my view, better understood as proxies for the much vaster and more abstract concept of environmental degradation, and the concept of safe operating-space is a proxy for concepts such as ecosystem integrity that are not directly subject to quantification. They provide a basis for the construction, within social systems, notably law, of models of scientific knowledge of ecosystems that can then be used to generate legal and political communications – but not in the form of blueprints for, or roadmaps to, sustainability that work backwards from ecological objectives to the various forms of behaviour that will be required to realise them.[26] State-based collective decision making based upon some conception of societal values or upon the public good, combined with legislation that takes the

crossed. This generates a zone of uncertainty around each threshold. The nature and size of that zone is critical in determining where to place the planetary boundary.

Ibid., at 3.

24 This is hardly a metaphor, in the minds of some observers. See, for example, Peter Burdon, Exploring Wild Law: The Philosophy of Earth Jurisprudence (2011); Cormac Cullinan, *Wild Law: A Manifesto for Earth Justice* (Totnes: Green Books, 2011).

25 Frank Biermann, '"Earth System Governance" as a Crosscutting Theme of Global Change Research' (2007) 17 *Global Environmental Change*, 326–37; Frank Biermann, *Earth System Governance: World Politics in the Anthropocene* (Cambridge MA: The MIT Press, 2014); Will Steffen, et al., 'Planetary Boundaries: Guiding Human Development on a Changing Planet' (2015) 347 *Science*, 736–48. Biermann appears to be an exception as he recognises non-governmental actors as agents, that is, actors possessing governance authority, but most of his attention is devoted to the participation of civil society organisations in norm-creation within governmental and intergovernmental *fora*; public-private partnerships; and epistemic communities such as networks of science. His calls for reform of earth system governance are focused entirely on state-based agencies and institutions, notably strengthening the United Nations' capacity to oversee partnerships and creating additional intergovernmental agencies and organisations: Biermann, this note above, chapters 3 and 4.

26 In the absence of direct communication between social systems, each system, in order to interact with others, works from a model of those other systems; see Gunther Teubner, *Law as an Autopoietic System* (Oxford-Cambridge MA: Wiley-Blackwell, 1993), 78–80.

form of social engineering, have failed to keep humanity within the safe operating space defined by the planetary boundaries for good reason, having to do – in part – with the nature of environmental degradation and – in part – with the interactions between society and nature.

II.1 The Uniqueness of the Ecological Challenge

The distinction between humanity as a force and humans as agents helps us to understand why ecological degradation is so difficult for governance systems and structures to grasp. The complexity and dynamism of ecosystems render causal links between perturbation and consequence difficult to identify because of the indirect, unpredictable manner in which ecosystems respond to perturbation. Harmful effects are thus observed at some distance in time and space from the interventions that brought them about. As Kerry Whiteside observes, prudential reasoning cannot be relied on to discover the links between our actions and their environmental effects; they are rendered visible to us through the mediation of scientists. Once actors know what impacts are being caused by their actions, they may still fail to change their behaviour: and because these impacts arise behind the backs of actors, as it were, in the form of unintended consequences of activities oriented towards other goals, the fact of harmful outcomes does not necessarily generate a sense of stigma associated with wrongdoing.[27] Even actors committed to reducing their ecological footprints often lack the means to do so: it serves little use to condemn driving in a city in which public transport is inadequate, turning on lights in a region in which electricity is generated by coal, or consuming produce grown on industrialised farms in a market in which organic produce is expensive.

Among the myriad objectives pursued by environmental civil society organisations and movements is the subordination of economic to ethical logic: economic actors should either be brought to recognise and act in accordance with their ethical obligations towards the environment, or they should be compelled by political authorities to act in accordance with the public good. Ecological objectives have a clear public interest nature and, arguably, should

[27] Kerry H. Whiteside, *Precautionary Politics: Principle and Practice in Confronting Environmental Risk* (Cambridge MA: The MIT Press, 2006), 93.

therefore be pursued only through public institutions.[28] It seems, at first glance, that this could hardly be otherwise: it is often assumed that such an ethically oriented law would have to be produced by a political authority that could legitimately claim to speak both on behalf of, and in the name of, an already-constituted public. The authority of law is thus grounded either discursively, or through the concordance of the substance of legal rules with the material aims to be pursued. If the latter, this amounts to saying that the validity of legal rules depends on the validation by science of their content; in other words, the way is paved for a thorough-going technocracy. To avoid such an unpalatable outcome, the possibility of creating the means for public participation in the production of scientific knowledge is entertained, but very often this objective is merely evoked without further discussion of how it is to be pursued or what its implications might be. As to the form of law in this scenario, it is highly material and instrumentalised, taking the form of social regulation designed to engineer a particular outcome. In short – ironically, given the ethically charged nature of the project – it is a highly cognitive form of law: the validity of legal rules depends not on the manner of their adoption or their grounding in shared understanding or on any other ethical-political grounds, but on the material results that their implementation brings about.[29]

Promoting environmental integrity may be a matter of ethical-political conviction, but acting on this conviction is an immense cognitive challenge. Even if actors have excellent information about the environmental impacts of their activities and can find the means to act on that information, the complexity of human inputs and environmental consequences would overwhelm even the most conscientious and resourceful among us. Law conceived of as social regulation, and politics conceived of as collective decision making, are not up to the challenge even at a local or regional level, and are completely overwhelmed at a global level. Furthermore, environmental regulation possessing the complexity required to steer actors' behaviour in sustainable directions would result in an unbearably dense thicket of legal rules. The quantity of information and the

[28] Armin von Bogdandy, Matthias Goldmann and Ingo Venzke, 'From Public International Law to International Public Law: Translating World Public Opinion into International Public Authority' (2017) 28 *European Journal of International Law*, 115–45.

[29] Niklas Luhmann, *Law as a Social System* (Oxford: Oxford University Press, 2004), p. 196 et seq.

speed with which it must circulate within society indicate the need for a networked approach which facilitates the transmission of information about scientific conclusions, the environmental risks generated by economic actors, consumer behaviour, and related issues across various nodes, permitting actions to be observed and responded to without the need for extensive coordination, deliberation, or consensus.[30]

There is yet another reason for the strong cognitive tendency of environmental law, namely, the time of ecosystems. The complexity and resilience of ecosystems permit them to absorb change while maintaining critical functions – until, that is, their resilience is overcome by the rate or extent of those changes, when they can move very rapidly from one point of equilibrium, or basin of attraction, to another.[31] Due to the complexity of ecosystems and the rapidity with which degradation can occur once tipping points are reached, scientific insights into ecosystems are themselves subject to ongoing change.[32] When environmental legal rules take the form of material standards grounded in scientific knowledge, they must be constantly amended in order to stave off obsolescence. Scholars of ecological governance who work closely with ecologists have been arguing for decades that the objectives of environmental law must shift from the production of 'good' ecosystems – possessing desirable characteristics and resistant to change – to the maintenance of ecosystem resilience. These scholars call for legal regimes that are flexible, capable of learning and adaptation, and responsive to ecosystemic changes and the resulting changes in the scientific understandings of ecosystem dynamics.[33]

[30] See Ladeur, Chapter 12 in this volume.

[31] Crawford S. Holling, 'Understanding the Complexity of Economic, Ecological, and Social Systems' (2001) 4 *Ecosystems*, 390–405; J.B. Ruhl, 'Thinking of Environmental Law as a Complex Adaptive System: How to Clean Up the Environment by Making a Mess of Environmental Law' (1997) 34 *Houston Law Review*, 933–1002.

[32] Due to the extreme accelerations of ecological time under conditions of climate change, adjustments to scientific outlooks on the progression of phenomena such as melting ice caps, coral reef bleaching, and ocean temperatures are broadcast through the media with such alarming regularity that they cease to alarm.

[33] Governance regimes possessing these features are referred to collectively as adaptive management: Crawford S. Holling, *Adaptive Environmental Assessment and Management* (Caldwell NJ: The Blackburn Press, 1978); Carl Folke, et al., 'Adaptive Governance of Social-ecological Systems' (2005) 30 *Annual Review of Environment and Resources*, 441–73 (2005); Jonas Ebbesson, 'The Rule of Law in Governance of Complex Socio-ecological Changes' (2010) 20 *Global Environmental Change*, 414–22.

III Towards a New Paradigm of Global Ecological Law

One obvious candidate as a governance technique or technology capable of functioning relatively well within the approach sketched above is a calculative approach operating through goals, benchmarks, and indicators. This calculative approach is particularly well adapted to operate in the political economy, given the relative ease with which indicators can be translated into price signals and other information that is legible within markets. Perhaps the best known of the planetary boundaries is the 2°C limit for global warming – that is, average global temperature increases should be kept below 2° C from pre-industrial times.[34] The immense complexity of climate science clearly cannot operate as a blueprint for climate governance, any more than the planetary boundaries can so operate for the protection of global ecosystems. Instead, a wide array of indicators and metrics have been devised, including a standard unit of measure for greenhouse gases, methods of accounting for inventories of greenhouse gases sequestered in sinks, such as forests, wetlands, and soil, means of calculating emissions in various sectors of activity, and, importantly, carbon pricing.

These calculative approaches are in widespread use in national, transnational, and international law in a vast array of sectors. They are highly controversial, in particular, when they are connected directly, as in the sale of carbon emission permits, or indirectly, as in certification of consumer products, to market mechanisms.[35] The network logic through which these techniques operate is better suited to the time and space over which governance of ecological risk must extend, and vastly better adapted

[34] The 2°C limit has for some time been regarded as too high; the Paris Agreement sets it as an outer limit, with states called upon to aim instead for warming of no more than 1.5°C. The Intergovernmental Panel on Climate Change recently concluded that catastrophic impacts would result from a 2°C increase: Intergovernmental Panel on Climate Change, Global Warming of 1.5°C: an IPCC Special Report on the Impacts of Global Warming of 1.5°C above Pre-industrial Levels and Related Global Greenhouse Gas Emission Pathways, in the Context of Strengthening the Global Response to the Threat of Climate Change, Sustainable Development, and Efforts to Eradicate Poverty (2018).

[35] For such critical perspectives, see, for example, Chris Methmann, 'The Sky is the Limit: Global Warming as Global Governmentality' (2013) 19 *European Journal of International Relations*, 69–91; Erik Gómez-Baggethun and Manuel Ruiz-Pérez, 'Economic Valuation and the Commodification of Ecosystem Services' (2011) 35 *Progress in Physical Geography: Earth and Environment*, 613–28; Christoph Görg, *Societal Relationships with Nature: A Dialectical Approach to Environmental Politics*, in: Andrew Biro (ed.), *Critical Ecologies: The Frankfurt School and Contemporary Environmental Crises* (Toronto: University of Toronto Press, 2011), pp. 43–72.

to the complexity of this governance. The existence of multiple nodes that process and circulate information has important advantages over structures that depend on centralised forms of collective decision making requiring strong convergence on objectives and a high degree of consensus on the means through which these objectives are to be pursued. The diffuse nature of ecological damage and the myriad, apparently innocent decisions and acts that drive it, work against the translation of ecological risk into political risk,[36] or, to put it another way, these characteristics drastically reduce the resonance of societal concerns about ecological destruction for the political system. The economic system, on the other hand, is much more easily irritated by the ecological convictions held by consumers when the means are at hand to convey information about the ecological risks posed by products on the market, thus amplifying these irritations through a vast number of apparently innocuous decisions about purchases and investments.

Consider regulatory techniques used by transnational orders in the context of the management of the risks posed by chemical substitution. The actors primarily involved include state agencies, international organisations, private authorities, firms, and individuals in the roles of citizen, consumer, and stakeholder. Regulatory instruments include lists,[37] performance ratings,[38] self-evaluation

[36] Luhmann describes political risk in this context as the risk that an environmental measure 'will not pay off politically'; see Niklas Luhmann, *Risk: A Sociological Theory* (Abingdon: Routledge, 1993), p. 64. Conversely, a government could conceivably be punished at the ballot box for failing to address an ecological risk.

[37] An influential example is the International Chemical Secretariat's (ChemSec) SIN (Substitute it now) list of substances of very high concern (SVHC), which is simply a reproduction of the European Union chemicals regulation, REACH: available at: https://chemsec.org/business-tool/sin-list/about-the-sin-list, accessed 21 November 2018. Its deployment by ChemSec greatly amplifies the resonance of this list: for example, the names of producers of SIN-listed chemicals are also published: SIN Producers, available at: https://chemsec.org/business-tool/sin-producers, and chemicals on the list are presented in a searchable and highly accessible database: http://sinlist.chemsec.org, accessed 21 November 2018. This list is complemented by a 'SINimilarity list' of chemicals belonging to the same chemical group or having similar structures, available at: http://sinimilarity.chemsec.org, accessed 21 November 2018.

Another example of a listing approach is the Chemicals of High Concern list developed by the US civil society organisation Safer Chemicals, Healthy Families. Their Hazardous 100+ list draws from the lists of six regulatory agencies: https://saferchemicals.org/methodology, accessed 21 November 2018.

[38] Safer Chemicals, Healthy Families produces an annual report card of the chemical safety performance of large US retailers based in the first instance on publicly available data, available at: https://retailerreportcard.com//retailers, accessed 21 November 2018.

tools,[39] voluntary standards,[40] and certifications.[41] In a slightly different register are supply chain management tools developed by retailers, be they individually[42] or in collaboration with one another.[43] As is typical of global legal authorities, these actors reference one another, for example, by including one another's certifications or standards into their own performance criteria, and interact extensively with state-based legal instruments and institutions, for example, by incorporating legislative standards into their evaluative instruments. Incentives and sanctions often bleed into one another: firms with poor environmental reviews are invited to engage in processes to improve their performance and thus be rewarded with positive publicity. At the same time, by acting simultaneously on consumer preference, the behaviour of regulatory authorities, and firms and industry associations, they may, in some contexts, be capable of generating disincentives and possibly even sanctions in the form of obstacles to markets or lucrative contracts.[44] This is more obviously the case with supply-chain

[39] See, for example, BizNGO's Chemical Footprint Project, which relies mainly on carrots such as publication of (voluntarily produced) footprint reports and pledges of support by firms, available at: www.chemicalfootprint.org/results.

[40] These include the Higg Index produced by the Sustainable Apparel Corporation, available at: https://apparelcoalition.org/the-higg-index.

[41] The Green Chemistry and Commerce Council is one of the organisations that amplifies the impact of certification programmes by listing and grouping them on its website. Some prominent examples include Ecologo, available at: https://industries.ul.com/environment/certificationvalidation-marks/ecologo-product-certification, Green Seal, available at: www.greenseal.org, and GreenScreen Certified, available at: www.greenscreenchemicals.org/certified.

[42] Prominent examples include Walmart (Walmart, Supplier Sustainability Assessment: 15 Questions for Suppliers (2009), available at: http://az204679.vo.msecnd.net/media/documents/r_3863.pdf. See, also, Larry Catá Backer, 'Economic Globalization and the Rise of Efficient Systems of Global Private Law Making: Walmart as Global Legislator' (2007) 39 *Connecticut Law Review*, 1739–84) and The Gap, available at: www.gapinc.com/content/gapinc/html/sustainability/ca-transparency-insupplychainsact.html; see, also, Larry Catá Backer, 'Multinational Corporations as Objects and Sources of Transnational Regulation' (2007) 14 *ILSA Journal of International and Comparative Law*, 499–523.

[43] In the wake of the Rana Plaza disaster, the Alliance for Bangladesh Worker Safety was founded by a group of major apparel firms: see www.bangladeshworkersafety.org; see, also, Larry Catá Backer, 'Theorizing Regulatory Governance within its Ecology: The Structure of Management in an Age of Globalization' (2018) 24 *Contemporary Politics*, 607–30.

[44] See the discussion of the softening of the distinction between power and influence, and of the questionable association between power and the capacity to administer negative sanctions in Poul F. Kjaer, 'The Concept of the Political in the Concept of Transnational Constitutionalism: A Sociological Perspective', in: Christian Joerges

management, in which compliance with codes of conduct is the price of admission to business with the relevant firm, but a choice not to belong to the club of certified producers or top-ranked retailers could constitute a withholding of a benefit that is, in the light of its potential economic impact, not meaningfully different from a sanction.

Larry Catá Backer argues that clothing retailer The Gap's Code of Vendor Conduct is in essence a labour code imposed on its suppliers, similar both in its content and overall objectives to governmental regulation.[45] While clearly a self-interested move on The Gap's part, this self-interest will not be promoted without (at least the perception of) the promotion of the interests of the much wider constituency of workers in the supply chain. He notes that, unlike the context of state-based regulation, the constituencies at the centre of these regulatory efforts, that is to say,

> the business people operating supplier factories, or their subcontractors, the children and their families, and the local communities in which all of these activities occur ... seem to be cut out of the process. Things are done on their behalf. Working conditions are improved to better their environment. Business relationships are changed on the basis of values that might or might not be shared by local business. Yet there is little expectation that the objects of all these activities will actually participate actively in the formation and elaboration of standards and enforcement norms.[46]

As a result, 'control might be every bit as strong under the harmonizing regimes of economic private regulation ... as in the old days of direct political colonialism'.[47]

Backer is also aware, however, of the advantages of contract over public law in contexts such as these. He argues that state-based law could be reoriented away from public regulation for the pursuit of a particular set of values towards requirements for information disclosure, the information of which could then be deployed to guide consumption and investment decisions. Privately held values could, in this way, be channelled through decisions and behaviour within markets to generate incentives for economic actors to act in

(ed.), *After Globalisation: New Patterns of Conflict and Their Sociolgical and Legal Recontructions*, 309 (Oslo: ARENA, 2011), pp. 285–321, at 309.

45 Backer, n. 42 above, at 511.

46 Ibid., at 522.

47 Ibid., at 523.

the public interest.[48] In this manner, broad and deep consensus across multiple cultures on the public goods that should be pursued is not required – something that state-based political institutions are ill-suited to accomplish in any event.[49] Backer nevertheless sees an important role for the state in compelling the production of information, as well as verifying and circulating it, objectives which he argues that '[t]he state is in a unique position to ensure'.[50] However, in many contexts, the actors that are in the best position to produce high-quality information are those that generate the environmental risks about which information is sought, namely, firms. The necessary incentives could potentially be generated by states through negative sanction, as Backer suggests, but private transnational orders also have the capacity to impose sanctions on firms that fail to generate the necessary information. Furthermore, they do not face the jurisdictional boundaries within which state agencies must operate, and may, in some instances, be more effectively integrated into transnational networks through which information about non-compliant behaviour can be rapidly circulated. By increasing the resonance of such information, transnational orders put into play an effective, if indirect, sanctioning mechanism. Many such orders have a demonstrated capacity to translate communications by producing compact, but nevertheless complex, packages of meaning, or social components,[51] that do not transfer meaning across boundaries as such, but do make it more likely that information will be perceived within another social system as relevant.[52]

48 Larry Catá Backer, 'From Moral Obligation to International Law: Disclosure Systems, Markets and the Regulation of Multinational Corporations' (2007) 39 *Georgetown Journal of International Law*, 591–633, at 592–3.

49 Ibid., at 620.

50 Ibid., at 629.

51 Rudolf Stichweh, 'Transfer in Sozialsystemen: Theoretische Überlegungen', in: Vanessa Duss, et al. (eds.), *Rechtstransfer in der Geschichte: Legal Transfer in History* (Munich: Martin Meidenbauer, 2006), pp. 1–13, at 3.

52 Jaye Ellis, 'The Role of Translation in Transnational Governance' (2017) 22 *Tilburg Law Review*, 165–84. Poul F. Kjaer argues that many global legal norms are norms oriented toward connectivity; they are 'aimed at facilitating the separation, transmission, and incorporation of social components from one context to another': Poul F. Kjaer, 'Constitutionalizing Connectivity: The Constitutional Grid of World Society' (2018) 45 *Journal of Law and Society*, Special Supplement: Societal Constitutions in Transnational Regimes pp. 114–34, at 126– 7.

To the extent that these social components are influential, and possess the capacity not only to change incentive structures, but also, in some contexts, to sanction, the processes through which they are confected will come to be highly contentious. Many economic actors have seen this clearly, as manufactured controversies over the risks posed by tobacco, climate change, and chemical risk, all demonstrate. A result is that negotiation, deliberation, and contestation are pushed out of political and into scientific arenas, to the detriment of public perceptions of scientific knowledge and scientists. Once these battles have been fought and won, it would appear that the law has little to do but rather mechanically apply categories that have been shaped elsewhere.[53] This is a development that Luhmann warned against. Yet the complexity of ecosystems and the human impacts upon them create immense obstacles to a formal law featuring rules of general application. The function of a general rule such as the obligation to take reasonable care to avoid harming others is sharply limited in a context in which lawyers and judges cannot rely on prudential reasoning either to identify the content of the standard of care or to trace the causal links between a defendant's fault and a plaintiff's injury. But this does not mean that the norms of global ecological law must become cognitivised through and through. Rather, stabilisation of expectations could occur at different sites, notably, at the boundaries between social systems, where the processes of condensation and compacting of expert knowledge occur.

It might appear questionable as to whether digging down yet one more level will reveal a purchase for normative considerations, but there are important normative standards at work within these decision-making *loci*. Throughout the process of scientific knowledge generation,

[53] Franz L. Neumann describes this as the reduction of the role of judge to that of police officer: when legal rules cease to be general, law is reduced to 'a technical instrument for the execution of certain political objectives': Franz L. Neumann, 'The Change in the Function of Law in Modern Society', in: William E. Scheuerman (ed.), *The Rule of Law under Siege: Selected Essays of Franz L. Neumann and Otto Kirchheimer* (Berkeley-Los Angeles CA: University of California Press, 1996), pp. 101–41, at 134. Luhmann describes this state of affairs as the political system attempting to use the legal system as a mere means of implementing its own decisions, thus importing into law the logic of the political system and potentially endangering law's *autopoiesis*: Luhmann, n. 5 above, at 94–5. See, also, Michael King and Chris Thornhill, *Niklas Luhmann's Theory of Politics and Law* (Basingstoke: Palgrave Macmillan, 2003), p. 199. King and Thornhill describe a context in which the political system has made a determination regarding the existence of certain facts derived from scientific input, reducing the law to 'little more than an official stamp on decisions that have already been taken through political internalization of "scientific facts"'. Ibid., at 201.

decisions are being made – about the design of experiments, the manner in which results should be interpreted, when the drawing of a conclusion is warranted, and the implications of that conclusion, among others. Scientists require some means of communicating these decisions both to other scientists as well as to the political authorities and the media. Earth systems scientists are among those whose work is often subject to intense political and media scrutiny, so these communications can be of great moment. Scientists do not communicate, even to one another and certainly not to non-scientists, the whole complexity of their knowledge-generating activities; nevertheless, they must find ways to condense not only their data, observations and findings, but also the reasons why these should be received with confidence by various audiences. They rely, in this process, on references to standards, principles, and policies that stabilise expectations. The expectations in question are largely procedural, namely, that scientific knowledge will be produced in certain ways, according to methodologies or processes of developing and validating methodologies, that generate confidence in results. The rigour and reliability of scientific knowledge production and the extent to which scientific results generate confidence are represented by William Rehg as the *cogency* of scientific arguments.[54] He notes that demonstrations of cogency vary according to context; not surprisingly, scientists speak differently to colleagues in their sub-discipline than to those in other specialities, and differently again to non-scientists, including political and legal authorities. But Rehg also argues that these contexts are not closed off from one another; the standards used to reach assessments of cogency travel across them.[55] In many cases, notably, policy sciences, such as toxicology, boundary objects are deliberately constructed that permit the translation of scientific insights about the toxicity of substances into regulatory standards such as limitations on exposure.

Theodore M. Porter notes that, within certain communities, such as geologists in nineteenth-century London or contemporary particle physicists, trust in individual scientists may be an appropriate basis for assessing cogency, but it does not function well within larger scientific communities where scientists do not know one another, or in the emerging sub-disciplines in which clear standards for assessing cogency have yet to be negotiated.[56] Similarly, when courts or regulatory agencies make

[54] Rehg, n. 6 above, at 3–4.

[55] Ibid., at 241–2.

[56] Theodore M. Porter, *Trust in Numbers: The Pursuit of Objectivity in Science and Public Life* (Princeton NJ: Princeton University Press, 2001), chapters 8 and 9.

decisions that depend heavily on scientific input, means of methodological standardisation are sought.[57] There are many reasons for this: to ensure that public decisions are made upon the basis of highly reliable information; to bolster the legitimacy of regulatory and legal decisions; and to hide from view the crucial role played by scientific, policy, and legal judgment, for example. If the standardisation of research methodology is understood primarily as a means of generating objective scientific conclusions through the reduction of the space for the exercise of judgment, one might end up with mindless checklist approaches to the production of scientific knowledge.[58] But there is another possibility. The normative nature of the distillation of scientific communications about toxicity could be productively misunderstood,[59] permitting the law to lend a form to these communications, one that enhances their resonance in other social systems.[60] More in particular, the proceduralisation of assessments of cogency would permit the stabilisation of expectations within civil society, where decisions are being made about how best to act on commitments to environmental sustainability and, as a direct result, how to integrate or respond to the information communicated through certification, ratings or rankings, and other largely cognitive regulatory instruments. In short, if uncertainty, complexity, and the sheer quantity of information regarding environmental degradation and sustainability overwhelm the capacity of individuals and institutions to determine what action to take or what path to follow, the boundary-crossing concept of cogency permits reliance on condensed forms of communication based upon the processes of translation that these communications underwent as they crossed boundaries.

IV Conclusion

It must be recalled that these compact packages do not contain the distilled truth about the non-human world. A *jus gentium* for the Anthropocene would take as its starting point the unknowability of Gaïa, the subject with which humankind is faced. The non-human world remains beyond the grasp of any one social system, or, for that matter, some form of societal rationality that can constrain the geophysical force that is humanity without seeking to address human

[57] Ibid., at 197 et seq.
[58] Ibid., at 202 et seq.
[59] Teubner, n. 7 above, at 1453.
[60] Kjaer, this volume.

agents within society. As with global law in general, the bulk of its norms will be cognitive in nature, subject to learning in the face of disappointed expectation. But, for global environmental law to be more than a collection of standards and indicators, and for it to operate in a systematic manner, norms that govern the constitution of these instruments as well as their implementation in transnational networks will be required. Though some scholars critical of these calculative techniques fear that depending heavily on scientific conceptions of nature results in truncated, reductionist perceptions of the non-human world, this depends in great measure on what assumptions one makes about the way in which scientists see the world, and how they see themselves as observers of the world. Despite a certain tendency to view Earth systems scientists as so many Pygmalions, mistaking their models for the world, they are engaged in very human forms of knowledge acquisition, argumentation, and persuasion. In order for communications respecting their insights to resonate within other social systems, they must indeed be carefully prepared for transfer, losing nuance and subtlety along the way. The manner in which this preparation is accomplished is therefore of great importance. The validity of these rules cannot be made to depend on their correspondence to facts about the non-human world. It instead depends – in large measure – on the capacity of law to regulate the process through which scientific knowledge is placed at the disposal of networks operating through the political economy.

As noted, Niklas Luhmann warned against law that takes the form of goal-oriented programming, in which not only objectives but also precise standards are dictated to law by the political system.[61] He was particularly cognisant of the danger of such a loss of law's *autopoiesis* in its attempts to grapple with environmental risk and degradation. Given the immense complexity and opacity of ecosystems, public law for environmental protection that takes the form of social regulation would result in an elaborate mass of law by decree, subject to rapid change or reinterpretation, and would therefore be highly arbitrary.[62] The current trend in global law towards cognitive instruments to set standards and measure performance possesses certain advantages over state-based law, namely, the capacity to move smoothly across jurisdictional boundaries, and the

[61] Luhmann, n. 29 above, at 196 et seq.

[62] This would be true not only of ecological law but of any body of law that relies heavily on expert input.

close integration between science and economics, promoting rapid movements of information through transnational networks. If global law were to be comprised of nothing other than calculative instruments and vehicles, it would be very similar to the approach that Luhmann criticised: highly material, detailed environmental rules subject to rapid change, whose content depends on communications generated outside the legal system, notably, in science and in economics. But the form of law envisaged here is not limited to cognitive rules such as standards and indicators. If this were so, then global ecological law would risk collapsing in on itself. The content of these rules would be subject to rapid, unpredictable changes, driven by opaque processes of condensation of scientific insight that would be extremely vulnerable to influence and interference on the part of large firms, acting individually, through industry associations, or through apparently independent think tanks or civil society organisations. Members of civil society might eventually learn to distinguish reliable from compromised regulatory agencies and standards packages, but this process would be slow and fraught with error. Firms seeking to orient their behaviour in the light of standards and indicators would soon learn that the arbitrariness of these criteria and their mutability make them poor guides: firms could not predict whether significant investment in research and development or in the confection of sustainability policies and procedures would turn out to be misspent, as standards and indicators morph without warning. If confidence in the link between such standards and sustainability wanes, then the promises and threats on which transnational regulatory orders rely would be undermined. In short, stabilisation of expectations, through norms whose validity is resistant to learning in the face of disappointment, is essential to the viability of global law. In the field of ecology in particular, normativity is likely to have its greatest impact at the level of the translation and condensation of scientific insights into compact packages that are actionable in the political economy.

PART III

The Transformation of the Law of Political Economy in Europe

8

The Transformative Politics of European Private Law

HANS-W. MICKLITZ

I Bremen 1986/Copenhagen 2017

Poul Kjaer's conference on 'The Law of Political Economy – Transformations in the Functions of Law' throws me thirty years back to a conference in Bremen, organised by Christian Joerges and David Trubek on 'Critical Legal Thought'.[1] Bremen University, the Centre of European Legal Policy (*Zentrum für Europäische Rechtspolitik*, ZERP) and the University of Wisconsin managed to invite the then leading critical minds from the Ivy League in the United States and from 'left-wing' German universities, in particular, Frankfurt and Bremen. The introduction of Christian Joerges, David Trubek and Peer Zumbansen in the republication 25 years later in the *German Law Journal* highlights how subjective memory differs.[2] So will mine.

I.1 ZERP and the Single European Act

In the late 1980s, the social welfare state was on the decline in the EU Member States. Critical scholars who sympathised with the labour movement and had hoped for effective co-determination, or who invested

[1] Christian Joerges and David Trubek, 'Critical Legal Thought: An American-German Debate' (1989) 11 *Schriftenreihe des Zentrums für Europäische Rechtspolitik*, Volume 11, 1989, republished in a special issue of the *German Law Journal* (12) 2011, pp. 1–33.

[2] Christian Joerges, David Trubek and Peer Zumbansen, '"Critical Legal Thought: An American-German Debate." An Introduction at the Occasion of its Republication in the *German Law Journal* 25 Years Later', details in note above, available at: https://static1.squarespace.com/static/56330ad3e4b0733dcc0c8495/t/56b6f8bf2eeb8170481ecb6f/1454831807784/GLJ_Vol_12_No_01_Joerges.pdf; Peer Zumbansen provides for an intellectual justification of a reader to the book, the others comment as participants; Christian Joerges gives his personal account of the German intellectual history, while David Trubek explains why the American scholars were ready to come to Bremen in 1986.

scholarly and politically in consumer and environmental protection in order to establish a better and more just society, found themselves in a kind of identity crisis. Gradually, the political impetus on social regulation, on the 'Social' faded away.[3] At about the same time, in 1986, the EU adopted the Single European Act (SEA). The treaty amendment freed the EU from the political deadlock of the early 1980s, lifted market integration to the completion of the Internal Market and introduced social regulation to be achieved through majority decision making.

The foundation of the Centre of European Legal Policy in 1982 preceded the European development by few years. The small state (*Land*) of Bremen, 'The Freie and Hansestadt Bremen', was courageous enough to defy the then growing scepticism on Europe's future and invested in 'law and politics' (the name of ZERP) to promote 'Social Europe'.[4] From the 'big bang' of the SEA in 1986 onwards, the EU appeared, to many critical legal scholars around Europe, as an opportunity to overcome the decline of the national social welfare state through the rise of the 'Social' in the EU. The 'European Integration through Law' project[5] had granted lawyers all over Europe a prominent and leading position. As the EU was made through law,[6] 'Social Europe', should and, indeed, *could* also be promoted and achieved through law. Our state of mind, the young post doctorates of the Centre of European Legal Policy, is best to be characterised as a *mélange* of enthusiasm and German[7] idealism. The SEA and the idea of 'Social Europe' carried the young scholars (me included) down the 'bumpy road'[8] towards Brussels and Luxembourg.

[3] I am using the 'Social' in the meaning of Duncan Kennedy, 'Three Globalizations of Law and Legal Thought: 1850–2000', in: David M. Trubek and Alavaro Santos (eds.), *The New Law and Economic Development: A Critical Appraisal* (New York: Cambridge University Press, 2006), pp. 19–73.

[4] The name could be read as a dedication to Rudolf Wiethölter, *Rechtswissenschaft* (Frankfurt aM: Fischer Verlag, 1968), and his concept of 'political jurisprudence'.

[5] Mauro Cappelletti, Monica Seccombe and Joseph H.H. Weiler, 'Integration through Law: Europe and the American Federal Experience', in: Cappelletti, Seccombe and Weiler (eds.), *Integration through Law*, Vol. 1, Book 1 (Berlin: Walter de Gruyter, 1986).

[6] Walter Hallstein, *Der unvollendete Bundesstaat* (Düsseldorf-Vienna: ECON, 1969).

[7] Rüdiger Safranski, *Romantik: Eine deutsche Affäre* (Munich: Carl Hanser Verlag, 2007).

[8] Volkmar Gessner, 'Europas Holprige Rechtswege – Die rechtskulturellen Schranken der Rechtsverfolgung im Europäischen Binnenmarkt', in: Ludwig Krämer, Hans-W. Micklitz and Klaus Tonner (eds.), *Law and Diffuse Interests in the European Legal Order: Liber Amicorum Norbert Reich*, VIEW Schriftenreihe (Schrifrenreiche des Instituts für Europäisches Wirtschafts- und Verbraucherrecht), Band 3 (Baden Baden: Nomos Verlag, 1997), pp. 163–76.

I.2 Practice of Theory or Theory as Practice

And then this: a conference on 'Critical Legal Thought', meant to engage into a self-reflection, not only on what critical legal thought means or could mean, but also on what kind of purpose critical legal scholarship might have in the transformation of the nation state to the welfare state. The intense three days of presentations and discussions of the intimidating great minds from across the Atlantic left us (or rather, me) 'irritated'. Throughout the discussions, there was a mismatch in the understanding of what critical theory and critical legal scholarship stands for, and what its relationship to society should be. The editors, Christian Joerges and David Trubek, framed the tension later on in the following categories:[9]

- On the one hand, there is *Practice of Theory* – theory as representation of the world as it is, where theory is expected to produce guidance for social action. This was the dominating understanding of many critical legal scholars in the 1970s and 1980s in continental Europe. Theory had to serve a societal purpose, the building of a better and more just society, and later the building of Social Europe.
- On the other hand, there is *Theory as Practice* – which denies that the purpose of theory is to present the world. Theory is being understood itself as practice, a (an even better or ever better) normative vision that structures individuals, and helps to build a society. Theory's goal then is to change the way in which we think and NOT to contribute to change the world.

Grudgingly, I admit that the critical legal study scholars from Harvard, Wisconsin and Stanford shattered my belief and my conviction about *Practice of Theory*. Thirty years later, the deep gulf between the two understandings of 'Theory' are more alive than ever. They underpin the recent publication of Tamara Perišin and Siniša Rodin on *The Transformation or Reconstitution of Europe*,[10] which explicitly builds on Critical Legal Studies to analyse the role and function of the ECJ/CJEU in particular. However, many of the contributions are more in line with '*Practice of Theory*' than with '*Theory as Practice*'.[11] On the one side

[9] Joerges and Trubek, Introduction, n. 1 above, p. 7.

[10] The subtitle tells the message: 'The Critical Legal Studies Perspective on the Role of the Courts in the European *Union*' (Oxford: Hart Publishing, 2018).

[11] In their introduction to the book 'Transformation or Reconstitution of Europe: The Critical Legal Studies Perspective on the Role of the Courts in the European Union', the editors seem to be much more in line with Practice of Theory than with Theory as Practice.

are those who invoke the law to fight down neoliberalism, while, on the other, there are those who call for a new legal theory, for a normative vision to build society. Despite the similarities, the debate of the 1980s cannot be compared with those thirty or forty years later. There are at least two differences: the 'left' *versus* 'right' distinction in 'political jurisprudence' has lost its contours. The Great Crisis has catapulted the 'Political Economy of the Law' onto the agenda of critical legal scholarship. Yale set the agenda in 2016,[12] Copenhagen followed one year later. The political economy of law remained under scrutinised in 'Critical Legal Thought', which might explain why neither European integration nor globalisation played a role in the late 1980s.

I.3 Claim and Argument

In what follows, I focus on the EU, on European integration and on the transformative function of European law. The subject of my research is European private law. I will use the socio-legal research of my ERC (European Research Council) project on 'European Regulatory Private Law'.[13] As I was actively involved in the integration through law process, more precisely in building the 'Europe with a Social Face' aspect, the chapter is necessarily a kind of self-reflection on the role and function of leftist critical legal scholarship and on how law is transformed through its involvement for a political objective.[14] Thus, the chapter carries a strong flavour of ideological critique (*Ideologickritik*). The claim is a double one. It is not enough for a critical legal scholar to defend the rights of the weaker parties in the society and to understand private law as an integral part of the democracy. It is equally necessary to reflect critically upon the political function of critical legal scholarship. I will first look into what I call the 'expectation society'. The 'expectation society' is the product of the rise of the 'Social' in the 1920s as revitalised in the 1970s, and then transferred to the EU in the 1990s. Critical legal scholarship supported the transformation of the Common Market into the Internal Market with a Social Face. In their commitment to the 'good cause', they (me) did not hear the subterranean cracks of the European integration process. I will

12 David Singh Grewal, Amy Kapczynski and Jedediah Purdy, 'Law and Political Economy: Toward a Manifesto', 6 November 2017, available at: https://lpeblog.org/2017/11/06/law-and-political-economy-toward-a-manifesto.

13 See https://blogs.eui.eu/erc-erpl.

14 Requiring an engagement with Friedrich A. von Hayek, 'The Intellectuals and Socialism' (1949) 16 *Chicago Law Review*, 417–33.

reflect on the transformative function of European private law in the different stages of Europe building, integration through law, integration through governance, and integration beyond law. Law, this is my argument, has undergone a double transformation, in the use of law to implement the 'Social', and in the change of the level playing field, from the nation state level to the European level. European critical legal scholarship has accompanied this process first in a spirit of sympathy and support, and later in disappointment and ever sharper critique.

II Expectation Society and Critical Legal Scholarship

The rise of the 'Social' in the twentieth century left deep traces in the consciousness of the peoples. The West relied on the market and on democracy to tame the market powers and to establish the necessary balance between 'capital' and 'labour', while the East trusted in the state-run economy and the socialist state. The West, not least under pressure from the East, had to provide for the necessary 'socialist oil'[15] in the private law system in order to appease the grand opponents. The call for the 'Social' transformed private law into economic law.[16] The 'Social' had to be built not only within the private law system, but also through a regulatory frame beyond private law, most prominently enshrined in Otto Sinzheimer's concept of an 'economic constitution'.[17] The 'Weimar Legacy',[18] the rich tradition of critical jurisprudence, promoted the democratisation of industrial relations through co-determination and the insertion of fairness into economic relations. Similar discourses may be reported from France and the United Kingdom, albeit bound to national particularities.[19] Law, this has to be highlighted, was supposed to play a leading role in the design of an economic and political order meant

[15] Otto von Gierke, *Die Soziale Aufgabe des Privatrechts: Vortrag gehalten am 5. April 1889 in der juristischen Gesellschaft zu Wien* (Berlin: Springer, 1889), translated into English, with an introduction by Ewan McGaughey, 'The Social Role of Private Law' (2018) 19 *German Law Journal*, 1017–116.

[16] Heinz-Dieter, Assmann, Gert Brüggemeier, Dieter Hart and Christian Joerges (eds.), *Wirtschaftsrecht als Kritik des Privatrechts* (Königstein Ts: Athenäum, 1980).

[17] Otto Sinzheimer, *Grundzüge des Arbeitsrechts* (Jena: G. Fischer, 1921).

[18] Udi Greenberg, *The Weimar Century: German Émigrés and the Ideological Foundations of the Cold War* (Princeton NJ: Princeton University Press, 2014).

[19] Bob Hepple (ed.), *The Making of Labour Law in Europe: A Comparative Study of Nine Countries up to 1945* (London: Mansell Publishing, 1986). Bob Hepple and Bruno Veneziani (eds.), *The Transformation of Labour Law in Europe: A Comparative Study of 15 Countries 1945–2004* (Oxford: Hart Publishing, 2009).

to appease democracy and capitalism. The 1920s left deep traces in the state of mind of the people. They created and established the societal expectations of the citizens towards their states. One might understand the 1920s as a precursor of what became the national welfare state of the 1960s. The Great Crisis, the rise of 'neoliberalism' and the decline of the 'Social' has triggered research on possible parallels between the failure of corporatist Weimar and the road to Fascism.[20]

II.1. Rise of the Welfare State and the Birth of Social Europe

In the first twenty years after World War II, Western European politics focused on re-establishing the economy. The quick recovery of the world economy enabled the second rise of the 'Social'. The French 1968 revolution 'screamed'[21] for a more just society with balanced power relations in the economy and society. From France, the revolt spread throughout Europe and left deep traces in critical legal scholarship and in the role and function of law. The 1970s in Germany mirrored the debates within the Weimar Republic – co-determination in industrial relations and *democratic* legislative control over the fairness of economic relations. The unfinished Weimar projects, in particular those favoured by socialist and social-democratic parties, found their way into politics. Consumer policy entered the political area, and occupied political parties and political programmes around Europe. The production society turned into a consumption society. Law was to help to improve/democratise industrial relations to the 'better', law was to set a frame for consumer relations, compensating for the imbalance of power. The socialist and social democratic governments in Europe set the tone, reinvigorated social expectations.[22] Nation states set the law-making machinery in motion to meet long established (1920s) and newly created (1960) expectations.

In the late 1970s, the welfare state began to run into difficulties, not even ten years after the great departure. The many social laws needed to be enforced, not only by courts, but ever more by regulatory agencies.

[20] For a thorough debate, see Poul F. Kjaer and Niklas Olsen (eds.), *Critical Theories of Crisis in Europe: From Weimar to the Euro* (London-Lanham MD: Rowman & Littlefield, 2016).

[21] 'We can only start from where we are, from where we are but do not want to be, from where we scream.' John Holloway, *Change the World without Taking Power: The Meaning of Revolution Today*, 2nd ed. (London: Pluto Press, 2010), p. 4; Hans Lindahl, *Authority and the Globalisation of Inclusion and Exclusion* (Cambridge: Cambridge University Press, 2018), p. 177, with further examples from the opponents of globalisation.

[22] Fritz W. Scharpf, *Crisis and Choice in European Social Democracy* (Ithaca NY: Cornell University Press: 1991).

The 'failure rhetoric' made a quick career – regulatory failure, governmental failure, judicial failure, democratic failure. Nation states started to realise that they could not maintain their promises, and gradually began to back-peddle, radically in the United Kingdom under Margaret Thatcher, while more smoothly in France. The German situation is particular in that unification (1989) helped the then conservative government out of economic and political difficulties. The social benefits had to be financed. The rise of the welfare state is inherently connected to the increase in sovereign debt.

In 1986, the adoption of the Single European Act opened the gate for the European legislator. The SEA legitimated the agenda of the Centre for European Legal Policy at the University of Bremen. The European Commission generously promoted comparative research in private law. We, the young scholars in Bremen, committed to Social Europe, interpreted the mandate of the European Commission to build the Internal Market with a Social Face as a research agenda. Using the language of 'Critical Legal Thought', we exercised *Practice of Theory*[23] with limited self-reflection. Our three studies on product safety paved the way for the adoption of the Product Safety Directive 92/59.[24] We were involved in the preliminary drafting, together with European Commission officials, at the European University Institute. We were proud of participating in what we understood as an important political step forward to make sure that products could not only circulate freely in the EU, but also guarantee a sufficient level of safety to protect the citizens against injuries. Looking back, I remember Christian Joerges saying that we are abolishing the Article 36 TFEU defence, the right of Member States to defend their national laws on health and safety. For our part, we neither reflected seriously on the implications of the competence transfer from the Member States to the EU, nor on the social expectations.

II.2 Cracks and Ambiguities

The idea of a market with a social face, or even a Social Europe, is based upon a deep ambiguity. The message of the SEA looked so overtly

[23] Within ZERP in between 1986 and 1990, I was involved in three projects on product safety. After I left Bremen, I founded the VIEW as a research institute on consumer law and policy. The Series (Nomos Baden-Baden), now forty volumes, documents the engagement with building a Europe with a social face. See www.nomos-shop.de/reihen popup.aspx?reihe=214.

[24] Today Directive 2001/95 OJ L 11, 15 January 2002, pp. 4–17.

convincing. The Member States had unanimously agreed in the desire and the need to push European integration beyond market integration. The competence transfer simultaneously allowed the Member States to outsource unresolved social issues to the EU level. However, the opening of a new level playing field came at a price. Tentatively, the EU turned into the addressee of social expectations. The European Commission, which holds the monopoly to initiate legislative measures, was far too much attracted by the potential power gain through enlarged competences to be able to realise that increased competences come with increasing responsibilities, and that the shift in the level playing field could backfire.

In the aftermath of the Single European Act, quite similar to the heyday of the welfare state in the 1970s, the EU set the legislative machinery into motion in order to complete the Internal Market. The fall of the Berlin wall in 1989 and the promised enlargement of the EU in 1992 might even have encouraged the European Commission to accelerate the law making in the 1990s. The ECJ backed the power grabbing through generous interpretation of the competence rules.[25] The 'Integration through Law' project, now in the combination of market integration and social regulation went full steam ahead, promoted by critical legal scholarship. Early warnings against the Internal Market project, from Ernst-Joachim Mestmäcker, criticising the end of ordoliberalism,[26] or from Joseph H.H. Weiler,[27] questioning the abolition of the foundational balance between legal integration and intergovernmentalism fell on deaf ears. At a conference on human rights and social rights held at the European University Institute in 1990, I presented a paper on 'the right to safety'.[28] Joseph Weiler argued that harmonising product safety in the EU was *ultra vires*. Rather unaffected,

[25] ECJ Case C-233/94, *Germany* v. *Parliament and Council* [1997] ECR I-2405; ECJ Case C-270/12 Short Selling ECLI:EU:C:2014:18.

[26] Ernst-Joachim Mestmäcker, 'Auf dem Wege zu einer Ordnungspolitik für Europa', in: Ernst-Joachim Mestmäcker, Hans Möller and Hans-Peter Schwartz (eds.), *Eine Ordnungspolitik für Europa. Festschrift für Hans v.d. Groeben* (Baden-Baden: Nomos Verlagsgesellschaft, 1987), pp. 9–49, at 9–26.

[27] Joseph H.H. Weiler, 'The Community System: The Dual Character of Supranationalism' (1981) 1 *Yearbook of European Law*, 267–306, at 268; the scepticism shined through the whole project of social rights and fundamental rights in the aftermath of the SEA. Antonio Cassese, Andrew Clapham and Joseph H.H. Weiler (eds.), *European Union – The Human Rights Challenge, Human Rights and the European Community: The Substantive Law* (Baden-Baden: Nomos Verlagsgesellschaft, 1991).

[28] Hans-W. Micklitz, 'Consumer Rights', in: Cassese, Clapham and Weiler (eds.), n. 27 above, pp. 53–110.

the EU turned the legislative programme in the 'White Paper on the Completion of the Internal Market' into reality. Not so much in labour law, but definitely in consumer law, and later in non-discrimination law, the EU succeeded, with the help of the majority rule, in adopting a dense network of regulations and directives, all meant to improve the 'Social'. It took another decade or two before the design and the effects of the European Social was to materialise.

The more competences the EU assumed, the more the EU appeared as a political actor not only with regard to the market, but also – and in particular – with regard to the 'Social'. Gradually, the EU, the European Commission and lately the European Court of Justice became the target of social expectations. Over time, the ambiguities of the competence transfer began to unfold, with a long-lasting effect on the relationship of the European citizens towards their nation state and towards the EU, not to mention on critical legal scholarship. The Member States used the EU as a level playing field, either to degrade the 'Social' and/or to upgrade it. The Lisbon Agenda 2000 stands for degradation. By that time, Member States were ringing in a new approach to the handling of social regulation. They decided to turn 'the EU into the most competitive economy of the world'.[29] Social regulation had to be tested against 'economic efficiency'. The Member States used the EU first as catalyst and later as scapegoat. Labour law stands out as a prominent example. Up-levelling occurred when the Member States found it convenient to establish common rules for the Internal Market. This is particularly true for consumer law, which travelled comfortably piggyback with the completion of the Internal Market competence. Non-discrimination law served as the glue between the decline of labour law and the rise of consumer protection.[30] The outcome is mixed: on the negative side, an incremental EU labour law, which is dismantling national labour law; on the positive side, a non-discrimination law expanding from employment relations to the public sphere and a fully developed European consumer law.

II.3 Expectations

This is the rather mixed result more than thirty years after the adoption of the Single European Act. What is worse is that European citizens do

[29] See www.europarl.europa.eu/summits/lis1_en.htm.

[30] Richard Münch, *Die Konstruktion der Europäischen Gesellschaft. Zur Dialektik von transnationaler Integration und nationaler Desintegration* (Frankfurt aM: Campus Verlag, 2008).

not perceive the EU as promoting the 'Social' – even though it does – but as the opposite, as destroying the 'Social' – even though the Member States are the driver. The Member States rendered this distorted perception possible – through nested games.[31] They present themselves as the parties which had defended the 'Social' in Brussels, or even as those which had managed to increase the level of social protection, and the EU as the party which was ready to sacrifice the 'Social' on the altar of the Internal Market, upon the basis of market rationality and international competitiveness. Reality, however, is more complex: it seems as if the citizens follow the explanations of their national political leaders and thereby both misunderstand and misjudge the role and function of the EU. This is also due to the overtly complex competence structure, the division between law making at EU level and enforcement through the Member States, not least the insurmountable difficulty in assigning responsibilities in a multi-governance structure.[32]

The EU ended up with more competences that it could digest, handle and properly implement. Today, the EU looks like the 'bad guy' and the Member States like the 'good guy'. Citizens tend to glorify the golden age of the national welfare state. But what is the responsibility of critical legal scholarship which unwillingly contributed to the current state of affairs, in the conviction that it was supporting the building of 'Social Europe'?

II.4 Critical Legal Scholarship

The short love affair of roughly ten years between critical legal scholars and the Internal Market with a Social Face, a Social Europe – the golden 1990s – ended up first in dismay, then turned into a rising critique, and culminates in the current EU bashing. Today's critical legal scholarship accuses the EU of pursuing a 'neoliberal agenda',[33] of imposing the market rationality on the

31 Richard D. Putnam, 'Diplomacy and Domestic Politics: The Logic of Two-level Games' (1988) 42 *International Organization*, 427–60; George Tsebelis, *Nested Games: Rational Choice in Comparative Politics* (Berkeley-Los Angeles CA: University of California Press, 1990).

32 Raymond Breton, 'Identification in Transnational Political Communities', in: Karen Knop, Sylvia Ostry, Richard Simeon and Katherine Swinton (eds.), *Rethinking Federalism: Citizens, Markets, and Governments in a Changing World* (Vancouver: University of British Columbia Press, 1995), pp. 40–58.

33 Usually, the reference to neoliberalism serves as a substitute for a deeper debate on what exactly neoliberalism might mean.

'Social',[34] of transforming the nation state into a market state,[35] or even of undermining national democracies.[36] What has happened?

Until the late 1990s, the promotion of European integration did not need explanation and/or legitimation. The call for European integration guaranteed peace and prosperity. European integration through law relied on a 'common European legal culture'.[37] It seems as if this fundament was not stable enough for the building of a Europe *beyond* the market, and certainly not for managing the effects of the financial crisis and the Eurocrisis. However, this cannot explain the withdrawal of the intellectual support for the European project. There is certainly a generational dimension. All those intellectuals who shared memories of World War II passed away or are no longer in office. The generation which is now in power is not stamped by this experience and has a more sober look at the pros and cons of the European project.[38] The old and the new generation of *critical* legal scholars were united in the defence and the development of the 'Social', maybe with different connotations. The older generation focused on the imbalance of power and how law could compensate the deficiencies of the weaker parties. The younger generation relied on human and fundamental rights, sometimes in the belief that 'rights' may bring 'justice'.[39]

[34] Marija Bartl, 'Internal Market Rationality, Private Law and the Direction of the Union: Resuscitating the Market as the Object of the Political' (2015) 21 *European Law Journal*, 572–98. Gareth Davies, 'Freedom of Contract and the Horizontal Effect of Free Movement Law', in: Dorota Leczykiewicz and Stephen Weatherill (eds.), *The Involvement of EU Law in Private Law Relationships* (Oxford: Hart Publishing, 2013), pp. 53–70; see the contribution of Marija Bartl, focusing on consumer law, and that of Stefano Giubboni, focusing on labour law, Chapters 9 and 11 respectively, in this volume.

[35] Dennis Patterson and Ari Afilalo, *The New Global Trading Order: The Evolving State and the Future of Trade* (Cambridge-New York: Cambridge University Press, 2008); Philip Bobbitt, *The Shield of Achilles: War, Peace, and the Course of History* (New York: Anchor Books, 2003).

[36] Wolfgang Streeck, *How will Capitalism End?* (London: Verso, 2016).

[37] Franz Wieacker, 'Foundations of European Legal Culture' (1990) 38 *The American Journal of Comparative Law*, 1–29, Pierre Pescatore, The Law of Integration: Emergence of New Phenomenon in International Relations, based on the Experience of the European Communities (Leiden: Sijthoff, 1974).

[38] But see Julio Baquero Cruz, *What's Left of the Law of Integration? Decay and Resistance in European Union Law* (Oxford: Oxford University Press, 2018), stressing the legacy of Auschwitz for the building of Europe.

[39] Alexander Somek, 'The Preoccupation with Rights and the Embrace of Inclusion: A Critique', in: Dimitry Kochenov, Gráinne de Búrca and Andrew Williams (eds.), *Europe's Justice Deficit?* (Oxford: Hart Publishing, 2015), pp. 295–310.

In both variations, critical legal scholarship understands legal theory 'as Practice'. The law in action could not deliver the law which the legal theory advocated. Czeslaw Milosz distinguishes, in *The Captive Mind*, Alpha the Moralist, Beta the Disappointed Lover, Gamma, the Slave of History, and Delta the Troubadour.[40] Milosz is describing the behaviour of Polish intellectuals during Stalinist times. Each of the four shows astonishing similarities to the current behaviour of critical legal scholars in times of crisis. Alpha is still searching for the new individual that could replace the Kantian ideal. This kind of thinking exists in neo-Marxist theories and, amazingly enough, in behavioural science.[41] Beta is demoralised turning love into disappointment, and faces cynicism and self-destruction. European legal scholarship is full of Betas. Gamma is still pursuing the once set political objective against all resistance and sometimes even against her own conviction. Such an attitude is dominant in the day-to-day business of doctrinal European legal scholarship, critical and non-critical.[42] Delta is the opportunist, defending and criticising the EU at the same time – with passion. Many critical legal scholars will share Delta's bias. It is certainly tempting to take the exponentially growing critical literature on the EU and classify the authors and their scholarship along the lines of Milosz distinction. It remains for the critical legal scholars themselves to reflect on where they are standing. Such self-reflection might help to gain distance from ones' own research and maybe to burst into laughter – about oneself. Personally, I would put myself into the category of Delta, perhaps with a touch of Gamma, due to the legacy of my generation.

III The Transformative Function of European Law

The question on the 'political economy of law' and the 'transformative function of European law' reaches further and deeper. What is at stake is no longer 'practice of theory' or 'theory as practice', but the role of law itself in rapidly changing economic and political circumstances.

[40] Czeslaw Milosz, *The Captive Mind* (London: Penguin Books, [1953] 1980).

[41] Philipp Hacker, 'Nudging and Autonomy: A Philosophical and Legal Appraisal', in: Hans-W. Micklitz, Anne-Lise Sibony and Fabrizio Esposito, *Research Methods in Law and Consumer Law* (Cheltenham: Edward Elgar Publishing, 2018), pp. 77–118.

[42] See the textbooks on European law and the contributions in European law journals, such as the *Common Market Law Review*, *European Law Review*, and the *Yearbook of European Law*.

In referring to political economy, I am combining two strands: (a) the Marxist understanding of political economy and the role and function Marxism devotes to law;[43] and (b) the (critical) international political economy. Political economy looks like a method to analyse European private law, no longer through the rose-tinted glasses of what kind of law is needed to best support and defend the weaker party in the Internal Market with a Social Face, but whether law could at all help to improve the situation of the weaker party, and, if not, the economic and the political system has to be changed. Understanding political economy as a method leads to 'the transformations of the functions of the law' through the change of the level playing field, through the shift of the 'Social' from the nation state level to the EU. The 'political economy' puts the dismantling and transformation of the 'Social' upfront. It is no longer a question of the correct assessment of the achievements of EU law, on whether and to what extent the EU has upgraded or downgraded the 'Social'. The question is whether and, if so, to what extent law is the appropriate means to improve the 'Social'.

The 'transformations of the functions of the law' offers a new, to date under-researched, dimension. The function of the law has undergone a double transformation, the first results from the use of law to implement the 'Social', the second from the change of the level playing field. I will analyse the two issues one by one. The first invokes the question of whether there is a difference between the function of the law to build a market and to build the 'Social'. The second investigates what happens to law through the constant change of its function: from integration through law, over/through integration through governance, to integration beyond law. In each of the two, critical legal scholarship is heavily involved, shivering between Alpha and Delta.

III.1 Law between Politics and Economics

The current narrative in critical legal scholarship looks more or less like this: the EU is dismantling the social achievements that the national welfare state has established; therefore the EU is about to destroy labour law at both levels, individually and collectively; the EU is transforming consumer protection law into consumer law without protection,

[43] Note: law does not show up, at least not explicitly. In Marxist theory, law is part of the *Überbau* (superstructure); in neo-Marxist literature, for example, David Kennedy, 'Law and the Political Economy of the World' (2013) 26 *Leiden Journal of International Law*, 7–48), it is not exactly clear where the place for the law is meant to be.

submitting consumer law to the market rationality.[44] Non-discrimination law, instead, is and remains the darling dogma of leftist legal scholars.[45] In their quest to turn theory into practice (practice of theory), critical legal scholars tried to disconnect the 'Social' from the market. Political objectives, this was the argument, should prevail over economic constraints. The EU is blamed for having extinguished such attempts. In the EU, economics prevails over politics. At national level, critical legal scholarship all too often forgot about economics – the who pays, while, at the European level, critical legal scholarship tended to overlook politics – the addressees of European integration, society, and the people.

At about the time of the Bremen Conference, the *Land* (state) of Bremen was struggling hard with growing international competition. For the non-insiders, Bremen was one of the richest *Länder* (states) in post-World War II West Germany. The port was booming; shipping and steel were the backbones of the city. Bremen hosted a promising car-manufacturing company, called *Borgward*. The decline of the *Land* of Bremen is paradigmatic for all the coal and steel regions in Germany and Europe. Coal and steel were cheaper to import to Europe than to produce in Europe. Korea turned into a huge competitor in the shipbuilding industry. Bremen suffered from globalisation. Gradually, its competitive advantage vanished way. The workers in the coal, steel and shipbuilding industries were about to lose their jobs, just as elsewhere in West Germany, Belgium, France and the United Kingdom. Trade unions organised strikes against the closure of industries and claimed subsidies from the *Land* of Bremen in their struggle for survival. In the heated public debate, the mayor had to choose between two evils – rejecting the claim for subsidies or pumping taxpayer's money into dying industries through sovereign debt. The mayor chose the second variant, saved social peace and ruined the public finances of the *Land* of Bremen permanently. The formerly rich *Land* of Bremen is today economically dependent on the inter-*Länder* fiscal adjustment. The left sympathised with the strike of the workers and with the Bremen government. So did we, the members of ZERP. The voices raised against using taxpayers money to keep dying industries artificially alive, remained unheard. The commitment to the

[44] Marija Bartl on consumer law, Stefano Guibboni on labour law, and Jotte Mulder on competition law and environmental protection, Chapters 9, 10, and 11 respectively, in this volume.

[45] Alexander Somek, 'The Darling Dogma of Bourgeois Europeanists' (2014) 20 *European Law Journal*, 688–712.

defence of social achievements, of workers' rights and fair remuneration were celebrated as a political victory in stark contrast to the right-wing neoliberalism in Thatcher's United Kingdom.

A similar story can be told on the rise and fall of consumer protection. In 1969, the Social Democrats and the Liberal Party formed a coalition which lasted until 1982, when Helmut Kohl took over. During these thirteen years, the German government, under the leadership first of Willy Brandt and later Helmut Schmidt realised two major projects which had their origins in the Republic of Weimar – co-determination and the control of standard contract terms. The debates in the political *fora* turned around feasibility, the search for the appropriate and most effective solution to the benefit of the consumer. Economics did play a role only in so far as the government was concerned with not overburdening companies. The debates even on the costs were political rather than economic. There was no impact assessment and no cost-benefit analysis. The fight over the reach of consumer policy remained by and large a political fight. Consumer activists and their academic supporters – like myself – were campaigning for rules that protect the weaker party, the consumer against the supplier. There was next to no attention given to the fact that the poor consumers were paying for the protection of those consumers who were better off. It needed behavioural economics to disclose that the formula of 'the poor pay more' has gained a cynical dimension.[46] The poor are not just disadvantaged in their relation with the supplier, they also suffer from the economic burden imposed on them by the rich co-consumers. A certain uneasiness about consumer policy as a middle-class policy was brushed aside in the belief that consumer protection law would be to the benefit of all consumers, rich and poor, and that it was for the supplier and the manufacturer to cover the costs of the increased protection.

The EU brought economics back in, not immediately after having taking over the 'Social' in the aftermath of the Single European Act, but definitely from the adoption of the Lisbon Agenda in 2000 onwards. One might distinguish two stages in the development of the 'Social' in the EU. In the first stage, the EU tried to copy the national social welfare policies. The protective dimension of social regulation, the emphasis on the weak worker, the part-time worker or pregnant women, ranked high on the

[46] Omri Ben-Shahar and Carl E. Schneider, *More than you Wanted to Know: The Failure of Mandated Disclosure* (Princeton NJ: Princeton University Press, 2014); Omri Ben-Shahar, 'The Paradox of Access Justice, and its Application to Mandatory Arbitration' (2016) 83 *The University of Chicago Law Review*, 1755–817.

agenda. The consumer was still associated with the weaker party. The first consumer policy programme of 1976 breathes the spirit of imbalance of power, although both catchwords – 'weak party' and 'imbalance of power' – do not show up explicitly. There were undercurrents already in the 1980s and 1990s questioning the protective outlook. The oft-quoted ECJ *Gut Springheide* judgment, relying on circumspect consumers, dates back to 16 July 1998.[47] However, it needed the move towards economic efficiency to trigger the second stage of Social Europe 2.0, one where economics gained ground over politics, a process which is thoroughly analysed by Marija Bartl and Stefano Giubboni, Chapters 9 and 11 respectively, in this volume.

In labour law, it remained for the ECJ to set the tone of the debate for the forthcoming years. The *Laval Quartet*[48] stand out like lighthouses for the 'neoliberal move' of the EU. This was in 2005. The handling of the economic crisis in 2008 and the management of the Euro crises through the *Troika* were grist to the mills of leftist critics. Social rights were claimed to be sacrificed on the altar of a neoliberal market economy.[49] Economics – making the EU the most competitive economy or, less rhetorically, adjusting labour law to the changing global economic environment – were said to prevail over politics. The failed initiative to transform *Viking* into a European regulation on the right to strike[50] was perhaps the most blatant attempt of the European Commission towards deconstructing labour rights and promoting economic efficiency. The Lisbon Agenda, however, seems to have come to a halt. In 2017, the Posting Worker Directive was amended so to prevent wage dumping in reaction to *Laval*.[51] Whether the amendment serves the interests of the workers in the Western Democracies alone and keeps the Eastern European workers away from the national labour markets

[47] ECJ Case C-210/96 *Gut Springheide* 1998 I-04657.

[48] C-341/05 *Laval un Partneri* [2007] ECR I-11767, C-346/06 *Rüffert* [2008] ECR I-1989, C-319/06 *Commission* vs *Luxembourg* [2008] ECR I-4323, C-438/05 *The International Transport Workers' Federation and The Finnish Seamen's Union* [2007] ECR I-10779; Margherita Cornaglia, The clash between national social values and European economic freedoms in the European Court of Justice's collective labour law jurisprudence moving away from a proportionality-based assessment, LLM Thesis, EUI Florence, 2018.

[49] Claire Kilpatrick, 'On the Rule of Law and Economic Emergency: The Degradation of Basic Legal Values in Europe's Bailouts' (2015) 35 *Oxford Journal of Legal Studies*, 325–53.

[50] Two Commission proposals: on how to strike the balance between workers' right to strike and companies' right to freedom of movement of services (COM(2012) 130 final, 21.3.2012) and how the Member States are to apply the Posting of Workers Directive (COM(2012) 131 final, 21.3.2012).

[51] Directive 2018/97, OJ L 173/16.

remains to be seen. There are more nuanced voices on what could be called Social Europe 2.0, which do not deny the paradigm shift in European labour law, but stress the opportunities of transforming labour protection law into *the law of the labour market*, of reconnecting the 'Social' to the economy.[52] This is very much in line with the case study of Tommaso Pavone on the impact of the ECJ judgment *Porto di Genova*,[53] which destroyed the power of the trade union, but enabled the recovery of the economy around the port. What would have happened to the *Land* of Bremen if the EU had prevented the mayor from subsidising the dying industry?

Similar developments are to be reported from consumer law. Consumer law grew at the national level together with the rise of the social welfare state. Consumer law was consumer protection law, having, as its addressee, the weak party. The EU first copied and then changed the paradigm from national consumer protection law to European consumer law without protection. In implementing the Lisbon Agenda, the consumer policy programme 2002[54] aimed at substituting minimum harmonisation through full harmonisation. One single level playing field should free business from dealing with twenty-eight different consumer laws. The economies of scale were to prevail over different levels of protection, enshrined in different national cultures and traditions. The European Commission managed fully to harmonise the law on unfair commercial practices in 2005 and on consumer credit in 2008, but failed with regard to consumer contract law – unfair terms and consumer sales law. In contrast to labour law, the European Commission has not given up the 2002 policy agenda. The so-called Consumer Refit is just another

[52] Loïc Azoulai, 'The Court of Justice and the Social Market Economy: The Emergence of an Ideal and the Conditions for its Realisation' (2008) 45 *Common Market Law Review*, 1335–355, Paul Davies and Mark Freedland, *Towards a Flexible Labour Market: Labour Legislation and Regulation since the 1990s* (Oxford: Oxford University Press, 2007). Simon Deakin and Frank Wilkinson, *The Law of the Labour Market: Industrialization, Employment and Legal Evolution* (Oxford: Oxford University Press, 2005); Advocate General Miguel Poiares Maduro's Opinions in *Viking* and *Laval*.

[53] ECJ Case C-179/90 *Merci convenzionali porto di Genova SpA* v *Siderurgica Gabrielli SpA*. Reference for a preliminary ruling: *Tribunale di Genova – Italy*, European Court Reports 1991 I-05889, ECLI identifier: ECLI:EU:C:1991:464, Tommaso Pavone, 'From Marx to Market: Lawyers, European Law, and the Contentious Transformation of the Port of Genoa', *Law & Society Review*, 2018, 1, early view.

[54] Communication from the Commission of 7 May 2002 to the European Parliament, the Council, the Economic and Social Committee and the Committee of the Regions – 'Consumer Policy Strategy 2000–2006' [COM (2002) 208 final – Official Journal C137/ 2 of 08.06.2002.

attempt at what the European Commission failed to achieve with the Consumer Rights Directive in 2011.[55]

In contrast to the 'ugly four' in labour law, in consumer law the ECJ is shivering between the protection of the weaker party in the Spanish mortgage cases and the promotion of economic efficiency through the average consumer unfair commercial practices. A serious debate, however, on who benefits from the rules, the 'weak poor' or the 'rich circumspect' consumer, is missing. Consumer law is stuck at both ends, in economics because economic efficiency is not really taken seriously, and politically because the distinction between the weak and the circumspect consumer is not fully thought through. Consumer lawyers, just like labour lawyers, are critical of the move towards full harmonisation, be it implemented by the European Commission or the ECJ,[56] but shy away from discussing the distribution of the costs between consumers.

III.2 Law and the Changing Paradigms of Integration

Elsewhere, I distinguish between the three stages of building the EU: integration through law, integration through governance, and integration beyond law.[57] At each stage, law changes its function. In the foregoing analysis, I have explained how European private law has been used to realise the Internal Market and how the 'Social' is transformed through the shift from national level to EU level. The function of the law remained relatively stable. EU law making and the growing case law of the ECJ provide ample evidence. Insisting on the integration through law paradigm, despite the economic crisis, the euro crisis and now the political crisis, are starting to look weird. Integration through law turns into an 'as if' rationale; *as if* it were still possible and feasible to continue integration building along the lines of the Treaty of Rome and the SEA. It suffices to recall the thicket of consumer information rights or the 100 ECJ judgments in

[55] Review of EU consumer law – New Deal for consumers, https://ec.europa.eu/info/law/law-topic/consumers/review-eu-consumer-law-new-deal-consumers_en; Hans-W. Micklitz and Norbert Reich, 'Crónica de una muerte anunciada: The Commission Proposal for a "Directive on Consumer Rights"' (2009) 46 *Common Market Law Review*, 471–519.

[56] ECJ C-183/00, González Sánchez, [2002] ECR I-3901; Thomas Verheyen, 'Full Harmonization, Consumer Protection and Products Liability: A Fresh Reading of the Case Law of the ECJ' (2018) 26 *European Review of Private Law*, 119–40.

[57] Hans-W. Micklitz, *The Politics of Justice in European Private Law: Social Justice, Access Justice, Societal Justice* (Cambridge: Cambridge University Press, 2018), pp. 163.

consumer law.[58] In a worst-case scenario, EU law is hanging in the air, a subject for research, but disconnected from the real world, from the political economy of the Member States and the EU. Is this the legacy of integration through law? Critical legal scholarship on the mismatch between the autonomous legal order and the national legal orders is growing, albeit, usually, without much self-reflection.

Whilst integration through law is self-explanatory, 'integration through governance' and 'integration beyond law' need clarification. The latter two find their common origin in three non-binding policy documents: the already-mentioned Lisbon Agenda 2000, the Constitutional Charter 2000, and the White Paper on Governance 2001.[59] Integration through governance is to be understood as the political answer of the EU and the Member States to the limits of the 'integration through law' paradigm. 'Integration beyond law' combines the move towards economic efficiency to be counterbalanced through constitutionalisation via fundamental rights. In political practice, 'integration through governance' precedes 'integration beyond law'. Critical legal scholarship invested in governance and, until today, in constitutionalisation in order to 'rescue' what is left of the 'Social' at EU level. This is particularly true with regard to the constitutionalisation of private law.[60] (Experimental) governance is about to turn into an overarching concept that explains the transformation of the EU and the Member States.[61] The quest for

[58] Betül Kas and Hans-W. Micklitz, *Rechtsprechungsübersicht zum Europäischen Vertrags- und Deliktsrecht* (2014–2018) – EWS (Europäisches Wirtschafts- und Steuerrecht 2018, 181-219 and 241-300 Seiten (Teil I und Teil II (Part I and II)) – Analysis of the case-law of the ECJ in European contract and tort law.

[59] See https://ec.europa.eu/europeaid/sites/devco/files/communication-white-paper-governance-com2001428-20010725_en.pdf.

[60] Olha O. Cherednychenko, *Fundamental Rights, Contract Law and the Protection of the Weaker Party: A Comparative Analysis of the Constitutionalisation of the Contract Law, with Emphasis on Risky Financial Transactions* (Munich: Sellier European Law Publishers, 2007); Chantal Mak, *Fundamental Rights in European Contract Law: A Comparison of the Impact of Fundamental Rights on Contractual Relationships in Germany, the Netherlands, Italy and England* (Alphen a/d Rijn: Kluwer Law International, 2008); Gert Brüggemeier, Aurelia Colombi Ciacchi and Giovanni Comandé (eds.), *Fundamental Rights and Private Law in the European Union* (Cambridge: Cambridge University Press, 2010).

[61] Mark Dawson, *New Governance and the Transformation of European Law: Coordinating EU Social Law and Policy* (Cambridge: Cambridge University Press, 2011), Charles F. Sabel and Jonathan Zeitlin, 'Learning from Difference: The New Architecture of Experimentalist Governance in the EU' (2008) 14 *European Law Journal*, 271–327. Charles F. Sabel and Jonathan Zeitlin, 'Experimentalism in the EU: Common Ground and Persistent Differences' (2012) 6 *Regulation & Governance*, 410–26.

economic efficiency, however, was perceived much more as a threat than as an opportunity to rethink the 'Social'.

In integration through governance, the Open Method of Co-ordination (OMC) is centre stage. Via the OMC, the European Commission tried to influence labour law both outside and beyond the formal competence of the Treaty. Fabrizio Cafaggi and Horatia Muir Watt[62] used the thinking behind the OMC to embark on a deeper analysis on the new modes of governance in European private law. Much more concrete is the attempt of the Ius Commune Series on Private Law edited by Walter van Gerven.[63] The idea behind Ius Commune is the convergence of national private laws through national courts and European Courts. Judicial networks help to organise the exchange between national and European Courts. However, the European Commission pursued a different avenue. It tried – in vain – to initiate negotiations between business and consumer organisations at EU level to elaborate commonly agreed standard terms.[64] Much more successful has been the strategy of the European Commission to extend the New Approach on Technical Product Standards to harmonising the law on services, most visibly in the field of regulated markets.[65] The EU celebrates the New Approach as a success story, as it allows it to harmonise the conditions under which products can be legally marketed EU-wide. In the ongoing liberalisation and partly privatisation, the EU relied on sector-related standardisation for market-building purposes. There would

[62] Fabrizio Cafaggi and Horatia Muir-Watt (eds.), *Making European Private Law: Governace Design* (Cheltenham: Edward Elgar Publishing, 2010); Fabrizio Cafaggi and Horatia Muir Watt (eds.), *The Regulatory Function of European Private Law* (Cheltenham: Edward Elgar Publishing, 2009).

[63] Walter van Gerven, 'Needed: A Method of Convergence for Private Law', in: Andreas Furrer (ed.), *Europäisches Privatrecht im wissenschaftlichen Diskurs* (Bern: Stämpfli Verlag), pp. 437–60, and Fabrizio Cafaggi, 'Rethinking Private Regulation in the European Regulatory Space', in: Cafaggi (ed.), *Reframing Self-Regulation in European Private Law* (Alphen a/d Rijn: Kluwer Law International, 2006), pp. 3–75. For an overview of the Ius Commune Casebooks for the Common Law of Europe (edited by Dimitri Droshout), see www.bloomsburyprofessional.com/uk/series/ius-commune-casebooks-for-the-common-law-of europe/?SeriesName=Ius+Commune+Casebooks+for+the+Common+Law+of+Europe&SeriesFullTitle=Ius+Commune+Casebooks+for+the+Common+Law+of+Europe.

[64] Hugh Collins, 'Why Europe Needs a Civil Code' (2013) 21 *European Review of Private Law*, 907–22.

[65] Contributions in Marta Cantero and Hans-W. Micklitz (eds.), *Standards, Contracts and Codes: Streamlining Transnational Norm-production and Norm-enforcement*, Edward Elgar Publishing, forthcoming 2020.

be no internal market for telecom, for energy or for transport without the technical standards which had been developed over time. The Banking Union and the key role technical standards are playing, fit well into this picture.

The EU created a comprehensive 'contractual underworld', which lies beneath the surface of contract and tort law, but which – in practice – works as a substitute for the politically impossible harmonisation of the law on services through secondary EU law. One might argue that these technical standards are to be separated from contract and tort, at least as long as there is no formal reference in the contract to the use of technical standards. Such convincing distinctions overlook that it is not so much contract law but technical standards that set and define the conditions for cross-border transactions. European law has changed its function and its form.[66] Critical legal scholarship circulates around transparency, accountability, legitimacy, and judicial review. But legitimacy and accountability are, strictly speaking, not legal criteria. Transparency has made its way into secondary EU law and could be regarded as a horizontal European principle. The difficulty, however, is to materialise the principle and to give it shape. Overall judicial review is regarded as the means of last resort, if not of last hope. In its recent case law, *Frabo, Elliott* and *TÜV Rheinland*,[67] the ECJ accepted jurisdiction for harmonised European standards and seems ready to exercise some form of procedural control over the making of technical standards, and may gradually transform accountability into liability. Can courts compensate for the loss of the legal form? Critical legal scholarship is fascinated by the new integration paradigm and at the same time sceptical about its potential to realise the European Social beyond the competence borders or within the competence borders through new enforcement techniques.

Integration beyond law brings together two conflicting strands of integration, the rise of economic efficiency, which goes hand in hand with the rise of constitutionalising private law through human rights and fundamental rights. To date, the EU has not succeeded in fully implementing economic efficiency against which European social regulation is tested.

[66] Yane Svetiev, 'European Regulatory Private Law: From Conflicts to Platforms', in: Kai Purnhagen and Peter Rott (eds.), *Varieties of European Economic Law and Regulation: Liber Amicorum for Hans Micklitz* (New York: Springer International Publishing, 2014), pp. 153–77.

[67] Case C-171/11, Fra.bo [2012] ECR I-000, Case C-613/14, James Elliott Construction [2016] ECR I-00, Case C-219/15, Schmitt [2017] ECR I-00.

The attempts look half-hearted, mainly designed to legitimate the move from minimum to full harmonisation. However, the EU managed to implant into the EU legal system the worker-citizen, the consumer-citizen and the entrepreneur-citizen.[68] This goes along with the transformation of the labour law and consumer law not only into the incriminated law of the labour market and the consumer market but into the law of the labour and consumer market *society*. EU critical legal scholarship is focusing on the economisation of the society, of submitting each and every part of the society, even those habits that are not directly related to concrete economic transactions, to the rationality of the Internal Market.

The constitutionalisation of private law is at the forefront of European legal scholarship. Human rights and fundamental rights are mobilised to shield both the workers and the consumers against the detrimental effects of the economic crisis and the euro crisis. More than 50 per cent of all preliminary references to the ECJ invoke the Charter of Fundamental Rights, most prominently, the right to effective judicial protection.[69] Their ubiquitous character allows them to give each and every private law conflict a constitutional – human rights, fundamental rights – twist. The ECJ is, within limits, willing to use human rights and fundamental rights as arguments to correct national private laws.[70] The flood of references may lead to guiding principles of constitutionalised European private law, against which national private law has to be measured. Is this the total constitution of which we should not be afraid?[71] But is it possible to build a European society around individual rights alone, however sacrosanct these rights might be? Where is the collective function of the 'Social', where is the solidarity which cannot be shaped in the rights language? Critical legal

68 Michelle Everson, 'The Legacy of the Market Citizen', in: Jo Shaw and Gillian More (eds.), *New Legal Dynamics of European Union* (Oxford: Clarendon Press, 1995), pp. 73–90. Market citizenship in general is said to be inherently limited. In contrast, Niamh Nic Shuibhne, 'The Resilience of EU Market Citizenship' (2010) 47 *Common Market Law Review*, 1597–628, believes that market citizenship may offer more than we presume.

69 Marek Safjan and Dominik Düsterhaus, 'A Union of Effective Judicial Protection: Addressing a Multi-level Challenge through the Lens of Art 47 CFREU' (2014) 33 *Yearbook of European Law*, 3–40.

70 Federico Della Negra, 'The Uncertain Development of the Case Law on Consumer Protection in Mortgage Enforcement Proceedings: Sánchez Morcillo and Kušionová' (2015) 52 *Common Market Law Review*, 1009–32.

71 Mattias Kumm, 'Who Is Afraid of the Total Constitution? Constitutional Rights as Principles and the Constitutionalization of Private Law' (2006) 7 *German Law Journal*, 341–69.

scholarship all too often focuses on the destructive potential of the EU, but falls short of recognising that the EU is trying to build a European society *beyond* the market, not only, but also, through law.[72]

IV Conclusion

This chapter should be read as an ideological (self-)critique of the role and function of critical legal scholarship in the rise of the 'Social' after 1960, first, at national level, later, at EU level. Critical legal scholars have all too often understood critical legal theory as *practice of theory*, in which law is there to help to protect the weaker parties in society and to compensate for the imbalance of power. The decline of the welfare state and the 'neoliberal move' in the EU teaches us that law can be politicised not only to promote the 'Social' in the name of justice but also to deconstruct the 'Social' in the name of economic efficiency.

The revival of the political economy provides for an opportunity to rethink the role of law in the secular compromise between capitalism and democracy. This requires us to look into the politics *and* the economics of the law. To date, the two camps in the debate are not really communicating with each other; quite to the contrary, they are looking at each other in 'hermeneutics of suspicion'. Duncan Kennedy[73] distinguishes between critical legal scholars who are governed by *constitutional ambition* and those advocating *modesty as 'internal' politics*, referring to Mattias Kumm, as a protagonist for the former, *versus* Gunther Teubner and Christian Joerges, as protagonists for the latter.

[72] Micklitz, *Politics of Justice in European Private Law*, n. 57 above, *passim*.

[73] Duncan Kennedy, 'A Political Economy of Contemporary Legality', Chapter 4 in this volume, and Kennedy, 'The Hermeneutic of Suspicion in Contemporary American Legal Thought' (2014) 25 *Law & Critique*, 91–139.

9

Socio-Economic Imaginaries and European Private Law

MARIJA BARTL

I Introduction

The aim of this chapter is to explore how our ideas about the economy and the market shape the way we think about the law, as well as how ideas about the law condition our understanding of what market is and what it 'needs'. There are several reasons why we should explore this broad question through the prism of private law. One reason will be obvious to private lawyers: while sociologist have always underlined the immense importance of private law, and particularly contract law, for the institution of markets,[1] private law scholarship and practice has been often understood as being insulated from political considerations,[2] and presumably concerned mainly with corrective justice based upon rules logically deduced from first-order principles of personal freedom and the 'will theory'. But how far can these discourses actually be isolated? Secondly, and perhaps more importantly, private law plays an important role in making and correcting markets and economies: the rule of law, understood as the enforcement of contracts and the protection of private property, has been portrayed as being core to economic development by financial and developmental institutions

[1] For instance, Max Weber, *Economy and Society*, new ed. (Oakland CA: University of California Press, 1992), p. 666 et seq.

[2] James Gordley, *The Philosophical Origins of Modern Contract Doctrine* (Oxford: Clarendon Press, 1993), p. 216. Similar points were raised also by P.S. Atiyah, *The Rise and Fall of Freedom of Contract* (Oxford: Oxford University Press, 1979), or Duncan Kennedy, 'From the Will Theory to the Principle of Private Autonomy: Lon Fuller's Consideration and Form' (2000) 100 *Columbia Law Review*, 94–175, and are still professed by Ernest J. Weinrib, *The Idea of Private Law* (Oxford: Oxford University Press, 1995).

such as the World Bank or International Monetary Fund.[3] The EU has, in contrast, attempted to constrain market forces through private law; for instance, by means of consumer law, which has become one of the core elements of its more 'Social' face.[4] Ultimately, then, the question that this chapter raises is one of *what* we are actually saying when we say that we use the law, and private law in particular, as means to correct markets: What is our underlying conception of either the market or the law?

The argument that I would like to advance in this chapter is that legal and economic discourses, independently of whatever their participants would like to assume, share a set of fundamental pre-understandings as the relation between the subject of the legal-political order and the social whole – which has, in this way, co-instituted a particular kind of society in different historical periods.[5] These shared pre-understandings ensure that the law and legal discourse tend to support, rather than subvert, the tenets (if not particulars) of socio-economic organisation. However, by uncovering this entanglement, we unearth a potentially subversive role for the law. To the extent that the law and legal discourse unsettle the shared pre-understandings as to the relation between the subject and the social whole, and offer alternative imaginaries as to the role of the law in society, a broader change in social imaginary may ensue.

To develop this argument, this chapter relies on the concept OF social imaginaries,[6] that is to say, 'the ways people imagine their social

[3] The stress on the enforcement of contracts and protection of property as the main component of the rule of law was particularly strong in the early 1990s; today, the hierarchy remains: 'Rule of law captures perceptions of the extent to which agents have confidence in and abide by the rules of society, and in particular the quality of contract enforcement, property rights, the police, and the courts, as well as the likelihood of crime and violence.' See http://info.worldbank.org/governance/wgi/pdf/rl.pdf.

[4] Daniela Caruso, '*Qu'ils mangent des contrats*: Rethinking Justice in EU Contract Law', in: Dimitry Kochenov, Gráinne de Búrca and Andrew Williams (eds.), *Europe's Justice Deficit?* (Oxford: Hart Publishing, 2015), pp. 367–80.

[5] Cornelius Castoriadis, *The Imaginary Institution of Society: Creativity and Autonomy in the Social-historical World* (Cambridge-Malden MA: Polity Press, 1997).

[6] The interpretation of the concept in this chapter draws on both psychoanalytic and constructivist/communitarian uses of the concept, and, in particular, I acknowledge my debt to Castoriadis; Charles Taylor, *Modern Social Imaginaries* (Durham NC: Duke University Press, 2004); Sheila Jasanoff and Sang-Hyun Kim, *Dreamscapes of Modernity: Sociotechnical Imaginaries and the Fabrication of Power* (Chicago IL: University of Chicago Press, 2015), and Ngai-Ling Sum and Bob Jessop, *Towards a Cultural Political Economy: Putting Culture in its Place in Political Economy* (Cheltenham: Edward Elgar Publishing, 2013).

existence, how they fit together with others, how things go on between them and their fellows, the expectations that are normally met, and the deeper normative notions and images that underlie these expectations'.[7] In the first part of the chapter, I develop a theoretical account, arguing that different economic, political and legal discourses converge around shared, and historically determined, pre-understandings (social imaginaries) as to what constitutes the socio-economic whole, who can act on it and how.

I further elaborate this argument by exploring the transformations of private law as a response to different imaginaries of the economy, politics and society in the last two centuries. I present three basic socio-economic imaginaries (the birth of the political economy; the market as a political project; and, finally, the market as a means of rationalisation), and show the ways in which these imaginaries have analogues in supportive legal imaginaries, rules and practices – even if legal discourse may have been blind to its very dependence upon wider social imaginaries.[8]

In the second part of the chapter, I turn to European private, and, in particular, consumer, law in order to demonstrate how a new socio-economic imaginary enters and settles in European consumer law and policy. Taking as a starting point the European Commission's communications on consumer policy, I illustrate how, over the last thirty years, different imaginaries of the market and the economy have shaped the horizons in EU consumer law. Finally, in the third and last part of the chapter, I illustrate some of the important impacts of the new economic imaginary on European private and consumer law. These include both the understanding of the subject of European Private Law (EPL) as well as the relation of the subject to the social whole.

When it comes to the limitations of the argument, there are several. First, the articulation of three socio-economic imaginaries against the background of the transformation of private law should not be seen as an exercise in historical reconstruction, but rather as an analytical framework that allows us to theorise the relation between the law and the economy in the context of EPL. Second, the historical references are based mainly upon secondary literature. For periodisation, I rely on several important contributions, including those of Duncan Kennedy[9]

[7] Taylor, *Modern Social Imaginaries*, n. 6 above, p. 23.

[8] Atiyah, *The Rise and Fall of Freedom of Contract*, n. 2 above, reviewed by Betty Mensch, 'Freedom of Contract as Ideology' (1981) 33 *Stanford Law Review*, 753–72.

[9] Duncan Kennedy, 'Three Globalizations of Law and Legal Thought: 1850–2000', in: David M. Trubek and Alvaro Santos (eds.), *The New Law and Economic Development: A Critical Appraisal* (Cambridge: Cambridge University Press, 2006), pp. 19–73.

and Christoph Schmid.[10] Third, 'the focus' of the chapter is on the question of how stability is maintained over time, whereby the first part of the chapter articulates how the dominant imaginaries have been institutionalised in the rules of private law. A different story needs to be told about how social change is wrought: while a prelude to this topic may be found in the second part of the chapter, which discusses the penetration of the new economic imaginary in consumer law policy, social change and the law is the topic of a different and more ambitious project. The last limitation is geographical: given that the focus of the chapter is on EPL, I do not deal with the broader global history of economic or legal thought, but mainly focus the West European debate in the last 200 years.

II Social Imaginaries: The Bridge between Law and the Economy

Social imaginaries are collectively held, and are often the institutionalised, beliefs, ideas, images and fantasies that underwrite our lived experience.[11] They represent shared pre-understandings as to what constitutes our social existence – how the economy, society, human relations, nature and politics fit together[12] – thereby providing a basic infrastructure for meaning making, the reduction of complexity, and the ordering of social reality.[13] Social imaginaries are historical creatures, 'creating for each historical period its singular ways of living, seeing and making its own existence',[14] with its own temporalities, geographies and knowledge.

If social imaginaries present a shared basis for making sense of our social existence, they must also include imaginaries of the economy,

[10] Christoph U. Schmid, *Die Instrumentalisierung des Privatrechts Durch die Europäische Union: Privatrecht und Privatrechtskonzeptionen in der Entwicklung der Europäischen Integrationsverfassung*, 1. Aufl, Schriftenreihe Des Zentrums für Europäische Rechtspolitik der Universität Bremen (ZERP), Bd. 61 (Baden-Baden: Nomos, 2010).

[11] The reason I resort to the concept of imaginaries is at least twofold. First, having its origin in psychoanalysis, the concept builds on the recognition of the fragility of the shared, taking seriously the constitutive role of the individual imagination and leaving more space for fantasies and inconsistencies. At the same time, it is still apt to aid in the understanding as to why certain changes may be more fundamental than others: why some lead to a new society, while the others leave us in the old world (Sum and Jessop, *Towards a Cultural Political Economy*, n. 6 above.)

[12] For Charles Taylor, modern social imaginary stands on three pillars – the distinction between public and private spheres, the economy as a distinct sphere, and finally the idea of collective self-determination. Taylor, *Modern Social Imaginaries*, n. 6 above.

[13] Sum and Jessop, *Towards a Cultural Political Economy*, n. 6 above.

[14] Castoriadis, *The Imaginary Institution of Society*, n. 6 above.

politics or law, and how they work together in the constitution of our social world. More specifically, I will argue that, because economic, political and legal imaginaries find their common foundation in deeper social imaginaries, they will share similar pre-understandings, at least at two different levels. First, they will share pre-understandings as to the nature of the social world, and the degree to which this world is transformable. Economic, political and legal imaginaries jointly institute the imagined boundary between the social and natural, the constructed and the given, the transformable and fixed. Second, economic, political and legal imaginaries will share similar pre-understanding as to agency in the socio-economic processes, and in particular how subjects/actors/collectivities/groups can intervene in the socio-economic process in order to change the social whole.

An example of a successful social imaginary that has set the ground for the transformation of the economy, politics and law is what is often referred to as neoliberal political rationality.[15] Neoliberal imaginary has both grounded the understanding as to the appropriate social whole on which to intervene and how to do so. First, in this imaginary, the social whole is mostly seen as being synonymous with the market (be it global, international or national). Second, the mode of intervention on this social whole is not only to optimise the functioning of existing markets, but, more importantly, to spread its rationalising principles to other spheres where they were absent. Finally, in this imaginary, subjects and social actors (consumers, workers, employers, trade unions, etc.) have a common interest to work together in order to improve market functioning, achieve rationalisation of social processes, and improve international competitiveness.

This social imaginary has been articulated institutionalised, through various disciplinary discourses and practices. As I show in later parts of this chapter – which refer to legal discourse and practice – it has found its expression in a certain understanding of the law's appropriate role. That is, on the one hand, understanding law as means to facilitate and harness markets and, on the other, a particular way in which legal subjects have been articulated. It was the actors who were expected to contribute to market dynamism that were assigned specific rights, duties, responsibilities and capacities to deliver on this goal. This is, of course, not to say that there have been no legal interventions in the EU that do not adopt

[15] Mark Beeson and Ann Firth, 'Neoliberalism as a Political Rationality: Australian Public Policy since the 1980s' (1998) 34 *Journal of Sociology*, 215–31.

a more 'interventionist' stance, such as the general data protection regulation (GDPR), but such interventions have remained few, and unless sufficiently institutionalised, their 'survival' has often been under attack.[16]

In what remains of the section, I articulate different transformations of private law in response to different imaginaries of the economy, politics and society during the past two centuries. I will show how three different economic imaginaries have their counterparts in supportive legal imaginaries, rules and practices.

II.1 The Birth of Political Economy and Classical Legal Thought

One of the tectonic shifts that consolidated in the eighteenth century was the *discovery* of political economy.[17] The economy became visible as a sphere governed by a set of interdependent natural-like processes, when the 'naturality', with all its predictable law-like qualities, stemmed from modelling the social world as a series of interactions between predictable (i.e. rational self-interested) individuals.[18] This political economy became both the object of, and the limitation to, governmental intervention: the question of the *desirability* of intervention depended for the most part on establishing the *possibility* of intervention: to wit, how far is the economy transformable through political and legal intervention?

Among classical economists, two main answers were given to this question: on the more optimistic side, Adam Smith furthered a positive case for the market.[19] Even if he acknowledged that market processes may sometimes be disruptive, ultimately, this process was a natural means to progress. The natural human propensity to self-interest and barter becomes a common good in a self-regulated market.[20] Others, like

[16] The introduction of innovation (https://ec.europa.eu/epsc/publications/strategic-notes /towards-innovation-principle-endorsed-better-regulation_en) is possibly a direct challenge to precautionary principle (www.politico.eu/article/consumer-protections-europe-big-business-sharks-circle).

[17] In his seminar contribution, Foucault discusses the birth of political economy from Physiocrats; see Michel Foucault, Arnold I. Davidson (ed.) and Graham Burchell (trans.), *The Birth of Biopolitics: Lectures at the Collège de France, 1978–1979* (Basingstoke: Palgrave Macmillan, 2008).

[18] Ibid.

[19] Adam Smith, *An Inquiry into the Nature and Causes of the Wealth of Nations* (Chicago IL: University of Chicago Press, 1977).

[20] Ibid.

Ricardo, or Malthus, took a slightly more pessimistic attitude: while the market process may bring about much human suffering, especially for less fortunate peoples, there is little point in intervening to help them since any such intervention would be counter-productive.[21] If one regulates wages, it will ultimately harm the poor because it will lower employment. If one limits hours of work, it will ultimately harm those who want to work more to ensure the livelihood of their extended families. If one prohibits usury, one will see the emergence of a black market. Intervention, in fact, makes things worse; the best we can do is to let the natural course of things run its course.

Both of these positions presuppose a self-regulated, given or non-transformable quality of the market economy: political intervention (through the law) would either impede progress or would be futile. Such naturalised views of the economy were further sustained by a broader shift to 'positivism' in social sciences, which viewed society more generally as operating upon the basis of scientific laws akin to gravity.[22] This transformation has been accompanied by the development of specific technologies of observation and government, such as statistics, which enabled the observance of regularities in various populations, with regard to specific problems or times.[23]

At least four symmetries between this economic thought and discourse, on the one hand, and private and particularly contract law, on the other, are observable during the 'classical' period. By observing these symmetries, then, we can infer the shared pre-understandings that make these two spheres – so to speak – work to maintain the existing social order – even if they may not be seen as linked.

First, the naturalism that spanned market thinking also spanned private law.[24] If the naturalised imaginaries of the market hinged on the predictability of its operation, in so far as they could be scientifically deduced from a vision of the social order that hinges on the rational (and natural) behaviour of self-interested individuals, we can see a similar naturalising tendency reflected in the deductive character of private and

[21] Thomas Robert Malthus, *An Essay on the Principle of Population* (Oxford: Oxford University Press 2008).

[22] Auguste Comte, *The Positive Philosophy of Auguste Comte* V1 (Whitefish, Literary Licencing, 2014).

[23] Alain Desrosières, 'How to Make Things which Hold Together: Social Science, Statistics and the State', in: Peter Wagner, Björn Wiitrock and Richard Whitley (eds.), *Discourses on Society: The Shaping of the Social Science Disciplines* (Dordrecht: Springer, 1990), 195–218.

[24] Gordley, *The Philosophical Origins of Modern Contract Doctrine*, n. 2 above, p. 218.

contract law. Quite contrary to public law,[25] private law could have been inferred rationally from the higher natural principles, such as individualism and free will,[26] by scholars or experts, rather than through a political process. Upon the same basis, private law claimed universality, justified both by belief in the generality of such deductive 'exercises', as well as a naturalised understanding of the individual and (corrective) justice.[27]

Second, both the market and private law imaginaries had a similar *subject* in mind. They both relied on a subject that is an autonomous, formally free individual, who must be ready to bear the consequences of their actions in the marketplace. Such individuals were expected to deliver public benefit(s) by looking after their own affairs (private vice, public virtue) – while they, instead of any public authority, are trusted to know their own interests best. In this sense, the safeguarding of individual liberty became important, as a matter of political theory, political economy, and law.

We may find the third parallel in the relation between the subject and the social whole, as framed in both political economy and private law. The political economy of the times was an order in which the innumerable interactions of individuals (micro level) gave rise to a certain natural, spontaneous (macro) order.[28] Private law quite neatly resembles this picture. The idea of free, autonomous and responsible individuals, and their wills, were to engage in their individual dances within the institutions of property and contract law – thus creating an organic society bottom up, a variant of what ordoliberals were later to call the 'private law' society.[29]

Fourth, there is a common concern with dynamism in both political economy and private law. The emergence of political economy in the eighteenth century is closely linked to the formation of national markets, which enabled intensified interaction across the national territory.[30] The same goes for early civil codes, such as the *Code Civil des Français* or

[25] Duncan Kennedy, 'Three Globalizations of Law and Legal Thought', n. 9 above.

[26] Atiyah, *The Rise and Fall of Freedom of Contract*, n. 2 above.

[27] Duncan Kennedy, 'Three Globalizations of Law and Legal Thought', n. 9 above.

[28] Smith, *An Inquiry into the Nature and Causes of the Wealth of Nations*, n. 19 above.

[29] Stefan Grundmann, 'The Concept of the Private Law Society: After 50 Years of European Business and European Business Law' (2008) 16 *European Review of Private Law*, 553–81; Nuno Manuel Pinto Oliveira, 'The Private Law Society and Contract Law Application' (2009) 5 *European Review of Contract Law*, 29–40.

[30] Karl Polanyi, *The Great Transformation: The Political and Economic Origins of Our Time*, 2nd ed. (Boston MA: Beacon Press, [1944] 2001).

Napoleonic Code, which were intended as both a means of market making and nation making.[31] The formalism and abstractness of contract law, then, not only parallels but also enables the pursuit of market dynamism.[32] As subsequent critics of the process of 'materialisation' make clear, any de-formalisation of contract that considers the particulars of the transaction (as it concerns persons or goods) moves us out of the domain of 'pure contract'.[33]

The underlying conception of politics behind both the economic and the legal imaginaries in this period is that of *futility*. The naturalised conceptions of the market require as little political intervention as possible, while the logical rules of private law are not open to politics at all. What typifies the imaginaries of this time is thus a shared pre-understanding of how social change takes place. While both economic thought and private law focus on the micro-level social structure – to wit, the individual – be it as a pursuer of self-interest or as the formally equal subject of private law, social change is imagined as an organic bottom-up process, driven by both capable individuals and market-driven technological change. The role for politics – or the law – for social change is limited at best.

II.2 The Market as a Political Project: The Rise of the Social in Legal Thought

In the last quarter of nineteenth century, there arose an increasing political and legal confidence in Europe that the state should interfere in the operation of the 'free markets'.[34] While some early interventions had already taken place in the nineteenth century,[35] the emergence of unionisation and the labour movement as agents of social change greatly intensified the degree of intervention. Even though the history of labour movements across Europe differs,[36] it can quite safely be concluded that the strengthening of the labour movement was one of the major forces

[31] Pierre Legrand, 'Against a European Civil Code' (1997) 60 *The Modern Law Review*, 44–63.

[32] Weber, *Economy and Society*, n. 1 above.

[33] Ibid.

[34] Atiyah, *The Rise and Fall of Freedom of Contract*, n. 2 above; Ewan McGaughey, 'The Social Role of Private Law (Otto von Gierke, 1889)', translation (2018) 19 *German Law Journal*, 1018–116.

[35] Atiyah, *The Rise and Fall of Freedom of Contract*, n. 2 above.

[36] Sheri Berman, *The Primacy of Politics: Social Democracy and the Making of Europe's Twentieth Century* (Cambridge University Press, 2006).

that drove the expansion of the franchise and the subsequent 'social-democratisation' of politics in Western Europe.[37]

Keynesian macroeconomics,[38] which, in a very important way, denaturalises markets, has perhaps been one of the most obvious embodiments of the new social imaginary. Change was the socio-economic project of the time. In this imaginary, 'we' know how the economy operates and how to intervene in it: thus, political and legal intervention could be employed in order to ensure full employment and better distribution of economic benefits.[39] The reimagination of the market was also accompanied by a shift in political discourse. The concerns with justice, equality, or substantive freedom became increasingly important: be it in response to the threat of communism, or a genuine care for social justice, the market outcomes appeared increasingly to be at odds with the liberal principles of freedom or equality.[40] On the side of economic thought, marginalism, and the discovery of 'marginal utility', made it clear that the large inequalities of income and wealth were possibly not only morally wrong, but also economically unproductive.[41]

The imaginary of private, and contract law also fundamentally changes. Private law is increasingly seen as both the infrastructure of market economy, which sets the ground rules for the struggle among different groups and interests, as well as an institution which is distributive in its own right.[42] By the same token, scholars came to believe that changing the legal infrastructure led inexorably to changes in the economic outcomes.[43] The most visible consequence of the denaturalisation of private law was the contraction of contract law. An ever-greater number of fields and institutions were carved out of contract law, including labour law, social law, tenancy protection and consumer protection, all of which constituted separate legal sub-disciplines with different

[37] Ibid.

[38] David Laidler, 'Keynes and the Birth of Modern Macroeconomics', EPRI Working Paper Series 2-2005.

[39] Nicholas Wapshott, *Keynes Hayek: The Clash that Defined Modern Economics* (New York: WW Norton & Company, 2011).

[40] Atiyah, *The Rise and Fall of Freedom of Contract*, n. 2 above.

[41] Emil Kauder, *History of Marginal Utility Theory* (Princeton NJ: Princeton University Press, 2015).

[42] Robert L. Hale, 'Coercion and Distribution in a Supposedly Non-Coercive State' (1923) 38 *Political Science Quarterly*, pp. 470–94; Robert L. Hale, 'Force and the State: A Comparison of Political and Economic Compulsion' (1935) 35 *Columbia Law Review*, 149–201; McGaughey, 'The Social Role of Private Law (Otto von Gierke, 1889)', n. 34 above.

[43] Ibid.

values and ideologies.[44] This process of 'neo-feudalisation' of contract law, which introduced groups back into the heart of private ordering, was accompanied by the processes of 'materialisation' of private law.[45] That is to say, to the extent that contract law was still concerned with the individual, it was no longer the abstract, formally free and equal person, but rather a socially situated individual with attendant factual or material inequalities.[46] In both economic thought and policy, as well as private law, the socio-economic imaginary of this period comes with an important recognition of the existence of different social groups (be it that of workers, tenants, consumers or employers) and their differing interests. This represented an essential move beyond the individual of the classical period, whereby the social political and legal intervention were focused at the meso level of groups and collectivities.

The political imaginary of the time draws on the idea that politics is both a struggle and a compromise among groups with different interests. The ensuing legislative intervention into private law then aims to deliver a more balanced infrastructure for both political and economic exchange. Ultimately, this social imaginary stands on the shared pre-understanding that social change is possible through collective action and law, including private law. The main agents of change are groups, rather than individuals.

II.3 Markets as a Means of Rationalisation: Facilitative Law

The critique of the post-WW2 welfare state, built on the imaginary of the social, came from both the left and the right.[47] The New Left criticised a bloated welfare state and bureaucracy, with its disempowering, colonising effects on 'lifeworld(s)'.[48] The New Right presented the state as an intrusive, authoritarian institution, constraining market forces with economically negative consequences.[49] The economic stagnation of the end

[44] Ruth Dukes, *The Labour Constitution: The Enduring Idea of Labour Law* (Oxford Monographs on Labour Law, 2014); Schmid, *Die Instrumentalisierung Des Privatrechts Durch Die Europäische Union*, n. 10 above.

[45] Weber, *Economy and Society*, n. 1 above.

[46] Ibid. See, also, Friedrich Kessler, 'Contracts of Adhesion – Some Thoughts about Freedom of Contract' (1943) 43 *Columbia Law Review*, 629–42.

[47] David Harvey, *A Brief History of Neoliberalism* (Oxford: Oxford University Press, 2005).

[48] Jürgen Habermas, 'Legitimation Problems in the Modern State', in Habermas, *Communication and the Evolution of Society* (Boston MA: Beacon Press, 1979), pp. 178–206.

[49] Harvey, *A Brief History of Neoliberalism*, n. 47 above.

of the 1970s gave some credence to the arguments of the latter group, signposting what we may call the neoliberal revolution.[50]

When it comes to the imaginary of the market economy, in the 1980s one perceives a certain move towards the renaturalisation of the market, with the narrative of 'free market' and 'shock therapy' as a signpost. This return to liberalism, in its neoliberal variant, came, however, with some important novelties.[51] Above and beyond the free market, as a 'private sphere' that should be left free of governmental regulation, neoliberalism was also a broader critique of state institutions. In this imaginary, 'more market' was presented as a means of rationalisation of state institutions (government failure) and the economy.[52] The idea is that the introduction of competition and market incentives will rationalise (make more efficient, cost sensitive) both public institutions (new public management) and the private sphere (touching everything from privatising industries to the flexiblisation of labour).[53]

This double imaginary of the market ensured that, despite the failures of Shock Therapy and of the Washington Consensus in the 1990s, a powerful neoliberal project remained intact.[54] Perhaps markets left on their own do not really work, and some level of regulation may be necessary. Yet, viewing the market as a model for shaping social relations in order to achieve increased efficiencies across the social world, is a separate political project – and one broadly endorsed by politicians across the political spectrum from circa the second half of the 1990s.[55]

This new imagery of the market leads to new transformations of private law. If the perspective of private law was a micro perspective in the 'classical' period, focused on individuals, or 'meso' in the period of the focused on groups, from the end 1990s law and private law turns finally to the macro perspective of facilitating the market: private law becomes one of the instruments which contributes to the well-functioning market.[56] In such

[50] Ibid.

[51] Ibid.

[52] Colin Leys, *Market-Driven Politics: Neoliberal Democracy and the Public Interest* (London-New York: Verso Books, 2001).

[53] Harvey, *A Brief History of Neoliberalism*, n. 47 above.

[54] Ibid.

[55] Mark Beeson and Ann Firth, 'Neoliberalism as a Political Rationality: Australian Public Policy since the 1980s' (1998) 34 *Journal of Sociology*, 215–31; Harvey, *A Brief History of Neoliberalism*, n. 47 above.

[56] Marija Bartl, 'Internal Market Rationality, Private Law and the Direction of the Union: Resuscitating the Market as the Object of the Political' (2015) 21 *European Law Journal*, 572–98.

a framework, labour law, for instance, turns into the law of the labour market.[57] The main question behind labour law is no longer about the struggle between labour and capital, or employment relations between strong employer and weaker employee. Instead, the question becomes 'what kind of normative or regulatory framework is needed in order for labour markets to function in the interests of a range of societal goals, of which efficiency is one'.[58] The same move to the macro perspective of the market has also been observed in consumer law, mainly dominated by the EU. Thus according to Hans Micklitz, 'consumer protection law' has been turned by the EU into 'consumer law', which is more concerned with market functioning than consumer rights and protection.[59]

An important consequence of adopting the macro perspective of the market is that it comes with an implicit perception of shared interest among various groups and classes which come to constitute the (internal) market. The discourses of competitiveness, flexibility, empowerment, dynamism and progress all aim at the better utilisation of all of society's resources – ultimately to the benefit of all. The conception of the subject in private law changes as well. Markets, ever more defined in regional or global terms, need flexible and dynamic workers, who enjoy learning and moving around. The task of labour law, with its discourses of flexibility and learning, thus becomes a tool to support these human virtues.[60] Equally, consumer law, in order to serve its (internal) market-building role well, must aim to produce rational and circumspect consumers, who are able to shop cross-border, and contribute to better (internal) market functioning.[61]

Even if the civil law codifications of the nineteenth century (and their later cousins), which are in force across Europe, may present a certain resistance to this market-making instrumentalism in private law,[62] there is significant disagreement as to their relevance in the face of the 'penumbra' of contract law developing in liberalised public services, or through

[57] Dukes, *The Labour Constitution*, n. 44 above.

[58] Ibid., p. 103.

[59] Hans-W. Micklitz, 'The Expulsion of the Concept of Protection from the Consumer Law and the Return of Social Elements in the Civil Law: A Bittersweet Polemic', EUI Working Paper, 2012.

[60] Dukes, *The Labour Constitution*, n. 44 above.

[61] Micklitz, 'The Expulsion of the Concept of Protection from the Consumer Law and the Return of Social Elements in the Civil Law', n. 59 above.

[62] Martijn W. Hesselink, 'The Politics of a European Civil Code' (2004) 10 *European Law Journal*, 675–97.

the horizontal effects of treaty freedoms or non-discrimination principles.[63]

Finally, even the justice discourse changes in this period. Fundamental to the 'third way' conception of social justice, according to Hugh Collins, is the abandonment of the goal of relative equality among citizens, the equality of distributive outcomes.[64] Instead, the concern became social inclusion, that is, 'securing a minimum level of welfare' for each citizen, with a particular focus on members of various disadvantaged groups, so that they may all reach the necessary minimum to participate in social life.[65]

The political imaginary of the time draws on is the politics of common interest. All individuals and groups – worker, consumers, university teachers, etc. – need an economy that is competitive and well functioning. The compromises are, however, no longer the outcomes of struggle, in either economic policy or private law, but rather the outcome of rational economic assessment of what improves (Kaldor-Hicks) market efficiency. Ultimately, this social imaginary stands on the shared pre-understanding that change comes when the entire economy performs well, rationalised at a national and regional level by introducing market principles across social institutions and, internationally, by improving its competitiveness vis-à-vis other global competitors. Notably, the recent attempts to spread deep free trade agreements (FTA), such as the TTIP, which is the FTA between the EU and the United States, can be seen as attempts to expand 'market rationalising' principles to global trade, making them more akin to national and regional modes of market regulation. However, the more recent discursive strengthening of mercantilism in international trade policy, which came with the current US administration (Trump), goes back to underscoring competition and *quid-pro-quo*.

III Socio-Economic Imaginaries in European Consumer Policy

If the previous section discussed the symmetries between economic thought and policy, on the one hand, and private law discourse and

[63] Hans-W. Micklitz, 'The Visible Hand of European Regulatory Private Law – the Transformation of European Private Law from Autonomy to Functionalism in Competition and Regulation' (2009) 28 *Yearbook of European Law*, 3–59.

[64] Hugh Collins, 'Discrimination, Equality and Social Inclusion' (2003) 66 *The Modern Law Review* 66, 16–43.

[65] Ibid., p. 22.

rules, on the other, establishing the shared pre-understandings of how the economy, the law, and politics coalesce, this section focuses on describing the transition from the imaginary of the market as a political project to the imaginary of the market as a means of rationalisation in the EU.

The proxy used is the communications on consumer policy of the European Commission from early 1980s. Behind these policies, of course, there will have been struggles between actors with differing agendas, both from within and from outside the European Commission, and these policies have been received differently by the disparate audiences to whom they were directed. However, what these documents dazzlingly expose is the language, and the underlying imaginary, that the EU Commission used in order to achieve broader political support for its policy objectives.

When considering the interactions between market imaginaries and private law imaginaries in the EU, one must account for one specifically EU complication. The first question is how did the shift in the representations of the market transform EU consumer law? The second is what specific role, if any, has been played by an EU-specific imaginary of the *internal* market? The latter requires a great deal of sensitivity due to the institutional and substantive constraints under which the EU operates, for they may have considerable implications for the way in which the EU constructs the idea of the market.

Indeed, EU consumer protection law has always been 'the law of the internal market', at least in name.[66] Given the limited competences of the EU in the field of private law, European consumer legislation has been based upon the 'internal market' (now Article 114 TFEU) from its inception. However, what I try to show in what follows is that the entire 'world' may change while we still safely remain under the veil of internal market.

The first steps in consumer policy were taken from the 1970s. However, the first official *Commission consumer* Programme dates to 1981:

> Community is primarily concerned with the need to enable the consumer to act with *full knowledge of the facts*, and to hold the *balance between market forces*. To do this, he must be able to exercise the *five basic rights*,

[66] Christoph U. Schmid, 'The Instrumentalist Conception of the Acquis Communautaire in Consumer Law and Its Implications on A European Contract Law Code' (2005) 1 *European Review of Contract Law*, 211–27.

> which the preliminary programme conferred on him. They are: the right to protection of health and safety; the right to protection of economic interests; the right of redress; the right to information and education; and the right of representation (the right to be heard).[67]
>
> (my italics)

While not quite as ambitious as later communications, the 1981 Programme still imagines private law in conflictual terms, a law of interest and struggle. Consumers are expected to safeguard their interests, and, to that effect, they are equipped with consumer rights. This image corresponds to the socio-economic imaginary of the social, where it is struggle, and conflict, that 'balance' market powers.

In the 1991 Commission Consumer Programme, the first after the Single European Act (1986), the Commission elaborates the link between the internal market and consumer policy:

> In 1985 a programme was launched to give *a new impetus* to consumer policy. This *coincided with the publication of the White Paper on the Internal Market* and increased consciousness of the importance of addressing consumer concerns in the concentrated preparations for the Internal Market.[68]
>
> (my italics)

The Communication goes on to articulate how these rights (similar to those from 1981) will be delivered. First, when it comes to *consumer representation*, the Commission is interested in ensuring full representation of consumers in policy making, as well as providing support (including financing!) for the establishment of a strong consumer organisation, which could fight for consumers' interests. *Qua* 'consumer information', the Commission aims to provide consumers with an 'information service', focusing on delivering information from various sources. Other matters that need to be taken care of are *transparency*, including addressing concerns about biotechnology, through labelling. Finally, the Commission aims to take action in *Comparative Testing*.

While, in this programme, the Commission draws a clear link between the internal market and consumer protection, the imaginary of the market, and the consumer interests and rights underpinning it, are still

[67] See Council Resolution on a second programme of the European Economic Community for a consumer protection and information policy, 19 May 1981, available at: http://eur-lex.europa.eu/legal-content/EN/TXT/PDF/?uri=CELEX:31981Y0603(01)&from=EN.

[68] COM (90) 98 final, Three Year Action Plan for Consumer Policy in the EEC, available at: http://aei.pitt.edu/3712/1/3712.pdf.

understood in terms of conflict. The Commission goes even so far as to contemplate financing the emergence of strong consumer associations, which could fight for consumer interests effectively. In addition, the provision of information is still framed in terms of public obligations,[69] including the provision of factual information coming 'from various sources' (e.g. 'Sales promotion information is not of itself a sufficient basis for decision making for significant purchases'). Thus, while the Commission's position may be underpinned by the 'stakeholder' understanding of democracy, it was less 'managed' in comparison with what was to come later. In other words, the conflictual nature of 'common good' is still beyond doubt.

The Consumer Agenda of 1998 was already moving towards a less conflictual representation of the market. Consumers, in the changing world (globalisation and IT), need to become aware of the 'inter-linkages' between their interests and the interests of other stakeholders:

> A *new influence for consumer policy* that will have to be matched by a *new maturity on the part of consumers and their representatives.* If consumers are to play their role fully as equal stakeholders in society, they need to understand the *inter-linkages* between their *interests* and those of others . . . More specifically, as interests become more inter-linked, interactions need to be characterised by increased *cooperation.* Sometimes the respective interests of consumers and other groups will be mutually reinforcing, sometimes they will not and *tradeoffs* will have to be found. Consumers themselves can recognise and *accept such trade-offs* because they are not only consumers but *taxpayers, employees and beneficiaries of public policies too.* They can also accept that they have responsibilities and that their *immediate interests as consumers have to be reconciled with longer-term concerns for the environment and society.* EU consumer policy should therefore ensure that *consumer interests are equitably reconciled with those of other stakeholders.* This reconciliation of interests will usually be *a positive-sum game.*[70]
>
> (my italics)

Now, what is striking about this document is a clear shift towards the macro perspective of the market, and the discourse of common interest. The

69 Interestingly, the focus on information duties as means to overcome 'market failures' have been present since the 1980s in the Consumer Credit Directive, which was administered by the DG Market, instead of DG Consumer Protection. Stefan Grundmann, 'Information, Party Autonomy and Economic Agents in European Contract Law' (2002) 39 *Common Market Law Review*, 269–93.

70 COM ((1998) 696 final, Consumer Policy Action Plan 1999–2001, available at: http://aei.pitt.edu/6657/1/6657.pdf.

Commission makes consumers responsible for concerns that transcend their narrow group interests, and invites them to take seriously the interests of other stakeholders, including businesses, given that they are both taxpayers and employees. Moreover, this willingness to accept trade-offs is in the direct interest of consumers, in so far as such cooperation presents a positive-sum game. The market enlarges the size of the pie. This new mandated cooperative attitude to be expected from consumer representatives is particularly striking, given that many of these consumer representatives are financed by the EU.[71] Last, but not least, it is in this consumer programme that we also see the birth of the famous concept of 'consumer confidence', which is to dominate subsequent EU interventions.[72]

Just three years later, the 2001 Green Paper constitutes an important shift in the rethinking of the (internal) market imaginary:

> It is the cross-border movement of goods and services that allows consumers to *search out bargains* and innovative products and services and thus ensures that they *optimise their consumption decisions*. This cross-border demand *increases competitive pressure within the internal market* and allows for a more efficient and competitively priced supply of goods and services. This *virtuous circle* can only be achieved if the regulatory framework in *place encourages consumers and businesses to engage in cross-border trade. Different national laws* on commercial practices relating to business-consumer relations *can hinder this evolution.*[73]
>
> (my italics)

In the 2001 Communication, two important things occur. First, the Commission proposes a distinct internal market imaginary, reinterpreting the diversity of private laws as a barrier to intra-community trade. Thus, the internal market becomes an important framework in its own right. Furthermore, the Commission introduces 'costs and benefits' language into the equation, when 'cost-benefit' analysis with its welfare economics background clearly points to a market perspective to resolve questions of consumer law.

The second crucial change is an explicit concern with subjectivities. Consumers should be encouraged to optimise their consumption

[71] For one of the programmes, see: http://ec.europa.eu/chafea/consumers/funding/calls-for-tenders/tender-04-2018_en.htm.

[72] Thomas Wilhelmsson, 'The Abuse of the "Confident Consumer" as a Justification for EC Consumer Law' (2004) 27 *Journal of Consumer Policy*, 317–37.

[73] COM(2001) 531 final, 'Green Paper on European Union Consumer Protection', available at: https://eur-lex.europa.eu/legal-content/EN/TXT/PDF/?uri=CELEX:52001DC0531&from=EN.

decisions (become more cost rational) and thus improve overall market competitiveness in its cross-border dimension, and, consequently, benefit from better prices and better services. This is presented as the natural outcome of rational consumer behaviour in competitive markets. Most importantly, regulatory frameworks should encourage consumers to behave in such a way. Ultimately, this is for consumers' benefit in so far as the 'virtuous circle' of competitiveness is in the common interest.

The more current *air du temps* is captured by the last *Consumer Agenda 2012*:

> 1. Consumer policy as an essential contribution to Europe 2020
>
> Consumer expenditure accounts for 56% of EU GDP and is essential to meeting the Europe 2020 objective of smart, inclusive and sustainable growth. Stimulating this demand can play a major role in bringing the EU out of the crisis. To make this possible, the potential of the Single Market must be realised. Data show that consumers shopping online across the EU have up to 16 times more products from which to choose, but 60% of consumers do not yet use this retail channel. As a result of this reluctance, they do not fully benefit from the variety of choice and price differences available in the Single Market. Improving consumer confidence in cross-border shopping online by taking appropriate policy action could provide a major boost to economic growth in Europe. Empowered and confident consumers can drive forward the European economy.[74]

The document views consumer law and policy as a market-making tool. Consumer law is clearly linked to the macro perspective of the market, and its purpose is to stimulate demand and bring about economic growth, which is clearly in the common interest. Consumers have a distinctive *responsibility* to contribute to this project and 'drive forward the EU economy', mainly through shopping online – the core internal market imaginary in recent years. 'Protection' plays a marginal role in this narrative: the language is about confidence and empowerment, which are directed towards market making, rather than with any concern for consumer protection. More recently, the Commission has even started using slogans such as 'Justice for Growth' in order to promote further initiatives of the DG Justice in the field of consumer protection.[75]

[74] COM(2012) 225 final, 'A European Consumer Agenda – Boosting confidence and growth', available at: https://ec.europa.eu/commission/sites/beta-political/files/consumer_agenda_2012_en.pdf.

[75] See EU Commission Press Release, available at: http://europa.eu/rapid/press-release_MEMO-14-153_en.htm.

IV Socio-Economic Imaginaries and the Transformation of European Consumer Law

What are the hard law consequences of this shift in the underlying imaginary of the (internal) market for consumer protection in the EU? This an important question in so far as EU consumer policy was originally meant as a social policy – a way of getting closer to citizens – thus, the transformation in this arena tells a lot about the ways in which the 'Social' is envisaged in the EU.[76] The questions that we will pursue below are that of *who* the new subject in European consumer law is, and *how* this subject should relate to the social whole? In other words, how much of the previous discussion actually translates into legal provisions? Given the limited space, I will pick up some of the most important critiques that have been mounted against EU consumer law in the last decades in order to illustrate what consumer lawyers find problematical.

IV.1 The Subject of European Consumer Law

A number of scholars have noted that the EU has considerably changed the concept of a 'person' in private law.[77] The first critiques concerned the case law of the Court of Justice of the EU (CJEU), and its concept of the 'average consumer'.[78] This benchmark consumer, against whom the national law was tested, all too much resembled Adam Smith's economic man, introducing a standard that struck down forms of protection targeted at the 'not so up-to-standard' consumers. Others critiqued the concept of the person in the EU more generally:

> The combination of reducing persons to citizens, citizens to consumers, regarding the latter as instrumental to market building and moving towards horizontal and full harmonisation brings us very far away from contract law as a matter of justice.[79]

[76] Marco Dani, 'Rehabilitating Social Conflicts in European Public Law' (2012) 18 *European Law Journal*, 621–43.

[77] Schmid, *Die Instrumentalisierung des Privatrechts Durch die Europäische Union*, n. 10 above.

[78] Rossella Incardona and Cristina Poncibò, 'The Average Consumer, the Unfair Commercial Practices Directive, and the Cognitive Revolution' (2007) 30 *Journal of Consumer Policy*, 21–38.

[79] Martijn W. Hesselink, 'European Contract Law: A Matter of Consumer Protection, Citizenship, or Justice?', available at: https://papers.ssrn.com/sol3/papers.cfm?abstract_id=946727, p. 41.

In the 2000s, the new way of critique addresses the construction of internal market-useful subjectivities. As Micklitz has noted, 'with a weak consumer in need of protection, the internal market is not feasible. The Internal Market needs an active, informed and adroit consumer.'[80] Consumer law targeted at this kind of consumer aims both to constitute a particular kind of subjectivity, and rationality,[81] which puts those who do not fit into the desired model at various kinds of disadvantages. Not only do they have to pay for the forms of protection that they do not need, but also far less space and public funding is left for those activities from which they may profit.[82]

IV.1.a Dealing with Those Not up to Speed

If weak consumers are not the main target of the protection, what happens to those who fall below the 'standard'? The response to this question is particularly urgent because the liberalisation and privatisation of former public services makes these crucial services a subject of contract and consumer law. To deal with weak consumers, the EU introduced the concept of the 'vulnerable consumer', some time in the mid-2000s. The concept can be found in 'regulated markets' ('In this context, each Member State shall define the concept of vulnerable customers which may refer to energy poverty'[83]), but it is also penetrating more general consumer law (the Unfair Consumer Practices Directive: 'consumers particularly vulnerable to the practice or the underlying product because of their mental or physical infirmity, age or credulity'[84]).

Many authors have invested hopes in this concept as means to ensure a more socially minded consumer law, in particular, if linked to the concept of 'affordability'.[85] Yet, this confidence may be somewhat premature, for three reasons. First, while the term features in various policy

[80] Micklitz, 'The Expulsion of the Concept of Protection from the Consumer Law and the Return of Social Elements in the Civil Law', n. 59 above, p. 7.

[81] Bartl, 'Internal Market Rationality, Private Law and the Direction of the Union: Resuscitating the Market as the Object of the Political', n. 56 above.

[82] Geraint Howells, 'The Potential and Limits of Consumer Empowerment by Information' (2005) 32 *Journal of Law and Society*, 349–70; Oren Bar-Gill and Omri Ben-Shahar, 'Regulatory Techniques in Consumer Protection: A Critique of European Consumer Contract Law', University of Chicago Institute for Law & Economics Olin Research Paper, no. 598 (2012).

[83] Directive 2005/29/ECon Unfair Business-to-Consumers Practices, Recital 7.

[84] Ibid., Article 5.3.

[85] Hans.-W. Micklitz, 'Universal Services: Nucleus for a Social European Private Law', EUI Working Paper, 2009.

documents, it finds very little bite in practice. For instance, the third energy package, one of the most important venues in which the concept can be found, defines the obligations of Member States towards vulnerable consumers as follows: define the concept of a vulnerable consumer, prohibit the disconnections of vulnerable consumers in critical times, ensure the transparency of contractual terms, ensure that an independent dispute settlement mechanism is put in place, and ensure a single point of contact for any problems that consumers might face.[86] Yet, if targeted at vulnerable consumers in particular, these do not seem particularly well suited. The only *substantive* obligation towards vulnerable consumers is the prohibition of disconnection in critical times (itself an inspiration taken from the United Kingdom). As for the rest, providing formal rights of access, the transparency of contract terms, contact points and dispute settlement mechanisms are all measures that are less than ideal (as the Commission itself notes) for addressing the needs of *vulnerable* consumers.[87]

Second, to the extent that the concept of affordability should play a role, it comes with few actual enforceable claims, rights or remedies for consumers. Instead, the Member States are only encouraged to rely on social protection systems or energy efficiency improvements in providing protection.[88] Measures that are potentially more effective for ensuring the 'affordability' of energy supply that go further than just 'competitive price' – such as 'social tariffs' or 'default tariffs' – are actively discouraged.[89]

IV.2 The Relation of the Subject to the Social Whole

IV.2.a Focus on Information

In European Consumer Law, very few developments mark the shift to a different socio-economic imaginary in the same way as the increased focus on 'information provision'.[90] While, in the first decades of EU policy, consumers were meant to receive information from public sources, in order to be equipped to engage with other market actors,[91]

[86] Marija Bartl, 'The Affordability of Energy: How Much Protection for the Vulnerable Consumers?' (2010) 33 *Journal of Consumer Policy*, 225–45.
[87] Ibid.
[88] Directive 2009/72/EC, Electricity Directive (Third Package). See, for instance, Recital 45 or the Art 3/8.
[89] Bartl, 'The Affordability of Energy', n. 86 above.
[90] Howells, 'The Potential and Limits of Consumer Empowerment by Information'.
[91] See the previous section referring to consumer policies 1981 and 1991.

the later approach turns towards the provision of information by the providers of goods or services themselves.

The shift towards the provision of information as a core instrument in EU consumer policy was justified by the double service that it may perform: the provision of information empowers consumers, making them aware of what kind of goods or services they are purchasing.[92] At the same time, reducing information asymmetries between consumers and sellers is an important way of improving market functioning.[93]

The enthusiasm for this governance tool still holds strong in the EU policy, despite criticism.[94] Quite illustratively, if the last Consumer Agenda consists of sixteen pages, the policy paper 'Knowledge Enhancing Aspects of Consumer Empowerment' runs to thirty-two pages. But even in the Consumer Agenda itself, the information duties receive considerably more space than, for instance, 'vulnerable consumers' do.[95]

In terms of distributional effects, this is a rather questionable choice. As a matter of general consumer policy, the information provision does a poor job in either cleaning the markets or empowering consumers.[96] A considerable amount of scholarship in behavioural psychology and behavioural economics demonstrates this point – an issue that the Commission itself acknowledges in the 'Knowledge Enhancing' policy document.[97] What is more, however, the focus on information duties is a policy with sharply negative redistributive consequences. Those less well-off consumers are going to be disproportionality less able to make use of these mechanisms.[98]

IV.2.b Concerns for Access Take Prominence

Another important shift that we can observe with the move towards the new socio-economic imaginary is the increased concern with *access* to markets, which takes precedence over other concerns, such as social

[92] European Commission, 'Commission Staff Working Document: On Knowledge Enhancing Aspects of Consumer Empowerment, SWD(2012) 235 Final'.
[93] Ibid.
[94] It is not only scholars and consumer associations, but also the Commission itself, that have recognised the limits of the information paradigm. See European Commission, 'On Knowledge Enhancing Aspects of Consumer Empowerment'.
[95] Ibid.
[96] Bar-Gill and Ben-Shahar, 'Regulatory Techniques in Consumer Protection', n. 82 above.
[97] European Commission, 'On Knowledge Enhancing Aspects of Consumer Empowerment', n. 92 above.
[98] Bar-Gill and Ben-Shahar, 'Regulatory Techniques in Consumer Protection', n. 82 above.

justice or affordability. Access has gained prominence with the liberalisation and privatisation of formerly public utility sectors, such as telecoms, gas, electricity, postal services, and public transport, in so far as the state can no longer guarantee access.[99] A similar concern with access also underpins the horizontal dimension of the principle of non-discrimination – namely, ensuring a non-discriminatory access across the sale of goods, provision of services, or labour market.[100]

An increased interest in access merges two distinct normative concerns – while, in principle, it is concerned with 'not leaving anyone behind', the concern with access is also able to contribute to the internal market commitments by increasing market dynamism. Ideally, all consumers should be 'confident consumers' reaping the benefits of the internal market, with part of the mobile workforce moving flexibly to where market needs lie, or learning the skills that the market requires.[101]

What makes the concern with access resonate with the new socio-economic imaginary is that both access and access to justice are essentially procedural devices, which endorse a 'hands off' approach from the market itself, which is particularly handy within the context of the EU.[102] As Somek observes, 'what matters is that nobody is barred from availing oneself of an opportunity while it is taken for granted that the existence of the opportunity itself does not raise any questions of justice'.[103]

Several distributional consequences stem from this concern. To the extent that it becomes a substitute for the welfare state, and thus could be seen as being able to substitute or override some of its redistributive policy instruments, it may present a threat to any 'solidaristic' understanding of private law in the EU. Equally, the concern with access may

99 Peter Rott, 'A New Social Contract Law for Public Services? Consequences from Regulation of Services of General Economic Interest in the EC' (2005) 1 *European Review of Contract Law*, 323–45.

100 Hans-W. Micklitz, 'Social Justice and Access Justice in Private Law', in: Hans-W. Micklitz (ed.), *The Many Concepts of Social Justice in European Private Law* (Cheltenham: Edward Elgar Publishing, 2011), pp. 3–57.

101 Hans-Wolfgang Micklitz, 'Failure or Ideological Preconceptions – Thoughts on Two Grand Projects: The European Constitution and the European Civil Code', EUI Working Paper 2010/04, available at: cadmus.eui.eu/handle/1814/14016. In labour law, the question of inclusion/exclusion was one of the main justifications (also from the Left) to justify the lowering of labour protections for those with, for instance, permanent contracts.

102 Alexander Somek, 'From Workers to Migrants, from Distributive Justice to Inclusion: Exploring the Changing Social Democratic Imagination' (2012) 18 *European Law Journal*, 711–26.

103 Somek, n. 102 above.

yield regressive outcomes if we take into account the possible cross-subsidisation of its relatively sophisticated beneficiaries by the less well-off consumers.[104]

V Conclusion: Rationalisation and Common Interest

Early neoliberal discourse has, in many different ways, renaturalised markets: some of the most egregious examples of such thinking were the Washington Consensus, on the one hand,[105] and Shock Therapy, on the other.[106] Yet, while the idea that markets are self-regulating entities has become discredited, from the 1990s onwards, there has been a growing consensus across the political spectrum as to the epistemic-normative case for the market.[107] The market came to be seen as a means of rationalisation of social life: improving the allocation of scarce resources by introducing competition and incentives across private and public institutions.

This representation of the market as a means of rationalisation has had several important consequences in private law. First, we have seen the reinterpretation of fields such as labour law, or consumer protection, in macro terms of the market. Such reimagining rests on the idea of common interest: there is a limited need for the struggle between groups (between labour and capital, or between producers and consumers), in so far as they are all united in creating a virtuous circle of competitiveness and economic growth, which would make the EU the most competitive knowledge economy in the world.

Second, if market-incentives are seen as the best way of enhancing the rationality of the allocation of scarce resources, interventions should be supportive of market principles, rather than undermining them. We thus see certain types of intervention gaining the upper hand in private law (e.g. information duties, labelling, and various procedural rights), while recourse to social security (tax) seems to be the choice in areas where the provision of services is essential.

[104] OrenBar-Gill and Omri Ben-Shahar, 'Regulatory Techniques in Consumer Protection: A Critique of European Consumer Contract Law' (2013) 50 *Common Market Law Review*, 109–26.

[105] Andrew Lang, *World Trade Law after Neoliberalism: Reimagining the Global Economic Order* (Oxford: Oxford University Press, 2011).

[106] Martin Myant, *The Rise and Fall of Czech Capitalism: Economic Development in the Czech Republic since 1989* (Cheltenham: Edward Elgar Publishing, 2003).

[107] Harvey, *A Brief History of Neoliberalism*, n. 47 above.

Third, in so far as markets need 'participants' in order to function, private law legislation will focus both on encouraging participation and access, as well as model laws on those who are market-useful. It is the flexible worker and confident consumer – rather than the weak consumer and the protected employee – who are the main addressees of legislation; weak consumers will have to be accommodated through special provisions on access or vulnerability. Both competent consumers and flexible workers also bear particular responsibilities, in so far as market regulation is dependent on their correct functioning.

Yet the responsibilities that these new subjects have are different to those of the autonomous or responsible individuals of the nineteenth century. Classical contract law's subjects carried the responsibility for the contracts that they concluded. At the same time, their choices were epistemically prior to those of the public when it came to the choice of goals – they were the best judges of their own interest. Today, however, workers and consumers are not trusted to choose the right goals and preferences. Instead, they are increasingly made responsible for market making, through switching providers and changing jobs, ensuring competitiveness and dynamism.

Finally, what seems to be of major political significance is that private law, on the one hand, and the market, on the other, are progressively freed from conflict in the new socio-economic imaginary. The market is no longer a playground of genuine conflict between various groups, but is, instead, a space where one is struggling against (vulgarised) versions of 'efficiency' or part of a 'managed' conflict in the European Commission's stakeholder democracy. To the extent that conflicts are still spoken of, for instance, in front of the courts, the struggles are often framed as a conflict between labour versus efficiency (*Porto di Genova, Viking*),[108] or consumer protection versus the free circulation of goods, ultimately taking capital and material conflict out of the equation.

[108] Case C-179/90, *Merci convenzionali porto di Genova SpA* v *Siderurgica Gabrielli SpA*; Case C-438/05, *International Transport Workers' Federation and Finnish Seamen's Union* v *Viking Line ABP and OÜ Viking Line Eesti.*

10

The Transformative Socio-Economic Effects of EU Competition Law

From Producerism to Consumerism

JOTTE MULDER*

I Introduction

In the following, I will explore how a certain economic rationality is created, entrenched, and mobilised through European competition law and policy. More particularly, I will explore a question regarding European competition law's role in the transformation of frameworks of knowledge in particular market contexts, and reflect critically on this from an (EU) constitutional perspective.[1] I will argue that EU competition law, particularly cartel prohibition as dominantly interpreted by the European Commission and many national competition authorities, nudges towards a socio-economic orientation within Member States, which structurally favours interests on the demand side of markets (consumers) over and above that of the supply side (producers). The so-called modernisation and economisation processes of European competition law entrench a framework of decision making in the Member States that structurally favours this demand side of markets.

Whereas this may seem the preferred 'state of being' in most consumer-centric market societies, many Member States may accord a social function to the supply side of market that goes beyond their purely economic function and serves a broader social function that is reflective of a culture, social heritage, and identity. Producers may be accorded a central organising function in society that enables them to provide a socio-economic identity.

* The author is a legal counsel at the Authority for Consumers & Markets (ACM) and Assistant Professor at Utrecht School of Law (j.mulder1@uu.nl). The views in this contribution are solely those of the author and have been written on personal title.

[1] See the research agenda of Andrew T.F. Lang, 'The Legal Construction of Economic Rationalities?' (2013) 40 *Journal of Law and Society*, 155–71.

The protection of guilds (lawyers, waiters in France, pharmacists), certain ways of making products (pasta, wine, *reinheitsgebot* (the German 'Beer Purity Law')), or the size of stores and their opening times may all fulfil such social functions. Consumerist prioritisation may therefore clash with systems of governance that have historically been organised on a more neo-corporatist basis and accordingly incorporate *producerist* objectives or interests.

Although the Court of Justice of the European Union (formerly the European Court of Justice) has explicitly created avenues to accommodate such *producerist* interests within European competition law, there is a clear (economic) *consumerist* orientation within the modernisation and economisation processes that have shaped the European competition rules over the last decade or so. The 'consumerist turn' in European competition policy focuses on purposive rights and interests on the demand side of the market, in particular, primarily as an interest in competitive prices and choice for consumers. The legitimacy of this turn can be debated from the perspective of the European constitutional framework, which allows for social diversity and incorporates an express commitment to the accommodation of various modes of governance logics at Member State level.

I shall illustrate the transformative potential of EU competition law upon the basis of the European Commission's approach towards the liberal professions and a more recent example in the Netherlands, which demonstrates how EU competition law may transform a system of governance towards a logic of (economic) consumer welfare as a primary principle of socio-economic organisation whenever firms cooperate to achieve public interest objectives. I shall reflect on this finding from a normative perspective that is informed by the constitutional principle that a liberal society, such as the European Union purports to be, contains – by its very nature – a diversity of social spheres, and hence its institutions should act carefully in situations in which choices are made that implement a specific one dimensional valuation of a social context that may eventually inhibit socio-economic plurality. This normative preference for plurality is embedded within the constitutional foundations of the Treaty of Lisbon and resonates strongly with the case law of the Court of Justice of the European Union.

II Transformative Effects of the Economisation and Modernisation of EU Competition Law

EU competition law consists of a system of open norms. Of most relevance here is the cartel prohibition (Article 101 of the Treaty on the

Functioning of the EU (TFEU)) which prohibits firms from entering into agreements that restrict competition, but may be exempted from the prohibition in cases where cooperation leads to efficiencies that are beneficial for consumer welfare. In particular, the meaning of consumer welfare is a highly contested legal category. Clearly, such a system of open 'neutral' norms can be seized by powerful actors in order to entrench and mobilise agendas, and, it is argued, this is what happened when the European Commission – gradually in the course of the 1990s – adopted its own particular version of a consumer welfare approach.[2]

In the late 1990s, the European Commission initiated a more economic approach in European competition law.[3] One of the policy effects of this approach implied that only 'economic efficiencies' or the 'pro-competitive effects' of competition-restrictive agreements between firms would be accepted in order to fulfil the exemption criteria of the cartel prohibition.[4] One of the important effects that this has had on the legal assessment of the restrictions on competition is that decisive value was now to be attached to the objective qualification and concretisation in economic terms of the benefits claimed, which may be effectuated by restrictive agreements in order to qualify for an exemption from the cartel prohibition in Article 101(1) TFEU.[5] Upon this basis, the exemption criteria of Article 101(3) TFEU provide a common 'monetised' scale to evaluate the restrictive objectives of competition law.[6] In principle, all competition-restrictive interests are to be evaluated upon the basis of Article 101(3) TFEU.

In addition, and importantly, what is known as the 'modernisation' of EU competition law has – since 2004 – involved a decentralisation of the

[2] Heike Schweitzer and Kiran Klaus Patel, 'EU Competition Law in Historical Context: Continuity and Change', in: Kiran Klaus Patel and Heike Schweitzer (eds.), *The Historical Foundations of EU Competition Law* (Oxford: Oxford University Press, 2013), pp. 207–30.

[3] See Anne C. Witt, *The More Economic Approach to EU Antitrust Law* (Oxford: Hart Publishing, 2016).

[4] Guidelines on the application of Article 81(3) of the Treaty [2004] OJ C101/97; Guidelines on the applicability of Article 101 of the Treaty on the Functioning of the European Union to horizontal co-operation agreements [2011] OJ C11/1.

[5] Commission Guidelines on the application of Article 81(3) of the Treaty [2004] OJ C101/97; Commission Guidelines on the applicability of Article 101 of the Treaty on the Functioning of the European Union to horizontal co-operation agreements [2011] OJ C11/1; Lars Kjølbye, 'The New Commission Guidelines on the Application of Article 81 (3): an Economic Approach to Article 81' (2004) 25 *European Competition Law Review*, 566–77.

[6] Giorgio Monti and Jotte Mulder, 'Escaping the Clutches of EU Competition Law' (2017) 5 *European Law Review*, 635–56, at 635.

application of the competition rules.[7] This process had two significant and immediate effects. Firstly, the European competition rules were to be applied and enforced by both the national competition authorities and the European Commission simultaneously. This raised the need for uniform application of the competition rules and a subsequent explosion of instruments and knowledge-sharing instruments (such as the creation of the European Competition Network) in order to ensure that Article 101 TFEU would be applied by national competition authorities in congruence with the uniform guidelines of the European Commission. Secondly, undertakings themselves were, from now on, to 'self-assess' their status under the competition rules, whereas formerly they had been able to request official 'exemption decisions' from competition authorities. Again, to this end, the European Commission issued a plethora of guidelines, block exemptions and other soft law instruments to provide firms, and, in particular, their lawyers and economic consultants, with the tools to conduct such self-assessments.

The governance context that is of interest for the development of the argument that economisation and modernisation have potentially formative effects concerns that of (quasi) self-regulation. Competitors meet and may be stimulated, or sometimes required, to self-regulate within state governance systems in order to set standards for the pursuit of – sometimes deontological – objectives.[8] This may happen for technical standards, environmental objectives, labour conditions, minimum trade standards and so forth. Agreements that flow forth from the pursuit of such objectives may restrict competition, for example, through output restrictions, pricing agreements and prohibitions to trade in products that have been produced beneath certain trade standards.[9] Such private regulatory contexts raise competition law issues, since they are likely to restrict the independent operation of the undertakings in the markets concerned.[10]

[7] Rein Wesseling, *The Modernisation of EC Antitrust Law* (Oxford-Portland OR: Hart Publishing, 2000).

[8] See, for example, Laurens Ankersmit, 'Globalization and the Internal Market: Process-based Measures within the EU Legal Order' (2015, Ph.D. thesis, Vrije Universiteit Amsterdam); see, also, Harm Schepel, *The Constitution of Private Governance: Product Standards in the Regulation of Integrating Markets* (Oxford: Hart Publishing, 2005).

[9] Schepel, ibid.

[10] Schepel, n. 8 above; Björn Lundqvist, *Standardization under EU Competition Rules and US Antitrust Laws: The Rise and Limits of Self-regulation* (Cheltenham: Edward Elgar Publishing, 2014); Mislav Mataija, *Private Regulation and the Internal Market: Sports, Legal Services, and Standard Setting in EU Economic Law* (Oxford: Oxford University

When self-regulation leads to restrictions on competition, there exist, roughly, two 'escapes' within the European competition rules. Firstly, this occurs on the supply side of the market in which the self-regulation takes place. The Court has decided, in different, albeit connected, lines of case law, that the supply side of a market may be organised in a manner such that the companies involved are sufficiently restricted in their ability to regulate in a self-serving manner. This may be because the public law framework installs sufficient oversight and thus channels the private decision makers towards exclusively serving public interests or because the objectives pursued are legitimate, and both necessitate and justify some restrictions on competition.[11] In this case, the restrictions on competition can be *excluded* from the scope of the cartel prohibition in Article 101(1) TFEU. Secondly, as discussed previously, the demand side of the market may be sufficiently 'compensated' for the resultant restrictions on competition due to an increase in consumer welfare. Certain minimum technical standards may restrict competition on those standards, but can lead to quality increases in products that consumers are willing to pay for and thus positively contribute to consumer surplus. In this case, the restrictions on competition can be exempted from the cartel prohibition upon the basis of Article 101(3) TFEU.

Two important effects can be expected from the dual development of the economisation and modernisation of EU competition law. Firstly, that competition authorities within Europe should pursue cases upon the basis of the idea that where competing firms jointly pursue, for example, fair trade standards, they should only do so if they can demonstrate efficiency, and that consumers will directly benefit from the potential restrictions on competition. Hence, their actions should be completely in accordance with an understanding of what matters and what can be validated in terms of the market's willingness to pay for certain restrictions on competition. Secondly, in the process of the self-assessments, informal opinions and individual guidance, the competition authorities aim to internalise this economic, consumer-led market rationale into the responsive minds and calculus of the undertakings themselves.

Press, 2016); Giorgio Monti, *EC Competition Law* (Cambridge: Cambridge University Press, 2006), chapter 2, pp. 20–52; Renato Nazzini, 'Article 81 EC Between Time Present and Time Past – A Normative Critique of "Restriction of Competition" in EU Law' (2006) 43 *Common Market Law Review*, 497–536; Giorgio Monti, 'Article 81 EC and Public Policy' (2002) 39 *Common Market Law Review*, 1057–99.

[11] Based upon, for example, respectively Case C-185/91 *Reiff Bundesanstalt für den Güterfernverkehr* [1993] ECR I-5801 para. 22 and Case C-309/99 *Wouters* [2002] ECR I-1577.

The entrenchment of this economic rationality may have formative effects, in particular, given the fact that the importance of private regulation on the supply side of markets is increasing, and non-state actors determine a growing part of the conditions, rules and regulations that govern transnational trade.[12] In addition, and increasingly so, private regulatory initiatives pushed by NGOs and enhanced consumer awareness incorporates a responsiveness with respect to the pursuit of public – global – policy challenges, such as the protection of the environment, animal welfare, and human rights. Examples range from sustainability initiatives in the forestry sector to the setting of minimum standards for labour conditions in the clothing industry, and physical integrity rights in the extractive industry.[13] Such initiatives with wider welfare effects are costly and require investments that companies are often only willing to make if free-rider problems and first-mover disadvantages are resolved.[14] However, within this economic rationale, a group of companies that collectively adopt 'social objectives', such as a minimum fair-trade standard, will – within the framework of EU competition law – have to demonstrate that these measures are eventually beneficial for consumer welfare. For example, theoretically, a group of firms that collectively decide not to buy from suppliers that violate human rights is permitted only if consumer welfare increases in a quantifiable manner.[15]

Some (in particular, economists) will argue that this makes good sense, and posit that where pubic interests are at stake society wants to protect: and regulation is the answer.[16] The state can legislate, and, upon that basis,

[12] For example, Fabrizio Cafaggi, 'Transnational Private Regulation: Regulating Global Private Regulators', in: Sabino Cassese (ed.), *Research Handbook on Global Administrative Law* (Cheltenham: Edward Elgar Publishing, 2016), pp. 212–41.

[13] Respectively, the Forest Stewardship Council (FSC), the Bangladesh Accord, the Voluntary Principles on Security and Human Rights and the International Licensing Platform.

[14] The first-mover disadvantage concerns a situation where just one company decides not to offer certain unsustainable (often cheaper) products and may consequently loose a critical amount of customers to its competitors which remain selling the cheaper product. Such 'coordination' problems can be resolved if companies pursue welfare initiatives collectively. The free-rider problem concerns a situation in which a company invests in sustainability – for example, by virtue of a marketing campaign intended to inform consumers of the importance of fair trade – that may, consequently, benefit competitors that do not make such investments but nevertheless do benefit from consumers who are more willing to purchase sustainable goods.

[15] Such concerns were voiced in the context of the Bangladesh accord, see, for example, https://friendsoftheoecdguidelines.wordpress.com/tag/bangladesh-accord.

[16] For example, Maarten Pieter Schinkel and Yossi Spiegel, 'Can Collusion Promote Sustainable Consumption and Production?' (2017) 53 *International Journal of Industrial Organization*, 371–98.

take issues away from the market logic. However, regulation may not always be a realistic or feasible option. Moreover, as noted, governance structures may enable, stimulate or require the private sector explicitly to incorporate public interest objectives. Often, private regulation may also be a generic response from the private sector to a failure or unwillingness on the part of the nation state and conventional international law making to address cross-border challenges effectively.[17] It is suggested that, applied in this manner and context, the European competition rules have the potential to enforce and entrench a specific economic rationality that will have effects on the way in which undertakings pursue such interests.

It is illustrating, in this respect, to refer to two ideal type categories that can be used to point to the potential transformative effects of EU competition law. James Whitman introduced the ideal types of *consumerism* and *producerism* to discuss and compare the constitutive role of law in these respective imaginaries of society. A legal system orientated towards consumerism would be based around the idea that the individual as a consumer is primarily interested in low prices, product choice, and access to credit. The sovereignty of the consumer is prioritised within a legal system that structurally favours the demand side of a market. In contrast, the *producerist* legal system shifts attention to the supply side and focuses on the importance and centrality of the role of producers in society, combined with the dedication of a social function of *producer identity* in society. Clearly, any form of idealisation of the role of the producer within society risks being equated with a leaning towards fascism. However, producer identity has also been connected to positive social functions connected to culture, the arts and heritage, such as creating and retaining identity; modifying values and preferences for collective choice; building social cohesion; contributing to community development; and fostering civic participation.[18] These can all be seen as different stages in the appropriation of cultural content into the public life of members of society.

[17] Philip Schleifer, 'Creating Legitimacy for Private Rules: Explaining the Choice of Legitimation Strategies in Transnational Non-State Governance', EUI Working Paper 2015 RSCAS 2015/62.

[18] Pierre Bourdieu, *Distinction: A Social Critique of the Judgement of Taste* (London: Routledge Kegan & Paul, 1984); M. Sharon Jeannotte, 'Singing Alone? The Contribution of Cultural Capital to Social Cohesion and Sustainable Communities' (2003) 9 *International Journal of Cultural Policy*, 35–49. Robert D. Putnam, *Making Democracy Work: Civic Institutions in Modern Italy* (Princeton NJ: Princeton University Press, 1993).

Whitman juxtaposes Europe (conflated with Germany and France) as traditionally perceived to be oriented more towards the supply side, with the United States as cultivating the more fundamental consumerist interest. He notes that, as with all ideal-type approaches, legal systems do not correspond fully in all their characteristics with the posited ideal types, but he identifies some fundamental choices within these legal systems that do demonstrate differences that can be explained, at least in part, by the dominance of the (economic) consumer or producer interests.

II.1 Moving towards Consumerism: Liberating the Liberal Professions

In the course of the 1990s, in parallel with developing the more economic approach, the European Commission adopted a new policy with respect to the liberal professions in the Member States.[19] The sector is usually characterised by a high level of regulation, in the form of either state regulation or self-regulation by professional bodies. This regulation can affect, *inter alia*, the numbers of entrants into the profession; the fees or prices that professionals may charge and the permitted charging arrangements (e.g. contingency fees); the organisational structure of professional service undertakings; their ability to advertise; and the tasks which are reserved for the members of the profession. The European Commission acknowledged early on that some regulation in this sector is justified, but, as part of the more economic approach, it started to pursue an agenda on the basis of the idea that, in some cases, more pro-competitive mechanisms can and should be used, instead of certain traditional restrictive rules.[20] Former Commissioner of Competition Mario Monti (2003) explains the liberalisation policy of the Commission in this regard as follows:

> The present level of rules and regulation of liberal professions owe some debt to historical convention. How many are still needed in the modem world? Do they hinder or favour the development of the sector? Let me be provocative: Do they protect the consumers or the professionals? I propose to assess whether existing rules and regulations, which, remember, were devised and enacted in a very different economic context to that

[19] Liberal professions are occupations requiring special training in the liberal arts or sciences, for example, lawyers, notaries, engineers, architects, accountants and pharmacists.

[20] See, further, Ida Wendt, *EU Competition Law and Liberal Professions: An Uneasy Relationship?* (Leiden: Brill, 2012).

> which exists today, continue to serve the legitimate purposes of the protection of the public interest. I would also like to assess whether they are the most efficient mechanisms available in the current market situation. It is clear that across the [European Union] there are different regulatory mixes. As the study shows, different regulatory choices produce different outcomes in the market and it is possible that some regulatory mixes have more beneficial market outcomes than others. *It should be difficult to argue against those that have the least distorting effect on the workings of the market, while delivering the same, or even higher, turnover.*[21]
>
> (emphasis added)

On the one hand, in the first part of the speech, competition law is perceived as a constructive tool of European law, testing old conventions and requiring renewed articulation of the pursuit of public interests. On the other hand, in the second part of the speech, the idea emerges that self-regulatory systems should, however, be tested upon the basis of their 'efficiency' merits: 'It should be difficult to argue against those that have the least distorting effect on the workings of the market, *while delivering the same, or even higher, turnover.*'[22] As discussed, the competition rules, in particular, Article 101 TFEU as interpreted by the European Commission, place great emphasis on the benefits that consumers accrue from the process of competition. Solely by virtue of this fact, social relations between producers, which collectively pursue interests on the supply side of the market, are on a back footing. I argue that this amounts to a potentially significant formative effect of the competition rules with regard to governance structures in countries that, traditionally, have a more 'producerist' orientation.[23] The adoption of this efficiency-based rationale has been pushed in the incorporation and 'soft' review of national regulatory systems, which has largely been adopted by national competition authorities. Here, we see the beginnings of the mobilisation of a specific economic rationality – one that is capable of changing the socio-economic face of the Member States. The extent to which this push has resulted in structural reforms of (self-)regulatory systems is beyond the scope of this chapter, but two other case examples

[21] Mario Monti, Commissioner for Competition: European Commission, Competition in Professional Services: New Light and New Challenges; for Bundesanwaltskammer Berlin (2003), see: http://europa.eu/rapid/press-release_SPEECH-03-149_en.htm, last accessed 10 January 2019.

[22] Ibid.

[23] See James Q. Whitman, 'Consumerism versus Producerism: A Study in Comparative Law' (2007) 117 *Yale Law Journal*, 340–406, at 343.

from the Netherlands serve as an illustration of the potential formative effect this rationale may have on the pursuit of public interest objectives by private economic actors within a governance system that is traditionally focused on the supply side of markets.

II.2 Transforming Socio-Economic Regulation in the Netherlands

Competition law in the Netherlands is, today, completely based upon EU competition rules. Before its introduction in 1998, competition law was largely absent from the Dutch legal order and the Netherlands was often referred to as a 'cartel paradise' during that time. There were cartels in all sectors and branches of the economy, and it is estimated that there were as many unregistered cartels as there were registered cartels with the Ministry of Economic Affairs at the time.[24] Registered cartels ranged from dental prosthodontics, bailiffs, notaries, milk producers, and credit card companies. The relatively relaxed attitude towards cartelist behaviour can be explained because, historically, the Dutch system of social and economic policy making has been heavily consensus based, strongly reliant on the private sector, and often referred to as the 'polder' model.[25] This has been reflected in a plurality of advisory and consultative bodies that exist at all levels of policy making. Consensus-based policy making used to be most clearly reflected in so-called 'product boards' that would include all interested parties in a production chain within a public institutional framework that would be involved directly in the development of social and economic policy making, relevant to the economic sector involved. As such, policy concerning livestock would involve the product board for livestock, meat and eggs as an intermediary between government and industry in order to ensure a smooth transition between politics and industry interests. Consensus-based policy making remains a central feature of Dutch politics today.

However, whereas, before, the structures of policy making would only incorporate input from the industry within an otherwise traditional legislative procedure, recently, in contrast, the Dutch system of

[24] See www.volkskrant.nl/economie/zeshonderd-kartels-vragen-legale-status~a455732, last accessed 10 April 2018.

[25] Jaap Woldendorp, 'The Polder Model: From Disease to Miracle? Dutch Neo-corporatism 1965–2000', 2005 Ph.D. thesis, Vrije Universiteit Amsterdam, pp. 267–9. See, also, Bram Bouwens and Joost Dankers, 'Competition and Varieties of Coordination', in: Keetie E. Sluyterman (ed.), *Varieties of Capitalism and Business History: The Dutch Case* (Abingdon: Routledge, 2015), pp. 103–29.

governing has moved towards adopting governance structures which, as far as possible, outsource the pursuit of public-interest objectives to the private sector. The government coins this as a programme of so-called future-proof legislation that seeks to activate the 'self-organisational' potential of societal actors. This governmental approach is partly a response to the increasing complexities of societal challenges that often require transnational solutions and a recognition of the importance of creating regulatory flexibility towards innovation. In other words, this programme of future-proof legislation considers traditional legislation to be incapable of responding to the pace of change within society and is thus unable to respond fully to the needs of an innovation-based society. The main feature of the legislative reorientation as a whole is to stimulate development by virtue of which private actors increasingly incorporate public-interest objectives. In particular circumstances, this may lead to a clash with competition law. One field in which this has grown to be particularly visible is within the area of sustainability, specifically, the pursuit of social and green objectives upon the basis of industry initiatives.[26]

II.3 A Clash between Competition and Sustainability in the Netherlands

The first case that may illustrate this concerns the so-called Energy Agreement for Sustainable Growth (Energy Accord). The Energy Accord involved around forty organisations in the definition of a more sustainable energy and climate policy for the Netherlands.[27] The central government had organised so-called round tables with a wide array of

[26] A number of international publications have now looked at these Dutch cases. Monti and Mulder, n. 6 above, at 641; Anna Gerbrandy, 'Solving a Sustainability-Deficit in European Competition Law' (2017) 40 *World Competition*, 539–62; Gerbrandy, 'Addressing the Legitimacy Problem for Competition Authorities Taking into Account Non-Economic Values: The Position of the Dutch Competition Authority' (2015) 40 *European Law Review*, 769–81.

[27] The plan can be found at www.ser.nl/nl/publicaties/overige/2010-2019/2013/energieakkoord-duurzame-groei.aspx, last accessed 10 April 2018). See, for the preliminary competition law assessment by the Dutch competition authorities ACM: ACM, 'Notitie ACM over sluiting 5 kolencentrales in SER Energieakkoord', available at: www.acm.nl/nl/publicaties/publicatie/12033/Notitie-ACM-over-sluiting-5-kolencentrales-in-SER-Energieakkoord/, last accessed 10 December 2018). See, also, Erik Kloosterhuis and Machiel Mulder, 'Competition Law and Environmental Protection: The Dutch Agreement on Coal-Fired Power Plants' (2015) 11 *Journal of Competition Law & Economics*, 855–88.

organisations. These included regional and local government, employers' associations and trade unions, nature conservation and environmental organisations, and civil society organisations and financial institutions.[28] The Dutch government has framed these round-table negotiations and the outcomes at the time as 'agreements' both with and amongst the private sector with respect to the pursuit and attainment of sustainability objectives. Obviously, where such agreements include private actors that also compete in their respective market, issues with competition law may arise. From a competition law perspective, a problematic aspect of the early parts of the agreement concerned the closing down of coal-fuelled power plants from the 1980s. The energy companies that took part in the negotiations decided to close down the plants as part of an incentive path that would encourage the development of more sustainable energy sources in the long run. The trade association of the Dutch energy industry, *Energie Nederland* (EN) asked for an analysis from the Dutch Competition Authority (ACM) on whether the planned agreement on closing down coal power plants could be reconciled with Article 101 TFEU (and its equivalent in Article 6 of the Dutch Competition Act). The ACM qualified it simply as an agreement between undertakings within the meaning of the competition rules. The assessment of the ACM concluded that, firstly, the closure of coal power plants constituted an output restriction that would fall within Article 101(1) TFEU. By reducing production capacity, the undertakings involved would have less capacity to produce energy than they would have had without the agreement.[29] Secondly, it could not be exempted upon the basis of the exemption criteria of Article 101(3) TFEU.[30] For the latter analysis, the authority conducted an extensive cost-benefit analysis in accordance with the more economic approach set out by the European Commission. The value of the agreement's benefits was determined upon the basis of the costs of other (efficient) measures which, as a consequence, would not have to be taken (i.e. avoided costs). The ACM concluded that comparing the estimated price increase with the

[28] Interestingly, consumer interests were not represented.

[29] The production capacity that was to be closed under the agreement represented approximately 10 per cent of total production capacity available in the Netherlands.

[30] The criteria are: (1) The agreement contributes to an improvement of the production or distribution of goods or to the promotion of technical or economic progress; (2) The agreement allows consumers a fair share of the resulting benefit; (3) No restrictions that are not indispensable are imposed on the undertaking involved; (4) Competition is not eliminated in respect of a substantial part of the products or goods in question.

environmental benefits revealed that the agreement's expected drawbacks to consumers in terms of price for electricity would be substantially higher than the estimated value of the positive effects in terms of avoided costs. Subsequently, the closure of coal-fuelled power plants was removed from the accord.

The second case concerns the production of chicken meat. At the beginning of 2013, the main branch organisation on foodstuffs in the Netherlands announced that 'another chicken' would be introduced into Dutch supermarkets. Most of the organisations from the poultry sector, the chicken-meat producing industry and the supermarkets came together during a round-table meeting to discuss a more sustainable production of chicken meat ('the Chicken of Tomorrow'). The aim of these negotiations was to introduce a sectorwide sustainability impulse upon the basis of the introduction of a minimum standard for animal welfare. Dutch livestock holders responded to the increased attention within Dutch society to animal welfare and the explicit request from the Dutch government to incorporate animal-welfare objectives within the supply chain.[31] The Dutch government had indicated that the policy in this area should be informed and guided on the basis of sectorwide initiatives.[32] A sectorwide statement of intent was signed which committed the livestock sector, the meat-producing industry and retailers to move towards a *status quo* in which only sustainable produced meat would be sold from 2020 onwards. The 'Chicken of Tomorrow' initiative was introduced within this context.[33] Again, the ACM was invited to

[31] See in Dutch: Commissie van Doorn, 'Al het vlees Duurzaam: De doorbraak naar een gezonde, veilige en gewaardeerde veehouderij in 2020', 2 September 2011, available at: www.rijksoverheid.nl/bestanden/documenten-en-publicaties/rapporten/2011/11/23/al-het-vlees-duurzaam-de-doorbraak-naar-een-gezonde-veilige-en-gewaardeerde-veehouderij-in-2020/al-het-vlees-duurzaam.pdf, last accessed 10 December 2018. The case has led to some debate in the Netherlands: Laurens Ankersmit, 'Het einde van de kiloknallers? De grenzen aan zelfregulering van duurzaam vlees onder het kartelverbod' (2011) 23 *Actualiteiten Mededingingsrecht*, 149–55; Jotte Mulder, 'Een duurzame maatschappij, wat mag dat kosten?' (2015) 28 *NJB* (*Nederlands Juristenblad*), 1912–1920.

[32] Letter with the position of the Dutch government, 'Toekomst van de intensieve veehouderij' Official parliamentary documents: 28973 nr. 134, accessible at: https://zoek.officielebekendmakingen.nl/kst-28973-137.html, last accessed 10 April 2018.

[33] ACM assessment of the sustainability agreements 'Chicken of Tomorrow' (ACM/DM/2014/206028), January 2015, p. 2. The minimum standards that were part of the 'Chicken of Tomorrow' initiative concerned agreements on the keeping of a slower growing breed of chickens, more space for chickens upon the basis of a reduction of the number of chickens in a set space, improved conditions within the coops, stricter controls on animal-welfare standards, a more natural day-night rhythm, lowering of the use of antibiotics, the use of 100 per cent sustainable soya food and a number of other

assess this cooperation from a competition law perspective. The assessment of the ACM concluded that the sustainability initiative qualified as a restriction on competition in the retail market for chicken meat because 'regularly' produced chicken meat would no longer be for sale in Dutch supermarkets.

The ACM concluded that the initiative limited choice for consumers and removed a competitive benchmark. The analysis of the ACM aimed to provide guidance to companies that would want to implement such sustainability initiatives in the future as part of their self-assessment. For this purpose, the ACM, by way of 'guidance', conducted a 'willingness to pay' analysis.[34] It considered that the first condition of Article 101(3) TFEU (i.e. the contribution to the production or distribution of goods or to the promoting of technical or economic progress), would only be fulfilled if the measure would eventually lead to a higher consumer surplus, which was to be determined upon the basis of the willingness of consumers to pay more for the 'added' animal welfare. Consumer panels were asked to choose between different types of chicken meat that differed with regard to the level of animal welfare that was taken into account in the production of the meat. The economic analysis of the ACM concluded that the willingness to pay for the new chicken was not enough to justify the increase in the consumer price.[35] On balance, according to the study, there would be a negative effect on consumer surplus of 0.64 euro per kilogram of chicken

environmental measures. The initiative met with a lot of criticism, which, according to animal welfare organisations, would improve the conditions of chickens only marginally. Indeed, at first sight, the measures do look minimal and the improvements in chicken welfare would not be ground-breaking.

34 Economic assessment ACM, *Effects of the Chicken of Tomorrow – Costs and Benefits for Consumers* –Machiel Mulder, Sebastiaan Zomer (ACM) and Thomas Benning, Johan Leenheer (CentERdata), October 2014, available at: www.acm.nl/en/publications/publication/13761/Industry-wide-arrangements-for-the-so-called-Chicken-of-Tomorrow-restrict-competition, last accessed on 8 February 2019]). See, also, Kloosterhuis and Mulder, n. 28 above.

35 Ibid., p. 26. On balance, according to the study, there would be a negative effect on consumer surplus of 0.64 euro per kilogram of chicken breast. Moreover, the ACM considered that it would be preferable if, instead of introducing a minimum standard, consumers would be better informed about animal welfare upon the basis of labels. This could then also become part of a broader commercial strategy of a supermarket to attract consumers who value these sustainable products. According to the ACM, it would therefore be more appropriate if sustainability initiatives were to focus on measures to improve animal welfare by educating consumers and stimulating consumer confidence in other types of production, as part of a competitive process eventually leading to increases in consumer surplus.

breast.[36] Moreover, the ACM considered that it would be preferable if, instead of introducing a minimum standard, consumers were better informed about animal welfare upon the basis of labels. This could then also become part of a broader commercial strategy of a supermarket to attract consumers who value these sustainable products. According to the ACM, it would therefore be more appropriate if sustainability initiatives were to focus on measures to improve animal welfare by educating consumers and stimulating consumer confidence in other types of production, as part of a competitive process.[37] The initiative was, subsequently, abandoned.

The outcome in the two cases led to calls from civil society actors and the economic sectors concerned for a reconsideration of the constraints of competition law with respect to sustainability initiatives. It initiated a broader debate within the Netherlands regarding the right balance between EU competition law and sustainability. Importantly, the Dutch government considered the way in which the competition law framework was applied to be an ongoing obstruction to its ambition to involve non-state actors increasingly in the formulation of socio-economic policy as part of the earlier discussed future-proofing of its legislative agenda. Subsequently, the Ministry of Economic Affairs was tasked with the challenge of resolving this tension.

II.4 The Position of the European Commission

This initially resulted in a legislative instruction document that set out some amended conditions for the ACM to take into account in its assessment. The main changes concerned, firstly, the fact that the positive long-term effects of the initiatives would have to be considered with respect to the agreement, in so far as it was part of a wider package of measures, *as a whole*. Secondly, the potential positive effects would not only have to take into account the long-term – future – users, but also the positive effects for *society as a whole*. These two criteria can be seen as a direct response to the two cases that were highlighted above, potentially leading to different outcomes of the ACM assessment.[38]

[36] Ibid., p. 26.

[37] ACM assessment of the sustainability agreements 'Chicken of Tomorrow' (ACM/DM/2014/206028), January 2015, p. 7.

[38] Arguably, if the Energy Accord would have been considered as a whole and, consequently, if the closing down of the coal plants would not have been considered in isolation, the outcome of the assessment may have been different. Perhaps, the fact that

However, when the draft instruction was put up for a so-called internet consultation, in which interested parties could provide comments on the draft proposal, the European Commission intervened.[39] The Commission objected to the new criteria and considered them to be contrary to European Competition law. In its letter to the Dutch government, the Commission emphasised that it considered the assessments of the ACM with respect to the two cases to be fully in accordance with EU competition law. Firstly, the Commission considered that the requirement to take into account the agreement as a whole was potentially confusing. The Commission acknowledged that it might be necessary to assess an entire package of agreements but posited that this was already part of the third condition of Article 101(3), which deals with the indispensability of the restrictions. Where an agreement that restricts competition is necessary for the benefits accrued by other parts of a package of an agreement, it may already fulfil the 'indispensability' condition of Article 101(3). This, of course, assumes that those benefits have been monetised. What is more interesting is that, with regard to the new instruction, the Commission also considered that it was not possible to consider the potential positive effects for society as a whole. This would be contrary to the text of Article 101(3) TFEU which explicitly refers to the positive advantages for the 'users' of the products or services:

> If certain policy goals are considered valuable for society as a whole, while not by the consumers in the relevant market, *regulation* is the right tool to safeguard them and not competition law. In other words, competition law does not stand in the way of regulation to achieve these goals, but cannot substitute for the absence of such regulation.
>
> (emphasis added)

Therefore, the Commission urged the government not to install the legislative instruction. In other words, the Dutch government could not simply ask or agree with the private sector in order to pursue

the closing down of the coal plants was an inherent part of a wider agreement, concerned with bringing together various societal actors with the intention of creating co-responsibility for the objective of a sustainable environment, could then have influenced the assessment. Moreover, with respect to the 'Chicken of Tomorrow', the willingness to pay assessment conducted by the ACM would have to be considered insufficient since the potential positive benefits for society as a whole would also have to be considered.

[39] Commission letter, attachment to Government Letter of Ministry of Economic Affairs to Parliament of 23 June 2016 (Kamerstukken II 2015/16, 30196, 463). The letter is accessible at: https://zoek.officielebekendmakingen.nl/blg-775505, last accessed 17 April 2018.

public-interest objectives if this would negatively impact on competition. Such competition-restrictive interests would have to be more actively regulated if they were to serve wider societal objectives. The rationale that underlies this response is concerned with a question of accountability. The competition rules provide accountability by way of the market. Private measures that aspire to the achievement of public interest are provided with legitimacy because they can be accounted for in terms of the market. This is to say, if the measures on balance manage to achieve an outcome that leads to an increase in consumer welfare, then there is no need for the political sphere to become involved and provide legitimacy to the development of measures that aspire to serve a public interest. If there is no such accountability for measures that aspire to serve the public interest, but which, in the process, limit competition, then they require another source of legitimacy in the form of direct government regulation.

The response of the Dutch government to this stance from the Commission has been to introduce a legislative proposal that has since been developed and now exists in draft form and creates the option of a so-called *declaration of general effect* with respect to private sustainability initiatives that meet certain criteria. Upon this basis, private sustainability proposals are turned into legislation and, this is the assumption, potential problems with EU competition law can be circumvented. This is the underlying rationale of this proposal, which aligns, for example, with the system of collective labour negotiations that operates upon the basis of a similar process of declarations of general effect. The main condition for eligibility for a declaration of general application is that there is a public sustainability interest involved. Accordingly, the proposed law seeks to incorporate mechanisms that ensure that, eventually, the government and parliament can weigh the involved interests and decide whether or not to provide an initiative with general binding effect. Upon this basis, the proposal seeks to resolve the tension with competition law by introducing a framework that structures private decision-making procedures in such a way that they will result in outcomes that serve the 'public interest' and can subsequently be turned into legislation. This is a highly interesting proposal which is currently still under consideration and harbours many potential issues from a EU law perspective, issues which I have discussed elsewhere.[40]

[40] See, further on this, Monti and Mulder, n. 6 above, at 642.

III An EU Constitutional Reflection on the Dutch Sustainability Saga

The Dutch sustainability saga revealed that the European Commission takes a position that is reflective of a rather traditional command and control 'state-centred' perspective with respect to state-market-society relationships. That is to say, the Commission in its communication to the Dutch state emphasised that Article 101 should not be interpreted so as to allow private entities to pursue objectives beyond consumer welfare whilst restricting competition in the process. For this scenario, regulation would be the preferred route to take. However, the position of the European Commission is not fully in accordance with the case law of the European Court of Justice. The Court of Justice has created avenues in its case law that do allow for private deontological structures – pursuing objectives going beyond consumer welfare – to be excepted from the scope of Article 101.[41]

This is understandable foremost because the European Union contains, by its very nature, a diversity of socio-economic models. With this, I mean to say, models to organise society in accordance with a certain normative governing principle that is related to a type of social ordering. A useful distinction is sometimes found in juxtaposing socio-economic models to align closer with market or non-market enabling principles. For example, labour market rules may sometimes fulfil a purely market-enabling function by reducing transaction costs and information asymmetries in wage-setting, and, consequently, can be said to be organised around a socio-economic organising principle that is essentially market enabling. However, this is, of course, not the rule; a major tension may exist between, for example, the right to strike and market interests. Depending on the normative orientation of a socio-economic paradigm, the right to strike may be institutionalised precisely to shield workers from the power that capital owners can exercise as the holders of capital. The underlying normative principle of organisation of both types of labour market rules are fundamentally different. One may be qualified as being embedded within a market logic since the underlying rationale follows the allocative logic of the market whilst the other is entrenched in non-market rationales and enables a structure of negotiated deliberative coordination, outside of the logic of wealth maximisation.[42]

[41] Ca4se C-209/07 *Competition Authority* v. *Beef Industry Development Society Ltd and Barry Brothers (Carrigmore) Meats Ltd* [2008] ECR I-8637, paras. 34–6 and Case C-309/99 *Wouters* [2002] ECR I-1577.

[42] See Alexander Ebner, 'Transnational Markets and the Polanyi Problem', in: Christian Joerges and Josef Falke (eds.), *Karl Polanyi: Globalisation and the Potential of*

One of the main objectives of European law is to create an internal market, and, consequently, the rules may be set up to change or modify the behaviour of a profession or style of government, and, consequently, influence the normative orientation of a socio-economic paradigm within a Member State. It may confront embedded conventions, value systems and understandings within a Member State. European competition law is an excellent example of this, gradually having evolved from a contested policy to a dominant legal system that is largely applied uniformly in all the Member States.[43] In some cases, EU law will therefore render a choice for a certain socio-economic model compatible, re-enforcing the conventions and understandings in a Member State, for example, by holding that competition-restrictive practices of law associations may be considered legitimate when the integrity of the law profession is at stake.[44] In other cases, the object of internal market law may expressly be to change the conventions and understandings, for example, by holding that the right to strike within a Member State is only allowed if it is exercised within a transparent system of governance and abides by the principle of proportionality.[45]

Between these two examples, there exist different shades of compatibility and incompatibility, depending eventually on the normative interpretation of the law. One of the major challenges for European legislators and adjudicators is to find the right balance. To what extent can European law legitimately influence the socio-economic orientations of the Member States towards one particular model and to what extent should it allow or even stimulate diversity in socio-economic outcomes?

The claim in this chapter rehashes a point made strikingly by Miguel Poiares Maduro and more recently by Clemens Kaupa that the *European economic constitution* is, in principle, neutral in this respect.[46] European

Law in Transnational Markets (Oxford-Portland OR: Hart Publishing, 2011), pp. 19–40, at 28.

43 For example, Adrian Kuenzler and Laurent Warlouzet, 'Traditions of Competition Law: Europeanization through Convergence?', in: Kiran Klaus Patel and Heike Schweitzer (eds.), *The Historical Foundations of EU Competition Law* (Oxford: Oxford University Press, 2014), pp. 89–124.

44 For example, Adrian Kuenzler and Laurent Warlouzet, 'Traditions of Competition Law: Europeanization through Convergence?', in: Kiran Klaus Patel and Heike Schweitzer (eds.), *The Historical Foundations of EU Competition Law* (Oxford: Oxford University Press, 2014), pp. 89–124.

45 Case C-341/05 *Laval un Partneri* [2007] ECR I-11767; Case C-438/05 *Viking Line* [2007] ECR I-10779.

46 Miguel Poiares Maduro, *We the Court: The European Court of Justice and the European Economic Constitution* (Oxford: Hart Publishing, 1998); Clemens Kaupa, *The Pluralist Character of the European Economic Constitution* (Oxford: Hart Publishing, 2016).

law should not therefore be applied so as to force a normative direction for a socio-economic paradigm. This can be argued based upon the fact that the TFEU incorporates an explicit concern for reconciling freedom of (economic) movement with the social structures of the Member States. It does so, specifically, by integrating a *dual commitment* within its legal infrastructure. The internal market laws determine that, although there is a commitment to intra-European free trade within open competitive markets that accommodate the free movement of goods, capital, services and workers, the Member States themselves retain control over domestic social interests that are able to override these market integration objectives. In fact, it could be argued that European law should strive to accommodate various socio-economic models. A multitude of socio-economic projects may be pursued within the framework of the Treaty. From a doctrinal perspective, such openness can be derived from enabling provisions (such as Article 114 TFEU) as well as from the fact that the Treaty provisions are often ambivalent, and allow for different interpretations. In addition, there exists the obligation based upon Article 4 TEU to respect national identities, inherent in their fundamental structures, political and constitutional, inclusive of regional and local self-government. Indeed, the European Court of Justice has provided abundant interpretations of internal market rules that allow for various socio-economic paradigms to exist within the internal market, depending on the social system that it has chosen to implement in segments of its economy. For example, social schemes designed upon the basis of the principles of solidarity, have been considered by the Court to be incompatible with the functioning of a sector upon the basis of a normative principle of capitalisation. Therefore, EU competition rules do not apply in full to sectors that are primarily organised upon the basis of solidarity principles, provided that there are some guarantees of institutional design that guarantee transparency and a coherent, active form of state supervision. In these cases, the Court explicitly recognises legitimate social structures at Member State level that do not 'fit' within the normative order of the competition.[47]

This builds on the idea that the diversity of preferences and orientations in the EU is the product of specific historical experiences, political contestation, societal learning and continuous political decision

[47] Case law starting with Case ECLI:EU:C:1993:63 (*Poucet Pistre*). See, for an overview, Tamara K. Hervey, 'Social Solidarity: A Buttress against Internal Market Law', in: Jo Shaw (ed.), *Social Law and Policy in an Evolving European Union* (Oxford: Hart Publishing, 2000), pp. 31–47.

making.[48] As such, despite globalising trends, the Member States vary greatly in terms of institutional preferences and structural policy differences.[49] In similar terms, the economic historian Werner Abelshauser, has, for example, underlined the resistance of the varieties of capitalism against economic integration, and argued that this resistance is an asset. Diversity is economically beneficial, rather than detrimental.[50] Within this perspective, law's expressive role is underlined in the sense of institutionalising normative preferences and reflecting – to some extent – a shared morality of a community at a given point of time.

IV Conclusion

There is a clear and sensible reason as to why competition law is sceptical of forms of private 'producerist' regulation. Most economic theory tells us that commercial entities operate upon the basis of incentives and as a rule, undertakings may therefore be presumed to act only in their self-interest. A collective pursuit of proclaimed wider societal objectives should therefore always be met with a healthy level of suspicion.

However, by installing the current interpretation of consumer welfare as an economic rationality, the European Commission should be aware that it contributes to the cognitive infrastructures of markets. In structuring the way that self-regulatory objectives are accorded relative value within the framework of competition law, this affects the way in which those resources are distributed between the supply and demand sides of markets, which, in turn, can transform the nature of governance within the Member States. It is constitutive of the way firms are to approach

[48] As submitted by Christian Joerges, 'Market Integration and Europeanisation of Private Law', Jean Monnet Project Conference Paper (May 2015), on file with author.

[49] These can for example be classified in benefit structures, methods of financing, service intensity, family policy, employment regulation, logic of governance and the regulation of industrial relations in Anton Hemerijck, 'The Self-Transformation of the European Social Model(s)', in: Gøsta Esping-Andersen (ed.), *Why we Need a New Welfare State* (Oxford: Oxford University Press, 2002), pp. 173–214, at 178. See, also, Pablo Beramendi, 'Inequality and the Territorial Fragmentation of Solidarity' (2007) 61 *International Organization*, 783–820.

[50] See Werner Abelshauser, 'Ricardo neu gedacht. Komparative institutionelle Vorteile von Wirtschaftskulturen', in: Werner Abelshauser, David Gilgen and Andreas Leutzsch (eds.), *Kulturen der Weltwirtschaft: Geschichte und Gesellschaft* (Sonderheft 2012), pp. 29–38; Werner Abelshauser (2014), 'Europa in Vielfalt einigen. Eine Denkschrift', available at: wwwhomes.uni-bielefeld.de/wabelsha/Denkschrift.pdf, last accessed 8 February 2018. On this topic, see, also, Giandomenico Majone, 'The Deeper Euro-Crisis or: The Collapse of the EU Political Culture of Total Optimism', EUI Working Paper LAW 2015/10.

objectives such as sustainability in the future and, to some extent, constitutive of a market economy that prioritises consumerist interests over sustainable producer identity. This may give rise to governance reorientations where national governance structures that are set up to allow the supply side of a market to develop standards and self-define to be reorganised towards consumerist interests. However, it is clear that primary law and the case law of the European Court of Justice allow and, arguably, prescribe that competition law has to be applied in the context of the liberal society that the European Union purports to be. Because societies and forms of governance evolve, it can be argued that competition law is infused with a constitutional requirement to accommodate the existing or evolving notions of the legitimate exercise of regulatory power that constitute a genuine, systematic and coherent part of the socio-economic model of a system of governance within a Member State.

11

On the Vanishing Functional Autonomy of European Labour Law

(And Some Dangerous Counter-Movements)

STEFANO GIUBBONI

I Introduction: The Dimensions of the Autonomy of Labour Law from a European Perspective

Lying at the intersection of the law of persons and the law of goods,[1] labour law has had – since its origins at the end of the nineteenth century – an ambivalent relationship with the market economy and – basically – with capitalism.[2] Drawing upon the classical theory by Gérard Lyon-Caen, according to whom labour law is first of all a set of rules governing the exploitation of human labour in a capitalist economic system,[3] it is possible to maintain that a modern market economy cannot be even theoretically conceived without labour law:

[1] Alain Supiot, *Critique du droit du travail* (Paris: Quadrige/Presses Universitaires de France, 2007), p. 10.

[2] Cesare Salvi, *Capitalismo e diritto civile. Itinerari giuridici dal Code civil ai Trattati europei* (Bologna: Il Mulino, 2015).

[3] See Gérard Lyon-Caen, 'Permanence et renouvellement du Droit du travail dans une économie globalisée' (2004) *Le Droit Ouvrier*, 49–56, at 49 et seq.), in which the renowned French labour law scholar draws upon an early work of his (dating to 1950) in which he had provided this very famous definition of labour law: 'Le Droit du travail est l'ensemble des règles qui régissent: 1. L'exploitation du travail humain en régime capitaliste; 2. Les instruments de la lutte ouvrière contre cette exploitation; 3. Les résultats de cette lutte, c'est-à-dire les modifications incessantes subies par le régime d'exploitation lui-même' – 'Labour law is a set of rules governing: 1. the exploitation of human labour within a capitalist economic system; 2. the tools available to workers to fight against such exploitation; and 3. the outcomes of this fight, i.e. the ongoing changes affecting the exploitation pattern itself' (see Gérard Lyon-Caen, 'Les fondements historiques et rationnels du droit du travail' (1951) *Le Droit Ouvrier*, pp. 1–5).

> c'est seulement dans une logique marchand que s'estompe la diversité des travaux humaines ... La notion moderne de travail n'apparait donc qu'à partir du moment où le travail est traité comme une marchandise par le pensée économique ...[4]

Labour law is first of all a set of rules applying to a capitalist economic system (in a sense, a legislative framework that shapes capitalist relations of production) in as much as it carries out a fundamental task, that is, building up the hierarchical relationship of legal subordination (i.e. the exploitation of the workforce) in the framework of a contract between formally free and equal parties.[5] The conflicting role of protection/ emancipation of workers[6] – which is at the basis of the autonomy of labour law to the extent that this role makes the latter different from private law and commercial law[7] – logically falls under the employer–employee relationship, without questioning the relations of production, which are instead legitimated in the framework of political compromises that are always exposed to the changing conditions of the social forces, and are therefore destined to yield reversible outcomes.[8]

Labour law cannot therefore be separated from the market economy since it represents one of the latter's constituting institutional elements, which furthermore actually shape it. Clearly, labour law is always fundamental for the construction of a certain pattern of the capitalist economy; this entails that its rules, which change and can be reversed over time, in as much as they are linked to the flow of class conflicts in history, do so also over space and within countries. At the same time (and the inextricable ambivalence of the relationship with market economy can be observed here), labour law has gradually got rid of the *bourgeois* individualistic approach of private law by asserting an autonomous social rationality based upon the implementation, in the framework of contractual relationships, of a protection regime (aimed at ensuring a certain

4 Supiot, n. 1 above, at 6. 'It is solely in the framework of a market rationale that the diversity of human labour blurs .... The modern notion of labour emerged only when economists started to treat labour as a commodity ...' See, also, what Marx wrote as early as 1844: 'The worker's existence is thus brought under the same condition as the existence of every other commodity ... Political economy considers labour in the abstract as a thing ....' Karl Marx, *Manoscritti economico-filosofici del 1844*, edited by Enrico Donaggio and Peter Kammerer (Milan: Feltrinelli, 2018), pp. 14 and 28.

5 Supiot, n. 1 above, at 9.

6 Ruth Dukes, *The Labour Constitution: The Enduring Idea of Labour Law* (Oxford: Oxford University Press, 2014).

7 Giuseppe Santoro-Passarelli, 'Le funzioni del diritto del lavoro' (2018) *Rivista italiana di diritto del lavoro*, pp. 339–53.

8 Gérard Lyon-Caen, *Le droit du travail. Une technique réversible* (Paris: Dalloz, 1995).

degree of economic and job security) of the worker as the weaker party. From this point of view, as has been pointed out recently,

> the history of labour law is a story of emancipation from private law since labour law was established as a set of rules governing legal and property relationships between parties in an unequal position. Rather, labour law even contaminates private law when inequality between the contracting parties is no longer limited to employment contracts.[9]

In western Europe, this process of emancipation, that is, of (partial) autonomy, of labour law from private law reaches its peak – although with very different layouts in relation to the various models of welfare capitalism that were established during the '*Trente Glorieuses*' – in parallel with the first phase of the establishment of the European Communities.[10] It can be said that the first phase of European integration, at least until the end of the 1970s, was an essential part of a broader historical process of transformation of capitalist economies of western countries,[11] a process in which the great compromise (at social and democratic level) between capital and labour came to life, particularly in the founding countries of the European Community.

In the framework of the democratic capitalism of the '*Trente Glorieuses*', the autonomy of labour law in Europe gathered momentum in relation to a twofold dimension, an 'internal' and an 'external' one, both being interrelated with one another. At an internal level, the process of the (partial) autonomy of labour law from private law represents a central aspect of the social paradigm of the second wave of globalisation, as described by Duncan Kennedy. By making use of a conceptualisation and periodisation which only partially overlaps with the one adopted by Kennedy,[12] and drawing upon Luca Nivarra, it can be deemed one of the main components of the paradigm – which

[9] Vincenzo Bavaro, 'Appunti su scienza e politica sul diritto del lavoro' (2016) *Lavoro e diritto*, pp. 707–18, at 708.

[10] Jean Fourastié, *Les Trente Glorieuses, ou la révolution invisible de 1946 à 1975* (Paris: Fayard, 1979).

[11] Andrew Shonfield, *Modern Capitalism. The Changing Balance of Public and Private Power* (Oxford: Oxford University Press, 1965); Gøsta Esping-Andersen, *The Three Worlds of Welfare Capitalism* (Cambridge: Polity Press, 1990); Peter A. Hall and David W. Soskice, *Varieties of Capitalism: The Institutional Foundations of the Comparative Advantage* (Oxford: Oxford University Press, 2001).

[12] See, too, Salvi, n. 2 above, at 13, who also proposes a periodisation being partly different from the one suggested by Duncan Kennedy, 'Three Globalizations of Law and Legal Thought: 1850–2000', in: David M. Trubek and Alvaro Santos (eds.), *The New Law and Economic Development: A Critical Appraisal* (Cambridge: Cambridge University Press,

characterises that specific historical phase of the development of capitalism – of 'orthopaedic law', in which:

> the legal rule becomes an orthopaedic tool of the parties' will. This is aimed at bringing it in line with different goals, even though not necessarily in contrast with the contractual autonomy principle (economic development and, at some stages, social justice).[13]

The mandatory nature of labour law – set out by state law or collective agreements with a view to redistributing (to different extents) the social power between capital and organised labour – is key to the success of such paradigm, albeit depending on the extremely diverging patterns of democratic capitalism at national level.

From an external point of view, such autonomy was guaranteed by the way in which the treaties establishing the European Communities initially shaped the process of the gradual and controlled opening of the common market.[14] It is well known that, particularly pursuant to the original version of the Treaty of Rome, the newly established Community lacked any legislative competences on social policy matters – as labour law is called in the Community jargon – with the only, and very partial, exception of relatively secondary matters, in particular at that time, such as equal treatment (in terms of pay) between male and female workers, and the rules governing paid holiday schemes. The conferment on Member States of full regulatory autonomy in relation to social policy was justified both on economic grounds (since the differences in the levels of protection between the various countries were deemed to mirror any existing gaps in terms of productivity) and, mainly, on political and

2006), pp. 19–73, at 37 et seq. The latter – in as much as he states that the development of the social law paradigm took place in the period from 1900 to 1968 – seems to fail to emphasise the strong historical discontinuity of the democratic and social constitutionalism that consolidated after World War II. Such discontinuity should instead be stressed considering in particular the history of western Europe – see, more recently, Omar Chessa, 'La dogmatica costituzionale dei diritti sociali tra struttura e sovrastruttura' (2016) *Lavoro e diritto*, pp. 269–90, and Marco Benvenuti, 'Democrazia e potere economico' (2018) *Rivista dell'Associazione italiana dei costituzionalisti*, pp. 1–110.

13 Luca Nivarra, *Diritto privato e capitalismo. Regole giuridiche e paradigmi di mercato* (Naples: Editoriale Scientifica, 2010), p. 10.

14 According to a model that – in line with Ruggie – has been defined elsewhere as 'embedded liberalism'; see John G. Ruggie, 'International Regimes, Transactions, and Change: Embedded Liberalism in the Postwar Economic Order' (1982) 36 *International Organization*, pp. 379–415; see Stefano Giubboni, *Diritti sociali e mercato. La dimensione sociale dell'integrazione europea* (Bologna: Il Mulino, 2003). See, also, Maurizio Ferrera, *The Boundaries of Welfare: European Integration and the New Spatial Politics of Social Protection* (Oxford: Oxford University Press, 2005).

constitutional grounds (in as much as the different traditions were closely intertwined with the history of the trade union movement in each country and with the diverse conceptions of the welfare state, embedded in the newly rebuilt national democracies).

The present chapter will endeavour to show the reasons why, starting from the end of the 1980s, the 'external' dimension of the autonomy of social law in Europe has gradually experienced a seemingly irreversible crisis due to a deep transformation of the political economy of the European integration process and, following the Treaty on European Union (TEU), of the economic constitution of the European Union (EU).[15] In the last decade, this crisis has worsened due to the transformation of the EU and its Member States into, respectively, a strong *Liberalisierungsmaschine* and *Konsolidierungsstaaten*[16] – as Wolfgang Streeck evocatively described the process[17] – thus representing today's most successful experiment of neoliberal 'hyper-globalisation'.[18] The erosion of the immunity of labour law – initially from the legal patterns of the integrated market, and then from economic and financial governance – has certainly contributed to reducing its autonomy also as to its 'internal' dimension (it has most probably played a decisive role in this process),[19] even though a relationship of mutual interaction exists between the two dimensions, and it is not possible to identify unambiguous and linear causal processes.[20]

In its turn, this transformation has contributed to the fuelling – especially in those countries that have suffered the most from its effects, such as Italy – of a sort of 'rejection crisis', as clearly demonstrated at political level (almost all over Europe) by the development of 'populist' and 'sovereignist' counter-movements: all of them are inspired – albeit for different and sometimes openly conflicting reasons – by deep feelings of social frustration typical of those who feel that they are the losers from globalisation, which is already leading to Brexit in the worst way possible.

[15] See Sections II and III below.

[16] Literally meaning 'liberalising machine' and 'consolidation states'.

[17] Wolfgang Streeck, *Gekaufte Zeit. Die vertagte Krise des demokratischen Kapitalismus* (Berlin: Suhrkamp Verlag, 2013), p. 141 et seq.

[18] Dani Rodrik, *Straight Talk on Trade* (Princeton NJ-Oxford: Princeton University Press, 2018), p. 48 et seq. See Section IV below.

[19] Salvi, n. 2 above, at 157 et seq.; Francesco Costamagna 'National Social Spaces as Adjustment Variables in the EMU: A Critical Legal Appraisal' (2018) 24 *European Law Journal*, pp. 163–90.

[20] Vincenzo Bavaro, 'Lineamenti sulla costituzione materiale dei diritti sociali del lavoro' (2018) *Lavoro e diritto*, pp. 243–68, at 261; Omar Chessa, n. 12 above, at 271.

Today, the EU, which is probably going through the most difficult moment of its history, is supposed to give responses which, however, seem to lack a coherent and shared approach, also because of the huge divisions (and economic conflicts) that emerged – during the financial and sovereign debt crises – between its major Member States.

In the concluding section, it will be argued that, in as much as it is impossible to have a common set of fundamental social standards and a unitary welfare state at European level, an almost unavoidable response to the legitimacy crisis affecting the EU consists in giving back to the Member States a higher degree of autonomy and 'social sovereignty'.[21] A first step in this direction was actually taken – as will be explained below – with the approval of the recent Directive (EU) 2018/957, which significantly modifies the rules concerning the posting of workers in the framework of the provision of services. However, such a defensive strategy – based upon the re-establishment of a higher level of autonomy of national social law systems – turns out to be manifestly inadequate, in as much as it is not embedded in a broader correction of the neoliberal and highly asymmetrical structure of European economic and financial governance.[22]

II The Crisis of the Rationale Justifying European Labour Law

As outlined above, the original 'decoupling' between supranational economic integration and national social constitution allowed for the construction of the common market upon a solid basis of substantive democratic legitimisation;[23] in greater detail, national labour law and

[21] See Section V below. As stated by Dani Rodrik, 'after all, the nation-state remains the only game in town when it comes to providing the regulatory and legitimizing arrangements on which the markets rely'; Rodrik, n. 18 above, at 13.

[22] Seen from a shrewd (or maybe 'populist' and 'sovereigntist') Italian perspective, the current European integration backlash is essentially due to the increasing conflict between, on the one hand, 'creditor' countries' (i.e. German) hegemonic interests and, on the other, the interests of the 'debtor' countries of the Eurozone (essentially Italy). Suffice it to say that, thanks to the mechanisms introduced since 2011 with a view to coping with the sovereign debt crisis, Germany, already in 2019, will eventually be able to bring its public debt close to the sacral 60 per cent threshold, whereas Italy will have to cope with a debt stock totalling 130 per cent of GDP, and will have to abide by a set of rules that, de facto, will make it impossible to comply with the treaties. Such unsustainable (and indeed profoundly unjust) asymmetry is perfectly outlined by Thomas Fazi and William Mitchell, *Sovranità o barbarie. Il ritorno della questione nazionale* (Milan: Meltemi, 2018), p. 199 et seq.).

[23] Fritz W. Sharpf, 'The European Social Model. Coping with the Challenges of Diversity', in: Sharpf, *Community and Autonomy: Institutions, Policies and Legitimacy in Multilevel Europe*, Frankfurt aM-New York: Campus Verlag, 2010), pp. 221–46; Christian Joerges,

social security systems ensured that such legitimisation underlay the transnational process of economic opening up.[24] When, starting in the second half of the 1970s, this model of separation between the economic sphere and the social sphere began to decline, the first harmonisation policies implemented by the European Economic Community (EEC) in the field of labour law (from the directives on collective redundancies and on transfer of undertakings, to the first wave of gender equality directives) were aimed at reinstating – wherever possible – the autonomy of the national labour law systems, immunising them against negative interference triggered by the competition process within the common market. The rules laid down by the supranational legislator actually set minimum standards of protection, which Member States had to comply with, while remaining free to maintain or introduce higher levels of protection.[25]

However, the model of (partial) upward harmonisation of national labour laws was put into question: with the exception of a short revival in the second half of the 1990s, the crisis officially broke out at the beginning of the new millennium (the watershed can conventionally be considered the famous Lisbon summit of March 2000). There were, of course, multiple reasons behind this crisis, but the two major turning points of the review process of the political economy related to European integration in those years – that is, the launch of the monetary union, on the one hand, and the eastern enlargement, on the other – are certainly decisive. It is not by chance that the crisis of the upward harmonisation through directives setting a minimum common floor of labour protection unfolded exactly as the legal basis of the treaties theoretically enabled the EU eventually to implement a form of social policy that could potentially be extended to almost the whole of national labour law (albeit with persistent exclusions of competence in the fields of pay, right of

'What is Left of the European Economic Constitution? A Melancholic Eulogy' (2005) 30 *European Law Review*, pp. 461–89.

24 Stefano Giubboni, *Diritti e solidarietà in Europa* (Bologna: Il Mulino, 2012), p. 31 et seq.

25 Simon Deakin, 'Labour Law as Market Regulation: The Economic Foundations of European Social Policies', in: Paul Davies, Antoine Lyon-Caen, Silvana Sciarra and Spiros Simitis (eds.), *European Community Labour Law: Principles and Perspectives. Liber Amicorum Lord Wedderburn* (Oxford: Clarendon Press, 1996), pp. 69–93; Phil Syrpis, *EU Intervention in Domestic Labour Law* (Oxford: Oxford University Press, 2007); Catherine Barnard, 'Fifty Years of Avoiding Social Dumping? The EU's Economic and Not So Economic Constitution', in: Michael Dougan and Samantha Currie (eds.), *50 Years of the European Treaties. Looking Back and Thinking Forward* (Oxford-Portland OR: Hart Publishing, 2009), pp. 311–42.

association, strike, and lockout, pursuant to Article 153, paragraph 7 of the Treaty on the Functioning of the European Union – TFEU). Indeed, that model suffered a crisis exactly when, through the Lisbon Treaty, 'the social drive of the constitutionalisation process reached its peak',[26] mainly as a result of the reinforcement of the EU's values and social goals and of the recognition, as EU primary law, of the EU Charter of Fundamental Rights.

The rationale of the model under analysis entails that national labour laws, and, more generally, national social law systems, should stay immune to the competition process and, at least in principle, to any type of competition between the different regimes that takes place within the common market.[27] Autonomy from market and competition law – a founding and constitutive trait of labour law – must be guaranteed also at an 'external' (supranational) level by protecting national social protection systems against the destructuring effects of negative integration, which paves the way to market liberalisation. This model, which had already been gradually stripped of legitimacy already during the 1990s, was completely overturned by the *Viking* and *Laval* case law.[28]

In these two renowned judgments, as well as in the case law that has coherently followed since then, the relationship between the internal market and national labour legislation is perfectly inverted. Domestic labour legislation is therefore subjugated to strict scrutiny by the Court of Justice of the European Union (CJEU)[29] against the exercise of fundamental economic freedoms. Under the constitutional guarantee enshrined in the treaties and in the EU Charter of Fundamental Rights,

[26] Hans-W. Micklitz, 'Judicial Activism of the European Court of Justice and the Development of the European Social Model in Anti-Discrimination and Consumer Law', in: Ulla Neergaard, Ruth Nielsen and Lynn M. Roseberry (eds.), *The Role of Courts in Developing a European Social Model: Theoretical and Methodological Perspectives* (Copenhagen: DJØF Publishing, 2010), pp. 25–61, at 36.

[27] Maximilian Fuchs and Franz Marhold, *Europäisches Arbeitsrecht* (Vienna: Verlag Österreich, 2018), p. 8 et seq.

[28] CJEU, Case C-438/05, *Viking*, and Case C-341/05, *Laval*. The vast literature on these judgments cannot be mentioned here: see, for example, Mark Freedland and Jeremias Prassl (eds.), *Viking, Laval and Beyond* (Oxford-Portland OR: Hart Publishing, 2014), and Catherine Barnard, 'The Calm after the Storm: Time to Reflect on EU (Labour) Law Scholarship Following the Decisions in *Viking* and *Laval*', in: Alan Bogg, Cathryn Costello and A.C.L. Davies (eds.), *Research Handbook on EU Labour Law* (Cheltenham-Northampton MA: Edward Elgar Publishing, 2016), pp. 337–60.

[29] To avoid confusion, this essay refers to the European Court of Justice (ECJ) as the Court of Justice of the European Union (CJEU) for decisions made prior to 1 December 2009 when the Treaty of Lisbon entered into force.

the transnational freedom to conduct a business tends to subjugate any national labour law provision (regardless of it stemming from statutory legislation or a collective agreement), subjecting any hindrance created by the latter to strict compatibility scrutiny against the rules of the internal market. From this new perspective, the protective function pursued by labour law loses its legitimation. Labour law regains legitimacy in so far as it is able to pass a proportionality test carried out in compliance with the primacy of the principle of allocative efficiency of market freedoms.[30] This implies that the higher the degree of protection guaranteed by domestic labour law rules is (and thus the stronger the restriction of employers' contractual freedom), the greater the 'justificatory pressure' on national systems will be, that is, the obligation upon Member States and trade unions – whichever the source – to justify such regulations. Therefore, higher levels of protection (compared to the standards set out in EU directives) guaranteed by national legal systems become potentially illegitimate, even those higher standards that were once allowed and even encouraged by EU upward harmonisation directives. This completely overturns the original normative function of EU labour law, since – instead of setting a minimum floor in terms of worker protection – it ends up determining an upper limit that, in principle, national law makers (and trade unions themselves) must respect in order to avoid jeopardising the efficient functioning of the market.

In this way, the protection against social dumping – which initially represented the primary rationale of the harmonisation social policy, now irreparably in crisis – becomes, at the very best, a potential reason for justifying the national labour law protective rule in the likely event that its legitimacy is questioned as a hindrance to transnational economic freedom. The original perspective is, once again, fully overturned: protection against the risks of social dumping no longer represents the starting point of an upward harmonisation process of protection standards in as much as the generalisation of the highest protection standards is no longer a viable solution in the enlarged EU; instead, it represents grounds for justifying the legitimacy of the more favourable national measure, in compliance with the constraints imposed by the rules of the internal market. The thrust towards lowering protection standards is constitutionally reinforced – especially for the 'debtor' countries of the Eurozone periphery – also by the convergent operational rationale

[30] Stefano Giubboni, 'Libertà d'impresa e diritto del lavoro nell'Unione europea' (2016) *Costituzionalismo.it*, pp. 89–133, at 55 et seq.

inherent to the EU's new economic and financial governance, which invariably requires bridging the gap of competitiveness with the best-performing countries by reducing social expenditure and by implementing 'structural reforms'; this means reducing labour costs, as well as introducing a higher degree of (numerical) 'flexibility', particularly in relation to lowering employment protection against dismissals for economic reasons.[31]

III The Functional Displacement of EU Labour Law

This new idea of (national) labour law as an obstacle to – and no longer as a precondition of – the correct functioning of the internal market has significant implications in many other respects. In this new model, in fact, the functions attributed to EU labour law, and especially the directives aimed at that type of harmonisation that Massimo D'Antona called 'functionalist', are reshaped and reinterpreted. This is where Gérard Lyon-Caen's take on the 'reversible' nature of employment law as a way to resolve the redistributive conflict between capital and labour really comes into play. Some examples, taken from the CJEU's recent case law, will help make the point.

The *Alemo-Herron* case[32] was focused on the interpretation of Directive 2001/23/EC on the protection of employees' rights in the event of transfers of undertakings. Through 'dynamic clauses' incorporated within individual employment contracts, the transferor company was obliged to apply to its employees the public sector collective agreement entered into by the employers' association of which it was a member. The transferor company was therefore also obliged to grant them any future wage increases deriving from collective bargaining in that sector. The controversy originated because the transferee (which was classified in a sector other than the transferor's) simply refused – in contrast with UK legislation that transposed Directive 2001/23/EC – to take over the employment conditions agreed on by the transferor, and

[31] Stefano Giubboni and Giovanni Orlandini, 'Dentro la crisi. Spunti comparati sull'impatto delle 'riforme strutturali' nel diritto del lavoro in Italia, Portogallo e Spagna' (2018) *Rivista giuridica del lavoro*, pp. 643–79.

[32] CJEU, case C-426/11, *Alemo-Herron*. In spite of a different outcome, the recent judgment issued in relation to joint Cases C-680/15 and C-680/11, *Asklepios*, does not change the CJEU's argumentation and interpretation – see, for further details, Stefano Giubboni, 'Freedom to Conduct a Business and EU Labour Law' (2018) 14 *European Constitutional Law Review*, pp. 172–90, at 185.

specifically the pay-related obligations deriving from such dynamic clauses. Considering these clauses to be detrimental to its freedom of association, the transferee resorted to court action, claiming that they were in breach of EU legislation, as well as calling for the case to be referred to the CJEU for a preliminary ruling.

In his conclusions, Advocate General Cruz Villalón had emphasised how these clauses, certainly allowed under Directive 2001/23/EC, could come into conflict not with the freedom guaranteed by Article 11 of the Convention for the Protection of Human Rights and Fundamental Freedoms (and Article 12 of the EU Charter of Fundamental Rights), but rather with the freedom to conduct a business, enshrined in Article 16 of the latter, namely, the principle of contractual freedom as a fundamental manifestation of entrepreneurial freedom. Nonetheless, the Advocate General had come to the conclusion that such a violation of the transferee's contractual freedom could not be ascribed to national law unless under the assumption that the obligation arising from those dynamic clauses was 'unconditional and irreversible'.[33] The CJEU, instead, took a different route: it held that such clauses theoretically imply a disproportionate limitation of the freedom to conduct a business, enshrined in Article 16 of the EU Charter of Fundamental Rights, in so far as the transferee does not have the possibility of participating in the collective bargaining process and thus in the conclusion of collective bargaining agreements, which – pursuant to UK law – apply following the acquisition of the undertaking. In the CJEU's opinion, the transferee is not given the possibility of effectively asserting its interests in a collective bargaining process to which it is a party, nor is it given the right – even considering its future economic activity – to negotiate the aspects determining the changes in the working conditions of its employees. As a consequence, the transferee's contractual freedom is seriously reduced to such an extent that such a limitation is liable to affect adversely the very essence of its freedom to conduct a business. It follows that, in the light of Article 16 of the EU Charter of Fundamental Rights, Directive 2001/23/EC is to be interpreted as precluding a Member State from adopting measures that, albeit more favourable to employees, go as far as to affect adversely the very essence of the transferee's freedom to conduct a business.

The judgment draws a clear dividing line with respect to the CJEU's previous case law. The reversed interpretation of the directive – which is

[33] Para. 58 of the conclusions by the Advocate General.

considered in the light of the freedom to conduct a business, as enshrined in Article 16 of the EU Charter of Fundamental Rights – leads to the actual overturning of its function: having been initially conceived as a tool for the protection of the continuity of employment relationships and conditions, Directive 2001/23/EC is turned into an instrument for the protection of the employer's interest in terms of ensuring the greatest profits from commercial transactions, making sure wage costs are kept to a minimum. The fundamental interest that is given protection – as is the case with the *Viking* and *Laval* judgments, in which such interest is protected against the collective action of employees – is certainty of the labour costs budgeted by the undertaking. Collective action and bargaining, by virtue of the proportionality test, are weakened and almost neutralised in relation to their typical role as tools for social struggles and claims, whose goal is to challenge business profitability in order to gain distributive outcomes that are more favourable to workers.[34]

The CJEU reasserted, in an even stronger way, this new trend of its case law in the Grand Chamber's judgment related to the *Anonymi Geneki Etairia Tsimenton Iraklis (AGET Iraklis)* case.[35] The focus was on the compatibility with Directive 98/59/EC on collective redundancies – read yet again in the light of Article 16 of the EU Charter of Fundamental Rights – of Greek Law No. 1387/1983, which allowed the public authority to deny a company the authorisation to effect collective redundancies in exceptional circumstances, and particularly in the event of exceptionally high levels of unemployment (and of the consequent risks of social and economic upheavals). In the case in hand – and precisely in the presence of exceptionally severe unemployment and social disruption – the relevant Greek authorities had denied the authorisation requested by *AGET Iraklis*, a subsidiary of a French multinational group, on the assumption that the corporate plan to decommission the plant had not been based on appropriate motives.

It is worth pointing out that, in transposing Directive 75/129/EEC on collective redundancies, the above-mentioned Greek law introduced to its legal system a protection scheme that was common to several countries at that time, for example, in France (where it has been reformed only relatively recently) and in the Netherlands (where it is still in place). However, although complying with a partially different line of argument

34 Bavaro, n. 20 above, at 255.

35 CJEU (Grand Chamber), Case C-201/15, *Anonymi Geneki Etairia Tsimenton Iraklis (AGET Iraklis)*.

from the extremely neoliberal one adopted by Advocate General Wahl, the CJEU inevitably came to the same conclusions by ruling that the Greek law was in conflict with the directive, interpreted in the light of the entrepreneur's contractual freedom. The national legislation, in fact, would deprive the provisions of Directive 98/59/EC of their effects, precluding the employer from implementing any redundancy plan whenever the company's adverse economic conditions might suggest such a choice on the basis of an assessment of economic profitability that cannot be hampered by a discretionary decision of the public authority. The CJEU yet again transforms a directive aimed at partial and minimum harmonisation into an instrument for the protection of 'the employer's business interests'.[36] The classical principle according to which law makers are, in principle, always allowed to provide higher levels of protection to employees than those set forth by European directives, is justified in view of the need to strike a 'balance' with the freedom to conduct a business and the related guarantee of the employer's contractual autonomy.[37] The overturning of the traditional protective function of EU labour law could not be more blatant: a proper '*autodafé de l'Europe sociale*'.[38]

IV Sources and Techniques of EU Labour Law in Times of Crisis

In the framework of such reconceptualisation of labour law as a hindrance to the proper functioning of the market, both the new course of the CJEU's case law on fundamental freedoms and on the role played by social policy directives, and the operational rationale of the economic and financial governance of the Eurozone merge together.[39] The new 'economic mythology' does not envisage a labour law framework that is different from the common law of

[36] Bavaro, n. 20 above, at 249.

[37] Giovanni Orlandini, 'Libertà di stabilimento versus diritto al lavoro: ancora un bilanciamento "sbilanciato" tra libertà economiche e diritti dei lavoratori' (2017) 153 *Giornale di diritto del lavoro e di relazioni industriali*, pp. 203–18.

[38] Alain Supiot, 'Les voies d'une vraie réforme du droit du travail', in: Supiot (ed.), *Au-delà de l'emploi* (Paris: Flammarion, 2016), pp. II–XLVII, at X.

[39] Phil Syrpis, 'The EU's Role in Labour Law: An Overview of the Rationales for the Involvement in the Field', in: Alan Bogg, Cathryn Costello and A.C.L. Davies (eds.), *Research Handbook on EU Labour Law*, Cheltenham-Northampton MA: Edward Elgar Publishing, 2016), pp. 39–40; Aristea Koukiadaki, 'The Legacy of the Economic Crisis for Labour Law in Europe', in: Bogg, Costello and Davies (eds.), *Research Handbook on EU Labour Law*, this n., pp. 64–88, at 66.

contracts;[40] at most, in its nuanced variants, it acknowledges an ideal type that substantially shifts the focus of labour protection from the employment relationship to the labour market, from employee protection to the promotion of employment or the facilitation of employment transitions. The flexicurity model ensures that the loss of 'external autonomy' of labour law also affects the 'internal' dimension of the relationship between social law and private law in the various legal systems of EU Member States.

The decline of the functional autonomy of European labour law put into question the role played by the sources of the European social policy. As authoritatively stated, in the field of social and labour policies 'the economic and financial crisis shook up the traditional hierarchy of sources and regulatory techniques, raising issues of democratic legitimacy and accountability for all the actors involved'.[41]

Reference has already been made to the implosion of the model of harmonisation through directives, practically removed from EU labour law sources at least following the great enlargement of 2004. Having experienced for some time now a growing crisis in terms of effectiveness, this model simply became unviable in such a heterogeneous and divided context; all of this, as noted above, occurred in spite of the apparent strengthening of the EU's legal bases in the field of social policies. A similar process of self-destruction was experienced by the European quasi-legislative collective bargaining framework (Article 155 TFEU), already envisaged in the Agreement on Social Policy annexed to the Protocol on Social Policy of the TEU as a new regulatory technique useful for the reactivation of a new virtuous circle for setting common minimum labour standards, which falls under the institutionalised exercise of the collective autonomy of the European social partners.

After an initial relatively successful phase, mainly characterised by the two directives on atypical employment in the second half of the 1990s, social dialogue and the pan-European inter-sectorial collective macro-bargaining soon underwent a relentless decline, up to the current standstill. As the European Commission's threat to exert its power of legislative initiative as a default option disappeared, employers' organisations actually have very little incentive to negotiate, and workers' unions, which formed a relatively united and homogeneous group up until the

40 Éloi Laurent, *Mitologie economiche* (Vicenza: Neri Pozza, 2017).

41 Silvana Sciarra, 'Il diritto sociale europeo al tempo della crisi', in: Elisabetta Catelani and Rolando Tarchi (eds.), *I diritti sociali nella pluralità degli ordinamenti* (Naples: Editoriale Scientifica, 2015), pp. 269–88, at 269.

enlargement, are now torn apart by cross-cutting conflicts that reflect the cleavages (north-south and west-east) engendered by the European disintegration process. Indeed, the marginalisation of the social partners' role has deeper and more complex roots, and is intertwined with the overall 'shift in location of labour law from the classic Community method towards the OMC (Open Method of Co-ordination) and bailouts',[42] which underlies the broader process of the normative and functional displacement of the traditional sources of European social policy.[43]

After being hailed as the new general soft-law tool for the positive integration of national social systems at the Lisbon summit in 2000, the OMC was generally welcomed as the new frontier of reflexive and promotional law, an inclusive mechanism capable of inducing the circulation and cross-fertilisation of best practices and of conjugating social rights and market forces by reconciling the need to reinforce the convergence processes of national economies, with the growing diversity of the different models of welfare capitalism within the EU.[44] Once again, after an initial phase of encouraging results during a period of economic growth more or less equally distributed throughout the continent, the crisis that broke out at the end of the first decade of implementation of the OMC revealed all the inconsistencies and ineffectiveness of the OMC.[45] The OMC was swallowed up by the EU's new crisis management law,[46] becoming nothing but a tool for the implementation of the opaque (hard) web of constraints imposed by the new Stability and Growth Pact.[47] It became one of the many channels for the transmission of the imperatives of what Wolfgang Streeck has called '*Politik des Konsolidierungsstaates*',[48] where room for the experimentation and reflexive harmonisation in the social field, which the OMC was intended

[42] Alan Bogg, Cathryn Costello and A.C.L. Davies (eds.), 'The Role of the Court of Justice in Labour Law', in: Bogg, Costello and Davies (eds.), *Research Handbook on EU Labour Law* (Cheltenham-Northampton MA: Edward Elgar Publishing, 2016), pp. 114–49, at 144.

[43] Claire Kilpatrick, 'The Displacement of Social Europe: A Productive Lens of Inquiry' (2018) 14 *European Constitutional Law Review*, pp. 62–74.

[44] Olivier De Schutter and Simon Deakin (eds.), *Social Rights and Market Forces. Is the Open Method of Coordination of Employment and Social Policies the Future of Social Europe?* (Brussels: Bruylant, 2005).

[45] Sciarra, n. 41 above, at 47 et seq.

[46] Ibid., at 270.

[47] Emilios Christodoulidis and Marco Goldoni, 'The Political Economy of European Social Rights', in: Stefano Civitarese Matteucci and Simon Halliday (eds.), *Social Rights in Europe in an Age of Austerity* (London-New York: Routledge, 2018), pp. 239–56.

[48] Literally meaning 'politics of the consolidation State'; see Streeck, n. 17 above.

for, is evidently eliminated and replaced by rigid uniform orientations aimed at the 'structural reform' of national systems.[49] This undoubtedly means – especially for the weakest Member States of the Eurozone – a reduction in workers' rights for the sake of market constraints and discipline.[50]

V In Search of the Lost Autonomy of European Labour Law between Risks and Opportunities

The classic EU labour law paradigm is thus going through a strong existential crisis. It is beyond any doubt a crisis in terms of effectiveness and, even more, in terms of legitimacy: as observed by Bob Hepple,[51] the whole system of the new European economic constitution puts 'a heavy burden of proof on advocates of employment rights to establish the superiority of regulation over ordinary market rules'. The standardising pressure exerted by market rules no longer encounters barriers aimed at protecting the autonomy and legitimate diversity of national labour law systems as conceived at the beginning of the integration process, when Otto Kahn-Freund wrote that 'there is nothing to show that even a functioning common market would, within an appreciable future, produce uniformity where for centuries there has been diversity'.[52] This, of course, does not mean that these differences will disappear in the near future: however, there is no doubt that the *Laval*, *Alemo-Herron*, and *AGET Iraklis* judgments all follow the same 'neoliberal trajectory',[53] fostering downward harmonisation of protection standards. Similarly, the obligations descending from the pervasive technocratic and quintessentially post-democratic system commonly known as 'European economic governance' go in the same direction, reinforcing the discipline imposed on profligate debtor states by financial markets.[54]

49 Rodrik, n. 18 above, at 51 et seq.

50 Koukiadaki, n. 39 above.

51 Bob Hepple, 'Factors Influencing the Making and Transformation of Labour Law in Europe', in: Guy Davidov and Brian Langille (eds.), *The Idea of Labour Law* (Oxford: Oxford University Press, 2011), p. 39.

52 Otto Kahn-Freund, 'Labor Law and Social Security', in: Eric Stein and Thomas L. Nicholson (eds.), *American Enterprise in the European Common Market: A Legal Profile*, Vol. I. (Ann Arbor MI: The University of Michigan Law School, 1960), pp. 297–458, at 304.

53 Lucio Baccaro and Chris Howell, *Trajectories of Neoliberal Transformation: European Industrial Relations since the 1970s* (Cambridge: Cambridge University Press, 2017).

54 Christodoulidis and Goldoni, n. 47 above, at 248 et seq.

EU labour law seems to have lost its fundamental function, which has been – and should be – that of ensuring the co-existence and interdependence of national social constitutions within the common marketplace,[55] thereby guaranteeing the diversity of the various models of democratic capitalism, without turning the economic and monetary integration into a standardising (and deforming) mould that benefits those economies to which the governance of the crisis has been asymmetrically tailored. But any attempt to revive the idea of EU labour law as an instrument for governing the interdependence of national labour constitutions is very difficult. In this regard, a paradox emerges: that of the 'impossible necessity' of EU labour law, described by Hugh Collins,[56] in as much as a European labour code would be both necessary, with a view to counteracting competition between different regulatory frameworks, and impossible, because of the increased diversity (and divergence) of national systems.

The difficulty stems from the overall functional displacement of the several techniques used to this aim. Not even through the constitutionalisation of a hard core of fundamental social rights in the EU legal system – a goal that has been pursued since the end of the 1980s, and has been apparently achieved by conferring on the EU Charter of Fundamental Rights the same legal value as the treaties – has the expected outcome been obtained. Conferring on economic freedoms and the freedom to conduct a business the same value as fundamental rights has paradoxically worsened, in the CJEU's latest case law, the constitutional asymmetry that should have been tackled through the development of an EU catalogue of social rights. On the other hand, due to the irresistible Teutonic opposition of Europe's reluctant hegemon, no credible proposals have been put forward to reform the economic and financial architecture of the EU with a view to complementing the incomplete and asymmetrical governance structure of the Eurozone. Moreover, no proposals have been tabled to strengthen the common budget adequately with a view to implementing even minimal countercyclical fiscal transfer policies, thus showing a pathetic lack of '*de facto*

[55] Florian Rödl, 'Constitutional Integration of Labour Constitutions', in: Erik Oddvar Eriksen, Christian Joerges and Florian Rödl (eds.), *Law, Democracy and Solidarity in Post-national Union: The Unsettled Political Order of Europe* (Abingdon: Routledge, 2008), pp. 152–71.

[56] Hugh Collins, 'The Impossible Necessity of a European Labour Law', in: Sam Muller, Stavros Zouridis, Morly Frishman and Laura Kistemaker (eds.), *The Law of the Future and the Future of Law* (Oslo: TOAEP, 2011), pp. 453–66.

solidarity', particularly between 'creditor' and 'debtor' countries, which is the real drive of European disintegration.

The revival of the necessary autonomy of social law should thus take other routes, which are, however, difficult to discern at the moment. It is nonetheless possible to make some assumptions to conclude this chapter.

The first consideration draws upon the new legislative framework that emerges from the recent (and already much criticised) approval of Directive (EU) 2018/957, which amends the rules on the posting of workers in the framework of a transnational provision of services. Without going into technical detail, it is possible to maintain that the new framework on the posting of workers at intra-EU level is now once again more in line with Member States' need to avoid wage dumping. In other words, this new legislative framework is (at least partly) similar to the one in place prior to the adoption of the neoliberal approach with the *Viking* and *Laval* judgments.

Directive (EU) 2018/957 actually incorporates a broad notion of pay by setting out that posted workers are entitled to be paid remuneration as determined 'by the national law and/or practice of the Member State to whose territory the worker is posted', including 'all the ... elements ... rendered mandatory by national law, regulation or administrative provision, or by collective agreements or arbitration awards which, in that Member State, have been declared universally applicable' (as per the new wording of Article 3, paragraph 1 of Directive 96/71/EC). The goal of combating the very common fraudulent practices concerning the calculation of the remuneration paid to workers is pursued through a number of provisions aimed at detailing which elements can be paid to employees as reimbursement of expenditure incurred.

In order to tackle the problems that emerged at case law level in relation to the enforcement of Directive 96/71/EC, Article 3, paragraph 8 has been complemented with a provision setting out that even those Member States in which collective agreements can be declared universally applicable may base themselves upon collective agreements that have not been declared as such provided that the relevant mechanisms at the basis of the universal applicability principle have not been used. This change concerns, in particular, those systems, such as the German one, in which the percentage of collective agreements declared universally applicable is very low, or such agreements are largely outnumbered by contracts under ordinary law. However, the efforts made to promote pay equality between national and foreign workers do not go further, due to the structural limits imposed by the principles of the internal market:

first of all, the non-discrimination principle, which confirms the original framework set by Directive 96/71/EC in relation to the regulatory function of collective agreements, and reasserts the applicability – as wage-setting mechanisms – only of those that have been declared universally applicable or that are actually complied with by all the national companies of the sector concerned. As a consequence, no solution is provided in relation to the application of collective agreements as anti-dumping mechanisms within those systems that feature weak institutionalisation of industrial relations (e.g. in Italy), and lack rules with a sufficient degree of effectiveness so as to ensure uniform and widespread compliance with them.

The second counter-movement aimed at reasserting some 'external' autonomy of labour law is not supported, as is the case with the directive on the posting of workers, by EU law, but develops (more or less explicitly) in opposition to the intrusiveness of the EU in various areas. In this regard, Italy's frantic political and institutional scenario provides insights that, in a future perspective, may go far beyond its national borders.

Beyond the transitional political compromise achieved at the last minute with the European Commission, the 'neopopulist' government which brings together *La Lega* (formerly the *Lega Nord*, known as the 'Northern League' in English-speaking countries) and the Five Star Movement (*Movimento 5 Stelle* (M5S)) has led to the approval of a budget law that openly challenges the rules enshrined in the new Stability Pact, based upon the (rather widespread) assumption that those rules clash with national interests, in addition to limiting the democratic choices of the Italian people. It is not by chance that the EU stability rules have been challenged with a view to passing two social reforms (concerning pensions and minimum income) that fulfil – in opposition to EU austerity policies – the main political promises on the agendas of the above-mentioned parties in the run-up to recent elections. It is evident that, for the two ruling parties in Italy, this first challenge to the constraints set out in the Stability Pact – a move that is aimed at regaining a significant part of national 'social sovereignty' – foreshadows an attempt to renegotiate those rules. Such renegotiation is expected to take place in the near future in the framework of the EU's new political scenario that will hopefully emerge from the next European Parliament election in May 2019, with the hope that other populist movements would gain momentum (especially in France, thanks to the so-called *Gilets Jaunes* or 'Yellow Vests').

A subtler, though extremely significant, counter-movement in the same direction can be observed in Italy in the Constitutional Court's case law, particularly in the way in which it shapes its interactions with the CJEU and, more generally, the limits on the openness of the national system to European integration. Unfortunately, it is not possible to conduct an in-depth analysis, which would require complex technical considerations, here:[57] however, in essence, what emerges is that – in particular, following judgment No. 269 of 2017 – the Constitutional Court clearly aims to regain centralised control of constitutionality whenever it rules on a case that entails a potential breach of the fundamental rights enshrined in both the Italian Constitution and the EU Charter of Fundamental Rights. On closer inspection, this is another way of reasserting what Italian law scholars call the 'theory of counter-limits', albeit with potentially far-reaching implications in the context of crisis affecting the European integration process. This approach is particularly effective in as much as it is likely, at least in theory, to reduce the possibilities for ordinary courts to submit a reference for a preliminary ruling to the CJEU and to limit unwanted interference from judges in Luxembourg.

Signs of resurgence of 'polemic constitutionalism' can be found in other countries as well.[58] This is yet another manifestation of the overall legitimacy crisis of the European integration process, to which unfortunately the EU – torn apart by conflicting national interests – seems no longer in a position to offer shared political responses. In the absence of such responses, the European political scene – drawing from Karl Polanyi's classical teaching – is once again dominated by counter-movements that, even through dangerous nationalist drifts, aim to protect society against the market, in the name of an illusory national 'social sovereignty'.[59]

[57] Valeria Piccone and Oreste Pollicino (eds.), *La Carta dei diritti fondamentali dell'Unione europea. Efficacia ed effettività* (Naples: Editoriale Scientifica, 2018).

[58] Massimo Luciani, 'Costituzionalismo irenico e costituzionalismo polemico' (2006) *Giurisprudenza costituzionale*, pp. 1643–68.

[59] Karl Polanyi, *The Great Transformation: The Political and Economic Origins of Our Time* (Boston MA: Beacon Press, [1944] 2001).

PART IV

Towards a New Law of Political Economy

12

The Future of Law – 'Serial Law'?

KARL-HEINZ LADEUR

I Preliminary Remarks: From the Rule of Law to 'Serial Law?'

The hierarchical, top-down perspective on law is still the dominant one (primarily in continental legal systems – there are some peculiarities in Anglo-American law): this principle finds its repercussion in public law in the doctrine of the 'delegation' of rule-making power by parliament to administrative agencies or the assumption that the law is 'applied' to cases, but that cases do not make law. Because this doctrine is untenable in practice, the principle is mitigated by the acknowledgement of 'judge-made law' or the recognition of 'broad' parliamentary delegations or 'quasi'-legal rules (administrative norms that are treated *as* legal norms to a certain limit). At the same time, there is a plethora of legal delegations that seem to fulfil the requirements of the delegation doctrine (at least in the formal sense) without really allowing for the formation of rational expectations on the of citizens and firms. One should go one step further and abandon the delegation doctrine for the practice of decision making in conditions of complexity (i.e. control *ex ante* should be superseded by a new control project, control *ex post*). One could openly accept the law-making power of administration and/or of private organisations (i.e. 'serial law' that is generated from a 'series' of experimental search processes in conditions of uncertainty). One could, perhaps, transcend the limits of systems theory that still presupposes the stable functions of societal systems of communication (i.e. for the legal system, the counterfactual stabilisation of (behavioural) expectations).[1] One could hope for further inspiration from a 'media theory' of law.[2]

[1] Niklas Luhmann, *Das Recht der Gesellschaft* (Frankfurt aM: Suhrkamp Verlag, 1995).
[2] Thomas Vesting, *Die Medien des Rechts*, 4 volumes (Weilerswist: Velbrück Wissenschaft, 2011–2015), English translation to be published by Edward Elgar Publishing.

Scott Lash takes the view that the media, and the culture of the media, bring to the fore late-modern forms of a rupture with representation, the clear distinction of rule and exception, norm and facticity, the universal and the particular, the inside and outside (e.g., of organisations and markets).[3] The media (scripture, books, films, television, press, computer networks) increasingly structure the heterarchical processes of self-organisation of the law and undermine clear conceptual distinctions. The 'media', in this sense, are not primarily characterised by 'the physicality of a specific medium', the book,[4] the computer network,[5] but by the modes of *(re-)configurations* of communications that are 'mediated' by the media in the technical sense. For example, for computer networks, the extreme 'plasticity' of the figures and forms of digitisation, 'the processural realization of information in time … as a traditional image … only for contingent reasons'[6] – the digital structure allows for the permanent transformation upon the basis of an infinite Combinatorics of fragments – it needs a learning 'algorithmic' order that can use the possibility to search for the potential stabilisation of patterns, of productive 'nodes' of interrelationships within informational processes in real time, and can test their practical viability. This finds its repercussion in the legal system, for example, in the emergence of 'contextual' contracting, which no longer presupposes stability of expectations *ex ante* because this would undermine the functionality of law in conditions of high complexity.[7]

This needs a broader comment. One might start from a perspective on Jean-Luc Nancy's theoretical reflections on the 'singular' ('*singulier*')

[3] Scott Lash, *Another Modernity: A Different Rationality* (Oxford-Malden MA: Blackwell Publishers, 1999), p. 265.

[4] Vesting, *Die Medien des Rechts: Buchdruck*, n. 2 above (Weilerswist: Velbrück Wissenschaft, 2013).

[5] Mark N.B. Hansen, *New Philosophy for New Media* (Cambridge MA: The MIT Press, 2004), p. 23; Vesting, *Die Medien des Rechts: Computernetzwerke*, n. 2 above (Weilerswist: Velbrück Wissenschaft, 2015); Rosalind Krauss, *'A Voyage on the North Sea': Art in the Age of the Post-Medium Condition* (London: Thames & Hudson, 2000), pp. 7, 35.

[6] Hansen, n. 5 above, p. 9.

[7] Charles F. Sabel and Jonathan Zeitlin, 'Neither Modularity nor Relational Contracting: Inter-Firm Collaboration in the New Economy' (2004) 5 *Enterprise & Society*, pp. 388–403; Charles F. Sabel and William H. Simon, 'Contextualizing Regimes. Institutionalization as a Response to the Limits of Interpretation and Policy Engineering' (2012) 110 *Michigan Law Review*, pp. 1265–308; Matthew C. Jennejohn, 'Innovation, Collaboration, and Contract Design', Columbia Law and Economics Working Paper No. 319, 2008, available at: http://papers.ssrn.com/sol3/papers.cfm?abstract_id=1014420; and Jennejohn, 'Contract Adjudication in a Collaborative Economy' (2010) 5 *University of Virginia Law and Business Review*, 173–90.

which can no longer be subsumed as the 'particular' (i.e. already characterised by universality or a general 'trait', as an 'example') under the general or universal.[8] This finds its political repercussion in the fact that the representative institutions (parliament, political parties, trade unions, etc.) are increasingly facing the resistance of the particular, which escapes from the generalisation of interests, of political strategies, of legal standardisation. Whether this leads into a self-destructive aporia or just aesthetic resistance from versions of protest without political demands addressed to institutions is not clear.[9] This can be left open, however, as these are phenomena of a crisis that the 'singular' which cannot just be the starting point for generalisation, stable universal norms, etc., and this needs our attention.

According to Scott Lash the combination between 'singulars' is precisely what the media are up to.[10] Élise Domenach takes a similar view when she ventures the assumption (following Stanley Cavell) that the media (literature, films, etc.) remind us that we have to look at specific 'singular' works in order to discover and experiment with new possibilities which we would not see if we were already involved in the search for understanding the universal.[11] What is at stake are the 'poietic possibilities', the never ending 'flow of analogies' that still need 'stop rules' if we do not want to risk complete chaos.[12] Otherwise, there could not be any 'order from chaos'.[13] Stanley Cavell has aptly formulated what the new challenge (after the end of the universality and generality of order), it is the paradox of 'finding *as* founding' (no emphasis in the original).[14] A foundation is found, not founded! This means that there is an entanglement of hierarchies, of the general and the singular, of persons and things, that allow only for the experimentation with forms and patterns that have no preliminary stability. In a legal perspective this would mean

[8] Jean-Luc Nancy, *Être singulier pluriel* (Paris: Editions Galilée, 1996).

[9] Karl-Heinz Ladeur, 'Protest als künstlerische Performance – Die Herausforderung der Grundrechtsdogmatik durch "Aktionskunst"' (2015) 54 *Der Staat*, pp. 97–112.

[10] Lash, n. 3 above, p. 267.

[11] Élise Domenach, 'L'ordinaire de Stanley Cavell comme lieu d'une anthropologie sceptique', in: Claude Gautier and Sandra Laugier (eds.), *L'ordinaire et le politique* (Paris: Presses Universitaires de France, 2006), pp. 53–104, at 90.

[12] Douglas Hofstadter and Emmanuel Sander, *Surfaces and Essences: Analogy as the Fuel and Fire of Thinking* (New York: Basic Books, 2013).

[13] See Henri Atlan, *Entre le cristal et la fumée: Essai sur l'organisation du vivant* (Paris: La Seuil, 1979).

[14] Stanley Cavell, *This New Yet Unapproachable America: Lectures* after *Emerson after Wittgenstein* (Chicago IL: University of Chicago Press, 1989), p. 77.

that we have to reckon with new quasi-subjects, nodes within networks of relationships, that introduce new aggregation of action potential beyond the organisation (and the individual subject). This is why one may talk about a 'society of networks'. Of course, what I have in mind is not Nancy's reference to the 'singular' ('*singulier*') which, in my view, remains enclosed in an aesthetic paradox, even though it might be regarded as an intellectual 'instigation' to make use of the heterarchy of interrelationships between things, persons, and possibilities, below the level of stable concepts in order to grasp the 'unrest' which comes to the fore in the legal system, and which cannot be tackled both upon the basis of a classical normativity of *rules* (and discursive rationality of argumentation) and a systems-theoretical approach to the law as a system of communication whose touch upon the facticity 'outside' is always filtered by a predetermined *eigen*-rationality[15] – which determines both what it 'sees' and how it 'sees': programmes (norms) may change, but the law's function itself remains the same. This is dubious because the *facticity* itself has become so disruptive that the dependence of the law on facts and social conventions, and the observation of clusters and patterns within the facts is itself transformed. Niklas Luhmann has anticipated the possibility that a 'cognitive rationality' might replace the rationality of the law. This is perhaps a one-sided look at an alternative to the presupposition of a stable function of the law. The law's function itself may undergo a process of transformation in conditions of rapid changes in the knowledge basis of society. Such a dependence of the law on the stability of facts can go unnoticed for a long time if the facticity itself changes only slowly and continuously.[16]

I will try to demonstrate the idea of a transformation of the legal system, of normativity, focusing on four domains, which are under the pressure of a highly dynamic and disruptive development of technologies and knowledge: the emergence of global administrative law (GAL) ('from above') and the challenge of 'high technology' for administrative law ('from above'). The development of communication structures in the Internet that undermine the hitherto established social norms on communication, and finally the evolution of new forms of management of

[15] Luhmann, n. 1 above.

[16] Michel de Certeau has taken the view that the 'normative *discourse*' only 'works' ('*marche*'), if it has been preceded by a historical 'story' ('*récit*'), a text that 'has articulated with something real and speaks in its name' ('*articulé sur du réel et parlant en son nom*'); see de Certeau, *L'invention du quotidien. 1. Arts de faire* (Paris: Gallimard, 1990), p. 218.

private contracts in the domain of 'high knowledge' that reacts to the phenomena of extreme complexity in technology.

II The Future Forms of Coordination between Global and Domestic Administrate Law

A reflection on the future of domestic and global administrative law may be helpful: in both fields, a new generative dynamic momentum comes to the fore, which is due to the rise of networks emerging beyond both classical liberal administrative law ('the society of individuals') and its focus on the abstract person.[17] This evolution demonstrates that administrative law can no longer be constructed with reference to classical patterns and their stabilisation by statute law. Meaning is no longer deposited in slowly evolving rules of experience nor in the legal text. It presupposes a dynamic modelling of a distributed domain of options and relations invoking a multiplicity of perspectives in 'real time' in an open context. Cooperation will not only occur in public-private networks alone, but also in 'inter-public' joint ventures that mobilise expertise beyond the limits of stable territorial competencies.[18] The transnational dimension of administrative law is nothing but an expansion of the multi-layered spatial relationships that emerge at domestic level. The discretion of administrative decision makers which finds its legitimation in the increasing importance of specialised knowledge that has to be generated within complex procedures and demands the use of adequate methods of control could be opened for the coordination of heterogeneous and polycentric knowledge bases of different countries and societies,[19] in the sense that, in transnational procedures, the aggregation and integration of global social norms and knowledge might be regarded as a new meta-rule also for the judicial control of administrative discretion. Considering the dynamic nature of the administration both in and of networks, more evaluation *ex post* and more indirect rule

[17] Richard B. Stewart, 'Accountability and the Discontents of Globalization: US and EU Models for Regulatory Governance', draft paper presented at Hauser Law School, New York University, 2006.

[18] For transnational cooperation of agencies, see David T. Zaring, 'Informal Procedure, Hard and Soft, in International Administration' (2005) 5 *Chicago Journal of International Law*, pp. 547–603.

[19] For the re-emergence of the methodological problems of a distinction between 'law and non-law', see Karl-Heinz Ladeur, 'Global Administrative Law', in: Peer Zumbansen (ed.), *Oxford Handbook of Transnational Law*, forthcoming.

making will be necessary:[20] 'steering' administrative practice *ex ante* by statutes or by the 'application' of informal rules of experience will not be sufficient. The new knowledge base of the 'society of networks' will allow for more self-organised rules and patterns, while, at the same time, the decreasing relevance of stable norms in both senses should lead to a focus on procedural norms which are designed with regard to the generation of new knowledge that will be useful for the evaluation *ex post*.

We are still in the process of experimentation, which will generate new forms of action, new procedures, and new types of coordination between public and private actors. It may well be the case that the role of the judiciary in this new evolutionary process will be negligible, not to mention codification by the legislator. What should be conceivable is a new type of cooperation between domestic agencies and the legislator, with the prospect of coupling transnational procedures of decision making and domestic legitimation and accountability of decision makers.[21] New elements of an intertwinement of domestic and transnational law might be developing.

III Data-Driven Technologies and the Model of 'Evolutive Networks'

The regulation of data-driven technologies can itself only follow a model of 'regulatory networks',[22] that is, under the transformed conditions of uncertainty, stable goals for the regulatory process can only be formulated to a limited extent. Such a strategy is useful only in so far as certain risks can be analysed and described beforehand – and these are the risks of the past. This is why the internal risk management of firms should be strengthened, first of all.[23]

During the last financial crisis, the internal institutions of the risk management of banks was weakened by a 'philosophy' that favoured the 'makers', at the expense of the staff that were responsible for the risk

[20] Rudolf Stichweh, 'Wissensgesellschaft und Wissenssystem' (2004) 30 *Schweizerische Zeitschrift für Soziologie*, pp. 147–65, at 147 and 155.

[21] See, generally, David Dyzenhaus, 'Accountability and the Concept of (Global) Administrative Law', IILJ Working Paper 2008/7, available at: www.iilj.org/publications/2008-7Dyzenhaus.asp, p. 13.

[22] Marc Amstutz, *Evolutorisches Wirtschaftsrecht: Vorstudien zum Recht und seiner Methode in den Diskurskollisionen der Markgesellschaft* (Baden-Baden: Nomos, 2002), p. 289.

[23] Katharina Reiling, *Der Hybride: Administrative Wissensorganisation im privaten Bereich* (Tübingen: Mohr Siebeck, 2016).

management. The latter were devaluated as the 'worriers', as opposed to the 'warriors' who run the risks and meet the challenges of the markets. This also led to a spread of salaries in favour of the former and to the detriment of risk managers. In the regulation of financial markets, it would be crucial to focus more on avoiding a clustering of risks that might accumulate in a way that would block the potential of the self-organisation of the market. However, concrete patterns of such a regulatory policy cannot be designed in advance, but only in real time by way of continuous observation of the markets and a conception of an 'evolutive regulation' upon the basis of a basic *ex ante* regulation that is focused on the access to knowledge needed for such a mobile strategy, whereas the core element of regulation should consist in the observation of risk indicators *ex post*. This could be the new heuristic for an appropriate regulatory strategy.

Clustering would then be regarded as a kind of 'network failure' that should be an important frame of reference for risk regulation in the 'society of networks': the network collapses and is no longer able to mobilise and make use of its potential for self-organisation and flexible self-transformation to meet the challenge of crises. The same could be assumed for the new technologies that can be called 'data driven', as well, (i.e. technologies in whose development no linear trajectory can be identified).

It is important to regard the volatility of the process that is to be regulated not only as a problem but also as a potential for a flexible smart regulation: regulation *ex ante* can easily fail under conditions of complexity, despite the fact that not only the regulation of financial markets but also that of complex technologies, such as nanotechnology or genetic engineering, generate an abundance of data that could also be employed by a public regulatory strategy.[24] For example, nanotechnology allows for the use of micro particles that that can be combined to other nanosubstances or genetically modified organisms as 'biomarkers' that allow for the observation of risks of clustering. This means that the computerisation of technological design could also be used for a strategy of flexible regulation that is based upon evolutionary learning algorithms. The recent transformation of genetic engineering (CRISPR) towards a new informational paradigm demonstrates the new challenge

[24] The limits of the traditional regulation of technology, i.e., to presuppose a linear development of a technology that follows a certain 'trajectory' is demonstrated by the recent evolution of genetic engineering that has considerably changed and can no longer be referred to a stable 'description'.

of emerging technologies that are mainly 'data driven': genetic engineering has developed a technique of 'reprogramming' plants ('genome editing'), a kind of computerisation that cannot be treated as traditional genetic engineering.[25] Whether it may be subsumed under the regulatory regime for genetic engineering is dubious. The problem has been exacerbated by a position recently taken by the European Commission on 16 April 2016 not to regard this new technology as 'genetic engineering' in the former sense but to opt for a new intense regulation of the risks of the new technology.[26] This will be a huge problem because of the extreme flexibility of the new technology that can no longer be clearly distinguished from methods of traditional plant breeding. This position has been confirmed by the CJEU in its judgment of 25 July 2018.[27]

The monitoring of rapidly changing environments and the distribution of potentially hazardous substances in the environment may also be too complex for humans to design. However, a new strategy that would observe the changing landscape of research and of technology could observe a close relationship between such an innovative strategy and the coming paradigm of the 'Internet of things': on the one hand, a 'web of sensors' could communicate data that are collected from nature; on the other hand, the 'web of nature' is modelled upon the basis of a new information technology conception, and both 'communicate' without a human interface.

Clearly, this does not mean that 'older' regulatory models should be abolished altogether. There should be a combination of elements of all three paradigms: as far as experience is available, the traditional model should not be abandoned, the prospect of organisational generation of knowledge should be taken into consideration as well, and still we need a new approach for the emerging data-driven technologies that can no longer be regulated according to the traditional paradigms – and this means before they are used in practice.

As far as technology is concerned, we will face a new challenge once nanotechnology plays a more important role, which is only a question of time: this new technology – if one may still speak of *one* technology at all – will

[25] Jan Grossarth, *Frankfurter Allgemeine Zeitung*, 4 September 2016, No. 83, p. 21.

[26] Available at: www.theecologist.org/News/news_round_up/2987595/new_gmos_are_not_gm_eu_folds_under_us_pressure.html.

[27] C-528/16, *Confédération paysanne* v. *Premier Ministre*; for a critique, see Karl-Heinz Ladeur, 'Die Entscheidung des EuGH zur Anwendung des geltenden Gentechnikrechts auf CRISPR/Cas9-Verfahren v. 25.72018 – eine Entscheidung gegen technologische Innovation!' (2018) 3 *Innovations- und Technikrecht*, forthcoming.

make the relationship between science and technology even more complex: nanotechnology will not just provoke a new process of reframing of the relationship between science and technology, it will also reverse the hitherto established hierarchy between both: technology no longer makes 'use' of science – rather, it is technology that changes nature and creates new versions of 'objectivity'.[28] This new disruptive transformation will no longer allow for *ex ante* evaluations of risks and of risk management. Risk-assessment technologies will, on the one hand, have to be integrated into the new technological trajectories and follow their evolution. On the other hand, the rise of 'smart systems' can be used for the generation of a huge amount of risk information by the systematic observation of technological 'applications'. This new turn will demonstrate once more the importance of information technology and its ubiquitous presence in systems that generate artificial knowledge.

IV The Governance of the Internet

IV.1 The Missing Social Norms and How to Generate Them

Another variant can be seen in the discussions about the limits of internet communications. The web communities on the Internet tend to regard every legal barrier to internet communications as an unacceptable interference in the individual's fundamental rights. This, too, is a manifestation of the deterioration of a balance of legally protected interests moving to create 'groupings' of interests (W. Benjamin). Against this background, which can only be illustrated summarily here, the development of internet connections, from a perspective of both social theory and the law, must be seen as a challenge, as it rips right through the differentiated construction of both the public sphere and that of privacy, as well as of the relationship of each and every one with the other.

Compared to this, forms of communication typical of the new media, such as blogs or social media posts, acquire a hybrid character.[29] In this context, this means that the factual, social, and legal conditions of the differentiation of the relationship between the private and the public spheres are convulsed.[30]

[28] Lorraine Daston and Peter Galison, *Objectivity* (New York: Zone Books, 2007).

[29] About the 'superficiality' of blog communications, see Andrew Sullivan, 'Warum ich blogge' (2009) 63 *Merkur*, pp. 103–14.

[30] Karl-Heinz Ladeur and Tobias Gostomzyk, 'Der Schutz vor Persönlichkeitsrechtsverletzungen in Blogs' (2011) 61 *Neue Juristische Wochenschrift*, pp. 710–15.

In particular, individuals can communicate with large numbers of unknown participants electronically or, more precisely, non-orally, and this derails the rules that govern the borderline between private and public issues. Electronic communications about 'private' issues take place in what is, in any case, a potentially public manner, so that the participants in the communications no longer address one another privately and individually, but frequently – and also quite unintentionally – can reach a large number of people, without the person generating the message always being able to control this, as was hitherto the case with the mass media. It might even be said that mass media forms can be reproduced within hybrid internet communications (by professional bloggers), but there are also the ambiguous figures of communicating individuals who suddenly themselves become semi-media when they set out to achieve mass dissemination of their communications and, surprisingly, actually succeed in doing so.

In the past, the oral nature of communications used to set factual limits to the dissemination of the private individual's messages, while the public media's right to express themselves was limited by the law. On the other hand, examples can be used to show that 90–95 per cent of information that is of general interest at local level is produced by the traditional media, while the new media just compile it in new ways and distribute it. This is why issues that are much more specialised are now reproduced. This leads to the bundling function of the classical media focused on the state and on the civic public realm losing out in significance.[31] A report from the United States' FCC calls this development 'the great unbundling'. The professionalisation of reporting standards and the concomitant centralisation of knowledge rules also benefited the legal protection of third parties and enabled criteria to be developed for processing knowledge or maintaining or limiting non-knowledge or silence.

IV.2 The Transformation of Internet Communication

The Internet is changing the procedural rules of knowledge and non-knowledge fundamentally: communications now only appear to be disseminated horizontally, with no beginning and no end, to be brought into being without any standards that could be used for evaluating the proficiency of the knowledge that they contain for the future.[32] This also

[31] US-Federal Communications Commission, 'The Changing Media Landscape in a Broadband Age' (June 2011), p. 127, available at: www.fcc.gov/infoneedsreport.

[32] Clarisse Herrenschmidt, *Les trois écritures: Langue, nombre, code* (Paris: Éditions Gallimard, 2007).

makes any legal control and monitoring of such standards more difficult – and not only factually. The most important battle fought by the American Civil Liberties Union (ACLU) against the chilling effects of juridification is symptomatic of the absence of any concept of a 'control project' for the Internet or of any overarching perspective.

Knowledge is still connected to a distributed heterarchical network that does not appear to leave any space for stable rules of attribution, separation or responsibility to develop and be centralised. The attention paid to knowledge is generated virally or by being infected by matrices, for which there are no prior regularities, and which allow no rules to develop to govern the social reflection of the limits of knowledge and non-knowledge (secrecy). This is logical, to the extent that, as Boris Groys puts it, in many of the new forms of communication on the Internet (in this case, referring to Google), 'man no longer speaks in the traditional sense'. He becomes a 'user' who 'applies the various different linguistic contexts, topoi or terrains or makes new ones'.[33] He lets 'words appear or disappear in different contexts – in a completely silent and purely operative extra- or metalinguistic form of practice'.[34] The flow of the process itself becomes the framework of reference of the 'synaptic self' or of the 'neuronal personality',[35] which is disturbed by 'censorship' (i.e. the external interruption of the process of relating). It might be thought that the fact that Germany's 'Pirate Party' (*Piratenpartei Deutschland*) has no political platform, together with, in particular, the rising interest in 'direct' democracy, is a manifestation of the viral character of the Internet itself, and thus of the heterarchical 'society of networks'. This corresponds to the emergence of a fleeting, oscillating subjectivity that is inherent to the immediate experience of fluctuating attention and refutes all forms of mediatisation, institutionalisation and representation of the aggregation of generalisable interests.

IV.3 New Institutions for the 'Society of Networks'

The development of the Internet marks a break with the rules and the regularities that changes social communications on the borderline

[33] Boris Groys, *Google: Worte jenseits der Grammatik (dOCUMENTA (13)* (Berlin: Hatje Cantz Verlag, 2012), p. 27.

[34] Ibid., p. 27.

[35] Joseph LeDoux, *Synaptic Self: How our Brains Become who we are* (London-New York: Penguin Books, 2003); Catherine Malabou, *Que faire de notre cerveau?* (Paris: Bayard Éditions, 2004); Malabou, *La Plasticité au soir de l'écriture: Dialectique, destruction, déconstruction* (Paris: Éditions Léo Scheer, 2005).

between the private and the public spheres. This also preferably calls for (complementary) new institutions of (alternative) conflict resolution that are attuned more to change, and less to conservation,[36] so as to allow for 'learning by monitoring'.[37] A practice of this kind can be observed in the 'relational (incomplete) contracts' of hi-tech companies,[38] in which conflicts are no longer soluble by external judges, but are more likely to be found in, and submitted to, modular procedural methods designed to enable the problem to be described and overcome in the context of a flow that goes beyond the traditional concepts of borderlines.[39] This does not rule out the possibility of external support, even from the state courts. But their role changes in the dynamic context of the Internet, with its focus on self-adjustment, in the sense of the primary task of underpinning the ability of internet communications to organise themselves. The problem of the law in the Internet in general, and the protection of personality rights in particular, has its basis in the fact that the web has undermined the weight of social norms that have structured communication in a most differentiated and subtle way.

The problems of data protection in the Internet are so manifold that not all can be raised in the context of this chapter. This is also the reason why they cannot be tackled by clear-cut rules to be imposed on the Internet in advance, from outside. The steering of data communication is impossible. This complexity can, however, be tackled by a version of proceduralisation of the legal order of the self-organisation process which the Internet undergoes as the 'network of networks'. The internal differentiation of the legal structure of the Internet may allow for the generation of new knowledge and its processing via specific institutions of the Internet.

A net-specific *problématique* of the implementation of legal controls consists in the discrepancy between the attention which the single data of the individual meets, on the one hand, and the values of the processing and relationing of data through data mining, the construction of personality profiles,[40] the observation of broad data flows, and the operation of linking data by both firms and by the state for reasons of security, on the other. The interest in the closure and disclosure of information are both legitimate.

36 Ladeur and Gostomzyk, n. 30 above.

37 Jennejohn, 'Contract Adjudication', n. 7 above.

38 Sabel and Zeitlin, n. 7 above, pp. 388–403, at 388.

39 Jennejohn, Contract Adjudication', n. 7 above.

40 Joseph Turow and Lokman Tsui, *The Hyperlinked Society: Questioning Connections in the Digital Age* (Ann Arbor MI: University of Michigan Press, 2008).

IV.4 The Necessity to Observe the Collective Effects of the Processing of Data Flows

It would be much more helpful to change the paradigm of the conception of data protection 2.0 to a focus on networks, that is, to have a closer look at the opportunities and risks of data processing in networks and to adapt its legal structure, which is still characterised by its origin in the offline world to the conditions of the media world.[41] The rapid proliferation and continuous linking of information in networks can no longer be adequately mirrored in the individual right to decide on the separate domains of action that are attributed to persons. This construction can no longer do justice to the hybridisation of legal constellations. For example, a firm can possibly generate a high information value by data mining, which does not correspond to the construction of an accumulation of infringements of individual rights to decide on the use of the data which are of no particular interest to the user himself. A hybrid construction which is more adapted to the collective trans-subjective component of the data in a network can bring a more flexible and adequate solution to this dilemma (see below).

A case for a reconceptualisation of data protection is the de-anonymisation of IP-addresses by both private persons and the public security agencies. In this respect, it should be taken into consideration that the Internet as the 'network of networks' cannot be dissolved into a number of linear relationships of exchange between individuals – the precondition of the older regime of the protection of privacy in telecommunications – but that the old telecommunications have been transformed into an online world with its own rationality of information processing and generation of new information products which is based upon the generation of collective and collateral effects between information. These trans-subjective effects can no longer be attributed to individual 'owners'. Examples of these new phenomena are *eBay* ratings[42] and ratings of professional achievements (teachers, professors, medical doctors etc.).[43] The ubiquitous nature of the Internet and its new logic also comes to the fore when we take a look at the transformation of the

[41] James Grimmelmann, 'Saving Facebook' (2009) 94 *Iowa Law Review*, pp. 1137–1206.

[42] In the United States, *eBay* offers an electronic mediation procedure via 'Square Trade', available at: http://pages.ebay.com/services/buyandsell/disputeres.html.

[43] See Rita J. Verga, 'Policing their Space: The First Amendment Parameters of School Discipline of Student Cyberspeech' (2007) 23 *Santa Clara High Technology Law Journal*, pp. 727–48.

relationship between different types of rights which have been developed and coordinated in the offline world and which subsequently migrate into the Internet. It is inevitable that this entails a major effect of destabilisation that has to be compensated by a rebalancing.

IV.5 The Self-Organisation of the 'Data Owners' vis-à-vis Private Actors Following the Example of 'Collecting Societies' in the Protection of Intellectual Property: A Model for Net Friendly Legal Instruments

A new 'control regime'[44] which is fine tuned to the functioning of the Internet and the processing of data and patterns of combination could, for example, consist in the public and private funding of self-organised private institutions for the protection of data in the Internet following the model of collecting societies in intellectual property law and practice. Such a new type of association of users might act as an 'information broker', in the sense of a representation of the hybrid public-private interests of the users that transcend their own limited privacy concerns, and are focused on the trans-subjective elements of data processing in the Internet. These associations could make contracts on the conditions of the use of data that are not of much concern for each individual. This approach could correspond to the new transborder effect, which is common for the internet use of data in as much as it raises the collective effects from mass transactions that hitherto did not have any relation except to a central agent (such as a broadcaster). This 'information broker' might make contracts on payment for the use of internet data or make contracts on the quality of the protection of privacy. This form might be a productive alternative to the bureaucratic form of data protection by the institution of a public officer for the protection of privacy (*Datenschutzbeauftragter*). This model could present the appropriate levels of flexibility and hybridisation (balancing individual and collective interests) which are required by the logic of the Internet, whereas traditional legal instruments and procedure are more based upon the expectation of the stability of rights and public goods.

A new control regime has to adapt to the volatility and ubiquity of internet communication by flexible self-organisation of legal positions that are involved in a procedural mode of permanent self-transformation. It has to react to the fact that even identities are no

[44] Harrison C. White, *Identity and Control: How Social Formations Emerge*, 2nd ed. (Princeton NJ: Princeton University Press, 2008), p. 245.

longer stable, but are 'sampled' and open to transformation. One can even go so far as to assume that networks themselves become quasi-subjects in their own right.

IV.6 The 'Network Contract' as a New Paradigm of Private Law for the 'Social Media'

First of all, it should be recognised that, besides other legal arguments for the liability of social-media providers, primarily, the relationship between users and social media is a contractual one. In the American literature, this type of contract is regarded as an '*adhesion contract*'.[45] In legal practice, this means that the contract has the legal value of a more or less one-sided submission to the contract because conditions are normally formulated by only one partner of the contract (i.e. the 'provider'). The construction of a contractual relationship seems to be adequate because one partner, the provider, offers the possibility of using the communication services, whereas the other, the user, gives his or her consent to the use of the data that he or she places on his or her account for advertising strategies. This mutual consent brings about a relationship of reciprocity: the user can expect the conditions of use not to be changed arbitrarily. The provider lays open the conditions of use and the commercial use of the data for advertising, in particular. An exclusion of any forms of advertising is not a choice which is open to the users. The specific contractual relationship that is brought about in this constellation is characterised by the fact that a high number of similar 'exchange' contracts are concluded at the same time, and that conditions of use are formulated by the provider. However, at the same time, there is a second level of inter-relationships among the users themselves, which is not just a multiplication of a standardised version of a contract, although, in this case, the relationships between the participants including the user – the user-relationships – form a 'triangular' contract. The consent of the user to make use of the data for advertising only makes sense in the event that the other users allow for this use, too. This constellation might allude to the recent construction of 'network contracts'[46] – with a principled construction of this new type of

[45] See the seminal article by Friedrich Kessler, 'Contracts of Adhesion – Some Thoughts about Freedom of Contract' (1943), Yale Faculty Scholarship Series Paper 2731, available at: http://digitalcommons.law.yale.edu/fss_papers/2731.

[46] Gunther Teubner, *Networks as Connected Contracts* (Oxford: Hart Publishing, 2011).

contract, although Stefan Grundmann is more prudent in this regard.[47] The sense of such a construction could consist in the consequence that the triangular nature of the contract does not remain at the factual level but can, instead, lead to ideas about a specific 'hybrid' institutional component. The relationship is a 'hybrid' one, in as much as it can be located beyond the level of the bilateral exchange contract, but below the level of a 'company' (or, even less so, a corporate association). One has to bear in mind that this is not a normal case of a predetermined setting of 'general terms and conditions' that supplement the consent of the partners on the reciprocal rights and obligations, but of a one-sided competency of the provider to define the main duties of the user and to change them whenever he or she deems it appropriate.[48] The differentiation of the informational scheme of Facebook's sites mirrors, in a way, the 'hybrid' character of the 'regulatory' structure of the network: Facebook has, apart from the site on which the general terms and conditions are laid out,[49] a separate site on 'governance',[50] which contains rules of procedure on the change of rules, etc. This construction might look promising, although, as a consequence, only those members that click on this site[51] will obtain the information on the procedures.

The trans-subjective ('hybrid') component of the contract is to be seen in the fact that the purpose of the contract is not to be formulated clearly in advance. The relationships within the network are prone to continuous change, they evolve upon the basis of communication processes, which, first of all, are freely formulated and are integrated into a vast open network of relationships that allow for a plethora of communicative options. It is only at a secondary step that the provider observes these inter-relationships and tries to design the possibility of 'surfing' on this network with the modelling of a commercial type of interest.

[47] Stefan Grundmann, 'Die Dogmatik der Vertragsnetze' (2007) 207 *Archiv für die civilistische Praxis*, pp. 718–67, at 757.

[48] Robert Terenzi, Jr, 'Friending Privacy: Toward Self-regulation of Second Generation Social Networks' (2010) 20 *Fordham Intellectual Property, Media and Entertainment Law Journal*, pp. 1049–1106.

[49] See www.facebook.com/legal/terms.

[50] Available at: www.facebook.com/fbsitegovernance.

[51] A few years ago, Facebook announced a change in the 'terms of use' on the governance site and opened a voting procedure for the week of 1 June to 8 June 2012; however, only a tiny fraction of the users that remained far below the quota participated; see 'Die Mitbestimmung ist rein virtuell', *Frankfurter Allgemeine Zeitung*, 6 June 2012.

Advertising in the 'social media' does not follow the traditional patterns of addressing a mass public; instead, it is characterised by the observation and 'appropriation' of specific communicative networks that are spontaneously generated by the users. These differentiated networks process personalised information on consumer interests that may be recorded by advertising firms. This is also the reason why the consent of the users for the reprocessing of personalised profiles cannot be determined in detail *ex ante*.

This new constellation might fit into the new framework of 'networks of contract' which might help develop new rules for the management of a hybrid 'network interest' between exchange and collective interests.[52] This 'network interest' is emergent and heterarchical; at the end of the day, it can only be adopted for purposes of advertising if this is consented to by the users. The provider cannot just follow his or her own interest, but also has to support the processing of the networks of communications between the users by shaping an adequate institutional framework.[53] The relevance of the network of the inter-relationships between the users and the openness of the experimental development of communicative patterns and, at the same time, the evolving possibilities of personalised advertising could be a sound basis for the reformulation and concretisation of the preconditions of 'informed consent' in a dynamic environment.

V Civil Law and Contracting on High Technology Projects

The phenomenon of the self-organisation of legal relationships can also be observed in civil law where increasingly the self-organised components of a contextual law that develops in 'real time' comes to the fore in contractual practice.[54] In the domain of contracting on projects of high technology, or rather, 'high knowledge', the forms of bargaining and contracting become more and more fluid because the projects are so complex that it is difficult to figure out beforehand what is at stake: for example, in the process of developing innovative software, several people cooperate without determining *ex ante* whether they can or want to set

[52] See, generally, Teubner, n. 46.

[53] See James Grimmelmann, 'Privacy as Product Safety' (2010) 19 *Widener Law Review*, pp. 793–827, at 795.

[54] Ch. F. Sabel and Jonathan Zeitlin, 'Neither Modularity nor Relational Contracting. Interfirm Collaboration in the New Economy' (2004) 5 *Enterprise and Society*, pp. 388–403.

up a company, an exchange contract (of what type?) or whether someone is doing a favour to his or her friend. 'Visions' become the objects of contracts which have to be transformed into new relational procedures of mutual information.[55]

The methods adopted by the law of the 'society of networks' now being constituted are still in a state of flux. In my opinion, the new difficulties encountered when developing a constitution for the 'society of networks' are related to the fact that the networks develop to a considerable extent beyond the mediation of the state's legal system. One far from negligible effect of this is that the development of suitable institutions is also blocked, at least partly. Networks can be characterised negatively, first by the fact that they circumvent the classical distinctions between inside and outside, between market and organisation, and between public and private.[56] In particular, the dynamic of disruptive technologies leads to the development of 'epistemic communities', where knowledge is generated and processed. It is accompanied by volatile institutions of self-organisation, because the state law is not well attuned to observing and shaping networks. In this respect, Gunther Teubner's analysis of the 'self-constitutionalisation' of inter-organisational cooperation, etc., is exemplary.[57]

The unlimited way in which networks proceed corresponds to the rise of the concept of governance,[58] which indicates that the state and the law can rely less and less on 'decisions' as a means of binding and dealing with uncertainty. On the other hand, the institutionalisation of networks also calls for new forms of reconciliation with state law, whose relatively stable institutions need to be adapted to an experimental mode of observing development trajectories *ex post*, how they are confused by the introduction of multiple possibilities (replacing guidance), and the increase in transparency. Only a few comments can be made about this here.

It could be said that not only is the law further fragmented by the constraint to adjust to new heterarchical networks, but that the function of law itself is also fragmented: the law becomes more markedly

[55] F. Werk and A. Wittler, 'Vision statt Lastenheft', *Frankfurter Allgemeine Zeitung, Einspruch Magazin*, 7 February 2018, available at: https://fazarchiv.faz.net/document?id=FAEM__fazein_48385#start.

[56] Gunther Teubner, *Constitutional Fragments: Societal Constitutionalism and Globalization* (Oxford: Oxford University Press, 2008), pp. 7 et seq., and 158.

[57] See, generally, Teubner, ibid.

[58] Gunnar Folke Schuppert, *Governance und Rechtsetzung* (Baden-Baden: Nomos Verlag, 2011).

experimental in character as it makes individual partial functions available, which may structure private and private-public procedures of norm formation, for example, but may also come unstuck in the process. This applies in public international law, for example, to the development of emerging legal reforms beyond the boundaries of the state and this side of classical international law (responsibility to protect, global administrative law, etc.),[59] or to the preparation of the ability to develop contracts in complex operative networks without any clear purpose.[60] This includes new forms of mediation and conflict resolution, which also lead to the development of new law. These forms combine when, for example, new networks of evaluation (such as *eBay*) have to be taken into consideration by juridification approaches. This calls for new forms of monitoring and evaluation that systematically open the law up to a learning process. As a result, facticity and normativity are blurred in a new way. Juridification is called into play explicitly as a way of regulating private and private-public networks. This happens, for example, if specialised lawyers who are acquainted with the complexity of computer networks are engaged more as specialists for the determination of what the reasonable interpretation of an intransparent legal relationship might suggest. And, more often than not, such interpretations are accepted by the participants because they know that relational 'net subjects' have to adopt a flexible strategy for cooperation in conditions of uncertainty. Neither legal normative patterns of contractual coordination nor individual contracts can provide a satisfactory legal framework for the coordination of unclear perspectives on a dynamic project. In the past, legal forms presupposed the possibility of formulating more or less stable patterns of expectations and a correspondence with patterned forms of legal coordination of such expectations. However, in conditions of uncertainty, this is no longer the case. To date, there has been no law that is made for 'surfing a fluid reality'.[61] In many cases, this type of flexible law can only emerge in real

59 Jutta Brunnée and Stephen J. Toope, 'International Law and Constructivism' (2000) 39 *Columbia Journal of Transnational Law*, pp. 1–39, at 19; Charlotte Ku, *International Law, International Relations, and Global Governance* (Abingdon: Routledge, 2012), p. 13.

60 The law only becomes *ex post* when, for example, an unstructured hi-tech cooperation network (such as Silicon Valley) is 'translated' into a legal form, after the network's product has suddenly achieved a high market value: this is when the need arises to clarify what kind of legal relationship has actually come into being. The availability of fictions makes the law thoroughly suitable for this purpose. See, also, Jennejohn, 'Contract Adjudication', n. 7 above, p. 173.

61 Homa Bahrami and Stuart Evans, 'Super-Flexibility for Real-Time Adaptation: Perspectives From Silicon Valley' (2011) 53 *California Management Review*, pp. 21–39.

time or even *ex post* – if, for example, *Microsoft* offers a lot of money for the software that has been conceived by a group of loosely cooperating young people who did not think about such a prospect. One might call the patterns that emerge *ex post* from a practice of cooperation 'serial law', because of the preponderance of a 'series' of practical 'moves' in fluid reality.

It does not appear to make much sense to derive more extensive materials or formal demands of the law of networks from the principle of democracy if the state and administration are incapable of taking expertise into account. It would make rather more sense to integrate the demands on law making formulated *ex ante* by mobilising the instrument of subsequent improvement, with whose assistance the suitability of decision-making procedures could be evaluated *ex post*.[62]

VI The Limits of the Establishment of Institutions

As the flipside of this change, the change in the individuality of the 'society of networks' must also be taken into consideration from a legal perspective. How can a cognitive, epistemic link be maintained in a society whose institutions are so volatile and fragmented? This calls for a new collective model of 'order far from equilibrium' that is also compatible with the law.[63] In my opinion, its shortcomings are reflected not only in the field of data protection and the Internet, but also in the conflict about religion in the public realm (of school) and generally in the rise of a 'nomadically-inclined individualism', which rejects the influence of communications via third parties as illegitimate 'interference' and so hinders every process of the construction of stable institutions that would correspond to the law of the past. This is also the reason why more and more quasi-judicial adjudication by courts of arbitration or arbiters replaces state-based court practice: there is no stability in a factual, nor in a normative, sense. Arbitration and its frame of reference have themselves to generate legal solutions upon the basis of specific experience or expertise and not from general norms or patterns of practice. In this respect, the emergence of a 'web' of judgments that can give orientation to practitioners cannot easily be imagined. This extreme complexity of factual and normative issues casts some doubt on the idea of an

[62] Ladeur, n. 27 above.

[63] Ilya Prigogine and Isabelle Stengers, *Dialog mit der Natur* (Munich: Piper, 1990); Grégoire Nicolis and Ilya Prigogine, *Die Erforschung des Komplexen* (Munich: Piper, 1987), p. 77; Atlan, n. 13 above.

international court for the decision on conflicts about the 'application' of transnational treaties on investment protection: such a court would not be really democratically legitimated because it would no longer have a clear institutional integration into a state or an international organisation. It would – itself – be rather free floating. The problems of the emerging network society lie much deeper. They call into question the whole logic of the state or stable legal patterns of coordination. The law of the network society has to cope with a much more fundamental transformation of the whole structure of law.

Inside these networks, it is possible to discern signs of the development of a new relational person, who takes part in a variety of networks, for example, in the Internet, relating together the interests of a variety of 'societies of mind' (Marvin Minsky), corresponding to the 'society of the mind' that the cognitive sciences have observed at work in the human brain.

13

After Governance?

The Idea of a Private Administrative Law

RODRIGO VALLEJO[1]

'A world ends when its metaphor has died.'

Harold J. Berman, *Law and Revolution: The Formation of the Western Legal Tradition*, p. v.

I (Trans-)Formations of Political Economy: Private Regulation after the End of History

A raging inferno. This was the way in which the catastrophic fire at the *Ali Enterprises*' garment factory in Karachi, Pakistan, on 11 September 2012, was widely perceived by the victims, the 289 killed and over 600 seriously injured. When the fire broke out, as has been documented, only one exit was available for workers trying to escape from the blaze and all the windows were covered with iron bars.[2] The tormenting feelings of anguish, impotency and overall despair experienced by the victims, somehow also evoke those prompted by a very different kind of tragedy. Lost homes, bankrupt businesses, rocketing levels of unemployment, stagnant wages, bad credit, vanished life savings, increasingly 'austere' (or precarious) social security systems and strained fiscal capacities to stimulate the economy are just some of the enduring (re-)distributive manifestations of the worst financial cataclysm since 1929,

[1] Throughout earlier drafts of the present chapter, I have benefited from the generous advice and comments of several colleagues. Special thanks go to Antonina Bakardjieva, Edoardo Chiti, Sabine Mair, Hans Micklitz, and Urska Sâdl. The usual disclaimer applies. All web links were last accessed during March 2019.

[2] See, for example, Syed Shoaib Hasan, 'Deadly Karachi Blaze was "Waiting to Happen"', *BBC News*, 12 September 2012, available at: www.bbc.com/news/world-asia-19577450; and Imran Ayub, 'Desperate Jump for Life', *Dawn*, 12 September 2012, available at: www.dawn.com/news/748981.

despite (or because of) the regulatory and fiscal efforts to ensure some degree of 'stability'.[3] Similarly traumatised and in some way also feeling estranged, while ensconced in a hotel room in Hong Kong with its doors lined with pillows 'to prevent eavesdropping', Edward Snowden came to reveal the massive surveillance programmes disturbingly being deployed through digital devices by the United States' intelligence services.[4]

The fire in Karachi, the financial crises, and Snowden's revelations are seemingly three disparate events. Nevertheless, they are all linked by at least one common element. These events eloquently denote the significant degree of regulatory authority that private actors have currently gained in the field of public policy. In the case of Karachi, this authority is epitomised by the fact that just three weeks before the fire, the factory had had its basic health and safety standards certified by a renowned transnational private regulator, who was supposed to ensure compliance with some minimal human rights of *Ali Enterprises*' workers.[5] Moreover, in the case of the financial crises, such a regulatory authority is perhaps most conspicuously conveyed by the focal role that credit-rating agencies had in triggering the whole financial meltdown through their rating decisions on certain financial instruments.[6] Furthermore, in the case of Snowden, this authority is signified by the determinant role that big-tech firms and other telecommunications companies have played, as surveillance platforms, in the manipulation of information flows and coercion of online activities that are deemed to affect the strategic interests of powerful state or corporate agents, as Snowden's revelations had once disquietingly exposed.[7]

[3] See, mainly, Adam Tooze, *Crashed: How a Decade of Financial Crises Changed the World* (London: Penguin Books, 2018). On higher suicides rates, see James Gallagher, 'Recession "Led to 10,000 Suicides"', *BBC News*, 12 June 2014, available at: www.bbc.com/news/health-27796628.

[4] See, for example, the breakthrough interview by Glenn Greenwald, Ewen MacAskill and Laura Poitras, 'Edward Snowden: The Whistleblower behind the NSA Surveillance Revelations', *The Guardian*, 11 June 2013, available at: www.theguardian.com/world/2013/jun/09/edward-snowden-nsa-whistleblower-surveillance.

[5] Declan Walsh and Steven Greenhouse, 'Pakistan Factory Passed Inspection before Fire', *The New York Times*, 19 September 2012, available at: www.nytimes.com/2012/09/20/world/asia/pakistan-factory-passed-inspection-before-fire.html.

[6] On such a focal role, see, for example, Andreas Kruck, *Private Ratings, Public Regulations: Credit Rating Agencies and Global Financial Governance* (Basingstoke: Palgrave Macmillan, 2011); and Aline Darbellay, *Regulating Credit Rating Agencies* (Cheltenham: Edward Elgar Publishing, 2013).

[7] See, in general, Shoshana Zuboff, *The Age of Surveillance Capitalism* (London: Profile Books, 2019). On the latter, see, for example, Natasha Tusikov, *Chokepoints: Global Private Regulation on the Internet* (Oakland CA: University of California Press, 2016). On the former, see Kathleen Hall Jamieson, *Cyberwar: How Russian Hackers and Trolls Helped*

More broadly, these three events are only illustrative indications of a much larger phenomenon: the proliferation of a diverse, multifaceted and fast-evolving range of private regulatory practices within the landscapes of contemporary political economies.[8] Private regulation is certainly nothing new, not even within the history of modern law. Notwithstanding this, its presence has for a long time been relatively concealed from legal consciousness by the predominant dogmas of modern legal positivism, based upon its 'bright-line' approaches to the law/non-law and private/public distinctions.[9] What makes private regulation a central topic in public policy studies today, however, is the range and influence that this phenomenon has currently reached, in both qualitative and quantitative terms. Driven, to a large extent, by policies of (re-)privatisation, (re-)liberalisation, governmental outsourcing and financialisation, a varied *fauna* of private regulators has lately propagated in almost every policy field.[10]

An expanding wave of private regulatory authority is therefore significantly reconfiguring the topographies of contemporary political economies. A phenomenon that was exponentially boosted after the so-called 'end of history',[11] the currently ubiquitous 'turn to governance' therefore signifies a global landscape of renewed regulatory assemblages in which a diversified range of these 'new global rulers' hold a prominent place.[12] As

Elect a President: What we Don't, Can't, and Do Know (New York: Oxford University Press, 2018).

[8] See, in general, Thomas Hale and David Held (eds.), *Handbook of Transnational Governance: Institutions and Innovations* (Cambridge-Malden MA: Polity Press, 2011); and Peter Grabosky, 'Beyond Responsive Regulation: The Expanding Role of Non-State Actors in the Regulatory Process' (2013) 7 *Regulation & Governance*, 114–23.

[9] For a nowadays classical illustration, see, for example, Louis L. Jaffe, 'Law Making by Private Groups' (1937) 51 *Harvard Law Review*, 201–53. See, also, for a contemporary retrospective, Poul F. Kjaer, 'From the Private to the Public to the Private? Historicizing the Evolution of Public and Private Authority' (2018) 25 *Indiana Journal of Global Legal Studies*, 13–36.

[10] For an overview, Paul Verbruggen and Phillip Paiement, 'Transnational Private Regulation', available at: www.oxfordbibliographies.com/view/document/obo-9780199756223/obo-9780199756223–0226.xml.

[11] For an eloquent depiction, in quantitative terms, of such an expansive trend towards private or hybrid regulatory institutions at the international level during the 1990s, see Kenneth W. Abbott and Duncan Snidal, 'The Governance Triangle: Regulatory Standards Institutions and the Shadow of the State', in: Walter Mattli and Ngaire Woods (eds.), *The Politics of Global Regulation* (Princeton NJ: Princeton University Press, 2009), at pp. 49–62.

[12] See, mainly, Saskia Sassen, *Territory, Authority, Rights: From Medieval to Global Assemblages* (Princeton NJ: Princeton University Press, 2006), *passim*, pp. 141–271 (examining the kind of legal technologies and policy mechanisms that underlined such (re-)configurations). See, also, Tim Büthe and Walter Mattli, *The New Global Rulers: The Privatization of Regulation in the World Economy* (Princeton NJ: Princeton: University Press, 2011).

these inaugural examples suggest, instead of a regulatory state, transnational markets are thus already embedded in an intricate, polycontextural and increasingly multipolar web of 'regulatory capitalism'.[13]

In his landmark genealogical studies about the breakthrough of political economy as a modern governmental rationality, Michel Foucault also articulated a theory of crisis in this 'apparatus of governmentality'.[14] Drawing upon previous transitions from a paradigm of religious governmentality (i.e. the *pastorate*) into political governmentality (i.e. *raison d'état*) and to the current economic governmentality (i.e. the *political economy*), Foucault explains that the symptoms of such a crisis are manifested when simultaneous resistance practices to these predominant governmentalities, or 'counter-conducts' become intensified. In the case of the political economy, Foucault claims, such counter-conducts manifest themselves in recurring 'affirmations of an eschatology' that, through several terminologies, announces the 'suspension or completion of historical and political time when, if you like, the indefinite governmentality of the state will be brought to an end and halted [by] society itself'.[15] In his framing chapter to this volume, Poul Kjaer echoes these symptoms when diagnosing an implosive crisis in the contemporary governance paradigm which is characterised by, among other features, a 'holistic focus on "society", rather than the state or other institutional repositories of public power . . . as both the object and the subject of policy-making'.[16]

However, at least three puzzles remain in such an overall crisis diagnosis, which this chapter seeks to address. First, if law is not an epiphenomenon, but, instead, has a constitutive function in economic, social and political

[13] John Braithwaite, *Regulatory Capitalism: How it Works, Ideas for Making it Work Better* (Cheltenham: Edward Elgar Publishing, 2008) *passim*, at 23 (explaining ' . . . regulatory capitalism is not only about the regulatory state . . . It is also about regulation by industry associations of their large members and regulation of small producers by large producers who share the same chain of stewardship for a risk'). On such polycontextural and multipolar dynamics underlying these contemporary (re-)configurations, see, also, Lorenzo Casini, '"Down the Rabbit-Hole": The Projection of the Public/Private Distinction beyond the State' (2014) 12 *International Journal of Constitutional Law*, 402–28.

[14] Michel Foucault, *The Birth of Biopolitics: Lectures at the Collège de France, 1978–1979*, transl. Graham Burchell (Basingstoke: Palgrave Macmillan, 2008), at 70.

[15] See, specifically, Michel Foucault, *Security, Territory, Population: Lectures at the College De France, 1977–78*, transl. Graham Burchell (Basingstoke: Palgrave Macmillan, 2007), pp. 355–7, at 356.

[16] See his Introduction to this volume, p. 22. See, further, Poul F. Kjaer, 'From the Crisis of Corporatism to the Crisis of Governance', in: Poul Kjaer and Niklas Olsen (eds.), *Critical Theories of Crisis in Europe: From Weimar to the Euro* (Lanham MD: Rowman & Littlefield International 2016), pp. 125–39.

relations, as Kjaer correctly argues, what is the place of law and legal institutions within this governance paradigm? Second, more specifically, if form follows function, implicit in any analysis about the (trans-)formations in the function of the law of political economy is the task of identifying those current legal forms that are purportedly being transcended. Finally, given that competition law had such a determinant role in constituting the vindicated post-war 'turn to neo-corporatism', what role is competition law currently having, or could it have, in bringing about such a provocative outlook into a post-governance imaginary within political economies characterised by the expanding topographies of private regulators?

This chapter addresses these puzzles in the form of a proposition. This proposition is that the EU approach to the phenomenon of transnational private regulation could be productively understood, from a doctrinal perspective, in the form of an emergent 'private administrative law'. Underlying this proposition, it must be clarified from the outset, is the attempt to start sketching a conceptual framework that integrates these questions into a consistent doctrinal scheme which, by interconnecting the role of competition law within several private regulatory institutions, would operate as a baseline for examining the ongoing legal (trans-)formations from an internal perspective. This is not, however, a completely theorised proposition. Instead, it should be seen as part of an ongoing conversation about the constitutive place and significance of law within the overall transformations of political economy that we might currently be experiencing. While this chapter focuses only on exploring *some* of the foundations for this proposition, distinctive projections will, I hope, emerge for suitable theoretical guidance on some of its potential applications or implications. The aim of the chapter is, consequently, above all, programmatic.[17]

[17] The concept of a 'private administrative law', it must be clarified from the outset, is not new. As a way of framing certain private regulatory practices, it has been already suggested by several scholars but not methodically explored: see, for example, Harm Schepel, *The Constitution of Private Governance: Product Standards in the Regulation of Integrating Markets* (Oxford: Hart Publishing, 2005), at 285–338; Sabino Cassese, 'New Paths for Administrative Law: A Manifesto' (2012) 10 *International Journal of Constitutional Law*, 603–13, at 607; and Hans-W. Micklitz, 'Rethinking the Public/Private Divide', in: Miguel Poiares Maduro, Kaarlo Tuori and Suvi Sankari (eds.), *Transnational Law: Rethinking European Law and Legal Thinking* (Cambridge: Cambridge University Press, 2014), pp. 271–306, at 304. Throughout my ongoing Ph.D. research entitled 'The Idea of a Private Administrative Law', upon which the present chapter is based, my broader aim is to reconstructively explore the potential foundations, applications and implications of such a concept.

The argument unfolds in three steps: a methodological one (Section II), an analytical one (Sections III and IV), and a normative one (Section V). First, I am going to situate the idea of private administrative law, both theoretically and methodologically, as a distinctive approach within the juridical literature about private regulation (Section II). Second, such an idea is substantiated by contraposing the EU and the US approaches to private regulation through a comparative analysis of their leading antitrust case law on the topic. Upon this basis, two conceptions about private regulation are then distinguished analytically. These conceptions are: (i) private regulation as private ordering; and (ii) private regulation as police powers held by non-state actors. The distinction amounts, I contend, to two different justifications of the phenomenon, with quite divergent implications, which could respectively be aligned with the predominant approaches to private regulation in the United States and the EU (Section III).[18]

Upon the basis of this analytical distinction, Section IV examines how the EU, through several legislative instruments and its case law, has been configuring a distinctive criterion of validity on private regulatory practices. In contrast to the approach of the United States, this criterion does not rest solely in traditional doctrines of 'private autonomy' or 'state action', nor in the economic type of justifications alone (e.g. 'welfare', 'market integration' or 'economic freedom'), but in a broad spectrum of legitimate public policy purposes and good governance standards, both organisational and procedural, akin to those applicable to administrative agencies when exercising police powers. Upon this basis, I claim, the EU rules of recognition on private regulatory practices could be productively conceptualised, from a doctrinal perspective, in the form of an evolving private administrative law. The last step returns to the constitutive role of law to denote the overall significance of legal forms (Section V).

As a conceptual claim, the 'private administrative law' speech-act nevertheless seeks to trigger at least three types of performative interventions. First, it is insurgent to a set of commanding approaches that, under theories of sociological jurisprudence or so-called dynamics of 'constitutionalisation', have been giving 'Legal' (indeed, with a capital 'L') or even 'constitutional' status (and not only with a small 'c') to private regulatory organisations or regimes if certain conditions are

[18] In this way, my aim is to suggest some 'thinner' comparative distinctions into the 'thick' picture recently advanced by Poul F. Kjaer, 'Context Construction through Competition: The Prerogative of Public Power, Intermediary Institutions, and the Expansion of Statehood through Competition' (2015) 16 *Distinktion: Journal of Social Theory*, 146–66.

met.[19] Second, it supplements Global Administrative Law's (GAL) predominant focus on procedural regularity and governmental actors, by illuminating a series of institutional, formal and substantive dimensions to private regulatory practices that have also been articulated by EU legal authorities in these respects, which come closer to the European tradition of administrative law.[20] Finally, the idea of a 'private administrative law', as a conceptual project, performatively seeks to de-fetishise theories of private ordering, which are increasingly gaining analytical predominance within this juridical field.[21]

II Beyond Facts or Norms: Private Regulation in the Search for (Legal) Meaning

Private regulation has become a prevailing topic in public debates and policy making during the twenty-first century. In terms of research agenda, a leading role in this regard has been taken by social and political scientists. Through the use of different hashtags, such as 'self-regulation', 'private regimes', 'transnational business governance', or 'voluntary programmes', ever-more explanatory studies on the topic are being produced, sometimes meticulously integrating insights from history, economics or other disciplines. These studies currently amount to a prolific set of scholarship that has largely contributed to make private regulation a more visible and discernible phenomenon.[22]

[19] For an overview, see, for example, Gregory Shaffer, 'Theorizing Transnational Legal Ordering' (2016) 12 *Annual Review of Law and Social Science*, 231–53, at 242–6. See, also, Martin Loughlin, 'What Is Constitutionalisation?', in: Petra Dobner and Martin Loughlin (eds.), *The Twilight of Constitutionalism?* (Oxford: Oxford University Press, 2012), pp. 47–70.

[20] For a latest retrospective on the global administrative law approach, see Benedict Kingsbury, Megan Donaldson and Rodrigo Vallejo, 'Global Administrative Law and Deliberative Democracy', in: Anne Orford and Florian Hoffman (eds.), *The Oxford Handbook of the Theory of International Law* (Oxford: Oxford University Press, 2015), pp. 526–42; and, including a map of its European sources, Lorenzo Casini, 'Global Administrative Law Scholarship', in: Sabino Cassese (ed.), *Research Handbook on Global Administrative Law* (Cheltenham: Edward Elgar Publishing, 2016), pp. 548–72.

[21] On the relevance of understanding doctrinal controversies as part of a broader 'juridical field', Pierre Bourdieu, 'The Force of Law: Towards a Sociology of the Juridical Field' (1987) 38 *Hastings Law Journal*, 814–53, at 831 (defining the juridical field as 'a social space organized around the conversion of direct conflict between directly concerned parties into juridically regulated debate between professionals acting by proxy').

[22] For an overview of such literature, see Liliana Andonova and Yixian Sun, 'Private Governance'. www.oxfordbibliographies.com/view/document/obo-9780199756223/obo-9780199756223-0226.xml.

Since its post-1989 outbreak, however, the private regulation phenomenon has become a wide-ranging conundrum for law and legal thought.[23] In my view, to a relevant extent such a conundrum derives from the disruptive effect that the phenomenon produces in the binary ways through which lawyers regularly frame legal events, as represented, among others, by an entrenched private/public dichotomy.[24] By way of illustration, in his *The Idea of Private Law*, Ernest Weinrib influentially formulated an immanent conception of private law as an internally coherent and distinctive legal order of correlative rights and duties, comprehensively structured upon the ideals of individual autonomy and corrective justice.[25] Such a configuration, however, becomes, arguably, disrupted by a private regulation phenomenon which, by and large, operates through plurilateral relationships, in the name of safeguarding general interests, and frequently has (re-)distributive effects.

Likewise, in his *The Idea of Public Law*, Martin Loughlin vindicates an immanent conception of public law structured upon a relational dimension between a sovereign and her subjects, of a hierarchical nature, manifested through institutionalised ruling practices and sustained in its authority by a prudential discourse of political right.[26] In the intricate, polycontextural and multilayered era of governance, however, such a hierarchical imaginary of political jurisprudence no longer seems to hold.[27] In other words, Weinrib and Loughlin's immanent conceptions about private/public law, as reciprocally autonomous domains of legal thought and practices, jointly reassert the 'modern imaginary' of a comprehensive, but mutually exclusive,

[23] Mislav Mataija, *Private Regulation and the Internal Market: Sports, Legal Services, and Standard Setting in EU Economic Law* (Oxford: Oxford University Press, 2016), at 6–9 (outlines it nicely: 'Can it be seen not just as one social phenomenon among many others, but as law in its own right – even if it is not formally recognized by the State or embedded in State measures in some way? What are the consequences for our implicit understandings of law, democracy, and the State of recognizing that private regulation can be "law", in some sense of the word?').

[24] Harm Schepel, 'Private Regulators in Law', in: Joost Pauwelyn, Ramses Wessel and Jan Wouters (eds.), *Informal International Lawmaking* (Oxford: Oxford University Press, 2012), pp. 356–67 (distinguishing between 'bright-line' and 'grey-zone' approaches to private regulation and indicating a gradual progression towards the latter).

[25] Ernest J. Weinrib, *The Idea of Private Law* (Oxford: Oxford University Press, [1995] 2012).

[26] Martin Loughlin, *The Idea of Public Law* (Oxford: Oxford University Press, 2004).

[27] Julia Black, 'Decentring Regulation: Understanding the Role of Regulation and Self-Regulation in a "Post-Regulatory" World' (2001) 54 *Current Legal Problems*, 103–46; Orly Lobel, 'The Renew Deal: The Fall of Regulation and the Rise of Governance in Contemporary Legal Thought' (2004) 89 *Minnesota Law Review*, 342–470.

private/public spheres.[28] It is this 'modern imaginary', which conforms the conceptual basis of political economy as modern governmentality, the one which is increasingly becoming challenged by some of the spanning 'features' of the private regulation phenomena.[29]

The *problématique*, however, seems to run into a deeper level of western legal (un-)consciousness. The idea of public law (Loughlin) and the idea of private law (Weinrib) are both premised on the mythological figure of a *Leviathan*, as influentially devised by Hobbes, symbolising a sovereign as holding an ultimate monopoly of legal and political authority. This profound cultural archetype, constitutive of legal modernity, is the one purportedly being disrupted by the private regulation phenomenon.[30] Culturally, we might be experiencing telluric times, as Harold Berman's epigraph suggests. Alongside the perceived fragmentation of several modern legal orderings, the very same body of the king seems to be (re-)splintering.[31]

Theoretically, this scenario has prompted at least two broad types of legal responses to the private regulatory phenomenon. A first type of response, to be termed the 'normativist approach', in itself has two subcamps. One is represented by the *denialists*. As private regulation does not conform to conventional legal doctrines, it is normally based upon voluntary agreements (i.e. on 'consent', rather than 'coercion') or soft-law mechanisms (i.e. guidelines, best practices, indicators, algorithms etc.), the denialists contend, private regulation might be an interesting sociological phenomenon, but it is not legally relevant beyond some rather low-level forensic questions (e.g. standards of due diligence or

[28] See, for example, Norberto Bobbio, 'The Great Dichotomy: Public/Private', in: Bobbio (ed.), *Democracy and Dictatorship: The Nature and Limits of State Power* (Cambridge-Malden MA: Polity Press, 1989), pp. 1–21. See, also, Charles Taylor, *Modern Social Imaginaries* (Durham NC: Duke University Press, 2004), Chapter 4.

[29] Fabrizio Cafaggi, 'The Many Features of Transnational Private Rule-Making: Unexplored Relationships between Custom, Jura Mercatorum and Global Private Regulation' (2015) 36 *University of Pennsylvania Journal of International Law*, 875–938.

[30] See, for an examination about the terms and significance of such a challenge, Neil Walker, 'Epilogue: On Regulating the Regulation of Regulation', in: Fabrizzio Cafaggi (ed.), *Reframing Self-regulation in European Private Law* (Alphen aan den Rijn: Kluwer Law International, 2006), pp. 347–57. On Hobbes as providing the deep grammar of legal modernity, see, for example, David Dyzenhaus and Thomas Poole (eds.), *Hobbes and the Law* (Cambridge: Cambridge University Press, 2012).

[31] See, most provocatively, Gunther Teubner, 'The King's Many Bodies: The Self-Deconstruction of Law's Hierarchy' (1997) 31 *Law & Society Review*, 763–87; and Hent Kalmo and Quentin Skinner (eds.), *Sovereignty in Fragments: The Past, Present and Future of a Contested Concept* (Cambridge: Cambridge University Press, 2010).

burdens or proof). The prominent place that this view still holds in contemporary legal consciousness is represented, for example, by the enduring influence of the so-called '*Meroni* doctrine', concerning the nature and scope of private regulation within EU Law.[32]

The other sub-camp within such a normativist approach is represented by the *assimilationists*. Because private regulators are currently making sensitive policy choices, which are the marks of sovereign powers, the assimilationists hold, as a matter of logic, that they must conform in their organisation or operation to the kind of standards that have been devised within the western legal tradition for the legitimate exercise of sovereign powers. It is this cosmopolitanist impetus, premised on an abstract and universal 'ideal of reason' which, in my view, has mainly been driving the normativist agenda of the so-called 'constitutionalisation of private regulation' throughout its 'turn to publicness'.[33]

The second type of theoretical response to the private regulatory phenomenon conveys a range of 'empiricist approaches'. Instead of proclaiming how private regulators should operate, the empiricists delve into the practice to explain of how private regulators do, in fact, operate. Elaborated mainly upon the analytical lens of global/transnational legal pluralism, in any of its several variations,[34] this approach has essentially translated into a proliferating range of socio-legal studies about the private regulation phenomenon, normally based upon qualitative methods.[35]

[32] See, for example, Linda Senden, 'The Constitutional Fit of European Standardization Put to the Test' (2017) 44 *Legal Issues of Economic Integration*, 337–52 (quarrelling with such an entrenched view on the basis of some latest legal developments).

[33] See, for example, paradigmatically, those research agendas triggered by Armin Von Bogdandy, Philipp Dann and Matthias Goldmann, 'Developing the Publicness of Public International Law: Towards a Legal Framework for Global Governance Activities' (2008) 9 *German Law Journal*, 1375–1400; Mattias Kumm, Anthony F. Lang, James Tully and Antje Wiener, 'How Large is the World of Global Constitutionalism?' (2014) 3 *Global Constitutionalism*, 1–8; and Colin Scott, Fabrizio Cafaggi and Linda Senden, 'The Conceptual and Constitutional Challenge of Transnational Private Regulation' (2011) 38 *Journal of Law and Society*, 1–19.

[34] Ralf Michaels, 'Global Legal Pluralism' (2009) 5 *Annual Review of Law and Social Science*, 243–62.

[35] Albeit with important conceptual and methodological differences, see, in general, Gralf-Peter Calliess and Peer Zumbansen, *Rough Consensus and Running Code: A Theory of Transnational Private Law* (Oxford: Hart Publishing, 2010); Gunther Teubner, *Constitutional Fragments: Societal Constitutionalism and Globalization* (Oxford: Oxford University Press, 2012); and Terence C. Halliday and Gregory Shaffer, 'Transnational Legal Orders', in: Terence C Halliday and Gregory Shaffer (eds.), *Transnational Legal Orders* (Cambridge: Cambridge University Press, 2015), pp. 3–73.

By articulating the idea of private administrative law, this chapter seeks to push the legal debate beyond these two strands of the literature, through the adoption of a hermeneutic approach to the private regulatory phenomenon. Instead of evaluating the extent to which private regulators should be making policy choices, under standards of transcendental reason (i.e. norms), or analysing the diverse types of 'concrete orderings' that conform the current private regulatory *fauna*, in search of some empirically verifiable truths (i.e. facts), this hermeneutic frame entails confronting the question about the legal meaning of such a private regulatory phenomena. In this sense, such a frame places itself 'beyond facts and norms' by specifically adopting a phenomenological approach to private regulation from an EU law perspective.[36]

This chapter thus intends to move beyond the state of the art by inducing a transition from the ubiquitous vocabulary of 'legitimacy' (which is a sociological phenomenon) into the vocabulary of 'validity' (which is a strictly legal phenomenon) by analysing comparatively the determinant role that EU law and US law have had in shaping private regulatory practices. What is meant by EU law and US law is actual legal sources, including legislation and case law, both of which, as will be explained below, express significant differences in these respects. To this extent, the idea of private administrative law purports to instil a methodological transition within the private regulatory field from an 'external perspective' (i.e. that of the 'observer' of law-like practices) into an 'internal perspective' (i.e. that of the 'participant' in these practices) drawing upon the methodological parameters of legal doctrine. Such a transition, as will be argued, illuminates the constitutive place of law within the struggles of contemporary political economies and the institutional significance of legal forms.

[36] In adapting such a phenomenological approach to the study of private regulatory practices, I have mostly drawn inspiration from Hans Lindahl, *Fault Lines of Globalization: Legal Order and the Politics of A-Legality* (Oxford: Oxford University Press, 2013); and Martin Loughlin and Samuel Tschorne, 'Public Law', in: Mark Bevir and R.A.W. Rhodes (eds.), *Routledge Handbook of Interpretive Political Science* (Abingdon-New York: Routledge, 2015), pp. 324–37 (distinguishing such phenomenological approach, theoretically and methodologically, from both descriptive and normative interpretivism). For an appraisal on such an approach, see, also, Emilios Christodoulidis, 'Lindahl's Phenomenology of Legality' (2014) XVI *Etica & Politica/Ethics & Politics*, 940–55.

III Private Ordering and Private Police Powers: Comparative Approaches to Private Regulation

Several terminological stipulations are in order here. For the purposes of this chapter, the concept of private regulation conveys, very generally, the exercise of discretionary regulatory authority by private (i.e. non-state) actors. 'Discretionary' refers to the involvement of a private actor as an active issuer in the regulatory process, with the legal capacity to make autonomous choices within the means and specificities on a broad range of social goals. 'Regulatory' describes the sustained and focused attempt to alter the behaviour of market participants according to defined rules, standards or principles, with the intention of producing a broadly identified outcome or outcomes, which may involve mechanisms of rule making, monitoring or enforcement. Finally, 'authority' means the generalised acceptance of their ruling capacity as prima facie appropriate or justified. Private regulation entails, in this sense, the methodical engagement of private actors in the practice of subjecting the behaviour of market participants to enacted norms through rule making, monitoring or enforcement, in the name of fulfilling public interests.[37]

The latter element is key. The declared commitment to fulfil public interests, meaning a 'legitimate (social) purpose' that transcends mere rent seeking or an intimate sphere of 'pure' private autonomy, more generally, is what would differentiate 'private regulation' from mere 'private action'. It is also what differentiates 'private regulation' from illicit forms of social authority, such as those performed by mercenaries, structures of organised crime or *mafias* in general. This definition also excludes private involvement in regulatory functions that normally do not imply the exercise of discretional forms of authority, or, if so, only in much diminished forms, such as the provision of office materials or garbage-collection services in state procurement. Finally, its focus on market behaviour differentiates private regulation from other technologies or institutions of social control that operate through psychiatric, sexual or confessional relations, which come closer to Foucault's more expansive notion of disciplinary power.[38]

[37] In articulating this definition, elements have been drawn mainly from Julia Black, 'Critical Reflections on Regulation' (2002) 27 *Australian Journal of Legal Philosophy*, 1–35, especially, at 21–7; Mataija, n. 23 above, at 2–3; and Colin Scott, 'Regulation in the Age of Governance: The Rise of the Post-Regulatory State', in: Jacint Jordana and David Levi-Faur (eds.), *The Politics of Regulation: Institutions and Regulatory Reforms for the Age of Governance* (Cheltenham: Edward Elgar Publishing, 2004), pp. 145–74.

[38] See, in general, Michel Foucault, *The Essential Works of Michel Foucault, 1954–1984: Power*, Vol. 3, edited by James D. Faubion (New York: The New Press, 1997).

Upon this conceptual basis, I claim, two legal conceptions about the validity of private regulation could be comparatively distinguished. These conceptions are respectively termed private regulation as 'private ordering' (United States), and private regulation as 'private police powers' (EU). Both conceptions, it is important to stress, transcend the orthodox/denialist approaches to the public-private distinction by acknowledging that private actors can have some legal authority to safeguard public interests. However, these conceptions essentially diverge regarding the type of public interests that private regulators are entitled to protect. In particular, they diverge on whether private regulators are prima facie entitled to pursue public policy objectives beyond market efficiency (e.g. environmental sustainability, health and safety protection, or social solidarity), even when their regulatory choices produce anticompetitive effects.

In the case of the United States, in general, whenever private regulation produces anticompetitive effects, its validity ultimately depends on whether it probes to correct market failures or to reduce transaction costs according to strictly constructed 'consumer welfare' tests. In other words, unless the measure could qualify as state action/aid or be exempted from antitrust scrutiny, the scope of private regulation in the United States is, in principle, somehow reduced only to market efficiency aims. Such an approach is signified by its landmark case law, where the US Supreme Court has stated that, despite any commendable social purposes which might vindicate a private regulatory measure, such an alleged justification is 'not a reason, cognizable under the Sherman Act, for doing away from competition'.[39]

In the case of the EU, the approach is noticeably different. In contrast to the US Supreme Court, the CJEU has taken a broader approach to what kind of public interests private regulators can prima facie validly pursue, as in *Bosman* or *Bernard*.[40] Moreover, according to Article 101 TFEU, EU

[39] *National Soc'y of Prof Engineers* v. *United States* [1978] US Supreme Court 435 U.S. 679. See, also, *Federal Trade Commission* v. *Indiana Federation of Dentists* [1986] US Supreme Court 476 U.S. 447. Although within the vast US case law there are cases pointing towards a more open frame of reference, they are generally treated as idiosyncratic exceptions within US Antitrust Law that would confirm this general rule: see, for example, *Appalachian Coals, Inc* v. *United States* [1933] US Supreme Court 288 U.S. 344.

[40] See, with further references to previous case law on this point, *Union royale belge des sociétés de football association ASBL* v. *Jean-Marc Bosman, Royal club liégeois SA* v. *Jean-Marc Bosman and others and Union des associations européennes de football (UEFA)* v. *Jean-Marc Bosman* [1995] Court of Justice of the European Union Case C-415/93 ECR I-4921 at paras. 85–6 (holding that '. . . there is nothing [in EU Law, as specified by Article 48 of the Treaty] to preclude individuals [i.e. in this case, sporting associations, when

legal authorities have admitted private regulators validly to pursue public policy objectives, even if their measures produce restrictive effects on competition that cannot strictly be justified on market-efficiency grounds. These public policies have included health and safety or environmental protection,[41] and, more recently, safeguarding financial stability,[42] cultural diversity,[43] and ensuring legal compliance.[44]

These comparative legal differences, I contend, elicit at least two models for explaining and justifying the private regulatory practices that are currently at stake in any perceived transformations of the political economy through legal means. The first model, which is predominant in the United States, understands private regulation as private ordering. This model essentially explains private regulation as the capacity of certain social groups, especially business communities, to 'opt out of the legal system' in the exercise of their self-determination capabilities in order to provide more optimal rules for social or economic interactions from the perspective of aggregate welfare.[45] Private ordering, in this sense, has been generally

acting as private regulators] from relying on justifications on grounds of public policy, public security or public health. Neither the scope nor the content of those grounds of justification is in any way affected by the public or private nature of the rules in question'); and *Olympique Lyonnais SASP* v. *Olivier Bernard and Newcastle UFC* [2010] Court of Justice of the European Union Case C-325/08 ECR I-2177.

41 See, for example, *CECED* [1999] European Commission Case IV.F.1/36.718-OJ L187/47.

42 *Asnef-Equifax, Servicios de Información sobre Solvencia y Crédito, SL* v. *Asociación de Usuarios de Servicios Bancarios (Ausbanc)* [2006] Court of Justice of the European Union Case C-238/05; EU:C:2006:734; [2007] 4 C.M.L.R. 6, para. 67 (holding that an agreement to exchange information about consumers' credit-worthiness, even if it was found to restrict competition, could be exempted if it is 'capable of helping to prevent situations of over indebtedness for consumers of credit as well as, in principle, of leading to a greater overall availability of credit').

43 *Föreningen Svenska Tonsättares Internationella Musikbyrå upa (Stim)* v. *Commission* [2013] Court of Justice of the European Union T-451/08 EU:T:2013:189; [2013] 5 C.M.L.R. 16, para. 73 (holding that 'in the application of Article [101 TFEU], the Commission is required to take into consideration the objective of respecting and promoting cultural diversity, in particular where the application of that article concerns an activity linked to culture').

44 *Protimonopolný úrad Slovenskej republiky* v. *Slovenská sporiteľňa AS* [2013] Court of Justice of the European Union C-68/12 EU:C:2013:71; [2013] 4 C.M.L.R. 16, paras. 33 and 35 (although the Court held that, in this case, the restriction failed to demonstrate its 'indispensability' for achieving the referred purpose). See, with further references, Giorgio Monti and Jotte Mulder, 'Escaping the Clutches of EU Competition Law: Pathways to Assess Private Sustainability Initiatives' (2017) 42 *European Law Review*, 635–56, at 647–50.

45 The nowadays classical reference is Lisa Bernstein, 'Opting Out of the Legal System: Extralegal Contractual Relations in the Diamond Industry' (1992) 21 *The Journal of Legal Studies*, 115–57.

conceived as a broad category which encompasses different types of societal regulatory regimes that are independently sustained through forms of 'order without law',[46] or 'justice without the state'.[47] Yet, whether in their conditions of organisation or operation, as well as in their distributive effects, when closely examined, the prominent forms of private orderings currently operating in contemporary political economies, beyond those 'bucolic expanses of Sasha County', appear to be supported on (and thus ultimately configured through) several state-law technologies and institutions – especially after their Chicago-school-led (trans-)formations.[48]

In this way, the significant regulatory authority of contemporary forms of private ordering has become predominantly aligned with libertarian or utilitarian justifications of the practice. Sustained mainly on a maximisation of consumer/investor preferences, according to a monetary quantification of those preferences, these justifications ultimately aim to channel private regulatory choices throughout purportedly preference-neutral social welfare parameters and marketisation rationales.[49] Here lies the performativity of private ordering. Rather than merely reflecting human preferences, the concept of private ordering partially produces those preferences by institutionally structuring them, through legal means, according to a certain vision of human relations that effectively insulates private regulatory practices from hetero-normative forms of limitations, dispute or change.[50]

[46] Robert C. Ellickson, *Order without Law: How Neighbors Settle Disputes* (Cambridge MA: Harvard University Press, 1991). See, also, Robert D. Cooter, 'Against Legal Centrism' (1993) 81 *California Law Review*, 417–29.

[47] Bruce Benson, *The Enterprise of Law: Justice without the State* (Pacific Research Institute for Public Policy 1990).

[48] See, for example, on how a 'more economic approach' to competition law has (re-)configured private regulatory authority through 'big-business' consolidation, Patrice Bougette, Marc Deschamps and Frédéric Marty, 'When Economics Met Antitrust: The Second Chicago School and the Economization of Antitrust Law' (2015) 16 *Enterprise & Society*, 313–53; and, for an examination of other legal technologies, including financial, tax, IP and even family law, IGLP Law and Global Production Working Group, 'The Role of Law in Global Value Chains: A Research Manifesto' (2016) 4 *London Review of International Law*, 57–79. See, already, in general, David Charny, 'Illusions of a Spontaneous Order: Norms in Contractual Relationships' (1995–1996) 144 *University of Pennsylvania Law Review*, 1841–58, at 1845.

[49] See, for example, Robert D. Cooter, 'The Theory of Market Modernization of Law' (1996) 16 *International Review of Law and Economics*, 141–72.

[50] For some incisive assessments, see *inter alia* Peer Zumbansen, 'The Law of Society: Governance through Contract' (2007) 14 *Indiana Journal of Global Legal Studies*, 191–233, especially 212–20, at 215–6 (explaining that: 'The L&E scholars' interest in

In terms of legal culture, it is the enduring influence of neoclassical approaches to law and legal thought which explain why this conception currently figures more prominently in United States.[51] Concerning transnational private regulatory practices, perhaps the most prominent articulations of such a conception can be found in some of the works of Robert Cooter, Gillian Hadfield and Eric Posner.[52] To a relevant extent, their emphases have been placed on explaining and justifying, from this perspective, the authority and operational autonomy of the so-called 'new *lex mercatoria*'. Despite this emphasis, private ordering does bring about a complete theory of private regulatory practices that is both analytically overarching and normatively consistent. This, for example, is Gillian Hadfield assessing the regulatory role of Internet Corporation for Assigned Names and Numbers (ICANN): 'The first task in structuring a truly competitive domain name dispute resolution system, then, is to recognize that public law must draw a sharp line between democratic and efficiency goals and ensure that only the latter are delegated to the private system.'[53]

The second model is the one which, in my view, more prominently figures within EU legal culture in its path to 'new governance'. This

social norms . . . is not in the societal basis of norm-making as part of a larger exploration of sites of political will formation, but reflect instead their intention to privatize, formalize, and de-politicize the complex phenomena of contemporary regulatory governance . . . Central is the authors' distinction between an allegedly neutral private law arena (the *market*) and a value-laden, political realm (the *state*)'; and Frederich Kratochwil, *The Status of Law in World Society: Meditations on the Role and Rule of Law* (Cambridge: Cambridge University Press, 2014), at 272–91, 288 ('In view of the indeterminacy of "logical" solutions even in well-defined games, as multiple equilibria exist, settling on one of the equilibriums even in games of coordination will involve "politics" rather than "rational demonstration." Thus "politics" emerges precisely because *binding decisions* have to be made in the absence of a compelling algorithm for choice').

51 Herbert Hovenkamp, *The Opening of American Law: Neoclassical Legal Thought, 1870–1970* (Oxford: Oxford University Press, 2015). On the possibility of overcoming such an enduring gravitation of neoclassical legal thought within US legal culture, see, also, Victoria F. Nourse and Gregory C. Shaffer, 'Varieties of New Legal Realism: Can a New World Order Prompt a New Legal Theory?' (2009) 95 *Cornell Law Review*, 61–137.

52 See, for example, Robert D. Cooter, 'Decentralized Law for a Complex Economy: The Structural Approach to Adjudicating the New Law Merchant' (1996) 144 *University of Pennsylvania Law Review*, 1643–96; and Eric A. Posner, *Law and Social Norms* (Cambridge MA: Harvard University Press, 2009). See, also, Gillian K. Hadfield and Barry R. Weingast, 'What Is Law? A Coordination Model of the Characteristics of Legal Order' (2012) 4 *Journal of Legal Analysis*, 471–514.

53 Gillian K. Hadfield, 'Privatizing Commercial Law: Lessons from ICANN' (2002) 6 *Journal of Small and Emerging Business Law*, 257–88, at 283.

model essentially justifies private regulation as a way to strengthen regulatory effectiveness and legitimacy, by fostering the engagement of citizens with those policy choices that affect them. Whether it comes in the form of discursive, experimentalist or reflexive governance strategies, among other variations, it is a model that seeks to enhance the self-regulatory capacities (or capabilities) of pertinent communities by stimulating reciprocal learning and adaptability.[54] In contrast to the utilitarian/libertarian commitments that predominantly underlie private ordering theories, this model could be broadly characterised as following a liberal or pragmatist inspiration to the phenomenon.[55] Generally grounded in multiculturalism and republican ideals of 'non-domination', I contend, private regulatory authority could be productively conceptualised under this model as different types of 'police powers' held by private actors.

'Police powers' is the traditional denomination given within occidental legal culture to justify the regulatory authority of shaping or restraining the behaviour of individuals in the name of fulfilling public interests, especially by enhancing the security, progress and overall well-being of the community.[56] The creation and concurrent delimitation of market economies, as manifestations of police powers, was for a long time relatively concealed from modern legal consciousness by predominant laissez-faire dogmas of classical liberalism. These dogmas typically portrayed markets as 'natural orders' which arose somehow spontaneously out of human interactions which, through the self-regulating mechanism of free competition, ensured 'everyone's welfare and justice in accord

[54] See, for example, Neil Walker and Gráinne de Búrca, 'Reconceiving Law & New Governance' (2006) 13 *Columbia Journal of European Law*, 519–94 (emphasising its potential for bolstering a 'reflexive universality'); and Michael Wilkinson, 'Three Conceptions of Law: Towards a Jurisprudence of Democratic Experimentalism' (2010) *Wisconsin Law Review*, 673–718.

[55] On such a contrast, see Amy J. Cohen, 'Governance Legalism: Hayek and Sabel on Reason and Rules, Organization and Law' (2010) *Wisconsin Law Review*, 357–88.

[56] The genealogy of 'police' has been traced all the way back into the classical Hellenistic commitment to the care for the *polis*. Far from being an outdated concept, associated to the *anciėn regime* of *Polizeistaat*, or confined now solely to the realm of criminology, the contemporary relevance of 'police' is displayed in the prominent place that different types of *policy* studies have taken up not only within law schools. On such genealogy, see, for example, Markus D. Dubber, *The Police Power: Patriarchy and the Foundations of American Government* (New York: Columbia University Press, 2005). See, also, Martin Loughlin, *Foundations of Public Law* (Oxford: Oxford University Press, 2010), Chapter 14 (tracing its modernising trajectories within European legal culture[s]).

with the standard of the individual's capacity to perform'.[57] Under the influence of these dogmas, the concept of police powers became essentially confined to those compulsory restraints imposed by legislative or governmental branches of the state on pre-political 'natural rights' (especially those subjective rights to individual liberty, freedom of contract, and private property), mainly through command and control forms, justified by the need to achieve legitimate economic or social purposes.[58]

What is distinctive about the concept of police powers, nonetheless, is that these legitimate social purposes (ends), the kind of activities that these powers encompass (tasks), as well as the modes in which they can be exercised (forms), have been historically and geographically contingent. During early modern times, police powers were *de jure* or *de facto* exercised to a large extent by a range of private organisations or non-state institutions, such as guilds, market towns, and chartered companies, mainly for the purposes of guaranteeing a peaceful urban setting for an orderly development of commerce and trade.[59] The transition from commercial to industrial forms of capitalism, alongside its subsequent processes of urbanisation and democratisation, entailed that police powers in the economic realm were increasingly taken up by a proliferating range of administrative agencies that seek to re-embed market relations in a broader set of public policy goals.[60]

The table 13.1 below sketches some of the main features which, in my view, characterise the differences between both conceptions of private regulation.

[57] Jürgen Habermas, The Structural Transformation of the Public Sphere: An Inquiry into a Category of Bourgeois Society (Cambridge MA: The MIT Press, [1962] 1991), at 79.

[58] A good illustration of that understanding comes from the classical study by Ernst Freund, *The Police Power, Public Policy and Constitutional Rights* (Chicago IL: Callaghan & Company 1904), available at: https://archive.org/details/policepowerpubl01freugoog. See, further, Ernst Freund, *Administrative Powers Over Persons and Property: A Comparative Survey* (Chicago: University of Chicago Press, 1928).

[59] Foucault, *Security, Territory, Population*, n. 15 above, pp. 311–61, at 335 (' . . . police is essentially urban and market based, or to put things more brutally, it is an institution of the market, in the very broad sense').

[60] On the historical trajectories of police powers, until their current configurations, see Braithwaite, n. 13 above, at 12–31. See, also, more broadly, Bernard E. Harcourt, *The Illusion of Free Markets* (Cambridge MA: Harvard University Press, 2011).

Table 13.1 *Conceptions of Private Regulation*

	Private Ordering	Private Police Powers
Predominance	United States	European Union
Explanation	Societal capacities, especially of business communities, to correct market failures or reduce transaction costs more optimally	Human capabilities for self-regulation by enabling their engagement with the collective issues that affect them
Justification	Consumer welfare	Safeguarding 'public interests' or 'legitimate social purposes' (normatively contingent, not reduced to market efficiency alone)
Validity test	Pro-competitive efficiencies / cost-benefit analysis	Proportionality
Political and Social Philosophy	Utilitarianism / Libertarianism	Liberalism / Pragmatism
Legal Culture	Neoclassical legal thought	Legal institutionalism

The first five categories of the table have already been sketched. If law is a cultural asset that both expresses and, at the same time, can further shape a polity's identity, the last category outlines the kind of cultural factors or commitments that such a distinctive approach to private regulation within the EU and United States might also reflect.[61] At this level, I conjecture, at least one distinctive factor could be traced within European legal culture, in contrast to that of the United States, as a conceivable candidate: an enduring legacy of legal institutionalism within European law and legal thought.[62] This factor represents, in my view, some enduring modernist features within European legal culture concerning the law of political economy, which could place such a particular EU approach to transnational private regulation within some distinctive historical trajectories and vernacular structures.

[61] On positive law as a cultural asset, see, for example, Lawrence Rosen, *Law as Culture: An Invitation* (Princeton NJ: Princeton University Press, 2006). See, also, Roberto Mangabeira Unger, *Law in Modern Society* (New York: Simon and Schuster, 1976), at 47 ('Each society reveals through its law the innermost secrets of the manner in which it holds men together').

[62] See, in general, Massimo La Torre, *Law as Institution* (Dordrecht et al: Springer Science & Business Media, 2010) (tracing the (dis-)continuities between old and contemporary institutionalism within European legal thought).

IV The Idea of a Private Administrative Law

It is well known how the EU increasingly developed, through different means, an active meta-regulatory strategy on different forms of private regulation. Rather than a unique grand-ideal to be consistently applied across all policy fields, this strategy has, to a relevant extent, been driven by contextual and pragmatic considerations. In general, it could be inferred that, when regulatory harmonisation through EU Law became politically unfeasible, the EU turned to post-regulatory strategies for market integration purposes. Along the way, and almost unconsciously, I contend, a private administrative law began to take shape.

IV.1 Private Administrative Law: The Legislative Sources

At a first level of analysis, this post-regulatory turn to private regulatory capacities is illustrated by a broad overview of EU internal market legislation (i.e. regulations and directives) and soft law instruments on the topic. Right from the 'New Approach to Technical Harmonisation' of the 1980s,[63] but also in the 'Better Regulation' agenda,[64] and the 'Social Partnership' policy,[65] as expressed in the 'Inter-Institutional Agreement on Better Law-Making' (at least in its 2003 version),[66] among other instruments,[67] the EU explicitly engaged in different forms of private regulation for the development and operationalisation of its policies. An equivalent approach can be observed in EU legislation. The General Product Safety Directive, the Services Directive,

63 For an early assessment see, for example, Jacques Pelkmans, 'The New Approach to Technical Harmonization and Standardization' (1987) 25 *Journal of Common Market Studies*, 249–69. On some of its contemporary trajectories see, for example, Harm Schepel, 'The New Approach to the New Approach: The Juridification of Harmonized Standards in EU Law' (2013) 12 *Maastricht Journal of European and Comparative Law*, 521–33.

64 On its current shape, see https://ec.europa.eu/info/law/law-making-process/planning-and-proposing-law/better-regulation-why-and-how_en; and Sacha Garben and Inge Govaere (eds.), *The EU Better Regulation Agenda: A Critical Assessment* (Oxford: Hart Publishing, 2018).

65 See, for example, Paul Craig, *EU Administrative Law* (Oxford: Oxford University Press, 2012), Chapter 8.

66 Interinstitutional Agreement on Better Law-Making 2003, available at: https://eur-lex.europa.eu/legal-content/EN/TXT/?uri=CELEX%3A32003Q1231%2801%29.

67 See, for example, European Economic and Social Committee, 'The Current State of Co-Regulation and Self-Regulation in the Single Market' (2005) EESC Pamphlet Series for an assessment of actual examples of co- and self-regulation. For a latest account, https://ec.europa.eu/digital-single-market/en/community-practice-better-self-and-co-regulation-cop.

and the Market Abuse Directive, among others, all consign an explicit supporting role to private regulation.[68]

What is interesting from a legal perspective, among other aspects, is that these legislative instruments within EU law not only explicitly refer to several modalities of private regulation, but at the same time also discipline these private regulatory practices through a range of formal, procedural and substantive conditions of validity. In their formal dimension, for example, these instruments convey duties of clarity, publicity and prospective application. In their procedural dimension, they are accompanied by duties of representation, transparency, as well as opportunities for the review of regulatory measures both *ex ante* and *ex post*. In their substantive dimension, they include duties of good faith, legality 'with applicable laws and fundamental rights', and, in particular, the obligation that private regulatory measures must be of an 'added value to the general interest'.[69]

As can be observed, these conditions of validity for private regulatory practices differ notably from those which typically inform private or commercial action. Rather, they are more akin to those conditions of validity that have been incrementally made applicable to administrative agencies when exercising their own police powers.

IV.2 Private Administrative Law: The Judicial Sources

The second legal source comes from analysis of the EU case law concerning private regulatory practices. Drawing mainly from the free movement and competition law cases that private regulators have confronted within the EU legal order, this case law has been relatively consistent in both giving further shape and complementing, with some additional elements, the formal, procedural and substantive conditions of validity of private regulation already stated at the legislative level. For what is

[68] For a broad overview and analysis, see Mataija, n. 23 above, pp. 15–16 and 23–4.

[69] See, among others, Interinstitutional Agreement on Better Law-making, n. 66 above; European Union, 'The "Principles for Better Self- and Co-Regulation"' (*Digital Single Market*), available at: https://ec.europa.eu/digital-single-market/en/cop-principles-better-self-and-co-regulation. See, also, on standardisation agreements, Guidelines on the applicability of Article 101 of the Treaty on the Functioning of the European Union to horizontal cooperation agreements 2011 para. 257 et seq. (establishing a range of formal, procedural and substantive conditions of their validity, such as 'fair, reasonable and non-discriminatory' access to the standard or 'transparency' and 'unrestricted participation' during their procedure of adoption).

relevant in these respects, this case law could be helpfully synthesised in two main elements.[70]

Firstly, at a methodological level, when assessing the rationality of a private regulatory measure, the CJEU has regularly circumscribed its role to a determination of whether the measure is 'necessary and proportionate for the achievement of a legitimate aim', in the same way as when generally assessing a government's exercise of police powers. It has applied, however, a different kind of proportionality test to private regulators. As in *Déliege*, *Angonese* and *Viking*, the CJEU has accepted, on the one hand, a wide spectrum of 'legitimate purposes', even broader than those allowed to states.[71] On the other hand, as in *Wouters* and, to some extent, in *Erny*, it has considered a narrower range of 'less restrictive measures' while granting private regulators a wider margin of appreciation than that available to states.[72]

Secondly, at an institutional level, the case law has also assigned a crucial role to good governance standards as a condition of validity for private regulatory choices. In its organisational dimension, the focus has been mainly put on a biased composition of decision-making bodies[73] and conflict of interests policies.[74] In its operational dimension, the focus has been on the lack of transparency and openness in their proceedings,[75] and on the opportunities for a fair hearing, rationality and

[70] For a detailed analysis of the case law in reference to a range of doctrinal and theoretical debates within EU Economic Law, see Mataija, n. 23 above, Chapters 2–3.

[71] See *Christelle Deliège* v. *Ligue francophone de judo et disciplines associées ASBL, Ligue belge de judo ASBL, Union européenne de judo (C-51/96) and François Pacquée (C-191/97)* [2000] Court of Justice of the European Union Joined cases C-51/96 and C-191/97 para. 43. *Roman Angonese* v. *Cassa di Risparmio di Bolzano SpA* [2000] Court of Justice of the European Union Case C-281/98 para. 42. *International Transport Workers' Federation and Finnish Seamen's Union* v. *Viking Line ABP and OÜ Viking Line Eesti* [2007] Court of Justice of the European Union [Grand Chamber] Case C-438/05 paras. 74 and 90.

[72] See *JCJ Wouters and Others* v. *Algemene Raad van de Nederlandse Orde van Advocaten* [2002] Court of Justice of the European Union Case C-309/99 para. 110. In the case of *Georges Erny* v. *Daimler AG – Werk Wörth* [2012] Court of Justice of the European Union Case C-172/11, see paras. 41 and 47–51.

[73] *API – Anonima Petroli Italiana SpA and Others* v. *Ministero delle Infrastrutture e dei Trasporti and Others* [2014] Court of Justice of the European Union [Fifth Chamber] Joined Cases C-184/13 to C-187/13, C-194/13, C-195/13 and C-208/13.

[74] *Motosykletistiki Omospondia Ellados NPID (MOTOE)* v. *Elliniko Dimosio*, No. Case C-49/07 (Court of Justice of the European Union [Grand Chamber] July 1, 2008); and *Ordem dos Técnicos Oficiais de Contas* v. *Autoridade da Concorrência*, No. Case C-1/12 (Court of Justice of the European Union [Second Chamber] 28 February 2013).

[75] See, for example, Guidelines on the applicability of Article 101 of the Treaty on the Functioning of the European Union to horizontal co-operation agreements, Section 7 on Standardisation Agreements (*passim*, at para. 280).

judicial review.[76] These have been some of the institutional design benchmarks that EU legal authorities have established, in these respects, for private regulatory practices.

Upon these bases, at least three conclusions can, plausibly, be sustained. First, according to the range of doctrinal, legislative and judicial legal sources that have been briefly examined, private regulation has been incrementally devised by EU legal authorities as a distinctive realm of human activities, autonomous (but not totally independent) from the realms of both 'state action' and 'private/commercial action'. The second conclusion is that this realm of human activities, as it has been devised within the EU, especially in its commitment to the broad spectrum of public interests aims beyond sole market efficiency that private regulators could prima facie pursue, denotes a distinctive EU approach to the topic that has been termed as 'private police powers' to differentiate it from the 'private ordering' approach that is predominant within the United States.[77]

Finally, the type of requirements that the EU legal authorities have established as validity conditions of private regulatory practices, which typically characterise (but do not equate) those applicable to EU administrative agencies, becomes the ground for a third conclusion. The EU rules of recognition on private regulation could therefore be productively conceptualised, from a doctrinal perspective, in the form of an administrative law that has been incrementally emerging within the private sphere.[78] Just as those early years of a pre-legislated administrative law, when its rules, standards or

[76] *David Meca-Medina and Igor Majcen* v. *Commission of the European Communities* [2006], Court of Justice of the European Union [Third Chamber] Case C-519/04 P para. 45; and, most controversially, *Laval un Partneri Ltd* v. *Svenska Byggnadsarbetareförbundet, Svenska Byggnadsarbetareförbundets avdelning 1, Byggettan and Svenska Elektrikerförbundet* [2007] Court of Justice of the European Union [Grand Chamber] Case C-341/05 paras. 116 and 119. See, also, Case 222/86 *Union nationale des entraîneurs et cadres techniques professionnels du football (Unectef)* v. *Georges Heylens and Others* [1987] ECR 4097, paras. 13-16; Case C-18/88 *Régie des télégraphes et des téléphones* v. *GB- Inno-BM SA* [1991] ECR I-5941, paras 35-37; and Case C-506/04 *Graham J. Wilson* v. *Ordre des avocats du barreau de Luxembourg* [2006] ECR I-8613.

[77] Imelda Maher, 'Competition Law and Transnational Private Regulatory Regimes: Marking the Cartel Boundary' (2011) 38 *Journal of Law and Society*, 119–37, at 122 (' . . . by prohibiting cartels the EU ensures that it decides to what extent and in what circumstances and under what conditions such potentially powerful transnational private regulatory regimes should be permitted to operate').

[78] A clarification: rather than in its foundational role of the whole legal system, as in Kelsen's *Grundnorm*, the term 'rule of recognition' is being employed here in its more forensic connotation (i.e. those contingent secondary rules, identifiable within the legal system, establishing the conditions of validity for primary rules of obligation) as also specified by

principles were doctrinally drawn from an inductive reconstruction of internal organisational and operational frameworks or competent courts and tribunal decisions, currently, it could be said, a distinctive field of private administrative law is incrementally taking shape.[79]

Among EU legal scholars and practitioners, it has become recurrent to observe a number of tensions or even inconsistencies between EU internal market law, competition law, and the new governance approaches to regulatory policy. As a potential way to overcome these problems, in a recent contribution to this debate, Giorgio Monti and Jotte Mulder have suggested the desirability of advancing towards the articulation of an 'overarching internal market test' formed by a 'converged application' of the existing EU competition and free movement rules to new governance policies. If structured around a conceptual framework that could 'more cohesively' integrate existing standards concerning 'the input and output legitimacy of competition restrictive measures', they contend, such a test could contribute to transcend a persistent recourse within EU legal reasoning to 'static categories … mostly developed around conventional state-centred understandings of dominium and imperium'.[80]

My claim is that the idea of a private administrative law, as has been incipiently constructed alongside this analytical step of the argument, already provides such a conceptual framework. As a legal doctrine, however, the concept of a private administrative law should not be understood as a ready-made model of validity to be deductively imposed on reality. Instead, this concept would operate as the grammar according to which the formal, procedural or substantive conditions of validity of private regulators can be continuously articulated, tested and contested. Forensically, some degree of legal uncertainty is therefore inevitable, because the terms of recognition cannot but ultimately be appraised according to those conflicting demands of

Hart: see H.L.A. Hart, *The Concept of Law*, 2nd ed. (Oxford: Oxford University Press, 1994), pp. 94–9.

[79] For a recent overview of such methodological commitments underlying the early developments of modern administrative law within Europe, see Martin Loughlin, n. 56 above, at 435–48 (analysing the conceptual trajectories that continental [i.e. French, German] and English legal systems have had in these respects, albeit differing upon whether the legal control of administrative action was to be considered within the competence of ordinary courts or solely specialised ones). For a similar approach in the case of the United States, see, mainly, with further references, Jerry L. Mashaw, *Creating the Administrative Constitution: The Lost One Hundred Years of American Administrative Law* (New Haven CT: Yale University Press, 2012).

[80] Monti and Mulder, n. 44 above, at 656.

legal predictability and appropriateness to be judicially determined in the circumstances of the case.[81]

One interesting question to leave open is the extent to which this approach might lately be receding within the EU, as well as the reasons that might explain or justify this legal (trans-)formation. At least two recent decisions could serve as indications of such a change. On the one hand, the *Energy Accord* and *Chicken of Tomorrow* judgments.[82] On the other hand, the decision to erase all references to co-regulation or self-regulation strategies in the new version of the Interinstitutional Agreement on Better Law-Making.[83] Do these decisions entail backing off from post-regulatory strategies? Are the emphases on regulatory impact analysis and post-implementation assessments within the new Interinstitutional Agreement indications of a retreat into a neoclassical 'bright-line' private/public divide? Are they perhaps an indication of a 'United-States-ean' turn in EU law by moving into a 'more economic approach' also in private regulation? Articulated as a distinct scheme of intelligibility, alternative to an over-arching legal monism or an incommensurable legal pluralism, the private administrative law doctrine, by focusing on existing rules of recognition, proposes a conceptual baseline to envisage these and further questions, which will stimulate, I hope, renewed angles into this juridical field.[84]

[81] Fernando Atria, *On Law and Legal Reasoning* (Oxford: Hart Publishing, 2002), *passim*, 161–71, at 168 ('what the law is for the case cannot be known before deciding how the competition between predictability and appropriateness ought to be resolved'). See, also, illustratively, Harm Schepel, 'Rules of Recognition: A Legal Constructivist Approach to Transnational Private Regulation', in: Horatia Muir Watt and Diego P. Fernández Arroyo (eds.), *Private International Law and Global Governance* (Oxford: Oxford University Press, 2014), pp. 202–11.

[82] The so-called *Energy Accord* and *Chicken of Tomorrow* are two private regulation initiatives recently adopted in the Netherlands. Both of these initiatives comprised broad societal self-regulatory agreements to reduce the output of certain types of goods in order to safeguard some kind of sustainable development in their respective markets. Although these agreements were developed under the sponsorship of the Dutch government, both were ultimately declared illegal by the national competition authority. The decision became socially and politically contested, to the extent that the Dutch government activated a legal path for its regularisation. However, the European Commission intervened in the debate through a letter during the 'notice and comment' stage of the Dutch policy proposal, reaffirming the decision taken by the national competition authority. Although not a formal decision, this intervention ultimately proved to be quite an influential 'judgment' on the part of the European Commission in channelling the final outcome of the respective cases. For an instructive analysis, see Monti and Mulder, n. 44 above.

[83] Interinstitutional Agreement on Better Law-Making 2016, available at: https://eur-lex.europa.eu/legal-content/EN/TXT/?uri=uriserv:OJ.L_.2016.123.01.0001.01.ENG.

[84] See, for example, Dimitri van den Meerssche, 'European Perspectives on Constitutional Pluralism(s): An Ontological Roadmap' (2018) 9 *Transnational Legal Theory*, 1–31,

V The Return of History in Transnational Private Regulation and the Significance of Legal Forms

Regulatory entrepreneurs contesting US climate policy.[85] Developing countries defying scavenger investors.[86] Systemically important banks (and retailers) performing as focal nodes of peripheral sustainability endeavours.[87] Global digital corporations *de facto* transformed into data protection agencies.[88] These or other controversies and proliferating forms of political action, which are challenging the foundations, scope, and modalities of private authority in contemporary political economies, arguably signify the 'return of history', (not only) in transnational private regulation.[89] By examining the comparative role that competition law has had in partially configuring

whose insightful binary about the configuration of contemporary EU legal thought, in this way, I seek to transcend. In addition, my focus upon existent but contingent 'rules of recognition' also intends to conceptually broaden those proposed scholarly frames that, while being resistant to strong forms of legal or constitutional pluralism as well, have tended to ground contemporary private regulatory authority in some kind of delegation theory by government. In this sense, see, for example, for a careful analysis and positioning, Peter Lindseth, 'Agents Without Principals? Delegation in an Age of Diffuse and Fragmented Governance' in: Fabrizzio Cafaggi (ed.), *Reframing Self-regulation in European Private Law* (Alphen a/d Rijn: Kluwer Law International, 2006), pp. 107–30.

85 See, for example, for further references, Michele M. Betsill, 'Trump's Paris Withdrawal and the Reconfiguration of Global Climate Change Governance' (2017) 15 *Chinese Journal of Population Resources and Environment*, 189–91.

86 Jerome E. Roos, *Why not Default?: The Political Economy of Sovereign Debt* (Princeton NJ: Princeton University Press, 2019).

87 See, for example, respectively, Benjamin J. Richardson, *Fiduciary Law and Responsible Investing: In Nature's Trust* (Abingdon: Routledge, 2013); and Geoffrey Lawrence and Jane Dickson, 'The Political Economy of Agri-Food: Supermarkets', in: Alessandro Bonanno and Lawrence Busch (eds.), *Handbook of the International Political Economy of Agriculture and Food* (Cheltenham: Edward Elgar Publishing, 2015), pp. 213–31.

88 In a relatively overlooked implication of the so-called 'right to be forgotten' established by the CJEU, see, for example, www.google.com/webmasters/tools/legal-removal-request?complaint_type=rtbf&hl=en&rd=1 (explaining that: 'when you make your request, *we will balance* the privacy rights of the individual concerned with the interest of the general public in having access to the information, as well as the right of others to distribute the information' [emphasis added]). See, also, in response, https://medium.com/@ellgood/open-letter-to-google-from-80-internet-scholars-release-rtbf-compliance-data-cbfc6d59f1bd. I thank Thomas Streinz and Sabine Mair for insightful exchanges on the background and implications of the *Google Spain* case.

89 Jennifer Welsh, *The Return of History: Conflict, Migration, and Geopolitics in the Twenty-First Century* (Toronto: House of Anansi Press, 2017). See, also, David Kennedy, A *World of Struggle: How Power, Law, and Expertise Shape Global Political Economy* (Princeton NJ: Princeton University Press, 2016); Hans Lindahl, *Authority and the Globalisation of Inclusion and Exclusion* (Cambridge: Cambridge University Press, 2018).

such private regulatory authority, this chapter illustrates the constitutive place that legal institutions significantly hold in the perceived (trans-)formations currently underway.[90] Enabled through legal forms and reflexively self-actualised through authoritative judgments concerning the legality, illegality (or a-legality) of pertaining practices, it also documents why, albeit conceptually subtly, such an emphasis is utterly decisive.[91]

Alongside his governmentality studies, Michel Foucault also reminds us how, in all their subversive potential, 'counter-conducts' regularly stand in a symbiotic relationship with those very same paradigms that they seek to subvert.[92] Throughout the perceived legal 'conundrum' about the private regulation phenomenon, such an insight may well be replicating in most of contemporary legal approaches to the topic.[93] In articulating the idea of a private administrative law, jurisprudentially, the distinction drawn from both legal monism and legal pluralism has been conceptual. However, the fact that the distinction is conceptual does not mean that the law, as a matter of conceptual truth, is any of these. The model of law that a given legal culture follows is an interpretative question to be settled by the way in which the participants in that culture understand their own legal practices from an internal perspective.[94] Hence, *pace*

[90] See, for example, in addition, A. Claire Cutler and Thomas Dietz (eds.), *The Politics of Private Transnational Governance by Contract* (Abingdon: Routledge, 2017); and Mark Findlay, *Law's Regulatory Relevance?: Property, Power and Market Economies* (Cheltenham: Edward Elgar Publishing, 2017).

[91] Simon Deakin, David Gindis, Geoffrey Hodgson, Kainan Huang and Katharina Pistor, 'Legal Institutionalism: Capitalism and the Constitutive Role of Law' (2017) 45 *Journal of Comparative Economics*, 188–200, at 192 (' . . . when Hayek, Williamson and others overemphasize custom and private ordering, to the neglect of the essential role of the state, they end up treating the state aspects of law as secondary and epiphenomenal. In this respect their position is similar to that of Marx'); Robert W. Gordon, 'Critical Legal Histories' (1984) 36 *Stanford Law Review*, 57–125, at 100–13 and 108–9 (explaining that while epiphenomenal approaches to law and legal thought seek 'to lift the veil of legal form to reveal the living essences of power and need, the program of the critics is to lift the veil of power and need to expose the legal elements in their composition').

[92] See, for example, Michel Foucault, 'Omnes et Singulatim: Towards a Critique of Political Reason', in: James D. Faubion (ed.), *The Essential Works of Michel Foucault, 1954–1984: Power*, Vol. 3 (New York: The New Press, 1997), pp. 298–325, at 324; Michel Foucault, *The Will to Knowledge – Volume 1 of The History of Sexuality* (London: Penguin Books, [1978] 2008), at 95.

[93] See mainly, perceptively, Ralf Michaels, 'The Mirage of Non-State Governance' (2010) *Utah Law Review*, 31–46.

[94] Ludwig Wittgenstein, *Philosophical Investigations*, GEM Anscombe transl., 3rd ed. (Oxford: Basil Blackwell, 1967), at N116.

Harold Berman and Michel Foucault, to the extent that these world-making imaginaries about the place of law and political authority structuring the project of modernity are actually becoming (trans-)formed, genealogically, indeed 'a world ends when its metaphor has died'.[95]

[95] Fernando Atria, 'Living under Dead Ideas: Law as the Will of the People', in: Claudio Michelon and Maksymilian Del Mar (eds.), *The Anxiety of the Jurist: Legality, Exchange and Judgement* (Abingdon: Routledge, 2013), pp. 101–40. See, also, tectonically, Neil Walker, 'Out of Place and out of Time: Law's Fading Co-ordinates' (2010) 14 *Edinburgh Law Review* 13–46; and Martin Loughlin, 'The Constitutional Imagination' (2015) 78 *Modern Law Review*, 1–25.

14

The Transnational Dimension of Constitutional Rights

Framing and Taming 'Private' Governance beyond the State*

LARS VIELLECHNER

I Introduction

The concept of constitutionalism, as it was established in the modern nation state, is generally acknowledged as the zenith of legal evolution.[1] Today, this specific conjunction of democracy and the rule of law, including fundamental rights protection, has spread almost worldwide. Under the impact of the development commonly called 'globalisation',[2] or differentiation of 'world society',[3] in the social sciences, however, the extraordinary capacity of the constitutional state seems to have reached its limits. Indeed, many cross-border issues cannot be effectively regulated by national law. Some sociologists therefore presumed that law would lose significance in the future.[4] Yet, to date, there is no evidence of a decline of law. On the contrary, the emerging world society reveals an urgent need for conventional means to stabilise expectations and to resolve disputes that is satisfied by a double transformation of law.

* Reprinted with permission from (2019) 8 *Global Constitutionalism*, 639–61.

1 See Frank I. Michelman, 'W(h)ither the Constitution?' (2000) 21 *Cardozo Law Review*, 1063–83; Dieter Grimm, 'The Achievement of Constitutionalism and its Prospects in a Changed World', in: Petra Dobner and Martin Loughlin (eds.), *The Twilight of Constitutionalism?* (Oxford: Oxford University Press, 2010), pp. 3–22.

2 Anthony Giddens, *The Consequences of Modernity* (Stanford CA: Stanford University Press, 1990), pp. 63–78; Saskia Sassen, *A Sociology of Globalization* (New York: Norton, 2007), pp. 11–44.

3 Niklas Luhmann, *Theory of Society*, Vol. 1 (Stanford CA: Stanford University Press, 2012), pp. 83–99.

4 See Luhmann, *A Sociological Theory of Law* (London: Routledge and Kegan Paul, 1985), pp. 255–64.

On the one hand, international law extends to those subject matters that used to be reserved as the internal affairs of the states, including trade and ecology, but also certain aspects of criminal law and human rights.[5] For this purpose, states have created several international organisations. Some of them even dispose of their own courts. At global level, the World Trade Organization, including its Dispute Settlement Understanding, is one of the best-known examples.[6] At regional level, the European Union, including its Court of Justice, is particularly advanced in its development.[7] Here, the genesis of a new kind of public authority beyond the state, which acts with direct effect on the individual, has also called for the ensuring of fundamental rights protection.[8] To this end, the former Court of Justice of the European Communities has first invoked the European Convention on Human Rights and the common constitutional traditions of the Member States as general principles of law.[9] Meanwhile, Article 6(1) of the Treaty on European Union refers to a written Charter of Fundamental Rights.[10]

International and European law making sometimes fail, however, due to a lack of consent or pace among the states. On the other hand, therefore, transnational governance arrangements, which are constituted by contract mainly among non-state actors, step in to fill the gap.[11] The arrangement that allocates domains on the Internet offers

[5] See Joel P. Trachtman, *The Future of International Law: Global Government* (Cambridge: Cambridge University Press, 2013); Eyal Benvenisti, *The Law of Global Governance* (Leiden: Brill, 2014).

[6] See Deborah Z. Cass, *The Constitutionalization of the World Trade Organization: Legitimacy, Democracy, and Community in the International Trading System* (Oxford: Oxford University Press, 2005); John H. Jackson, *Sovereignty, the WTO, and Changing Fundamentals of International Law* (Cambridge: Cambridge University Press, 2006).

[7] See Joseph H.H. Weiler, 'The Transformation of Europe' (1991) 100 *Yale Law Journal*, 2403–83; Kaarlo Tuori, *European Constitutionalism* (Cambridge: Cambridge University Press, 2015).

[8] See Pierre Pescatore, 'Les droits de l'homme et l'intégration européenne' (1968) 4 *Cahiers de droit européen*, 629–93; Manfred Zuleeg, 'Fundamental Rights and the Law of the European Communities' (1971) 8 *Common Market Law Review*, 446–61.

[9] ECJ, Judgment of 12 November 1969, Case 29/69, *Stauder* v. *Stadt Ulm* (1969) *European Court Reports*, 419–26, at 425; Judgment of 17 December 1970, Case 11/70, *Internationale Handelsgesellschaft* v. *Einfuhr- und Vorratsstelle für Getreide und Futtermittel* (1970) *European Court Reports*, 1125–39, at 1135.

[10] Treaty of Lisbon Amending the Treaty on European Union and the Treaty Establishing the European Community, 13 December 2007, Art. 6, C:2007:306:13.

[11] See Gunther Teubner, 'Global Private Regimes: Neo-Spontaneous Law and Dual Constitution of Autonomous Sectors?', in: Karl-Heinz Ladeur (ed.), *Public Governance in the Age of Globalization* (Aldershot: Ashgate Publishing, 2004), pp. 71–87; Lars Viellechner, 'The Constitution of Transnational Governance Arrangements: Karl Polanyi's Double Movement in the Transformation of Law', in: Christian Joerges and Josef Falke (eds.), *Karl Polanyi, Globalisation and the Potential of Law in Transnational Markets* (Oxford-Portland OR: Hart Publishing, 2011), pp. 435–64.

the most sophisticated instance of this to date (Section II). It will be argued here that a new approach to the horizontal effect of constitutional rights may both account for the emergence of such arrangements and offer a solution to the problem of their legitimacy. According to this understanding, constitutional rights at the same time enable and restrict transnational regulation. In this way, they guarantee a comprehensive protection of freedom under conditions of globalisation (Section III). As long as transnational governance arrangements are not able to generate constitutional rights of their own, however, the national legal orders must complement them (Section IV). Hence, for the time being, the legitimacy of law in world society may only be ensured through the dialectical interaction of its various constituents (Section V).

II Transnational Law

The new forms of transnational governance emerging beyond both states and international organisations escape from the conventional categories of political and legal thinking (Sub-section II.1). They result in a peculiar type of transnational law (Sub-section II.2).

II.1 Description

The arrangement that allocates domains on the Internet may serve as an illustrative example. Although it is a unique phenomenon without precedent or equivalent, some, more general, conclusions on the evolution of law in world society may be drawn inductively from this model. The complex entity had not been systematically designed, but emerged rather accidentally and only consolidated in the course of its operation.[12]

In 1998, after a controversial debate between different interest groups ranging from private stakeholders to state governments, the Internet Corporation for Assigned Names and Numbers (ICANN) was founded

[12] See A. Michael Froomkin, 'Wrong Turn in Cyberspace: Using ICANN to Route Around the APA and the Constitution' (2000) 50 *Duke Law Journal*, 17–186; Milton L. Mueller, *Ruling the Root: Internet Governance and the Taming of Cyberspace* (Cambridge MA: The MIT Press, 2002).

as the institutional centre of the arrangement.[13] ICANN is a non-profit association pursuant to Californian law, incorporated in Los Angeles.[14] According to its by-laws, it is in charge of ensuring the stable and secure operation of the unique identifier systems of the Internet. Its board of directors includes representatives from all geographical regions of the world, but not from state governments, which have access only to its advisory committees.[15] The organisation thus occurred as an unparalleled compromise: While an international Internet organisation would have required membership of all states in the world, the unilateral regulation of the Internet by a single state, even if it were technically possible, appeared undesirable.[16]

Legally, ICANN acts upon the basis of multiple bilateral contracts.[17] On the one hand, it maintains contractual relations with several public and private institutions that administer the data files in which the top-level domains such as '.com' are inscribed.[18] On the other hand, ICANN was originally subject to a memorandum of understanding with the US government, which had supported early research on the Internet for military purposes and therefore long claimed supreme authority over its infrastructure.[19] Nevertheless, the US government had always remained on a latent position in this regard. Most recently, it has withdrawn its commitment altogether.[20] As a result, ICANN may take all

[13] Internet Corporation for Assigned Names and Numbers, founded 18 September 1998, available at: www.icann.org, last accessed 31 January 2019.

[14] Articles of Incorporation of Internet Corporation for Assigned Names and Numbers, as approved 9 August 2016, available at: www.icann.org/resources/pages/governance/articles-en, last accessed 31 January 2019.

[15] Bylaws for Internet Corporation for Assigned Names and Numbers, as amended 18 June 2018, available at: www.icann.org/resources/pages/governance/bylaws-en, last accessed 31 January 2019.

[16] See Wolfgang Kleinwächter, 'ICANN: Between Technical Mandate and Political Challenges' (2000) 24 *Telecommunications Policy*, 553–63; Susan P. Crawford, 'The ICANN Experiment' (2004) 12 *Cardozo Journal of International and Comparative Law*, 409–48.

[17] See Crawford, n. 16 above, at 414: 'a web of contracts'.

[18] Internet Corporation for Assigned Names and Numbers, Registry Agreements, available at: www.icann.org/resources/pages/registries/registries-agreements-en, last accessed 31 January 2019.

[19] Memorandum of Understanding between the US Department of Commerce and Internet Corporation for Assigned Names and Numbers, 25 November 1998, available at: www.icann.org/resources/unthemed-pages/icann-mou-1998-11-25-en, last accessed 31 January 2019.

[20] National Telecommunications and Information Administration Announces Intent to Transition Key Internet Domain Name Functions, 14 March 2014, available at: www.ntia.doc.gov/press-release/2014/ntia-announces-intent-transition-key-internet-domain-name-functions, last accessed 31 January 2019.

decisions of current administration independently. Second-level domains such as 'google.com' are allocated to individuals via numerous registrars, also under contract with ICANN, according to a 'first come, first served' principle.[21]

As each domain may only be registered once for reasons of unambiguous identification, disputes over their allocation soon began to arise.[22] In particular, the domain names that correspond to the names of celebrities and well-known trademarks became highly contested. In the so-called 'cybersquatting'[23] cases, some Internet users registered for a large number of such domains intending to sell them at a profit to the persons and corporations concerned. In order to solve these disputes, ICANN finally established a special dispute settlement mechanism,[24] based upon the Uniform Domain Name Dispute Resolution Policy (UDRP).[25] The accreditation agreements require the registrars to include the UDRP as general terms and conditions in each domain registration contract.[26] According to Paragraph 4(a) UDRP, a complaint will succeed when three conditions are met:

> You are required to submit to a mandatory administrative proceeding in the event that a third party (a 'complainant') asserts to the applicable Provider, in compliance with the Rules of Procedure, that (i) your domain name is identical or confusingly similar to a trademark or service mark in which the complainant has rights; and (ii) you have no rights or legitimate

[21] Internet Corporation for Assigned Names and Numbers, Registrar Accreditation Agreement, available at: www.icann.org/resources/pages/approved-with-specs-2013-09-17-en, last accessed 31 January 2019.

[22] See Jeffrey J. Look, 'The Virtual Wild, Wild West (WWW): Intellectual Property Issues in Cyberspace' (1999) 22 *University of Arkansas at Little Rock Law Review*, 49–89; Jessica Litman, 'The DNS Wars: Trademarks and the Internet Domain Name System' (2000) 4 *Journal of Small and Emerging Business Law*, 149–65.

[23] John D. Mercer, 'Cybersquatting: Blackmail on the Information Superhighway' (2000) 6 *Boston University Journal of Science and Technology Law*, 290–312.

[24] See Luke A. Walker, 'ICANN's Uniform Domain Name Dispute Resolution Policy' (2000) 15 *Berkeley Technology Law Journal*, 289–311; Laurence R. Helfer and Graeme B. Dinwoodie, 'Designing Non-National Systems: The Case of the Uniform Domain Name Dispute Resolution Policy' (2001) 43 *William and Mary Law Review*, 141–274.

[25] Uniform Domain Name Dispute Resolution Policy, 26 August 1999, available at: www.icann.org/resources/pages/policy-2012-02-25-en, last accessed 31 January 2019.

[26] Internet Corporation for Assigned Names and Numbers, Registrar Accreditation Agreement, available at: www.icann.org/resources/pages/approved-with-specs-2013-09-17-en, last accessed 31 January 2019.

> interests in respect of the domain name; and (iii) your domain name has been registered and is being used in bad faith.[27]

ICANN has recognised five different institutions in their capacity as dispute resolution service providers.[28] The group includes not only private organisations, such as the National Arbitration Forum based in Minneapolis,[29] but also the Arbitration and Mediation Centre of the World Intellectual Property Organization, an international organisation.[30] According to Paragraph 15(a) of the Rules for Uniform Domain Name Dispute Resolution Policy (UDRP-Rules), each panel appointed to decide a domain dispute must comply with the provisions of the UDRP, while it may autonomously complement its rules if necessary:

> 'A Panel shall decide a complaint on the basis of the statements and documents submitted and in accordance with the Policy, these Rules and any rules and principles of law that it deems applicable.'[31]

Because of its access to the registers, ICANN may even electronically enforce its own law. According to Paragraph 3(c) UDRP, it will cancel, transfer or modify a domain name upon receipt of a panel decision that requires such action.[32] Some commentators regard this sanction as an 'electronic equivalent of the death penalty'.[33] Yet, ICANN cannot prevent subsequent lawsuits before national courts. Paragraph 4(k) UDRP expressly provides for such a remedy:

> The mandatory administrative proceeding requirements set forth in Paragraph 4 shall not prevent either you or the complainant from

[27] Uniform Domain Name Dispute Resolution Policy, 26 August 1999, § 4(a), available at: www.icann.org/resources/pages/policy-2012-02-25-en, last accessed 31 January 2019.

[28] Internet Corporation for Assigned Names and Numbers, List of Approved Dispute Resolution Service Providers, available at: www.icann.org/resources/pages/providers-6d-2012-02-25-en, last accessed 31 January 2019.

[29] National Arbitration Forum, Domain Name Disputes, available at: www.adrforum.com /domains, last accessed 31 January 2019.

[30] World Intellectual Property Organization, Arbitration and Mediation Center, Domain Name Dispute Resolution, available at: www.wipo.int/amc/en/domains/index.html, last accessed 31 January 2019.

[31] Rules for Uniform Domain Name Dispute Resolution Policy, as approved 28 September 2013, § 15(a), available at: www.icann.org/resources/pages/udrp-rules-2015-03-11-en, last accessed 31 January 2019.

[32] Uniform Domain Name Dispute Resolution Policy, 26 August 1999, § 3(c), available at: www.icann.org/resources/pages/policy-2012-02-25-en, last accessed 31 January 2019.

[33] David G. Post, *Governing Cyberspace, or Where Is James Madison When We Need Him?*, June 1999, available at: www.temple.edu/lawschool/dpost/icann/comment1.html, last accessed 31 January 2019.

> submitting the dispute to a court of competent jurisdiction for independent resolution before such mandatory administrative proceeding is commenced or after such proceeding is concluded. If an Administrative Panel decides that your domain name registration should be canceled or transferred, we will wait ten (10) business days (as observed in the location of our principal office) after we are informed by the applicable Provider of the Administrative Panel's decision before implementing that decision.[34]

Hence, although a single state could neither comprehensively nor effectively regulate cross-border affairs, such as the infrastructure of the Internet, national courts may occasionally intervene in processes of transnational governance.

II.2 Interpretation

Transnational governance arrangements such as the one that allocates domains on the Internet hold a peculiar legal status. They escape from the thought patterns fixated on the state. In particular, they transcend the conventional dichotomies that have long dominated this tradition.

Firstly, transnational governance arrangements undermine the distinction between international and national law.[35] On the one hand, they cannot be qualified as international law, since they are neither created by inter-state treaties nor do they regulate inter-state relations. ICANN is a corporation according to Californian private law, and the rules issuing from the arrangement primarily address individual Internet users. Nevertheless, the World Intellectual Property Organization, as an international organisation, serves as a dispute resolution service provider under the UDRP. On the other hand, these arrangements cannot be classified as national law, since they neither emanate from national legislation nor do they exclusively affect national affairs. Although ICANN was subject to a contract with the US government and defers to national courts in domain disputes, it autonomously regulates the allocation of Internet domains across the globe.

Secondly, transnational governance arrangements subvert the distinction between public and private law.[36] On the one hand, regarding their

[34] Uniform Domain Name Dispute Resolution Policy, 26 August 1999, § 4(k), available at: www.icann.org/resources/pages/policy-2012-02-25-en, last accessed 31 January 2019.

[35] See Paul Schiff Berman, 'From International Law to Law and Globalization' (2005) 43 *Columbia Journal of Transnational Law*, 485–556; Harold Hongju Koh, 'Why Transnational Law Matters' (2006) 24 *Penn State International Law Review*, 745–53.

[36] See Gunther Teubner, 'Contracting Worlds: The Many Autonomies of Private Law' (2000) 9 *Social and Legal Studies*, 399–417; Peer Zumbansen, 'Neither "Public" nor

source, they result from the cooperation of various actors, both state and non-state. ICANN had long acted in agreement with the US government, which, at global level, recedes to a representative of particular interests for its part. At the same time, the advisory committees of ICANN comprise stakeholders from numerous other states and interest groups. On the other hand, regarding their subject matter, these arrangements touch not only upon the relationships of individual Internet users, but also upon concerns of society at large. Thus, the regulation of the Internet in general, and the allocation of domains in particular, are regarded as services of general interest because of their significance for enabling global information and communication.[37] The European Commission therefore concluded that ICANN takes 'decisions of a kind that governments would, in other contexts, expect to take themselves in the framework of international organisations'.[38]

Finally, regarding their medium, transnational governance arrangements break the distinction between statute and contract.[39] On the one hand, they are unable to enact rules that are generally binding. For this reason, ICANN, which was itself created by contract, allocates domains to individual Internet users *via* several registrars through bilateral agreements. On the other hand, all registration agreements indirectly impose a collective orientation by incorporating the dispute resolution mechanism of the UDRP as general terms and conditions. From this symbiosis, or 'network',[40] of contracts thus emerges a new form of collective order.

Transnational governance arrangements gain a relative autonomy by exclusively following their own 'secondary rules',[41] as defined by H.L.A.

"Private", "National" nor "International": Transnational Corporate Governance from a Legal Pluralist Perspective' (2011) 38 *Journal of Law and Society*, 50–75.

37 See Abdullah A. Al-Darrab, 'The Need for International Internet Governance Oversight', in: William J. Drake (ed.), *Reforming Internet Governance: Perspectives from the Working Group on Internet Governance* (New York: United Nations Information and Communication Technologies Task Force, 2005), pp. 177–83.

38 Commission of the European Communities, Communication from the Commission to the Council and the European Parliament, The Organisation and Management of the Internet: International and European Policy Issues 1998–2000, 11 April 2000, COM:2000:202:13.

39 See Gunther Teubner, 'Coincidentia Oppositorum: Hybrid Networks Beyond Contract and Organisation', in: Marc Amstutz and Gunther Teubner (eds.), *Networks: Legal Issues of Multilateral Co-operation* (Oxford-Portland OR: Hart Publishing, 2009), pp. 3–30; Marc Amstutz, 'The Constitution of Contractual Networks', ibid., pp. 309–46.

40 Gunther Teubner, *Networks as Connected Contracts* (Oxford-Portland OR: Hart Publishing, 2011).

41 Karel C. Wellens, 'Diversity in Secondary Rules and the Unity of International Law: Some Reflections on Current Trends' (1994) 25 *Netherlands Yearbook of International Law*, 3–37; Thomas Schultz, 'Secondary Rules of Recognition and Relative Legality in Transnational Regimes' (2011) 56 *American Journal of Jurisprudence*, 59–85.

Hart.[42] These secondary rules include not only rules of recognition, which allow for identifying the primary rules of obligation to be applied, but also rules of adjudication, which empower dispute resolution service providers to ascertain whether a primary rule of obligation has been violated on a particular occasion. Thus, Paragraph 15(a) UDRP-Rules prescribes all dispute resolution service providers recognised by ICANN to resolve disputes over domain names in accordance with the UDRP and all other rules and principles of law that they deem applicable.[43] In this way, the arrangement may operate self-referentially, similarly to the European Union, whose Court of Justice exclusively decides according to 'the law stemming from the treaty', which is hence considered as 'its own legal system'.[44]

III Transnational Constitutional Rights

Pursuant to a new approach proposed here, constitutional rights serve both as a foundation and as a limitation of transnational governance arrangements (Sub-section III.2). In this way, they also offer a solution to the problem of their legitimacy (Sub-section III.1).

III.1 Legitimacy

Since transnational governance arrangements such as that which allocates domains on the Internet are based on contracts and, therefore, are unable to enact rules that are generally binding, they do not raise a problem of legitimacy in the traditional sense of the term. On the contrary, contract by definition requires the approval of the parties so that it is regarded as 'the quintessential form of government with the consent of the governed'.[45] Within the national legal orders, such arrangements would be regarded as expressions of private autonomy

[42] H.L.A. Hart, *The Concept of Law* (Oxford: Clarendon Press, 1961), p. 91.

[43] Rules for Uniform Domain Name Dispute Resolution Policy, as approved 28 September 2013, § 15(a), available at: www.icann.org/resources/pages/udrp-rules-2015-03-11-en, last accessed 31 January 2019.

[44] ECJ, Judgment of 15 July 1964, Case 6/64, *Costa* v. *ENEL* (1964) *European Court Reports*, 585–600, at 593–4.

[45] Michael J. Trebilcock, *The Limits of Freedom of Contract* (Cambridge MA: Harvard University Press, 1993), p. 8. See also Reza Banakar, 'Reflexive Legitimacy in International Arbitration', in: Volkmar Gessner and Ali Cem Budak (eds.), *Emerging Legal Certainty: Empirical Studies on the Globalization of Law* (Aldershot: Ashgate Publishing, 1998), pp. 347–98.

and protected by constitutional rights, in particular freedom of contract and freedom of association. At the same time, however, national private law usually contains certain provisions of mandatory law that implement private autonomy and thus fulfil a constitutional function in the horizontal relations between individuals.[46] These provisions ensure that the parties have entered freely into a contract and protect the liberties of third parties from interference.[47]

Infringements on the freedom of contract and interference with the liberties of outsiders may also appear in the transnational context. On the one hand, unequal bargaining powers may considerably reduce party autonomy. Thus, the arrangement that allocates domains on the Internet holds a monopoly position in providing a service of general interest that is indispensable for realising freedom of information and speech under conditions of digital communication. It may therefore unilaterally impose the contractual terms for the registration of domains. On the other hand, such arrangements may significantly affect the liberties of third parties. Thus, the allocation of certain domain names may violate rights in names and trademarks.

Reformulated in this way, the issue may be addressed by a new approach to the 'horizontal effect'[48] of constitutional rights. According to this understanding, animated by systems theory of law,[49] constitutional rights are to be regarded as a social 'institution'[50] that upholds the differentiation of society and thereby indirectly generates collective order. Constitutional rights hence serve to enable and support the autonomous organisation of different social spheres, such as economics, religion, technology, arts and sciences, while, at the same time, preventing a single rationality from dominating society. Initially, the argument was

[46] See Dieter Grimm, 'Basic Rights in the Formative Era of Modern Society', in: Dieter Grimm, *Constitutionalism: Past, Present, and Future* (Oxford: Oxford University Press, 2016), p. 65.

[47] See Franz Bydlinski, *Privatautonomie und objektive Grundlagen des verpflichtenden Rechtsgeschäftes* (Wien: Springer, 1967).

[48] For the doctrine of 'horizontal effect' of constitutional rights within the state, see Stephen Gardbaum, 'The "Horizontal Effect" of Constitutional Rights' (2003) 102 *Michigan Law Review*, 387–459; Johan van der Walt, *The Horizontal Effect Revolution and the Question of Sovereignty* (Berlin: De Gruyter, 2014).

[49] See generally Niklas Luhmann, *Law as a Social System* (Oxford: Oxford University Press, 2014); Gunther Teubner, *Law as an Autopoietic System* (Oxford: Blackwell, 1993).

[50] Niklas Luhmann, *Grundrechte als Institution: Ein Beitrag zur politischen Soziologie* (Berlin: Duncker and Humblot, 1965).

advanced only with regard to the relationship between the political and the other social spheres within the state,[51] but its scope may be generalised, especially in the transnational context, which lacks a central political legislator.[52]

Such a conception reverses the supposedly 'classical'[53] function of constitutional rights as negative, or defensive, rights of the individual against the state in a double sense. On the one hand, it extends the circle of rights holders, including not only individuals, but also other social systems and institutions, in particular processes of societal self-regulation. Nevertheless, it does not abandon the protection of the individual and the system of remedies based upon subjective rights. On the other hand, this conception broadens the group of those obliged to respect constitutional rights, binding not only the state, but also other social systems and institutions that could develop totalitarian tendencies.

Philosophical and historical enquiries confirm that such a conception of constitutional rights only restores their original function. From a philosophical point of view, the understanding of constitutional rights as the defensive rights of the individual against the state reduces Immanuel Kant's notion of right, which had a decisive influence on modern constitutionalism. It does not reconcile the freedom of one with the other, in general, according to a universal law of freedom, but only that of the citizen with that of the state.[54] From a historical point of view, referring back to the French Revolution, constitutional rights had initially served as guiding principles for transforming the social order in accordance with the principles of freedom and equality. Only

[51] Ibid., p. 187.

[52] See Gunther Teubner, 'The Anonymous Matrix: Human Rights Violations by "Private" Transnational Actors' (2006) 69 *Modern Law Review*, 327–46; Karl-Heinz Ladeur and Lars Viellechner, 'Die transnationale Expansion staatlicher Grundrechte: Zur Konstitutionalisierung globaler Privatrechtsregimes' (2008) 46 *Archiv des Völkerrechts*, 42–73.

[53] Bernhard Schlink, 'Freiheit durch Eingriffsabwehr: Rekonstruktion der klassischen Grundrechtsfunktion' (1984) 11 *Europäische Grundrechte-Zeitschrift*, 457–68; David P. Currie, 'Positive and Negative Constitutional Rights' (1986) 53 *University of Chicago Law Review*, 864–90.

[54] See Ernst-Wolfgang Böckenförde, 'Fundamental Rights as Constitutional Principles: On the Current State of Interpreting Fundamental Rights', in: Ernst-Wolfgang Böckenförde, *Constitutional and Political Theory: Selected Writings*, Vol. 1 (Oxford: Oxford University Press, 2017), pp. 235–65, at 258.

afterwards did they fall back to their function as rights of defence against the state.[55]

III.2 Foundation and Limitation

In this view, constitutional rights serve both as a foundation and as a limitation of constitutional governance arrangements such as the one that allocates domains on the Internet.

On the one hand, they enable and protect these arrangements not only because they make use of their private liberties, but also because they contribute to creating an order that benefits the entire society and is not available elsewhere.[56] As a matter of fact, there is no consensus on creating an international organisation that could assume the task of allocating domains on the Internet. At the same time, the regulation of the Internet by a single state, such as the United States, would not be acceptable from a normative point of view, even if it were technically feasible. From an epistemological perspective, finally, societal self-regulation of the Internet may appear even superior to regulation by either national legislation or international treaty making. In complex subject matters, political regulators sometimes lack the knowledge required in order to take fully informed decisions.[57] Especially in the field of technology, which is subject to rapid evolution, they may encounter insurmountable cognitive limits. By contrast, transnational governance arrangements, which are deeply embedded within the respective social spheres, may instantly absorb the implicit knowledge dispersed there. For example, ICANN evolved from an initiative around the computer scientists and technicians who invented the Internet domain system.[58] As this development demonstrates, societal interaction in transnational governance arrangements may not only, and even not primarily, serve selfish ends, but enable movements of research and processes of innovation, the findings of which others may profit from as well. In its regulatory activity, the arrangement that allocates domains

[55] See Grimm, n. 46 above, p. 76.

[56] See Karl-Heinz Ladeur, 'Discursive Ethics as Constitutional Theory: Neglecting the Creative Role of Economic Liberties?' (2000) 13 *Ratio Juris*, 95–116; Thomas Vesting, 'The Autonomy of Law and the Formation of Network Standards' (2004) 5 *German Law Journal*, 639–68.

[57] See generally Friedrich A. von Hayek, 'Die Anmaßung von Wissen' (1975) 26 *Ordo*, 12–21.

[58] See Mueller, n. 12 above, pp. 73–208.

on the Internet is therefore protected by the constitutional rights to freedom of information and speech.[59]

On the other hand, however, horizontal constitutional rights as proposed here also constrain transnational governance arrangements, notably to avoid their self-destruction and excessive expansion. To this purpose, they not only comprise a negative, that is defensive, but also a positive component.

In a negative sense, they provide protection for both shareholders and outsiders against transnational governance arrangements.[60] For example, in the so-called 'cybergriping'[61] cases, in which domain names reproduce the names of persons or brands supplemented by pejorative suffixes, such as 'sucks', in order to express criticism, ICANN must respect not only personality and intellectual property rights, but also the right to freedom of speech.

In a positive sense, horizontal constitutional rights as proposed here allow for equal participation and consideration in transnational governance arrangements when they hold a monopoly in providing a service that is indispensable for realising freedom.[62] Since there is no central political legislator in the transnational context, the positive component is particularly important. It would be inadequate, however, to speak of 'democratisation'[63] in this regard. More precisely, the issue is to render

[59] See Achilles Skordas, 'Self-Determination of Peoples and Transnational Regimes: A Foundational Principle of Global Governance', in: Nicholas Tsagourias (ed.), *Transnational Constitutionalism: International and European Models* (Cambridge: Cambridge University Press, 2007), pp. 207–68; David R. Johnson and David G. Post, 'Law and Borders: The Rise of Law in Cyberspace' (1996) 48 *Stanford Law Review*, 1367–1402, at 1393: 'If there is one central principle on which all local authorities within the Net should agree, it must be that territorially local claims to a right to restrict online transactions (in ways unrelated to vital and localized interests of a territorial government) should be resisted. This is the Net equivalent of the First Amendment, a principle already recognized in the form of the international human rights doctrine protecting the right to communicate.'

[60] See Gunther Teubner and Vaios Karavas, 'http://www.CompanyNameSucks.com: The Horizontal Effect of Fundamental Rights on "Private Parties" within Autonomous Internet Law' (2005) 12 *Constellations*, 262–82.

[61] Rebecca S. Sorgen, 'Trademark Confronts Free Speech on the Information Superhighway: "Cybergripers" Face a Constitutional Collision' (2001) 22 *Loyola of Los Angeles Entertainment Law Review*, 115–52; Adam Goldstein, 'ICANNSucks.biz (And Why You Can't Say That): How Fair Use of Trademarks in Domain Names Is Being Restrained' (2002) 12 *Fordham Intellectual Property, Media and Entertainment Law Journal*, 1151–86.

[62] See Viellechner, n. 11 above, pp. 453–4; Gunther Teubner, *Constitutional Fragments: Societal Constitutionalism and Globalization* (Oxford: Oxford University Press, 2012), pp. 136–9.

[63] But see Oliver Gerstenberg, 'Private Law, Constitutionalism and the Limits of the Judicial Role', in: Craig Scott (ed.), *Torture as Tort: Comparative Perspectives on the Development of Transnational Human Rights Litigation* (Oxford-Portland OR: Hart Publishing, 2001), pp. 687–703.

transnational governance arrangements 'responsive'[64] towards their societal environment. In this way, they are required to take into account the conflicting interests of the persons and institutions affected by their activities.[65] For example, as ICANN holds a monopoly in allocating domains on the Internet and communication on the Internet is impossible without a domain, the rights to freedom of information and speech, as well as the right to equality, ensure that applications for second-level domains that have not yet been registered are not arbitrarily rejected. Moreover, when ICANN intends to create new top-level domains, such as '.xxx' for pornographic sites, it must equally consider the conflicting rights to freedom of speech, freedom of profession and concerns of youth protection.[66]

Such a conception of constitutional rights may provoke a double objection. A critique from an internal point of view may reveal a self-contradiction. Apparently, this conception aims at both differentiation and integration of society simultaneously. At times, it calls for protection of social systems and institutions in order to maintain a variegated order. At other times, it allows for intervention so as to improve participation in social systems and institutions.[67] A critique from an external point of view may further detect a category error. Allegedly, this conception tries to solve problems of collective self-determination by employing means of individual self-determination. In this way, it seems to overstretch the capacities of constitutional rights.[68]

In the transnational context, which lacks a central political legislator, however, these objections lose significance. When both states and international organisations fail, society must necessarily regulate itself. Collective order may then only result accidentally from societal interaction.[69] Intentional design is only possible by means of

[64] Lars Viellechner, 'Responsive Legal Pluralism: The Emergence of Transnational Conflicts Law' (2015) 6 *Transnational Legal Theory*, 312–32.

[65] See also Gunther Teubner, 'Substantive and Reflexive Elements in Modern Law' (1983) 17 *Law and Society Review*, 239–85.

[66] See Patty Chan, 'Safer (Cyber)Sex with .xxx: The Case for First Amendment Zoning of the Internet' (2006) 39 *Loyola of Los Angeles Law Review*, 1299–1337.

[67] See Oliver Lepsius, *Steuerungsdiskussion, Systemtheorie und Parlamentarismuskritik* (Tübingen: Mohr Siebeck, 1999), p. 70.

[68] See Oliver Lepsius, 'Braucht das Verfassungsrecht eine Theorie des Staates? Eine deutsche Perspektive: Von der Staatstheorie zur Theorie der Herrschaftsformen' (2004) 31 *Europäische Grundrechte-Zeitschrift*, 370–81, at 380.

[69] See Karl-Heinz Ladeur, 'The Role of Contracts and Networks in Public Governance: The Importance of the "Social Epistemology" of Decision Making' (2007) 14 *Indiana Journal of Global Legal Studies*, 329–51.

contract.[70] Under these conditions, the internal relationship between democracy and constitutional rights needs to be reformulated. It must be adapted to the changing circumstances in order to ensure a constant protection of freedom.

IV Transnational Legal Process

An adequate protection of constitutional rights in the transnational context has not yet been achieved. For the time being, it may only succeed through a dialectical process that oscillates between the internal constitutionalisation of transnational governance arrangements (Sub-section IV.1) and the external constitutionalisation provided by the national legal orders (Sub-section IV.2).

IV.1 Internal Constitutionalisation

Systems theory of law claims that transnational governance arrangements are able to establish their own constitutions.[71] As its proponents explain, these societal constitutions do not result from any visible act of constituent power. Rather, they emerge incrementally and pass through several stages of evolution, similar to the common law. Purportedly, each process of juridification presupposes latent constitutional norms that are created at the very time of their application and hence remain inseparable from the ordinary norms.[72] Constitutional norms of this kind include not only rules of recognition, such as Paragraph 15(a) UDRP-Rules, but also fundamental rights.

Indeed, some panels appointed to decide domain disputes invoke the right to freedom of speech, although the UDRP does not explicitly provide for such a right. They notably proceed in this way when they deal with issues of 'cybergriping'. In an early case, a dispute resolution panel appointed by the Arbitration and Mediation Center of the World Intellectual Property Organization proclaimed in a principled manner:

> Although free speech is not listed as one of the Policy's examples of a right or legitimate interest in a domain name, the list is not exclusive, and the

[70] See Peer Zumbansen, 'The Law of Society: Governance through Contract' (2007) 14 *Indiana Journal of Global Legal Studies*, 191–233.

[71] See Gunther Teubner, 'Societal Constitutionalism: Alternatives to State-Centred Constitutional Theory?', in: Christian Joerges, Inger-Johanne Sand and Gunther Teubner (eds.), *Transnational Governance and Constitutionalism* (Oxford-Portland OR: Hart Publishing, 2004), pp. 3–28.

[72] Ibid., p. 18; for a more detailed account, see Teubner, n. 62 above, pp. 73–123.

> Panel concludes that the exercise of free speech for criticism and commentary also demonstrates a right or legitimate interest in the domain name under Paragraph 4(c)(iii). The Internet is above all a framework for global communication, and the right to free speech should be one of the foundations of Internet law.[73]

Several other panels share this view. Yet, they employ different methods in order to reach their aim. Some of them refer to the right to freedom of speech guaranteed by the First Amendment to the Constitution of the United States of America.[74] Others determine the applicable law according to the rules of private international law of the competent national jurisdiction.[75] Still others refuse to apply national law in these transnational disputes as a matter of principle. Instead, they rely on the Universal Declaration of Human Rights of the United Nations,[76] international treaties, such as the International Covenant on Civil and Political Rights,[77] or the European Convention on Human Rights,[78] as well as general principles of law.[79] Finally, some panels apply national and international law sources simultaneously.[80]

More recently, many panels simply follow the large number of precedents rendered on the same issue.[81] A noteworthy decision not only identifies a specific right of the UDRP that allows using a trademark as

[73] WIPO AMC, Decision of 6 July 2000, Case D2000-0190, *Bridgestone Firestone, Inc. et al.* v. *Jack Myers.*

[74] WIPO AMC, Decision of 5 August 2000, Case D2000-0536, *TMP Worldwide Inc.* v. *Jennifer L. Potter*; Decision of 10 July 2009, Case D2009-0693, *Sutherland Institute* v. *Continuative LLC.*

[75] WIPO AMC, Decision of 22 April 2004, Case D2004-0014, *Howard Jarvis Taxpayers Association* v. *Paul McCauley*; Decision of 2 July 2008, Case D2008-0647, *Sermo, Inc.* v. *CatalystMD, LLC.*

[76] WIPO AMC, Decision of 14 November 2007, Case D2007-1379, *Chelsea and Westminster Hospital NHS Foundation Trust* v. *Frank Redmond*; Decision of 10 November 2014, Case D2014-1590, *Fiskars Corporation* v. *Whois Privacy Service/James Taverner.*

[77] WIPO AMC, Decision of 23 November 2009, Case D2009-1295, *Coast Hotels Ltd* v. *Bill Lewis and Unite Here.*

[78] WIPO AMC, Decision of 10 January 2002, Case D2001-1318, *British Nuclear Fuels Plc* v. *Greenpeace International*; Decision of 23 October 2006, Case D2006-1066, *Moss and Coleman Solicitors* v. *Rick Kordowski.*

[79] WIPO AMC, Decision of 18 January 2008, Case D2007-1461, *1066 Housing Association Ltd* v. *Mr. D. Morgan*; Decision of 8 March 2016, Case D2016-0110, *Visit Faroe IslandsP/F* v. *Pilot Whale, Save the Whales.*

[80] WIPO AMC, Decision of 23 September 2014, Case D2014-1331, *Petroleo Brasileiro SA – Petrobas* v. *Ivo Lucio Santana Marcelino Da Silva.*

[81] Among the first decisions employing this reasoning were WIPO AMC, Decision of 13 February 2008, Case D2007-1887, *Thorsten Rathmann* v. *Administrator Lunarpages and Customer of Lunarpages*; Decision of 17 April 2008, Case D2008-0274, *Escada AG* v. *Phil Mitchell.*

a domain name in order to express criticism, but also extracts the precise content of this right from previous decisions:

> [T]his Panel suggests that a registrant of a domain name is likely to have a right or legitimate interest in a domain name which is identical or confusingly similar to a mark of another party in accordance with paragraph 4(c)(iii) of the Policy if the following conditions are met: (a) the domain name has been registered and is being used genuinely for the purpose of criticising the owner of the mark; (b) the registrant believes the criticism to be well-founded; (c) the registrant has no intent for commercial gain; (d) it is immediately apparent to Internet users visiting the website at the domain name that it is not a website of the owner of the mark; (e) the respondent has not registered all or most of the obvious domain names suitable for the owner of the mark; (f) where the domain name is one of the obvious domain names suitable for the owner of the mark, a prominent and appropriate link is provided to the latter's website (if any); (g) where there is a likelihood that email intended for the complainant will be sent using the domain name in issue, senders are immediately alerted in an appropriate way that their emails have been misaddressed.[82]

Nevertheless, the dispute resolution practice is still unclear regarding both the foundation and the content of the right to freedom of speech under the UDRP. Regarding the foundation, some panels expressly speak of a fundamental right proper to the UDRP.[83] Others merely recognise a counter-right or a legitimate interest according to Paragraph 4(a)(ii) UDRP.[84] Yet others categorically deny their competence to take a decision of constitutional significance:

> Panelists are private citizens who are given a very limited brief by commercial contract between private parties, and accountable only to the private provider that has engaged them. Even if the consequences be limited to a single domain name, it is wholly inappropriate for a panelist to make a judgment with Constitutional import.[85]

[82] WIPO AMC, Decision of 25 February 2008, Case D2007-1947, *Fundación Calvin Ayre Foundation* v. *Erik Deutsch.*

[83] WIPO AMC, Decision of 6 November 2000, Case D2000-1171, *Migros Genossenschaftsbund* v. *Centro Consulenze Kim Paloschi*; Decision of 14 April 2004, Case D2004-0032, *Hollenbeck Youth Center, Inc.* v. *Stephen Rowland.*

[84] WIPO AMC, Decision of 5 September 2002, Case D2002-0596, *Akerman, Senterfitt and Eidson, P.A.* v. *American Distribution Systems, Inc. d/b/a DefaultData.com*; Decision of 22 October 2008, Case D2008-1234, *Union Square Partnership, Inc. et al.* v. *unionsquarepartnership.com Private Registrant et al.*

[85] WIPO AMC, Decision of 11 December 2006, Case D2006-1230, *InMed Diagnostic Services, LLC et al.* v. *James Harrison.*

Regarding the content of the right to freedom of speech under the UDRP, there is disagreement in two respects. On the one hand, opinions differ on the preliminary question of whether the use of a trademark with a pejorative suffix such as 'sucks' can cause a risk of confusion in the sense of Paragraph 4(a)(i) UDRP that would require justification.[86] On the other hand, decisions contradict each other on the question of whether the use of a trademark without a pejorative suffix is protected by the right to freedom of speech when the website thus designated contains criticism.[87]

The internal constitutionalisation of transnational governance arrangements such as the one that allocates domains on the Internet hence remains uncertain. Dispute resolution service providers may not only take divergent decisions, but also refuse to provide fundamental rights protection at all, especially since there is no obligation to follow precedents under the UDRP. There is only hope that external pressure might induce a self-restraint of transnational governance arrangements.

IV.2 External Constitutionalisation

As long as transnational governance arrangements do not guarantee adequate protection of constitutional rights, they must therefore be complemented by the national legal orders. In the arrangement that allocates domains on the Internet this is possible as Paragraph 4(k) UDRP explicitly allows for actions to be brought before national courts. Such kind of containment might be called 'external constitutionalisation'[88] and follow a model that is already established for the relationship between national legal orders and international organisations, as well as several international organisations

[86] On the one hand, WIPO AMC, Decision of 19 September 2000, Case D2000-0662, *Wal-Mart Stores, Inc.* v. *Richard MacLeod d/b/a For Sale*; Decision of 11 August 2016, Case D2016-0951, *Royal Institution of Chartered Surveyors* v. *Martin Rushton*; on the other hand, WIPO AMC, Decision of 26 January 2001, Case D2000-1015, *Lockheed Martin Corporation* v. *Dan Parisi*; Decision of 18 June 2001, Case D2001-0212, *The Royal Bank of Scotland Group Plc* v. *natwestfraud.com and Umang Malhotra.*

[87] On the one hand, WIPO AMC, Decision of 18 December 2000, Case D2000-1314, *Skattedirektoratet* v. *Eivind Nag*; Decision of 9 July 2014, Case D2014-0780, *Mr. Willem Vedovi and Galerie Vedovi S.A.* v. *Domains By Proxy, LLC/Jane Kelly*; on the other hand, WIPO AMC, Decision of 6 July 2000, Case D2000-0190, *Bridgestone Firestone, Inc. et al.* v. *Jack Myers*; Decision of 25 February 2008, Case D2007-1947, *Fundación Calvin Ayre Foundation* v. *Erik Deutsch.*

[88] For the distinction between an external and internal point of view in legal theory, see Hart, n. 42 above, pp. 86–8.

including the same member states among each other. According to this model, the various legal orders may, by means of mutual judicial assistance, compensate the gaps in the protection of constitutional rights that exist elsewhere.[89]

Thus, the Federal Constitutional Court of Germany has declared in its famous 'Solange' decision that it will only relinquish its competence to decide on the applicability of European Union law in Germany as long as the European Union guarantees a protection of fundamental rights 'which is to be regarded as substantially similar to the protection of fundamental rights required unconditionally by the Basic Law'.[90] Similarly, the European Court of Human Rights holds that state action taken in compliance with obligations resulting from the membership in an international organisation 'is justified as long as the relevant organisation is considered to protect fundamental rights, as regards both the substantive guarantees offered and the mechanisms controlling their observance, in a manner which can be considered at least equivalent to that for which the Convention provides'.[91] In the same vein, the Court of Justice of the European Union scrutinises the regulations of the European Union that implement resolutions of the United Nations Security Council sanctioning persons suspected of terrorism as long as the review procedure offered by the United Nations 'does not offer the guarantees of judicial protection'.[92]

The construction of a transnational dimension of constitutional rights is possible in all national legal orders across the Western tradition. It is particularly easy in Germany where the objective component of constitutional rights may serve as a gateway. The Federal Constitutional Court of Germany has already deduced several new dimensions from it, including an indirect horizontal effect in civil

[89] See, also, Nikolaos Lavranos, 'The Solange-Method as a Tool for Regulating Competing Jurisdictions Among International Courts and Tribunals' (2008) 30 *Loyola of Los Angeles International and Comparative Law Review*, 275–334; Antonios Tzanakopoulos, 'Judicial Dialogue in Multi-Level Governance: The Impact of the Solange Argument', in: Ole Kristian Fauchald and André Nollkaemper (eds.), *The Practice of International and National Courts and the (De-)Fragmentation of International Law* (Oxford: Hart Publishing, 2012), pp. 185–215.

[90] BVerfG, Decision of 22 October 1986, Case 2 BvR 197/83, *Solange II*, 73 *Entscheidungen des Bundesverfassungsgerichts*, 339–88, at 387.

[91] ECHR, Judgment of 30 June 2005, Case 45036/98, *Bosphorus* v. *Ireland*, § 155.

[92] ECJ, Judgment of 3 September 2008, Joined Cases C-402/05 P et al., *Kadi and Al Barakaat* v. *Council and Commission* (2008) *European Court Reports*, I-6351, § 322.

law,[93] a protective function of the state,[94] positive rights,[95] procedural guarantees[96] and organisational principles.[97] When other new dangers arise for fundamental rights in the transnational context, it becomes once more necessary to adapt the law to the changing circumstances. The constitutional principle of 'open statehood'[98] enshrined in the Basic Law for the Federal Republic of Germany then calls for ensuring protection of constitutional rights also with regard to transnational governance arrangements. In this respect, the objective component of constitutional rights may yet again prove to be a dynamic principle that adapts the law to social change and safeguards freedom in the face of alternating conditions.[99]

To date, the German courts have only ruled on domain disputes relating to the country code top-level domain '.de', for which the Deutsches Network Information Center eG (DENIC),[100] a private organisation authorised by ICANN and based in Frankfurt, Germany, distributes second-level domains. Here, they do not hesitate to invoke the right to freedom of speech guaranteed by Article 5(1) of the German Basic Law in 'cybergriping' cases. For example, the Higher Regional Court of Hamburg held, in a dispute concerning the domain 'awd-aussteiger.de', on which former clients criticised the business practices of a financial service provider:

93 BVerfG, Judgment of 15 January 1958, Case 1 BvR 400/51, *Lüth*, 7 *Entscheidungen des Bundesverfassungsgerichts*, 198–230, at 205–7.

94 BVerfG, Judgment of 25 February 1975, Joined Cases 1 BvF 1/74 et al., *Schwangerschaftsabbruch I*, 39 *Entscheidungen des Bundesverfassungsgerichts*, 1–95, at 41–4.

95 BVerfG, Judgment of 18 July 1972, Joined Cases 1 BvL 32/70 et al., *Numerus Clausus I*, 33 *Entscheidungen des Bundesverfassungsgerichts*, 303–58, at 330–5; Judgment of 9 February 2010, Joined Cases 1 BvL 1/09 et al., *Hartz IV*, 125 *Entscheidungen des Bundesverfassungsgerichts*, 175–260, at 222.

96 BVerfG, Decision of 20 December 1979, Case 1 BvR 385/77, *Mülheim-Kärlich*, 53 *Entscheidungen des Bundesverfassungsgerichts*, 30–96, at 57–61.

97 BVerfG, Judgment of 16 June 1981, Case 1 BvL 89/87, *Rundfunkentscheidung III*, 57 *Entscheidungen des Bundesverfassungsgerichts*, 295–335, at 320.

98 BVerfG, Judgment of 26 March 1957, Case 2 BvG 1/55, *Reichskonkordat*, 6 *Entscheidungen des Bundesverfassungsgerichts*, 309–66, at 362; Klaus Vogel, *Die Verfassungsentscheidung des Grundgesetzes für eine internationale Zusammenarbeit: Ein Diskussionsbeitrag zu einer Frage der Staatstheorie sowie des geltenden deutschen Staatsrechts* (Tübingen: Mohr Siebeck, 1964), p. 42.

99 See, also, Dieter Grimm, 'Return to the Traditional Understanding of Fundamental Rights?', in: Dieter Grimm, *Constitutionalism: Past, Present, and Future* (Oxford: Oxford University Press, 2016), pp. 183–96.

100 Deutsches Network Information Center eG, founded 1 December 1996, available at: www.denic.de, last accessed 31 January 2019.

> 'The defendant does not intend to promote unfair competition, but to criticise the plaintiff. This is as such not an unlawful undertaking. Rather the defendant may invoke the fundamental right to freedom of speech according to Article 5 of the Basic Law.'[101]

The external constitutionalisation of transnational governance arrangements may equally be achieved through the means of civil law. Thus, the Regional Court of Bremen dismissed an action of the public transport company *Bremer Straßenbahn AG* (BSAG) against the use of the domain 'bsagmeckerseite.de' because it did not find any likelihood of confusion pursuant to Paragraph 15(2) of the German Trade Mark Act or a violation of interests pursuant to Paragraph 12 of the German Civil Code.[102]

Civil law institutions also lend themselves for the external constitutionalisation of transnational governance arrangements in national legal orders that do not know of any horizontal effect of constitutional rights.[103] In the Anglo-American jurisdictions, common law might likewise assume this task. Thanks to its flexibility, it is especially well suited for such an undertaking.[104] Apart from this, even the national legal orders that rely on a rigorous state-action doctrine might follow the German model when it comes to confining transnational governance arrangements. As one commentator points out for the Constitution of the United States of America:

> We must decide on our own what makes better sense of our constitutional tradition. Is it more faithful to our tradition to allow these structures of control, the functional equivalent of law, to develop outside the scope of constitutional review? Or to extend constitutional review to the structures of private regulation, to preserve those fundamental values within our tradition? These are hard questions, though it is useful to note that they are not as hard to ask in other constitutional regimes. The German tradition, for example, would have less trouble with the idea that private structures of power must ultimately be checked against fundamental constitutional values.[105]

[101] OLG Hamburg, Judgment of 18 December 2003, Case 3 U 117/03, *awd-aussteiger.de* (2004) 7 *Multimedia und Recht*, 415–18, at 418 (my translation).

[102] LG Bremen, Judgment of 30 January 2003, Case 12 O 383/02, *bsagmeckerseite.de* (2003) 7 *Zeitschrift für Urheber- und Medienrecht – Rechtsprechungsdienst*, 360–2.

[103] See Robert Wai, 'Transnational Private Law and Private Ordering in a Contested Global Society' (2005) 46 *Harvard International Law Journal*, 471–86; Horatia Muir Watt, 'Private International Law Beyond the Schism' (2011) 2 *Transnational Legal Theory*, 347–428.

[104] See Henry H. Perritt, Jr., 'Towards a Hybrid Regulatory Scheme for the Internet' (2001) 16 *University of Chicago Legal Forum*, 215–322, at 280.

[105] Lawrence Lessig, *Code and Other Laws of Cyberspace* (New York: Basic Books, 1999), pp. 217–18. See, also, Paul Schiff Berman, 'Cyberspace and the State Action Debate: The

Some American courts have already taken this path. For example, a Court of Appeal held, in a dispute over a domain name that added a critical suffix to the designation of a shopping centre

> We find that Mishkoff's use of Taubman's mark in the domain name 'taubmansucks.com' is purely an exhibition of Free Speech . . . . And although economic damage might be an intended effect of Mishkoff's expression, the First Amendment protects critical commentary when there is no confusion as to source, even when it involves the criticism of a business.[106]

It does not seem appropriate, however, to apply national constitutional rights exclusively in cases that imply a cross-border aspect. Especially with regard to disputes over Internet domains, such a choice of law would be random and undemocratic as far as foreigners are concerned. The transnational dimension of constitutional rights should therefore be considered as a conflict-of-laws rule dealing with the relationship between national legal orders and transnational governance arrangements.[107] This rule does not refer to any single foreign legal order, either. Instead, it requires the applicable law in these cases to be determined according to a method called the 'substantive law approach'[108] in conflict-of-laws scholarship. A new substantive norm

Cultural Value of Applying Constitutional Norms to "Private" Regulation' (2000) 71 *University of Colorado Law Review*, 1263–1310.

106 CA (6th Cir), Judgment of 7 February 2003, Case 01-2648, *Taubman* v. *Webfeats and Mishkoff*, 319 F.3d, 770–80, at 778.

107 For the idea to transfer the concepts of conflict of laws to transnational governance, see Robert Wai, 'Transnational Liftoff and Juridical Touchdown: The Regulatory Function of Private International Law in an Era of Globalization' (2002) 40 *Columbia Journal of Transnational Law*, 209–74; Paul Schiff Berman, 'Conflict of Laws, Globalization, and Cosmopolitan Pluralism' (2005) 51 *Wayne Law Review*, 1105–45; Jacco Bomhoff, 'The Reach of Rights: "The Foreign" and "the Private" in Conflict-of-Laws, State-Action, and Fundamental-Rights Cases with Foreign Elements' (2008) 71 *Law and Contemporary Problems*, 39–71; Christian Joerges, 'A New Type of Conflicts Law as the Legal Paradigm of the Postnational Constellation', in: Christian Joerges and Josef Falke (eds.), *Karl Polanyi, Globalisation and the Potential of Law in Transnational Markets* (Oxford-Portland OR: Hart Publishing, 2011), pp. 465–501; Teubner, n. 62 above, pp. 150–73; Karen Knop, Ralf Michaels and Annelise Riles, 'International Law in Domestic Courts: A Conflict of Laws Approach' (2009) 103 *American Society of International Law Proceedings*, 269–74; Horatia Muir Watt, 'Conflicts of Laws Unbounded: The Case for a Legal-Pluralist Revival' (2016) 7 *Transnational Legal Theory*, 313–53; Christopher A. Whytock, 'Conflict of Laws, Global Governance, and Transnational Legal Order' (2016) 1 *UC Irvine Journal of International, Transnational, and Comparative Law*, 117–40.

108 Arthur Taylor von Mehren, 'Special Substantive Rules for Multistate Problems: Their Role and Significance in Contemporary Choice of Law Methodology' (1974) 88 *Harvard Law Review*, 347–71.

that comprises elements of all the legal orders concerned should, hence, be formed.[109]

Such an approach may raise serious concerns for its part. From a methodological point of view, it is extremely challenging. Not only does it place a special responsibility on judges, but it also requires comparative knowledge and skills that would need to be acquired through some new form of 'transnational legal education'.[110] Moreover, regarding democracy and separation of powers, the approach appears as highly problematic. It doubles the 'counter-majoritarian difficulty'[111] since judges are allowed to make rules by a possibly even arbitrary resort to foreign law. The assessment turns out more favourably, though, if it is acknowledged that the issue here is not to invalidate statutes enacted by a democratically elected legislator, but self-given rules of transnational governance arrangements. In this respect, the judges ensure that the legitimate concerns of all those affected by the rules, but not heard elsewhere, are duly taken into account.[112]

V Conclusion

The adequate standard of constitutional rights protection in the transnational context may then eventually arise from a dialectical process of mutual observation, recognition and contestation between national legal orders and transnational governance arrangements. While any competent court or arbitrator seized may take an authoritative decision, none of them may claim to have the last word. In this dialectical process of

[109] See, also, Eugen Langen, *Transnational Commercial Law* (Leiden: Sijthoff, 1973), p. 33; Graeme B. Dinwoodie, 'A New Copyright Order: Why National Courts Should Create Global Norms' (2000) 149 *University of Pennsylvania Law Review*, 469–580; Paul Schiff Berman, 'Towards a Cosmopolitan Vision of Conflict of Laws: Redefining Governmental Interest in a Global Era' (2005) 153 *University of Pennsylvania Law Review*, 1819–82; Gunther Teubner and Peter Korth, 'Two Kinds of Legal Pluralism: Collision of Transnational Regimes in the Double Fragmentation of World Society', in: Margaret A. Young (ed.), *Regime Interaction in International Law: Facing Fragmentation* (Cambridge: Cambridge University Press, 2012), pp. 23–54.

[110] Sébastien Lebel-Grenier, 'What Is a Transnational Legal Education?' (2006) 56 *Journal of Legal Education*, 190–5; César Arjona et al., 'What Law for Transnational Legal Education? A Cooperative View of an Introductory Course to Transnational Law and Governance' (2015) 6 *Transnational Legal Theory*, 253–86.

[111] Alexander M. Bickel, *The Least Dangerous Branch: The Supreme Court at the Bar of Politics* (Indianapolis IN: Bobbs-Merrill, 1962), p. 16.

[112] See Gerstenberg, n. 63 above, at 698–701; Paul Schiff Berman, 'The Globalization of Jurisdiction' (2002) 151 *University of Pennsylvania Law Review*, 311–545, at 520–1.

constitutionalising transnational governance arrangements, the national courts incur a 'double function',[113] or role splitting, that is already known from the implementation of public international law. On the one hand, they act as national agents. On the other, they support a transnational rule of law.[114] Arguably, the mere possibility of recourse to national courts may incite transnational governance arrangements to respect the appropriate legal standards.[115]

The judicial reconciliation of the various legal orders would be greatly enhanced if it were supported by a procedural commitment to deal with precedents that might be called 'default deference'.[116] Such a mode of decision making lies between *stare decisis* and persuasive authority. It allows for deviation from precedents, but only when there are convincing reasons. The mutual recognition and contestation of the various legal orders through the dialogue of judges and arbitrators may thus even bear some democratic potential. As it allows for articulating opposition, it can, at least to some extent, compensate for the lack of parliamentary legislation in the transnational context.[117]

113 Georges Scelle, *Précis de droit des gens: Principes et systématique*, Vol. 1 (Paris: Sirey, 1932), p. 43.

114 See Anne-Marie Slaughter, 'A Global Community of Courts' (2003) 44 *Harvard International Law Journal*, 191–219; Paul Schiff Berman, 'Judges as Cosmopolitan Transnational Actors' (2004) 12 *Tulsa Journal of Comparative and International Law*, 109–21; Sabino Cassese, *I tribunali di Babele: I giudici alla ricerca di un nuovo ordine globale* (Rome: Donzelli, 2009).

115 See Perritt, n. 104 above, at 266.

116 Andreas Fischer-Lescano and Gunther Teubner, 'Regime-Collisions: The Vain Search for Legal Unity in the Fragmentation of Global Law' (2004) 25 *Michigan Journal of International Law*, 999–1046, at 1039.

117 See Karl-Heinz Ladeur, 'Globalization and the Conversion of Democracy to Polycentric Networks: Can Democracy Survive the End of the Nation-State?', in: Karl-Heinz Ladeur (ed.), *Public Governance in the Age of Globalization* (Aldershot: Ashgate Publishing, 2004), pp. 89–118; Nico Krisch, *Beyond Constitutionalism: The Pluralist Structure of Postnational Law* (Oxford: Oxford University Press, 2010), pp. 264–76.

15

Counter-Rights

On the Trans-Subjective Potential of Subjective Rights*

GUNTHER TEUBNER

I Christoph Menke's Critique of Subjective Rights in Modernity

In his influential book, *Critique of Rights*, Christoph Menke has refined the time-honoured theory of subjective rights in important respects.[1] The following reflections build on his theory, but modify it with the argument that, after the transformations of late-modern society, the political relevance of subjective rights lies not so much in their role as individual entitlements. Rather, they have developed a trans-subjective potential in three dimensions – in the communicative, the collective, and the institutional, dimension. If this potential is to be realised, a liberation of the, as Menke calls it, 'pre-conceptual affection' of subjective rights in law, politics and society will be required.

In some respects, Menke bases his analysis on Niklas Luhmann, who has offered the most significant recent theory of subjective rights; Menke moves, however, beyond Luhmann at crucial points. Luhmann has attributed subjective rights a central role in the historical process of functional differentiation, but, in the end, he has described them merely as transitional phenomena on the path to a fully self-referential legal system and has denied them a relevant societal function, as soon as law has achieved its present-day autonomy.[2] This claim can only be upheld, however, if one assumes – as Luhmann does – that subjective rights have lost their quality of sources of law today.[3] As soon as one regards, in the

* Translation into English by Malte Frøslee Ibsen. I thank Vagios Karavas and Anton Schütz for their helpful comments.

[1] Christoph Menke, *Kritik der Rechte* (Frankfurt aM: Suhrkamp Verlag, 2015); English translation: Menke, *Critique of Rights* (Chichester: Wiley, 2020).

[2] Niklas Luhmann, *Ausdifferenzierung des Rechts: Beiträge zur Rechtssoziologie und Rechtstheorie* (Frankfurt aM: Suhrkamp Verlag, 1981), p. 96 et seq.

[3] Ibid., p. 65 et seq.

sense of legal pluralism, private ordering as an authentic legal order, only subjective rights – and, in particular, corporate-law-mediated property – can be viewed as its legal source and win an independent societal function, which, in times of transnationalisation, is even independent of state law.[4] It is subjective rights that, for Menke, represent law's central contribution to the constitution of late-capitalist societies, particularly to the establishment of societal power outside of the state. At the same time, he argues that subjective rights, if they are to play an emancipatory role, need to be transformed into 'counter-rights'. He offers crucial impulses for their critique and develops institutional imagination for what he calls a 'new law'.

He is likewise in debt to Jürgen Habermas for many insights, but he undertakes an important correction of his discourse theory. To be sure, in contrast to Kant, Habermas allows the empirical 'interests' of the participants as the point of departure for a rational discourse, which universalises these interests to justified norms. However, he also leaves these interests more or less unanalysed and focuses exclusively on procedural conditions of communicative rationality.[5] Menke criticises this as a mere proceduralisation, and stresses, by contrast, a new kind of materialisation, an orientation towards what he calls 'material drives and forces', towards the 'natural, arational'.[6] Menke foregrounds the other side of political judgement: instead of merely taking the procedural conditions of normative judgement into consideration, as Habermas does, he emphasises the materiality of a 'pre-conceptual affection',[7] in which he invests his hopes for emancipatory effect. He thus reorients attention towards the affective, emotional, arational dimension of judgement in a 'process of reflective transformation of sensible, affective evidence',[8] of which theories of rational argumentation take no account.

[4] On the quality of subjective rights as legal sources, see Pasquale Femia, 'Transsubjektive (Gegen) Rechte, oder die Notwendigkeit die Wolken in einen Sack zu fangen', in: Andreas Fischer-Lescano, Hannah Franzki and Johan Horst (eds.), *Gegenrechte: Recht jenseits des Subjekts* (Tübingen: Mohr Siebeck, 2018), pp. 343–56, at 349; on the legal character of transnational norms of private governments, see Gunther Teubner, 'Global Bukowina: Legal Pluralism in the World Society', in: Gunther Teubner (ed.), *Global Law without a State* (Aldershot: Dartmouth Gower, 1997), pp. 3–28.

[5] Jürgen Habermas, *Between Facts and Norms: Contributions to a Discourse Theory of Law and Democracy* (Cambridge MA: The MIT Press, 1996).

[6] Menke, n. 1 above, p. 158 et seq.

[7] Ibid., n. 1 above, p. 337 et seq.

[8] Ibid., n. 1 above, p. 377.

Menke's critique of the welfare state represents another original contribution to the analysis of late-modern societies.[9] Although he fully recognises massive conflicts between liberal and welfare state conceptions of law, he sees both captured in a *circulus vitiosus* of mutual failure: their critique only ever applies to the relations of domination of the other side, and, on their own, both, again and again, revert themselves into domination. This vicious circle ultimately derives from their common origin, from the *bourgeois* form of subjective rights. A possible 'new law' can only arise when this circularity of liberal and welfare state rights is broken.

In contrast to received versions of critical theory, which always aim at a critique of liberal-capitalist societies and most often towards a more or less vaguely developed vision of a socialist society, Menke wages a battle on two fronts. His critique is not only directed at liberal-capitalist formations with their intra-societal tendencies towards a concentration of power,[10] but just as much at socialist-communist formations with their totalising, tendencies of political aggregation.[11] Menke goes beyond both of these alternatives and seeks to formulate a theory of authentic political judgement, which, in the light of the obvious mal-developments of both alternatives, represents a remarkable attempt to work on political utopias. If one also takes into account his implicit critique of the post-structuralist quietists, the 'avant-gardists of the standstill',[12] then Menke is actually fighting a battle on three fronts.

However, most provocative of all should be Menke's ideas of a 'new law'.[13] His argument is characterised by multiple surprising twists and turns. His striking point of departure is Nietzsche's ideas about the slave rebellion against domination. Then, in a first turn, Menke does not follow Nietzsche in his negative evaluation of the slave rebellion, but reverts it into its opposite. A right to remain passive, a right not to participate, and a right to be taken into account in decision making, are invested with extremely positive connotations by Menke. In a next turn, he insists that the passivity of the slave mentality, which does not seek to rule over others, should not be deemed to be completely feeble. Rather, it is precisely in the suffering of passivity that Menke uncovers the emancipatory 'force of pre-conceptual affection', the force of sensitive receptivity, in which the subject suffers its

[9] Ibid., n. 1 above, p. 281 et seq.
[10] Ibid., n. 1 above, p. 177 et seq.
[11] Ibid., n. 1 above, p. 339 et seq.
[12] Ibid., n. 1 above, p. 159 et seq.
[13] Ibid., n. 1 above, p. 369 et seq.

obstinate affection. Menke understands the 'passivity of the sensible' 'dialectically as a force, as unrest or as negativity'. In a third turn, he finally cuts himself loose from the, at first remarkably one-sided, emphasis on the 'arational' affective receptivity, and argues for a 'materialist-dialectical mediation' of the pre-conceptual with rational normative argument, a mediation from which authentic political judgement is supposed to emerge. The mediation does not aim to rationalise affection, but rather, by contrast, to unfold the power of the arational against the rational – indeed, he insists that the 'sensible feeling . . . must be effective *against* its rationalization'. 'Counter-rights', which release such a political judgement, need to be institutionalised in politics, law and society.[14] Only when such counter-rights have been established is a political self-government of social practices possible. Counter-rights need to be established in such a way that 'they simultaneously must include everyone as capable of judgement while granting the powerless the right to be taken into account'.[15]

II Trans-Subjective Dimensions of Subjective Rights

Now, my contribution does not amount to criticising Menke's theory, but rather suggests that the theory be redirected towards trans-subjective rights. Both Menke's critique of existing rights, as well as his ideas for the counter-rights of a new law, need to be developed in this non-individualist direction. Menke attributes subjective rights almost exclusively to individual human beings, as was usual in the early phase of capitalism. Occasionally, he relates constitutional rights to social practices, but even then, he ultimately relativises them by referring back to individual actors.[16] Neither subjective rights for collective actors, characteristic of late capitalism, appear in Menke's argument, nor institutional guarantees for social practices – arts, science, education for example – as existing subjective rights, or as counter-rights in a 'new law'.

Menke's individualistic conception of subjective rights is intimately connected with his critique of the dark side of capitalism, inspired by Marx and Foucault. For Menke, subjective rights represent the central mechanisms of domination in *bourgeois* society, which oscillate between exploitation and

[14] Ibid., p. 381 et seq.
[15] Ibid., p. 400.
[16] Recent ambitious critiques of subjective right's reference to the mere individual can be found in Dan Wielsch, *Zugangsregeln: Die Rechtsverfassung der Wissensteilung* (Tübingen: Mohr Siebeck, 2008), and Vagios Karavas, *Körperverfassungsrecht: Entwurf eines inklusiven Biomedizinrechts* (Zurich: Dike, 2018).

normalisation.[17] In contrast, inspired by Luhmann and Derrida, I want to emphasise three non-individual dimensions of subjective rights based upon a critique of the dark side of functional differentiation, which I have described elsewhere in greater detail.[18] In the language of systems theory, this will cast a new light on the 'reification' of the individual will, criticised by Menke: firstly, in the dimension of inter-individual communication, secondly, in the dimension of collective action, and thirdly, in the dimension of communicative media. This should not only give a greater depth of focus to the analysis and critique of subjective rights in late modernity, but also expand the prospects for possible counter-rights in a future law.

III Subjective Rights Referring to the 'Reified Will'

III.1 Communication: Socialised Will

Menke consistently understands subjective rights only as referring to individual consciousness, to the 'empirical wills' of individuals as 'facts', as 'something given', which is determined through its legal form.[19] Against that, one should make clear that the alleged individual wills, to which subjective rights are supposed to refer, cannot be what is meant here. The will of subjective rights is always a socialised will, even in simple social interactions. Indeed, the will of the 'individual' is nothing more than a phenomenon produced by social communication, which is only subsequently attributed to 'persons', that is, to mere semantic artefacts, which are, in their turn, only generated by communication. Such a communicative will is therefore necessarily 'reified' in relation to the inner life of the individual people concerned.[20] This is not only

[17] Menke, n. 1 above, p. 177 et seq.

[18] Gunther Teubner, *Constitutional Fragments: Societal Constitutionalism and Globalization* (Oxford: Oxford University Press, 2012), p. 78 et seq. Specifically on the supplementary relationship between the social critiques of Luhmann and Derrida, Teubner, 'Economics of Gift – Positivity of Justice: The Mutual Paranoia of Jacques Derrida and Niklas Luhmann' (2001) 18 *Theory, Culture and Society*, 29–47, and Teubner, 'Dealing with Paradoxes of Law: Derrida, Luhmann, Wiethölter', in: Oren Perez and Gunther Teubner (eds.), *On Paradoxes and Inconsistencies in Law* (Oxford: Hart Publishing, 2006), pp. 41–64.

[19] Menke, n. 1 above, p. 177 et seq.

[20] The best theoretical account of the strict double-sidedness of consciousness and communication in Niklas Luhmann, *Social Systems* (Stanford CA: Stanford University Press, 1995), p. 103 et seq., and 278 et seq. The theory of objective interpretation proceeds from a different basis; see Ulrich Oevermann, *Strukturprobleme supervisorischer Praxis: Eine objektiv hermeneutische Sequenzanalyse zur Überprüfung der Professionalisierungstheorie* (Frankfurt aM: Humanities Online, 2001).

a sociological insight – lawyers, too, speak of an objectified will, which is opposed to the 'inner will' as an intra-psychological phenomenon, and which is, instead, interpreted in a typified way from the horizon of the other, from the needs of social interaction.[21] Menke, however, seems to locate the will, understood as 'something given', in individual consciousness and action. In any case, it remains unclear whether he also identifies other manifestations of will. If so, where? In the intention of the speaker – and only there? In the understanding of the recipient – and only there? In the intersubjective meaning? In the signification produced by autonomous communication, detached from the individuals' intentions? Or in the juridical re-construction of the will, in the reference of subjective rights?

If subjective rights refer to the 'will' of the subject, then this reference is, in itself, so indeterminate that it actually remains open to all possible formations of the will – for formations that are 'reified' or authentic, repressive or emancipatory, liberal, communist or dialectically mediated. Even Menke's 'pre-conceptual affection' is potentially present in the reference of subjective rights, implying that the Menkeian 'new law' is already potentially available. On closer inspection, what remains of the law's reference to the will is therefore not actually a question of the 'form' of the law, but rather a question of the 'form' of society, namely, how this will is understood in social communication under contingent historical circumstances, which, in its turn, influences the legal construction of the will.

III.2 Collective Actors: 'Will-Formation' of the Juridical Person

The contrast to the individual will is most clearly seen in the case of formal organisations and other collective actors. As is well known, the law not only invests individuals but also corporate organisations and collective actors with subjective rights, even with constitutional rights, something which has significantly contributed to establish these organisations as centres of private power.[22] Subjective rights have lost their sole reference to individuals in tandem with the rise of corporate organisations. Menke does not at all address this collectivist transgression, which

[21] In lieu of many others, see Klaus F. Röhl und Hans C. Röhl, *Allgemeine Rechtslehre: Ein Lehrbuch* (Cologne: Vahlen, 2017), § 78.

[22] For a critical analysis of the historical development of corporate actors and private government, see Joshua Barkan, *Corporate Sovereignty: Law and Government under Capitalism* (Minneapolis MN: University of Minnesota Press, 2013).

characterises today's organisation society –and he fails to do so even for civic associations, labour unions and political parties. But since collective actors actually have become legal subjects endowed with subjective rights, we must ask the question: Which 'wills' do subjective rights refer to? If it is only an aggregation of the members' individual preferences, as sternly decreed by methodological individualism in economics, then one gets lost in the Arrow paradox.[23] Therefore, one must take account of the supra-individual 'collective' dimension of organisations' rights – a dimension that can only be understood if one allows that organisations can, in themselves, have their own 'will', intentions, preferences, interests, rationality and their own capacity for action. All these organisational properties arise from complex communicative processes within the organisation, and are distinct from their members' individual preferences as well as from their mere aggregation.[24] Thus, in the organisations of contemporary political economy, a 'reification' takes place which is more drastic than in the interaction of individuals.

III.3 Communicative Media: Motivational Imperatives

Finally, in the institutional dimension of subjective rights, social institutions – arts, science, education, economy – appear as quasi-legal subjects.[25] In this dimension, subjective rights become 'subject-less rights', and the institutions become 'subjects without rights'.[26] The social institutions

[23] Kenneth J. Arrow, 'Social Responsibility and Economic Efficiency' (1977) 21 *Public Policy*, 303–17.

[24] For an extensive treatment, see Gunther Teubner, 'Enterprise Corporatism: New Industrial Policy and the "Essence" of the Legal Person' (1988) 36 *The American Journal of Comparative Law*, 130–55.

[25] For recent ambitious analyses of the institutional dimension of constitutional rights, see Thomas Vesting, Stefan Korioth and Ino Augsberg, *Grundrechte als Phänomene kollektiver Ordnung: Zur Wiedergewinnung des Gesellschaftlichen in der Grundrechtstheorie und Grundrechtsdogmatik* (Tübingen: Mohr Siebeck, 2014).

[26] For a critique of the individualistic bias in the concept of subjective rights and an emphasis of their trans-subjective dimension, see Andreas Fischer-Lescano, 'Subjektlose Rechte', in: Andreas Fischer-Lescano, Hannah Franzki and Johan Horst (eds.), *Gegenrechte: Recht jenseits des Subjekts* (Tübingen: Mohr Siebeck, 2018), pp. 377–420. He takes up the concept of subject-less rights, of the institutions, which are not themselves bearers of rights but are indirectly protected through basic rights, and generalises it for all situations traditionally grasped within the concept of subjective rights. Pasquale Femia distinguishes in a way similar to this text between traditional subjective rights and trans-subjective rights, but he differentiates these in discursive rights and collective rights, on the one hand, and 'rights without rule', on the other, with whose help energies for ecological interests are activated; Femia, n. 4 above. Malte Gruber

mentioned here are mere ensembles of norms, and are clearly distinguished from the above-mentioned organisations, because they are neither formally organised nor able to act on their own as collective actors. Accordingly, the law does not personify these institutions as the bearers of rights; instead, constitutional rights, in an institutional form, guarantee the autonomy of certain social domains of action against politics and other expansionary domains of action. Freedom of art not only invests the individual artist with a right, but also protects the autonomy of art as a communicative process, which includes the production of works of art, their reception, critique and dissemination. The same is true of freedom of speech, freedom of science, freedom of communication media, and freedom of association.[27] To be sure, this institutional dimension is somehow important to Menke, since he is unfailingly concerned with the constitution, the critique and the reformation of social domains of action, but he does not theorise the crucial role of subjective rights in these processes.[28] He understands institutions at best as normative frameworks for individual action. Why does Menke concede subjective rights to individuals alone and not to institutions, only human beings and not social systems, only actors and not discourses, only the subjective spirit and not the objective spirit? And does something akin to the will of functional systems of society exist, which can be distinguished from both individual wills and organisational wills, to which subjective rights refer?

At this point, the third dimension of the 'reification' comes to the fore. As discussed above, the individual will is already socialised in everyday interaction, just as in formal organisations, albeit in a different fashion. But the social will is also profoundly formed by functional systems. It thus degenerates to the shrunken will of *homo oeconomicus*, *juridicus*, *politicus*,

discusses how adequate procedures for the effectiveness of trans-subjective rights might be developed; see Malte-Christian Gruber, 'Fluide Zivilverfahren: Zur prozessualen Präsentation von Ermöglichungs- und Gegenrechten', in: Fischer-Lescano, Franzki and Horst (eds.), *Gegenrechte: Recht jenseits des Subjekts*, this note above, pp. 227–48.

27 Paradigmatically, on the freedom of science, according to the German Federal Constitutional Court: 'Art. 5 Abs. 3 Satz 1 GG determines that science, research and teaching is free. Hereby, according to wording and meaning, an objective foundational norm is established, which regulates the relationship between science, research and teaching to the state ... At the same time, this constitutional determination guarantees a right of freedom to anyone, who is active in these domains' (BVerfGE 35, 79 [112]).

28 Social theory (Constant, Simmel, Luhmann) has systematically uncovered the reciprocal enablement of individual freedom and the autonomy of communicative contexts of meaning, juridically speaking between the individual and institutional dimensions of rights. On a comprehensive treatment of this theme, see Cornelia Bohn, 'Twofold Freedom and Contingency' (2018) 22 *Simmel Studies*, 45–78.

medicalis, which, as a social phenomenon, reconstructs only a partial aspect of individual will-formation and effectively filters out the rest. The legal reference to the will of the subject is thus always already tied to the stern conditions of a single, highly specialised functional system. Accordingly, subjective rights refer to nothing but social pre-formed categories of individuality: 'preferences' or 'interests', 'desires'.[29]

The reference of subjective rights to the empirical fact of the will must therefore always also be understood as a reference to the rationality and normativity of one of the great functional systems. This, ultimately, is the meaning of the institutional theory of constitutional rights: the autonomy of the social systems of art, science, education, economy. This is why the double-sidedness of individual and institutional (collective) constitutional rights – as advanced by Carl Schmitt, but even more importantly by Helmut Ridder – is so important. And just as important is the double-sidedness of the subjective rights in private law, since they not only protect individual interests but also social institutions, as Ludwig Raiser, in particular, has shown.[30] The 'will' of subjective rights is thus always directed towards the binary code of one of the functional systems, limited by its programmes, oriented towards its rationality maximisation and motivated for acceptance by the communicative medium in question.

Indeed, in systems-theoretical terms, these communicative media – money, power, law, truth – are actually what is crucial for the third dimension of the social 'reification' of 'will'. This relationship between the communicative media and 'will', to which subjective rights refer, is not immediately comprehensible. Nevertheless, the contribution of communicative media lies precisely in creating the *motives* (!) for the acceptance of communication in their respective spheres of validity. Communicative media serve the 'function of rendering expectable the

[29] For a treatment, which is critical towards a one-sided economic functionalisation of subjective rights and for their compatibilisation with scientific and artistic meaning, see Dan Wielsch, 'Über Zugangsregeln', in: Michael Grünberger and Nils Jansen (eds.), *Privatrechtstheorie heute: Perspektiven deutscher Privatrechtstheorie* (Tübingen: Mohr Siebeck 2017), pp. 268–85; Wielsch, n. 16 above.

[30] Carl Schmitt, 'Freiheitsrechte und institutionelle Garantien der Reichsverfassung', in: Schmitt (ed.), *Verfassungsrechtliche Aufsätze aus den Jahren 1924–1954* (Berlin: Duncker & Humblot, [1931] 1985), pp. 140–78; Helmut Ridder, *Die soziale Ordnung des Grundgesetzes* (Opladen: Westdeutscher Verlag, 1975); Ludwig Raiser, 'Rechtsschutz und Institutionenschutz im Privatrecht', in: Raiser (ed.), *Die Aufgabe des Privatrechts* (Kronberg/Ts.: Athenäum Verlag, 1977), pp. 124–44. For a critical treatment, see Rudolf Wiethölter, 'Privatrecht als Gesellschaftstheorie? Bemerkungen zur Logik der ordnungspolitischen Rechtslehre', in: Wiethölter (ed.), *Festschrift für Ludwig Raiser* (Tübingen: Mohr & Siebeck, 1974), pp. 645–95.

acceptance of a communication in cases where rejection is probable'.[31] In this way, the communicative media pre-form the 'will' to which subjective rights refer. To be sure, the motivational power of communicative media is not directed towards mental states, but towards motives as social constructs – and this is our concern at present – which come with an assumption of different, albeit corresponding, states of consciousness. Communicative media thus form social motives and exercise an indirect influence on intra-psychological will-formation. The responsibility for falsifying authentic will-formation – which Menke criticises in the contemporary political economy as 'reification', 'fact', 'something given', 'empiricistic', and 'positivistic' – therefore lies with the motivational force of communicative media, more so than with socialisation of the will through interaction or organisation. More precisely: the 'pre-conceptual evidence' that Menke is looking for is blocked because, from the beginning, communicative media replace the initial evidence with a one-sided formation of motives controlled by either power, money, law or knowledge. In the perspective of media theory, subjective rights refer to a will to power, will to money, will to truth. To be sure, on the surface, subjective rights celebrate the autonomy of the individual human being, but, in reality, they compel the individual into Max Weber's 'iron cage of the future', here understood as the overpowering motivational compulsion of communicative media which are one-dimensionally oriented towards their rationality maximisation. But, in contrast to Marxian accounts, will-formation is not exclusively subject to the profit imperative of the capitalist economy, but also just as much subject to the power imperative of politics, the knowledge imperative of science, the innovation imperative of technology, the news-cycle imperative of information media, the standardisation imperative of the law.

If one sees the socialisation of the individual will in these three dimensions – the communicative interaction dimension, the collective actor dimension and the communicative media dimension – then it becomes possible to determine why and in what respects the reference of subjective rights to the 'nature of the will' not only implies the reification of the private will of the individual, as Menke describes,[32] but also the reification of social norm formation, which is generated through the mere positivity of communication, of both the collective and of the

[31] Niklas Luhmann, *Theory of Society*, Vol. 1 (Stanford CA: Stanford University Press, 2012), p. 190.

[32] Menke, n. 1 above, p. 266 et seq.

media. It is therefore no exaggeration to suggest that, even though individuals officially remain the subjects of subjective rights, their secret subjects in late modernity are instead social processes of interaction, of organisation and of the communicative media.

IV Counter-Rights of a New Law

Why is Menke so forgetful of society when theorising subjective rights? The motive for his (almost) exclusive concentration on the individual must, in the last instance, be the hope that he relies on the role that 'pre-conceptual affection' will play in a new law. As already mentioned, Menke's 'counter-rights' aim at releasing the affective energies. Only when the 'right of passivity' empowers this affection – in its dialectical mediation with normative argumentation – can authentic political judgement be realised.[33] However, Menke locates this affective power exclusively in the consciousness of individual human beings and not – in opposition to consciousness – in autonomous social communication. In Menke's work, social communication, at most, fulfils the role of a public order, which determines the normative framework for the release of pre-conceptual affection.

But here one must ask does social communication not itself contain the wholly different potentialities for pre-conceptual affection which we are used to finding in individual consciousness?[34] The challenge here is to connect with Émile Durkheim's advances in this direction and to give his, not psychological, but strictly sociological, formulations of '*colère publique*', '*conscience collective*' or that of norms as '*faits sociaux*' a theoretical form, which is defensible today. One has to recognise that also affective communication – just as much as cognitive or normative communication – has selective effects and can create affective horizons,[35] as 'affective own worlds'.[36] The question that must be addressed to Menke's theorem of pre-conceptual affect is does not sociality in itself unleash a pre-conceptual, affective force, which realises a social surplus of affectivity beyond affectivity

[33] Ibid., p. 337 et seq.

[34] Émile Durkheim, *The Division of Labor in Society* (New York: Free Press, [1883] 1933), p. 79 et seq., and p. 154 et seq. For a remarkable attempt to establish affective communication as independent in relation to affective mental states, see Paul Reinbacher, 'Sozialkapital als affektive Struktur sozialer Systeme' (2017) 43 *Swiss Journal of Sociology*, 15–36; Paul Stenner, 'An Outline of an Autopoietic Systems Approach to Emotion' (2005) 12 *Cybernetics and Human Knowing*, 8–22.

[35] Reinbacher, n. 34 above, p. 24.

[36] Luc Ciompi, 'Ein blinder Fleck bei Niklas Luhmann? Soziale Wirkungen von Emotionen aus Sicht der fraktalen Affektlogik' (2004) 10 *Soziale Systeme*, 21–9.

in consciousness?[37] To be sure, this pre-supposes that 'cognition and emotion, rationality and feeling, sense and affect are not only treated at the individual level, but also in the collective dimension as correlative concepts'.[38] In particular, the socialisation of the will in the three different dimensions also changes the view of a 'new law', which promises to release new affective potentials not only in individual consciousness, but also in social communication.

At this point, we must clarify, in more precise terms, the meaning of 'pre-conceptual affection', before it is identified as an independent communicative occurrence and not merely as a mental state. Here, we need to make reference to the legal paradox, as discussed by Niklas Luhmann and Jacques Derrida. It is not sufficient to understand 'pre-conceptual affection' in communication merely as a social equivalent for individual emotions. Substantially, it is a veritable matter of squaring the circle. It is a matter of the compatibility of the incompatible, which – impossible as it may be – is nevertheless realised in the present context: it is a matter of the (in-)compatibility of law's experience of its environment and law's experience of the world. In more precise, system-theoretical terms, one must make a tripartite distinction between (1) law's internal environment as a self-construction within the law, (2) law's external environment, and (3) the world as the background for any possible observation, which the observation can nevertheless not observe itself. The external environment of the law (2), against which the law closes itself through legal operations, cannot be directly experienced via these operations. But the external environment of the law (2) can be experienced indirectly as the re-entry of this environment within the self-descriptions of law, and it appears as enacted environment (1). This is law's inner environment, law's reality construct of its environment. The world (3), however, is the blind spot of the law/non-law-distinction, its invisible unity, its paradox[39] – and this very difference between the world (3) and law's external environment (2) is neglected by Menke when he discusses Luhmann's systems-theoretically conceptualised environment of the legal system.[40] He misses Luhmann's point that '. . . for a systems-theoretical concept of the world, this means that the world is the totality of what constitutes system and environment for each system.'[41]

[37] For a preliminary sketch of this communicative power, in particular in the case of *pouvoir constituant* in constitutional pluralism, see Teubner, n. 18 above, p. 61 et seq.
[38] Reinbacher, n. 34 above, p. 17.
[39] Luhmann, n. 31 above, p. 83 et seq.
[40] Menke, n. 1 above, p. 112.
[41] Luhmann, n. 31 above, p. 89.

At this point, the squaring-the-circle-problem reappears: the law is able to react only indirectly to its external environment (2). It does so only with law-specific distinction in its internal environment (1). It remains, however, inescapably exposed to the world (3), although it cannot observe the world (3) via its law-specific distinctions. In the law, this squaring problem is intensified through the compulsion to make decisions. One either ignores the world through *stare decisis* in the received legal distinctions, or one exposes oneself to the decision-making problems of being exposed to the world-experience.

Now, there appears to be a connection at this point between, on the one hand, a world so understood (3), which, as a paradoxical unity of law's distinction/designation, cannot be observed, but which, at the same time, is the basis for all legal distinctions, and, on the other, the 'pre-conceptual affection' which experiences a pre-reflexive evidence. The question is, while a mediated access to the external environment (2) through irritation and re-entry producing an internal environment (1) is, at any rate, possible, whether there also exists a 'genuine' access to the world (3), which can never, to be sure, be produced by means of distinction and designation, but can, perhaps, be produced in affection, meditation, art, mystical experience, and non-linguistic communication? 'Pre-conceptual affects' would then not merely be a sensitive opening towards the external environment (2), emphatic experience of the other and suchlike, but would rather be a pre-conceptual experience of the world (3), an immediate experience of the world not yet carved out by distinction and designation. While Luhmann warns against losing oneself in such paradoxes and recommends that one hides the world-paradox between ever-new distinctions, Jacques Derrida demands that one exposes oneself to such paradoxical experience and brings this experience back into the legal argument.[42] A theory of justice would have to be grounded in such an oscillation between the self-transcendence of law and the re-immanentisation in the legal doctrine of subjective rights.[43]

[42] Jacques Derrida, 'Force of Law: The Mystical Foundation of Authority' (1990) 11 *Cardozo Law Review*, 919–1046.

[43] On this view of justice, see Gunther Teubner, 'Self-Subversive Justice: Contingency or Transcendence Formula of Law?' (2009) 72 *Modern Law Review*, 1–23, available at SSRN: http://ssrn.com/abstract=1416033. For an intriguing discussion, see Ino Augsberg, 'Gerechtigkeit als Transzendenzformel', in: Lars Viellechner (ed.), *Verfassung ohne Staat* (Baden-Baden: Nomos, 2019), pp. 81–102.

With regard to Menke, one would have to ask, besides this – not wholly unknown – form of experience in our inner life, whether communication, collective action and the communicative media could not also mediate an independent 'arational', affective access to the world. If Menke postulates a subjective counter-right to pre-conceptual evidence of experience (as a pre-condition for political judgement), could this be interpreted as a right to the 'world' in the above-sketched sense (3)? A right – individual, but also collective – to experience the world (3) 'before' it was dissected through distinction and designation? A right to expose communication to the world, to exposing it to the paradox of distinction and designation? A right to passivity, non-participation, receptivity, which would markedly distinguish itself from the conventional subjective right? More concretely, would concept-less experience be supported not only, as is customary, by a subjective right to freedom, which is, in reality, only granted within the framework of social systems imperatives, such as market imperatives or scientific imperatives, but rather through an – individual, but also collective – right to suspension of both legal imperatives as well as that of social systems imperatives?

Such counter-rights would allow access to the 'world' through concept-less intuition, but they would also enable a normative judgement, which frees itself from judgements one-sidedly controlled by money, power or science. Here, the analogy to Kant's analysis of aesthetic judgement comes to the fore, as suggested by Menke and others, which, as such, represents nothing less than a squaring of the circle in its mediation of affect and reason. And it is not only jurists but indeed all professions that are haunted by this squaring problem, at least those from which judgement is expected under the imperatives of decision making – assisted by, and simultaneously abandoned by, science – in situations of *non-liquet*.

The counter-rights would thus not only be positioned against the individual will of *bourgeois* subjective rights, but also, and first and foremost, against those social structures which 'reify' the 'wills', the 'interests', the 'preferences', and the 'needs of the patients' to 'given facts'. If the counter-right to political judgement is to be strengthened against these socialised 'inherent rights' then one would have to determine specifically for each social domain how, and at which point, a new law could institutionalise counter-rights. In my view, constitutional rights would be the most adequate legal category in this regard – not in their traditional effect against the state, however, but rather in their horizontal effects against social constellations of power. Completely in line with Menke, such constitutional rights would be oriented towards enabling authentic political judgement, distinguished according to the social context in question.[44] Since the threats to constitutional right differ from context to context, the counter-rights in organisations would have to be differently arranged than counter-rights in interaction or in various functional systems. Counter-rights would then not only be a matter of unleashing 'pre-conceptual affection' in individual consciousness, as Menke imagines, but also in the above-mentioned three dimensions of sociality: communicative, collective, and medial. What could this mean for each dimension?

IV.1 Affective Communication

Does this exist – pre-conceptual affection as a purely communicative phenomenon in interactions? And not only in the more common understanding that communication releases psychological effects in the participating individuals, or that it 'transfers' affects from one individual to the other, but rather in the strict sense that communication, as such, produces independent and markedly different formations of meaning?[45] To be sure, the communication of pre-conceptual meaning seems a contradiction in terms, since this would imply communication by way of the linguistically non-communicable. It seems counter-intuitive to insert counter-rights at this point, since law ultimately communicates linguistically through the reference of subjective rights to the will. That is to say, law produces information about the law as well as about the will by means of concepts.

[44] On the contextualisation of basic rights in different social domains of action, see Gunther Teubner, 'The Anonymous Matrix: Human Rights Violations by "Private" Transnational Actors' (2006) 69 *Modern Law Review*, 327–46, at 338 et seq.; Isabell Hensel and Gunther Teubner, 'Horizontal Fundamental Rights as Conflict of Law Rules: How Transnational Pharma Groups Manipulate Scientific Publications', in: Kerstin Blome, Andreas Fischer-Lescano, Hannah Franzki, Nora Markard and Stefan Oeter (eds.), *Contested Regime Collisions: Norm Fragmentation in World Society*, Cambridge: Cambridge University Press, 2016), pp. 139–68.

[45] This is the central challenge to which the sociology of emotions must respond, if it is to offer an independent contribution relative to psychological theories of emotions. On this, see Reinbacher, n. 34 above. Also theories of the sense of justice, which thematise only the emotions of the participating human beings but not the affective dimension of legal communication as such, must answer to this challenge. In opposition to Luhmann, who wants to drive emotions out of communication and limit them exclusively to psychological experience and there to an 'immune function of the psychological system', Parsons is much more sensitive to the independence of communicative affects, when he identifies 'affects' with a sociologically and symbolically generalised medium of the system of action; see Luhmann, p. 274 et seq; Talcott Parsons, *Social Systems and the Evolution of Action Theory* (New York: Free Press, 1977), p. 214 et seq.

But it is similar to the case of aesthetic communication in literature. The aesthetic message of its words cannot be found in its content, but rather in what cannot be verbally communicated, and yet it is found precisely in that which can be co-communicated in words, which goes beyond what can be said: 'Art functions as communication although – or precisely because – it cannot be adequately rendered through words (let alone through concepts).'[46]

It needs to be emphasised again that the communication of concept-less affects is in no way reduced to its effects on individual emotions, that is releasing affects in psychological processes. Instead, what matters is the specific signification that communication of affects creates, in distinction to individual feeling. The difference of consciousness and communication implies that – like communication in literature – a genuine communication of the linguistically non-communicable takes place *beside* the communication of content. The difference in interaction between action and suffering emphasised by Menke is not only characteristic of human consciousness, but precisely also of social communication.[47] Accordingly, counter-rights must not only be directed to individual feeling, but with equal intensity also to the social communication of pre-conceptual affects.

A great potential of such counter-rights for affective communication would lie in simple social relations of a more private character – that is, in everyday communication beyond institutionalised politics and other functional systems.[48] Here, pre-conceptual affects are spontaneously communicated, whether linguistically or non-linguistically. It is not without reason that the opinion polls of authoritarian states – as well as in the corporate world – take such a keen interest in private affective communication for purposes of social control. Indeed, it is not without reason that these relations are often targeted by massive technologies of manipulation, political propaganda and, in particular, corporate commercials. Nor is it

[46] Niklas Luhmann, *Art as a Social System* (Stanford CA: Stanford University Press, 2000), p. 19; see, also, p. 52 et seq.

[47] Menke, n. 1 above, p. 350 et seq.

[48] For a focus on the potential for resistance in private everyday communication, see Nofar Sheffi, 'Resistance as Contract Law-Making', *Manuskript Frankfurt*, 2016; in a like manner, Grahame F. Thompson, 'The Constitutionalisation of Everyday Life?', in: Eva Hartmann and Poul F. Kjaer (eds.), *The Evolution of Intermediary Institutions in Europe: From Corporatism to Governance* (Basingstoke: Palgrave, 2015), pp. 177–97.

without reason that massive technologies of control and censorship have recently been developed on the Internet against the dissemination of privately communicated moods and emotional states. This shows that counter-rights against state and corporate modes of disciplining of both the emotional life of the individual and affective communication in simple social relations must be all the more robustly institutionalised.

IV.2 Collective Actors

The communicative power of pre-conceptual affection is probably most clearly expressed in its collective dimension.[49] Not only must individuals be equipped with counter-rights, as Menke suggests, but also collective actors, since it is only the latter that give counter-rights political potency in organised protest and increase the chances of their enforceability in legal processes. One of the most important challenges for the 'institutional imagination' (Roberto Unger)[50] of a new law is how to conceptualise collective counter-rights, so that not only political programmes can be developed, but also pre-conceptual affection can be articulated within social movements, organisations, associations, labour unions and NGOs, so they can produce collective political judgements in mediation with conceptual determinations. Here, it is not only a matter of constitutionally protecting individual motives, but rather also of enlarging the social spaces for collective will-formation in procedures tailored for the purpose.

Protest movements are paradigmatic candidates for collectively articulated affective communication. In their early phase, at any rate, protest movements are, to a large extent, characterised by spontaneously articulating affective grievance, discontent, accusation, engagement and belonging, without developed theories or explicit programmes of political action. These are explicitly not articulated as surges of individual emotions, but rather as

[49] Mascareno speaks from the perspective of organisational sociology of the ability of certain collective actors for systemic compassion in contrast to individual affects within organisations Aldo Mascareno and Camilo Drago, 'Nothing more than feelings? De la compasión individual a la compasión sistémica en las organizaciones modernas' (2016) 3 *Economía y Política*, 85–117. He draws on Grahame Thompson, *The Constitutionalization of the Global Corporate Sphere?* (Oxford: Oxford University Press, 2012), p. 80 et seq., who distinguishes between four types of organizations: cynics, bottom-feeders, enthusiasts, ethical producers. In the latter two types, collective affective communication may play an important role (Examples: Novo Nordisk, Lefrage, fair commerce, Eco-corporations, financial cooperatives).

[50] Roberto M. Unger, 'Legal Analysis as Institutional Imagination' (1996) 59 *Modern Law Review*, 1–23.

the affects of a collective actor, which, as a social movement, can unfold considerable communicative power.[51] Protest movements are the perfect example of the 'slave rebellion' in its present collective form, which Nietzsche criticised and whose productive potential Menke has now once again uncovered. To express publicly the suffering of injustice, instead of developing political alternatives, to articulate grievances without conceptualising them, to demonstrate passivity against the development of political alternatives, to claim the right to institutional non-participation, to avoid taking on political decision-making functions, to demand concern for their concerns from the rulers – all of these typical characteristics of the slave rebellion today point not to individual actors, but rather to collective protest movements. This includes their symbiosis with the news media that has effectively enabled their social and political successes, but which is precisely not supported by conceptually developed political objectives as much as on sheer affective communication.

And even though the actors of institutionalised politics usually reject all this as a naïve, un-political, un-thought-out and irrational form of politics, it is precisely such affective communication that needs to be supported by collective counter-rights. In fact, and even more radically, one cannot limit the scope of counter-rights to pre-conceptual collective affects to 'progressive', 'left' or 'emancipatory' protest movements, as they must also be extended to 'reactionary', 'right', 'community-seeking' movements, if this collective affective potential is not to be subject to political censorship from the outset. Here, the counter-rights of a new law must also unfold their effectiveness, even against considerable opposition from a public sphere, which – even though it understands itself as 'critical' – is all too willing to proceed to administrative bans against 'populist' movements. To be sure, it must also be emphatically emphasised that such extensive tolerance towards radical affective communication, from whatever side it arises, can only be realised according to the extent to which a self-confident law is able to forbid manifest violence and to enforce this ban effectively through manifest counter-force.[52]

[51] On this point, see John Markoff, *Waves of Democracy: Social Movements and Political Change* (New York: Routledge, 2015); Niklas Luhmann, *Theory of Society*, Vol. 2, Stanford CA: Stanford University Press, 2013), p. 154 et seq. On the relationship between social movements and their psychological environment, see Luca Tratschin, *Protest und Selbstbeschreibung: Selbstbezüglichkeit und Umweltverhältnisse sozialer Bewegungen* (Bielefeld: Transcript, 2016), p. 154 et seq.

[52] Menke, n. 1 above, p. 406, explicitly ascribes to the new law the right to enforce legitimately counter-rights with force.

IV.3 Communications Media

Finally, counter-rights would also be needed in the institutional dimension to protect the integrity of social domains of action against the expansive, indeed, even totalising, tendencies of other social domains of action. Institutional basic rights would have to be effective against the motivational imperatives of highly selective communicative media: seduction through money, negative sanctions of power, binding demands of law, scientific truth claims and technological feasibility fantasies. Counter-rights are thus directed against the 'structural violence' (Johan Galtung),[53] which radiates from any communicative media. They are directed against one-dimensional motivational imperatives and seek to liberate political judgement from these restrictions. They allow an access to the 'world' through 'pre-conceptual affection' and thus enable a different kind of normative judgement, which liberates it from the one-sidedness of conceptual determinations controlled by money, power or science.

While counter-rights would aim to neutralise the motivational imperatives of the highly specialised communicative media and thus correct for their corruption of judgement, at the same time, they would preserve the cultural achievements of social differentiation, which have their origins in the very motivational imperatives of the communicative media. This is how I understand the meaning of Menke's two-front battle, which is directed, on the one side, against the realities of capitalist societies, and against communist utopias of collective decision making, on the other. This explains Menke's critique of totalitarian socialisation and emancipatory de-differentiation. Instead, what is at stake is the furthering of social differentiation including its different communicative media, which must nevertheless – and this is the crucial point – be bound to their social responsibility through the enablement of authentic judgement.

V The Poly-Contexturality of Counter-Rights

According to Menke, counter-rights must follow different designs in politics, in law, and in society.[54] In politics, he aims for counter-rights to passivity, since passivity renders authentic political judgement possible. They should be realised as counter-rights to singularity against the totalising aggregative tendencies of socialisation. In law, by contrast,

[53] Johan Galtung, 'Institutionalized Conflict Resolution: A Theoretical Paradigm' (1965) 2 *Journal of Peace Research*, 348–97.

[54] Menke, n. 1 above, p. 372.

Menke argues for a differently conceptualised right to passivity, if one wants to overcome the 'givenness' of subjective rights. The goal would be the internal politicisation of positivistically 'reified' subjective rights. Menke ultimately aims towards an overcoming of the old politics and law through the enablement of dissent in society, which is guaranteed in both spheres through such a right to passivity. This should not be understood as simply a right to establish alternative theories or new ideologies, which would force themselves on life, but rather as a new 'form' of judgement formation in politics and in law. Menke's ultimate aim is a new 'politics' in both domains. After all, he develops a political theory of law, and not a theory of autonomous law.

In the end, Menke goes beyond the domains of politics and law, and explicitly focuses the counter-rights on society itself.[55] If society, first and foremost, appeared from the observer's perspective of government in Menke's theory, either as reference of law to the natural or as reference of politics to society, Menke now shifts the perspective. Counter-rights against social power should also be established in society itself, a kind of horizontal effect of counter-rights in parallel to the horizontal effects of established constitutional rights. They appear now as the 'good self-government of society', in so far as social counter-rights are to be effective 'in the conflict between participation and consideration'.

However, the enormous variety of social domains of action remains relatively vague and indeterminate. Most often, Menke speaks in a rather undifferentiated fashion about '*the*' society or about 'social practice' in the singular.[56] If one wishes to further this train of thought, then one would have to focus more strongly on the central transformations of late-modern society, that is, not only the functional differentiation of society, but also the differentiation of formal organisations, networks and social movements. Both existing subjective rights and future counter-rights will gain clarity and specificity if they become realised in different social domains and thereby necessarily assume different corresponding forms.[57] Menke's thoughts point, in a certain sense, themselves in this direction. As already mentioned,

[55] Ibid., p. 396 et seq.

[56] Ibid., p. 396.

[57] Here lies the starting point for demands to consider explicitly different social contexts in their specific form, within which subjective rights are realised (n. 16 above), for rights to body fragments; see Karavas, n. 16 above. This is also the central thesis of Pablo Holmes on the necessity of politicisation of the world society; Pablo Holmes, 'The Politics of Law and the Law of Politics: The Political Paradoxes of Transnational Constitutionalism' (2014) 21 *Indiana Journal of Global Legal Studies*, 553–83, at 582 et seq.

he determines counter-rights differently, depending on whether they appear in politics (as a guarantee for singularity) or in law (as a guarantee of the inner politicisation of law). This analysis would need to be carried through for other social domains – for the economy, science, art, the media, medicine – and should uncover highly diverse forms of *bourgeois* subjective rights, on the one side, and future counter-rights, on the other.[58]

Menke's counter-rights should thus be understood as institutionalising reflexivity in law, politics and society. Their task is to enable good judgement – the 'process of reflective conversion of sensible, affective evidence'[59] – in politics and in law, as well as within society. In politics, reflexivity breaks open political routines by privileging the singularity of the individual against the demands of aggregative politics. At the same time, counter-rights institutionalise reflexive politics in law. And reflexivity in society is going to be established by strengthening the irritability of one-dimensional domains of autonomy through their 'internal politicisation'.[60] The particularity of counter-rights would thus be visible in all domains by the fact that they do not simply proclaim alternative political programmes, theories, and ideologies, but instead facilitate communicative irritability, sensibility, feeling, the capacity for suffering, responsiveness, spontaneity, intuition, imagination – also/even mystical experience – against social concentrations of power.

Let me summarise my proposal relating to counter-rights. While Menke conceptualises them for individuals in politics, law and society, one would have to re-think them in three trans-subjective dimensions – the dimensions of communication, collective agency, and communicative media. If law is supposed to react adequately to the transformations

[58] Specifically for such a contextualisation of basic rights, see Ino Augsberg, 'Subjektive und objektive Dimensionen der Wissenschaftsfreiheit', in: Friedemann Voigt (ed.), *Freiheit der Wissenschaft: Beiträge zu ihrer Bedeutung, Normativität und Funktion* (Berlin: Walter de Gruyter, 2012), pp. 65–89, at 72 et seq; see, also, Hensel and Teubner, n. 44 above, p. 164 et seq.

[59] Menke, n. 1 above, p. 377.

[60] On self-politicisation of law, see Johan Horst, 'Gerechtigkeit als dialektischer Vollzug: Das Programm eines Rechts der Gegenrechte', in: Andreas Fischer-Lescano, Hannah Franzki and Johan Horst (eds.), *Gegenrechte: Recht jenseits des Subjekts* (Tübingen: Mohr Siebeck, 2018), pp. 249–76. Tanja Sheplyakova develops law-specific politicity and itsdependence on procedural elements; see Tatjana Sheplyakova, 'Klagen als Ausübung der "Gegenrechte"', in: Andreas Fischer-Lescano, Hannah Franzki and Johan Horst (eds.), *Gegenrechte: Recht jenseits des Subjekts* (Tübingen: Mohr Siebeck, 2018), pp. 205–26.

of late-modern societies, one would need to develop such counter-rights in two different directions. First, the individual counter-rights would be expanded to include counter-rights for collectives, organisations, social movements, networks, and functional systems, but also for simple social systems – not as substitutes for individual rights, but rather as their co-originary complements. Second, the counter-rights which Menke conceives as unitary would have to be pluralised: as counter-rights against the motivational imperatives of different communicative media, which would need to be arranged differently in different social contexts.

INDEX